The Dilemma of Constitutional Reform in Bosnia and Herzegovina

Studies in Territorial and Cultural Diversity Governance

Series Editors

Francesco Palermo
Joseph Marko
Roberta Medda-Windischer

VOLUME 25

The titles published in this series are listed at *brill.com/tcdg*

The Dilemma of Constitutional Reform in Bosnia and Herzegovina

Discussing Options with a View to EU Accession

Edited by

Maja Sahadžić, Tatjana Sekulić,
Nevenko Vranješ, and Jens Woelk

BRILL | NIJHOFF

LEIDEN | BOSTON

This publication is co-financed by the Know-how Exchange Programme sponsored by the CEI Fund at the EBRD contributed by Italy.

Library of Congress Cataloging-in-Publication Data

Names: Sahadžić, Maja editor | Sekulić, Tatjana editor | Vranješ, Nevenko editor | Woelk, Jens, editor
Title: The dilemma of constitutional reform in Bosnia and Herzegovina : discussing options with a view to EU accession / edited by Maja Sahadžić, Tatjana Sekulić, Nevenko Vranješ, Jens Woelk.
Description: Leiden ; Boston : Brill Academic Publishers, Inc, 2026. | Series: Studies in territorial and cultural diversity governance ; volume 25 | Includes bibliographical references and index.
Identifiers: LCCN 2025032139 | ISBN 9789004707870 hardback | ISBN 9789004707887 epub
Subjects: LCSH: Constitutional law--Bosnia and Herzegovina | Law reform--Bosnia and Herzegovina | Constitutional history--Bosnia and Herzegovina | Federal government--Bosnia and Herzegovina | Legislative bodies--Bosnia and Herzegovina | European Union--Bosnia and Herzegovina | Dayton Peace Accords (1995) | Yugoslav War, 1991-1995--Peace | Bosnia and Herzegovina--Politics and government--1992-
Classification: LCC KJK8205 .D55 2025 | DDC 342.49742--dc23/eng/20250725
LC record available at https://lccn.loc.gov/2025032139

Typeface for the Latin, Greek, and Cyrillic scripts: "Brill". See and download: brill.com/brill-typeface.

ISSN 2213-2570
ISBN 978-9-0047-0787-0 (hardback)
ISBN 978-9-0047-0788-7 (e-book)
DOI 10.1163/9789004707887

Contents

Acknowledgements

We would like to extend our sincere gratitude to Brill Publishing for their invaluable support in bringing this work to life.

Special thanks go to the editors of the series "Studies in Territorial and Cultural Diversity Governance", Joseph Marko and Francesco Palermo, for their insightful guidance and dedication throughout the process.

Without the Italian Embassy in Sarajevo, which provided necessary steering along the way, this vast intellectual platform would not have been feasible. The thanks extend to Nicola Minasi, former Italian ambassador to BiH, who came up with the initial idea, as well as to his successor, Marco Di Ruzza, who continued to support the project together with their former deputy Matteo Evangelista.

The Central European Initiative's (CEI) contribution is also highly appreciated as the academic effort was made possible thanks to their financial support.

A debt of gratitude goes to our copyeditor, Budislav Vojinović, who is the most meticulous and understanding of all of the copyeditors out there. His contribution has been instrumental in shaping the final outcome.

Lastly, the authors deserve gratitude as their participation in this project was outstanding. Though we may need to put in a little more effort to align our opinions, it seems that we are collegially closer.

Banja Luka, Milan, Trento, Utrecht, 31 March 2025

The Editors
Maja Sahadžić, Utrecht University
Tatjana Sekulić, University of Milano-Bicocca
Nevenko Vranješ, University of Banja Luka
Jens Woelk, University of Trento

Notes on Contributors

Neven Andjelic

is Course Leader BA International Relations at Regent's University London, where he teaches International Relations and Human Rights. He is also Adjunct Professor at University of Bologna. His latest book is *Covid-19, State-Power and Society* (Springer 2022).

Nikolina Babić

is Teaching Assistant at the Faculty of Political Science, University of Banja Luka. Her recent article is "Socialist and Social Democratic Parties in the Political System of the Republic of Srpska" (Defendologija 2021). Her research areas are political systems and local government.

Lejla Balić

is Associate Professor of Constitutional Law at the University of Sarajevo. Her scientific research interests are federalism, democratisation, parliamentary and electoral law, and European public law. She has published the monograph *European Union: Parliament and Democratization* (University of Sarajevo Press 2020.)

Damir Banović

is Associate Professor at the Faculty of Law, University of Sarajevo, where he teaches Philosophy of Law. His main research focus is on contemporary socio-legal theory, theory of collective rights, minority rights, consociationalism, and comparative federalism.

Dražen Barbarić

is Associate Professor at the Department of Political Science of the Faculty of Humanities and Social Sciences, University of Mostar, and Head of the Expert Team of the Institute for the Social and Political Research Mostar (IDPI). His areas of scientific interests are political theory, geopolitics, and security studies.

Tahir Herenda

is a Ph.D. candidate at the Faculty of Law at the University of Sarajevo, where he is also a Senior Teaching and Research Assistant. His research is focused on deeply divided societies.

Nedim Hogić
is a legal scholar and researcher of Comparative Public Law. He holds a Ph.D. from Sant' Anna School of Advanced Studies and an LL.M. from Harvard Law School. He is currently a Postdoctoral Research Fellow at the University of Oslo.

Harun Išerić
is Senior Research and Teaching Assistant in Administrative Law and Administration, and a Ph.D. candidate at the University of Sarajevo. His research interests encompass constitutional and human rights law, comparative administrative law and procedure, and elections and media.

Joseph Marko
is Professor Emeritus of Comparative Public Law and Political Sciences, University of Graz. He served as International Judge at the Constitutional Court of Bosnia and Herzegovina (1997–2002) and Politico-legal advisor of the UN Special Representative for the negotiations on re-unification of Cyprus (2015–2017). He is author of 4 monographs and more than 140 scholarly articles.

Goran Marković
is Full Professor of Constitutional Law at the Faculty of Law, University of East Sarajevo. His areas of interest are federalism, direct democracy and self-management, and systems of government. He published more than 100 scientific articles and four books. The recent books are *Ustavno pravo* and *Ustavni lavirint: Aporije ustavnog sistema Bosne i Hercegovine* (Službeni glasnik Beograd 2021).

Marko Romić
is a Ph.D. candidate in Public Law at the University of Belgrade and an Assistant Lecturer at the University of Banja Luka. Administrative law and public administration, legal history and state-church law are among his main academic interests. His book *Neustavnost zakona i upravni akti* was published in 2023 (Institute for Comparative Law, Belgrade).

Maja Sahadžić
is Assistant Professor of Constitutional Law at the School of Law and Researcher at Montaigne Centre for Rule of Law and Administration of Justice (Utrecht University), Visiting Professor (University of Antwerp), Senior Research Fellow (Law Institute in BiH), Fellow (Netherlands Institute of

Human Rights – SIM), and Affiliated Scholar (Centre for Comparative and Transnational Law at CUHK). She is Co-chair of the Committee on New Directions in Scholarship of the ICON S.

Tatjana Sekulić
is Associate Professor of Political Sociology at the Department of Sociology and Social Research, University of Milano-Bicocca. Main fields of her research concern the European integration in polycentric perspective; forced migration studies; new wars and contemporary conflicts; and democratic transition of post-totalitarian regimes.

Bojan Vlaški
is Assistant Professor of Administrative Law and Public Administration at the University of Banja Luka. He has written dozens of scientific papers that relate to the right to a good administration, public data, market competition, federalism, and intergovernmental relations.

Nevenko Vranješ
is Associate Professor of Political Science at the University of Banja Luka. His research interests are related to public administration, political systems, local self-government, and administrative law. Author of three books and many scientific articles, he assumed the office of the Human Rights Ombudsman of Bosnia and Herzegovina in September 2022.

Jens Woelk
is Full Professor of Comparative Constitutional Law at the University of Trento (Italy). He also works at the Institute for Comparative Federalism (Eurac Research) in Bolzano/Bozen. His research interests include federalism/regionalism, minority rights, and the constitutional transformation processes in Southeast Europe.

CHAPTER 1

A Methodological Note on the Role of Intellectual Work for Cooperation in Post-conflict Societies

Maja Sahadžić

Nearly thirty years after the General Framework Agreement for Peace in Bosnia and Herzegovina (also known as the Dayton Peace Agreement) was concluded, there are ongoing, intense discussions in both academic and public forums regarding the meaning and implications of designating Bosnia and Herzegovina (BiH) as a "complex state". In December 2022, Bosnia and Herzegovina was granted the status of a candidate country for EU membership, following an extended period of inaction stemming from unfulfilled duties under EU conditionality. Based on the Commission's March 2024 recommendation, EU leaders approved the start of accession talks in March 2024. But despite a number of misguided attempts at constitutional reform, the so-called Dayton Constitution (Annex 4 to the Dayton Peace Agreement), which must be revised in order to meet the EU membership standards, there is little indication that this will change anytime soon.

Therefore, it was crucial that the academic community investigates the various approaches for modifying the legal and constitutional framework to meet the demands of European integration. This is because scholarly expertise can help in preparing and orienting the decision on which option to adopt, with the decision evidently belonging to political institutions and to citizens. The Embassy of Italy especially acknowledged and promoted the academic cooperation in BiH because scholars and universities play a crucial role in the debate on constitutional issues and potential reform options. To this end, the Embassy of Italy organised two academic conferences (in November 2019 and December 2020) and invited scholars from BiH and Italian universities to participate in a series of informal discussions on fundamental constitutional issues.

After the initial contact, facilitated by the Italian Embassy, a group of academics from BiH and Italy collaborated to plan and prepare three workshops centred around important issues pertaining to the Dayton Constitution's core ideas and potential reform strategies (January–May 2021). The workshops have created a community of scholars from all over BiH by providing a platform for open and thought-provoking dialogue. This debate and the cooper-

 | DOI:10.1163/9789004707887_002

ation between academics from key BiH universities persisted and intensified especially through a collaborative effort on the first ever Glossary of Essential Constitutional Concepts in BiH.

The Glossary clarified, for the first time, the fundamental ideas of constitutional law in BiH. Targeting the general population, as opposed to only the academic community, posed a significant obstacle. As the scholarly community finds it difficult to comprehend the complexities of the system, one can only surmise the degree of difficulty faced by regular citizens. However, the rationale behind the Glossary was to provide a concise and organised explanation of the key ideas of Bosnian constitutional law as they pertain to its citizens. Hence, the Glossary's entries were written with the intention of being understood by both experts and non-experts.

Apart from this, recognising that the scholarly perspectives within the academic community of BiH occasionally diverge greatly constituted another significant obstacle. It is obvious that divergent theoretical stances could provide disparate results and jeopardise the coherence of the Glossary's development. Crucially, several subjects remained exceedingly delicate from a scientific and political standpoint. It was vital to establish as neutral an atmosphere as possible, take a pluralistic approach, and implement an internal check-and-balance mechanism in order to balance the approaches from a scientific and political standpoint. The main topics of discussion were not only which entries to choose for explanation and how to logically arrange the chosen entries to represent the intricate political and constitutional framework of BiH, but also, for example, whether or not to actively use case law in the entry writing process given its occasionally contentious nature.

As often in academia (and law), the focus on procedure helped for making progress in substance. In particular, the methodological approach used to guide the entry-writing process promoted a neutral atmosphere. A group discussion and debate were part of the process. As a result, thirty-five concepts were produced as entries, such as constituent peoples, entities, cantons, federalism, veto power, power-sharing, European integration, kind of government, and fundamental rights. The terminology in this Glossary was then derived from these concepts. On each single entry, academics were working in smaller groups of two or more, discussing concepts and trying to come to a consensus on controversial topics in order to draft the entry collectively. Crucially, the Glossary was written in all three of the official languages of BiH (Bosnian, Croatian, and Serbian) and in two scripts (Cyrillic and Latin). The Glossary's translation into English is a significant outcome as well, because it enables foreigners – such as international human rights activists, recently appointed diplomats in BiH, or simply enthusiasts interested in domestic constitutional law – to understand the fundamental ideas of the constitution.

Building mutual acceptance and trust was one of the main aims of the Glossary, which served as a basis for raising academics' understanding of their mutual reliance and mutual dependence. This resulted in a more cogent comprehension and perspective of the prospects for the future of the constitutional system and its possible modifications or adjustments.

In the final stage of the project, the editorial board members were motivated to put in a purely academic effort and publish an edited volume based on the key findings of a two-year research project and an intense academic debate on the primary concerns and fundamental ideas of the Constitution of Bosnia and Herzegovina. Therefore, this edited volume is the culmination of an extended undertaking. The authors have come together once more to examine the wisdom of the domestic and international Dayton participants in light of the experience of implementing the so-called Peace Agreement. They also intended to discuss the fundamental constitutional principles and institutional mechanisms of the Dayton constitutional system from the standpoint of comparative constitutional law and comparative government, rather than from the perspective of everyday politics. They examined BiH from the perspectives of EU enlargement and EU integration, as well as a post-socialist and post-conflict transitional society undergoing transformation.

To that end, the book offers an analysis "from within" Bosnia and Herzegovina, in contrast to many other analyses that were made "from the outside", often without a thorough understanding of the internal factors that affect the political and constitutional landscape. Importantly, the book maintains a diversity of disciplinary viewpoints because its authors are not only lawyers, but also political scientists and sociologists. Given that the majority of the book is devoted to discussing the BiH constitutional system, the legal approach is in fact highlighted. Thus, this book's outcome highlights not just fundamental information that is much too frequently absent from public discourse but also fundamental options for making political and legal decisions, which the authors openly address. In this sense, the book offers a novel perspective on how the complex BiH is framed by its constitution.

CHAPTER 2

A "Complex State", the Constitution, and EU Accession. Introduction

Jens Woelk and Nevenko Vranješ

1 Introduction

This book is about Bosnia and Herzegovina (BiH), the "complex State" (*složena država*).

Almost thirty years after the signing of the Dayton Peace Agreement, which includes the Constitution of Bosnia and Herzegovina, there have been no substantial reforms to the Constitution, despite demands from both domestic and international stakeholders. This is a result of the lack of political will and internal consensus among the holders of power in Bosnia and Herzegovina. Although EU accession is a declared political goal for years and the country was awarded the status of a candidate country for EU-membership in December 2022, no major or constitutional reforms have been adopted.

A network of scholars from Bosnia and Herzegovina has engaged in a scientific assessment of the constitutional system, the current situation, and its future perspectives. This is the first book examining BiH's complex constitutional system comprehensively, which is written by a plethora of well-known scholars from BiH, representing most major public universities in the country (Banja Luka, East Sarajevo, Mostar, and Sarajevo). Importantly, it gathers the main findings of a two-year research project and intense academic debate on the central issues and essential concepts of the Constitution of BiH. The project, which was financed by the Central European Initiative (CEI KEP Italy Project; 1 November 2021–31 December 2023), has created a network of scholars from major public universities in Bosnia and Herzegovina and from Italy, Austria, Belgium, the Netherlands, and the United Kingdom. It thus presents the "view from within" as academic analysis is based upon profound and direct knowledge of the situation as well as on hypotheses tested in teaching in front of students from Bosnia and Herzegovina.

This book draws from repeated and intense discussions among the same scholars who had engaged in a joint endeavour trying to clarify the essential

 | DOI:10.1163/9789004707887_003

constitutional concepts for themselves and for interested citizens.[1] The method is described in a methodological note on the role and potential of intellectual work for cooperation in post-conflict societies (Chapter 1, by *Maja Sahadžić*). Starting from the exploration of the basic notions in the Glossary, this volume goes deeper and presents an innovative insight into the constitutional framing of the "complex state". It is based on the multi-dimensional and interdisciplinary analysis that opens different perspectives: BiH as a pluri-national and multi-ethnic country, as a post-socialist and post-conflict transitional society in transformation, as well as the perspective of the EU-enlargement and EU-integration.

2 Three Foundational Questions

By contrast with other recent publications,[2] this volume does not present a comprehensive overview presenting the "Dayton system", but rather offers a profound and problem-oriented analysis of its main constitutional issues and problems, bringing together different disciplines, with a focus on law. In an evolutionary perspective, the analysis put forward by the authors is not limited to a mere illustration of the status quo but aims at examining the "complex state" in the perspectives of the challenges of Bosnia and Herzegovina's democratic transformation as well as of the objective of EU accession.

At the core of the book are **three "foundational" questions** related to the formation of identities and organisation of institutions, as well as of territorial government. They are three essential points of discussion with each containing several sub-questions that are intimately linked:

2.1 *Basic Values and Normative Principles, Rights, and Duties*

What are the basic standards by means of which to express cultural, socio-economic, and political identities and diversities in BiH? How to shape a sus-

1 This endeavour is briefly described in the methodological note of this volume. It resulted in the publication of a glossary which is freely accessible: Sahadžić, Maja, Banović, Damir, Barbarić Dražen and Marković Goran, eds., *Citizens, Constitution, Europe. Glossary of essential constitutional concepts in BiH*, published by the University of Sarajevo, Faculty of Law, 2023 (https://www.balcanicaucaso.org/eng/Projects2/Bosnia-and-Herzegovina-the-Constitution-and-EU-Accession/Citizens-Constitution-Europe).

2 For instance, mainly from a political science perspective, Banović, Damir, Gavrić, Saša, Barreiro Mariño, Mariña, *The Political System of Bosnia and Herzegovina. Institutions – Actors – Processes*, Springer 2021.

tainable vision for the future of both state and society? Which types of rights are necessary for the effective protection of individuals, groups, or communities? In many public debates, as well as in scholarly literature, individual rights of citizens are considered incompatible with the so-called "collective" rights of groups or communities: Is this a precondition for the functioning of a "civic", liberal, and democratic state? Is such a dichotomic conceptualisation of individual versus group rights part of the solution or part of the problem? And finally, what does political equality of citizenship mean in a complex state as BiH and how to frame it constitutionally? The first part of the book is dedicated to these questions.

2.2 *Institutional Organisation*

What sort of institutional set-up can translate these values, principles, rights, and duties into a functional system of representation and effective political participation? And what is necessary to make such a system fit for European integration? Any form of representative democracy needs a vision of who is to be represented by whom. Shall those who are elected represent the voters and their local or regional socio-economic interests in the respective electoral district, or rather protect the cultural identities of groups and/or their voters? Are these mutually exclusive alternatives or is it possible to design a model which can reconcile different objectives?

2.3 *Territorial Government*

Which system of territorial government may best guarantee these values, principles, rights, and duties in combination with the institutional make-up for the legislative, executive, and judicial powers? What kind of a federal system is BiH and what may be considered as an ideal combination of territorial and institutional organisation of powers for the future?

3 Foundational Questions Translated into Book Parts

These three essential issues are distinguished analytically and developed in the first two parts.

After an overview of the main constitutional developments in the 30 years of the post-Dayton order by *Nedim Hogić*, which also serves as an introductory basis for all chapters of the book, the following chapters of the **First Part** address the **fundamental constitutional principles**. The focus is on basic values and normative principles, rights, and duties. *Damir Banović* shows by analysing the case-law of the Constitutional Court of BiH that despite substantial changes, the system has not developed intrinsic values and principles that should or could be the normative guidelines for an efficient, democratic, inclusive, and multicultural state. According to *Goran Marković,* in Bosnia and Herzegovina some principles of federalism and consociation are missing or are prescribed in a way to guarantee the priority of consociational democracy over the elements of federalism. The three "Daytons", as nationally biased perceptions of the same text and the practical effects of these parallel worlds in the political system, are illustrated by *Dražen Barbarić*; indeed, the main consequences of the absence of "politics of recognition" is the lack of an accepted common frame or sense of a state. A profound analysis of the evolution of the leading cases of the European Court of Human Rights and the Constitutional Court of BiH is at the centre of *Joseph Marko's* chapter. *Marko* emphasises the dynamic dimension, which is essential for the evolution of the society and the system, and the limits in a democracy, which exclude mechanisms of segregation. Thus, the Dayton constitutional system cannot be interpreted as a "historic compromise" guaranteeing permanent corporate power-sharing in combination with territorial control through federal elements. The chapter concludes with a summary of normative standards to be implemented for future reform efforts:

The **Second Part** is dedicated to the **organisational consequences** which follow from the compromise in Dayton and from the discussion of the normative values, principles, and rights above. The chapters in the second part examine the institutional as well as the territorial organisation of BiH, but also consider them as essential for any other system of multi-level governance, from local self-government to the level of European integration. The problem of achieving a balance between different principles shapes almost every segment of BiH state organisation, and the issue of bicameralism in BiH is one of the most important. *Lejla Balić* stresses the consequences of the veto mechanisms, which lead to an ineffective and inefficient Parliamentary Assembly. In addition, the House of Peoples of BiH needs to be transformed by constitutional reform to ensure that all citizens are democratically represented; not only for the sake of implementing the judgements of the European Court of Human Rights. Shifting the attention to the executive powers, *Marko Romić* observes that the collective Presidency and the special constitutional position of the Council of Ministers represent peculiar characteristics of BiH in comparative terms, even vis-à-vis other complex countries in Europe. The "least dangerous branch of government" (Alexander Hamilton), the judiciary, is under strong pressure from all sides: *Jens Woelk*'s chapter looks closer into reform proposals regarding the High Judicial and Prosecutorial Council, the (foreign judges at the) Constitutional Court of BiH, and the issue of a Supreme

Court of BiH, all part of the European Commission's "constitutional conditionality". The potential of (improving) intergovernmental relations is explored by *Bojan Vlaški* starting from common interests of the State, the Entities and Cantons, which would be better served by intergovernmental agreements or bodies and the coordination mechanism for the European integration process than by mutual blockade or the High Representative's imposition. However, a culture of dialogue and out-of-court settlement of federal disputes, through arbitration and mediation mechanisms, needs to be developed. The second part ends with two chapters on the local and global contexts. In their chapter on the potential of local self-government in Bosnia and Herzegovina, *Nevenko Vranješ and Nikolina Babić* analyse the legal differences between the RS (unitary system), the FBiH (federal system, with 10 cantons as intermediate level), and Brčko District (as a unique local entity), claiming that the current organisation of local self-government in the entities (particularly its monotypic structure and omnibus competencies) does not align with their actual needs and the needs of the local population and could be subject to future reform. The wider international context is addressed by *Neven Andjelic* who comments on the lack of internal consensus, which still requires a broader international security arrangement for keeping the country together. While it does still appear as stable, the dramatic changes in the global context might provoke changes and instability, as the (divisive) question of formally joining NATO demonstrates.

Bosnia and Herzegovina's bid for membership in the EU adds a dynamic dimension to the above foundational issues, with the challenge of becoming part of a multilevel governance-system. Can the challenge of preparing the country for future accession to the European Union (EU) trigger sustainable transformation?

This is the main interest of the **Third Part**, in which the three "foundational" questions regarding the Constitution are put in the context of **how to reach the objective of EU accession.** This objective makes it necessary to manage the impact of EU integration and EU law in the domestic constitutional system, even before the country's accession. But what are specific challenges for the main constitutional principles following from EU-conditionality in the process of EU-integration? *Jens Woelk*'s chapter explores the constitutional impact of the EU's conditionality for membership. Starting from the specific character of the EU's legal integration and from the European Commission's Opinion (2019), it analyses options, with a particular view to the question of a specific "integration clause". And is there a particular view from a specific citizens' perspective? What kind of political and civic actions are needed for reconsidering constitutionality as an important element of a peace building process leading to sustainability? In her chapter, *Tatjana Sekulić* reconstructs the evolution of citizenship in Bosnia and Herzegovina, from a historical-political perspective, distinguishing between the two concepts of citizenship as status, i.e. membership in a modern democratic polity, and as identity, i.e. belonging to a specific ethnonational community. The chapter continues with a discussion of the different consequences of these concepts in the Dayton Constitution and the transformation for EU accession. May citizens' assemblies open a way out of BiH's dilemma and are they even possible in divided societies? Analysing the recent experience of two citizens' assemblies – one in the deeply divided city of Mostar, and another for the whole country – the chapter by *Harun Išerić and Tahir Herenda* sheds light on the potential efficacy of citizens' assemblies as instruments for fostering constructive dialogue and decision-making within societies marked by divisions. Thus, in essence, the third part of the volume discusses the challenge of adapting the internal structures as a precondition for future accession to the European Union and how to achieve this.

Overall, this book assesses the specific experience of the unique federal and consociational system and the constitutional situation following from the Dayton Peace Agreement. The intention is to make reform options for the constitutional challenges posed by the objective of EU accession visible. In their Conclusions, *Maja Sahadžić and Tatjana Sekulić* point out how the debate about those options emerges in all chapters as part of a mutual learning process in respect to diverse perspectives and positionings of the authors.

4 Conclusions

The specific knowledge about the situation, the challenges and the options is relevant for local and regional scholars and, ideally, politicians as well as "internationals", active in Bosnia and Herzegovina and in the Western Balkans (and in Brussels or other capital cities) in their capacity as diplomats or other. But it shall also offer conceptual keys and policy tools which may become useful for any other post-conflict context, multi-ethnic states, and societies, in an increasingly complex world.

The authors and editors hope that students, researchers, practitioners in government, international organisations, NGOs, minority associations, activists, academic and professional libraries, will use this book for understanding and going deeper into the intriguing questions of the "complex State" as such, but also for challenging traditional concepts and notions with a fresh approach. As a generation has passed already, since 1995, when the Dayton

Peace Accord has been brokered and signed, the situation has evolved considerably, both in Bosnia and Herzegovina as well as globally. To exit from its constitutional impasse and to proceed in its democratic transformation, Bosnia and Herzegovina urgently needs constructive discussion based on solid academic analysis and knowledge. Only on such a basis, serious, honest, and open dialogue on the country's future is possible.

Ivo Andrić, a great connoisseur of the Bosnian-Herzegovinian mentality, observed in the famous "Travnik Chronicle" that "Four religions live on this narrow, hilly and scarce piece of land (...) and each expects salvation from somewhere outside, and each from the opposite direction".[3] It is difficult to think of how to summarise the situation more efficiently. But it also implies that when "salvation" will be sought within BiH, it will be possible to adopt a spirit of compromise and a minimum of consensus on which to build the future of BiH. An important reminder.

Because of the richness of its diversity, Bosnia and Herzegovina was commonly considered a "Yugoslavia in miniature". But just as its rich diversity also represents the world at a small scale, the crisis of the multicultural community that it experienced also reflects the global challenge of accommodating diversity.[4] "Andrić made hatred eternal by linking it with borders and darkness, which irreversibly are part of a human condition."[5] In response, for Dževad Karahasan, the process of overcoming evil was the most important thing, and he considered bridge-building a "Bosnian method", because "the job of the *neimar* (bridge builder) is to find the resources to rebuild a bridge in the world in which it was destroyed".[6] And one can build on the fundamental characteristic of the Bosnian-Herzegovinian cultural system, which is pluralism. Indeed, the fundamental relation within its peculiar "dramatic" cultural system, as Karahasan calls it, consists in the tension between its different parts, which allows the single parts to preserve their original nature instead of excluding or devouring each other.[7] The "openness of Bosnian culture to the complex influences of other cultures does not come from its lack of identity, or from its poor awareness of that identity, but from its readiness to acknowledge

3 This quote used in Bojan Vlaški's chapter has been "borrowed" for this introduction, as it is such an apt summary of the situation of Bosnia and Herzegovina, in its transition and beyond.

4 Czyżewski, Krzysztof, A writer and war. Karahasan, the rebel, in *New Eastern Europe*, 1–2 (LV), 2024, 170–179 (179).

5 Idem, 174.

6 "The Bosnian Discourse on the Method" is one of the chapters in Karahasan, Dževad, *Sarajevo, Exodus of a City* (Kodansha International, New York, Tokyo, London, 1994).

7 Karahasan, Dževad, *Sarajevo, Exodus of a City*, 6–7.

the relevance and soundness of the attitudes of other cultures."[8] Again, this is an apt summary and at the same time a reminder.

Together, both reminders show the way forward, for the debate on constitutional reforms in Bosnia and Herzegovina and beyond.

Bibliography

Banović, Damir, Gavrić, Saša, Barreiro Mariño, Mariña, *The Political System of Bosnia and Herzegovina. Institutions – Actors – Processes*, Springer 2021.

Czyżewski, Krzysztof, A writer and war. Karahasan, the rebel, in: *New Eastern Europe, 1–2 (LV), 2024*, 170–179.

Karahasan, Dževad, *Sarajevo, Exodus of a City* (Kodansha International, New York, Tokyo, London, 1994).

Sahadžić, Maja, Banović, Damir, Barbarić, Dražen and Marković, Goran, eds., *Citizens, Constitution, Europe. Glossary of essential constitutional concepts in BiH* (Sarajevo: University of Sarajevo, Faculty of Law, 2023), https://www.balcanicaucaso.org/eng/Projects2/Bosnia-and-Herzegovina-the-Constitution-and-EU-Accession/Citizens-Constitution-Europe.

8 Idem, 64.

CHAPTER 3

Politics and History of Constitutional Development in Bosnia and Herzegovina

Nedim Hogić

1 Introduction

As Dražen Barbarić observes in this volume, the Bosnian Constitution, adopted within a larger framework of the peace negotiations in December of 1995, has established a mixture of liberal and consociational elements within a federal state. Unlike the previous Socialist Republic of Bosnia and Herzegovina, which explicitly and sometimes implicitly used only the ethnic quotas as a consociational mechanism,[1] the DPA adopted both federal and consociational elements for the same reason: the protection of collective ethnic rights. The consociational character is enshrined in the numerous provisions of ethnic veto, consensus-seeking mechanisms, and segmented autonomy, as noted by Goran Marković (in his chapter in this volume), in all federal units, primarily the two entities, Republika Srpska (RS) and the Federation of Bosnia and Herzegovina (FBiH). From the standpoint of federalism, the division of the state into two entities, one of which (FBiH) is also divided into ten cantons, testifies to a decentralising tendency that served the purpose to secure the ethnic control over territories. But, at the time of its drafting, the Constitution did not make clear the nature of this federalisation. Indeed, the state had few express prerogatives and no sources of income (e.g. through taxation). Rather than focusing on the rights that belonged to the citizens, the constitutional text dealt with the obligations of the entities in great detail. Both entities had the right to enter special and parallel relations with the neighbouring countries as if the constitution drafters intended to recreate an embryo of Yugoslavia. To that extent, the commitment towards the establishment of a customs union in the letters exchanged at the signing of the Dayton Peace Accords between Slobodan Milošević and Alija Izetbegović, the then leaders of Bosnia and Serbia, and U.S. Secretary of State Warren Christopher could be regarded as a future proof.[2] Another paradox was that the constitution, which elevated the

1 Marko, Joseph, "Bosnia-Herzegovina: the role of the judiciary in a divided society," *Const. Rev.*, 5, 2019, 194–196.

 | DOI:10.1163/9789004707887_004

rights of the three constituent peoples (Serbs, Bosniaks, and Croats), excluding all non-members of the three groups from full rights to representation, concluded with a long list of international human rights treaties that were to apply for the highest level of protection of human rights to be secured.[3] In any event, the Constitution, negotiated in Wright Patterson base in Dayton, Ohio, and signed in Paris, seemed open to diverse interpretations.

2 Reactions from Domestic and International Audiences

The Constitution's immediate reception upon its adoption was undoubtedly negative if not hostile and did not, despite some evolutionary movements, change over the years. No representative of the three major ethnic groups in the country openly endorsed it. The Bosniak political class believed that it gave the RS far too much autonomy, effectively rewarding the Serb leadership for ethnic cleansing, and that regionalisation of BiH would be a more sensible option for decentralisation. The Croat political elite, in particular after the adoption of the amendments to the FBiH constitution in 2002,[4] saw the Bosnian constitutional system as genuinely unfair to them as it locked them in the FBiH entity where Croats were a minority. The position of the Serb political elite evolved from outright rejection, that characterised the first few years following the adoption of the DPA, to the protectors of the constitution, claiming that its original meaning was the creation of a state with wide, almost confederal-like characteristics. The Constitution ignored the rights of all those not belonging to the three constituent peoples, who were excluded and discriminated by its provisions. In the wider sense, the DPA's territorial arrangements and the boundaries of the two entities that left many outside their pre-war residence occupied the public discourse of the first years. Various opinions of domestic and regional scholars concerning the state's constitutional structure greatly differed, referring to it as a unitary decentralised state, sui generis federation, and a confederation.[5]

---

2 Dayton Peace Accords Side Letters, *Yale Law School*, Lillian Goldman Library, The Avalon Project, 1995. https://avalon.law.yale.edu/20th_century/day23.asp#17.

3 Annex I to the BiH Constitution.

4 Vanjek, Dejan, "Bosnia and Herzegovina: A Country of Two Constituent Units and Three Peoples" in *The Forum of Federations Handbook of Federal Countries*, 2020, 65–82.

5 Sokol, Smiljko and Smerdel, Branko, *Ustavno pravo*, (Zagreb: Informator, 1998), 303–305. Bakšić-Muftić, Jasna, Razumijevanje Dejtonskog ustava 10 godina kasnije. *Zbornik radova Pravnog fakulteta u Splitu*, 42(1–2), 2005, 67–92. Karan, Siniša, "Form of Government in

The Constitution fared no better with the international audience. Save for the few involved in its drafting,[6] academic responses to the BiH Constitution were, and remain, overwhelmingly negative. Unfinished,[7] straitjacket,[8] creating an institutional overkill,[9] a compromise between ethno-territorial partition, and human rights protection[10] are just some of the descriptions and adjectives used to describe it. With almost no participation of either civil society or political parties other than the pre-war ruling three and with little care about other elements of the armistice agreements, such as demobilisation or transitional justice, the Constitution was far away from the spirit of the liberal 1990s, in comparison to other solutions adopted in the 1990s, such as the South African constitution or the Good Friday Agreement.[11]

And yet, despite the overwhelmingly negative attitude, its lack of ownership amongst the general population, and its overall complexity, the Constitution of Bosnia and Herzegovina has survived for three decades with only one amendment adopted, introducing the condominium and a wide autonomy of the Brčko District. Surprisingly resilient to change, it remains the site of contention and of reform proposals and battles.

3 Institutional Drivers of Constitutional Development

The main drivers of constitutional developments in Bosnia and Herzegovina were two institutions characterised by foreign presence, the BiH Constitutional Court and the Office of the High Representative. Acting together, but only sometimes in concert, these two institutions have significantly changed the constitutional paradigm of the country, strengthening central institu-

---

Bosnia and Herzegovina/Oblik državnog uređenja Bosne i Hercegovine" *Godišnjak fakulteta pravnih nauka*, 4(4), 2014, 156–167.

6 Szasz, Paul C., The protection of human rights through the Dayton/Paris peace agreement on Bosnia. *American Journal of International Law*, 90(2), (April, 1996), 301–316.

7 Marko, Joseph, 1–2 Sveske za javno pravo, 3, 2010.

8 Perry, Valery, Constitutional Reform in Bosnia and Herzegovina: Does the Road to Confederation go through the EU?. *International Peacekeeping*, 22(5), 2015, 490–510.

9 Woelk, Jens, "Bosnia-Herzegovina: Trying to build a federal state on paradoxes", *Constitutional Dynamics in Federal States–Sub-national Perspectives*, 2012, 109–139.

10 Waters, Timothy W. "The Naked Land: The Dayton Accords, Property Disputes, and Bosnia's Real Constitution," 40 *Harvard Journal of International Law*, 1999, 68.

11 O'Brien, James C. "The Dayton Constitution of Bosnia and Herzegovina, in Framing the state in times of transition," 2010, 344–345. https://www.usip.org/sites/default/files/Framing%20the%20State/Chapter12_Framing.pdf

tions without essentially challenging the ethnonationalist character of the state.

3.1 *Office of the High Representative*

The Office of the High Representative (OHR) oversees the civil implementation of the DPA (according to its Annex X). This encompasses foreign aid, rehabilitation of infrastructure, economic reconstruction, establishing political and constitutional institutions, promoting respect for human rights, and the holding of democratic elections.[12] Annex X also gives the High Representative creative freedom to broadly interpret the civilian implementation of the peace settlement.[13]

The so-called Bonn powers expanded the OHR's powers adding the competence to adopt binding decisions, and to remove public office holders who do not uphold their obligations under the DPA.[14] While the legal interpretation of the OHR's authority is becoming increasingly contested,[15] the influence of its decisions regarding removals and the legislative activity cannot be overstated. Even the obligation in the DPA that the entities had to align their constitutions with the BiH Constitution was, after a failure of the negotiation process in 2002, fulfilled by the OHR imposing the respective amendments.[16] The institutional reforms driven by the OHR that took place mainly between 1996 and 2010 have led to the creation of numerous institutions at the state level. Relatively successful reforms have created more than 60 institutions at the state level in the process of reforming the police, military, taxation authority, and

---

12 Art. II Annex X to the Dayton Peace Agreement.

13 Id. "The High Representative is the final authority in theater regarding interpretation of this Agreement on the civilian implementation of the peace settlement."

14 Peace Implementation Council (1998) Bonn Conclusions. https://www.ohr.int/pic-bonn-conclusions/?print=pdf. The Peace Implementation Council is an international quasi-governance body monitoring the situation in Bosnia and Herzegovina. It includes representatives from 55 countries and international organisations. The PIC is managed by the Steering Board, its executive arm. Its members are Canada, France, Germany, Italy, Japan, Russia, the United Kingdom, the European Union, and Turkey. It appoints the High Representative. In 2022, Russia withdrew from participation in this body and the financing of the OHR.

15 Banning, Tim, "The Bonn Powers of the High Representative in Bosnia Herzegovina: Tracing a Legal Figment", *Goettingen J. Int'l L.*, 6, 2014, 259.

16 Vanjek supra note 2. On 19 April 2002 a constitutional reform was enacted in both Entities on the basis of the Mrakovica-Sarajevo Agreement concluded under the auspices of the High Representative by the main political parties in the country. In the end, the reform was imposed by the OHR.

other institutions. Transfer agreements concluded between the entities facilitated the state assuming part of the authority for the judiciary in the creation of the High Judicial and Prosecutorial Council.

The OHR, despite being tasked with, inter alia, facilitation of the dialogue[17] did not, as time progressed, engage in mediation much. Instead, by a proactive interpretation of the mandate, its three main roles became to remove public officials, to impose laws (later to be confirmed by the BiH Parliamentary Assembly), or to strike down or temporarily suspend laws. The OHR was seen critically by many as being a profoundly undemocratic way of governing Bosnia and Herzegovina[18] and already in 2007, plans for its closure were drawn (known as "Agenda 5+2").[19] These plans have failed for two reasons. First there was disagreement between the EU member states and the United States and the United Kingdom over whether the immediate closure would risk peace and stability, and second, because of doubts whether the EU's political influence alone would stabilise the country. The imposition of decisions remains a cornerstone of the narrative for the RS politicians who believe that the impositions are a deviation from the original meaning of the Dayton Peace Accords, which was to create a common state with only very limited competences and a small number of state bodies, leaving the important competences to the entities instead.[20]

3.2 *BiH Constitutional Court*

The role of the Constitutional Court of BiH, composed of nine justices, four from the FBiH, two from the RS, and three appointed by the President of the European Court of Human Rights (ECtHR), in developing constitutional solutions as the ultimate domestic arbiter of constitutional and legal disputes cannot be overstated. The Court's jurisprudence has shaped the political and legal life of the country. Its decision U-5/98, usually referred to as "constituent peoples" case, led to the harmonisation of the entity constitutions with the BiH Constitution and an expansion of the constituency of peoples as a sui

17 Annex X to the DPA, Article II d.

18 See e.g.: Knaus, Gerald and Martin, Felix, "Travails of the European Raj", *Journal of democracy*, 14(3), 2013.; Dijkstra, Gerrit S.A. and Raadschelders, Jos C.N. "The High Representative in Bosnia-Herzegovina: The Unusual Institutional Arrangement of a Non-Authoritarian, yet Controlled, Democracy", *World Affairs*, *185* (2), 2022, 285–311.

19 OHR, "Agenda 5+2" see: (https://www.ohr.int/agenda-52/), and Tirak, Goran, "The Bosnian Hiatus: A Story of Misinterpretations", *CEPS Policy Brief*, 2010, 219.

20 Toal, Gerard, "Republika Srpska will have a referendum": the rhetorical politics of Milorad Dodik. *Nationalities Papers*, *41*(1), 2013, 166–204.

generis mode of protection of collective rights.[21] In U-9/00, deciding on the OHR's intervention in the creation of the Border Police in BiH, the Court established that the OHR is, similar to international institutions that existed in Austria and Germany after the Second World War, an institution of dual nature, both international and domestic. The court's 2003 judgment, dealing with constitutionality of the establishment of a national-level tariffs regime, interpreted Art. I.4 as an obligation to establish the joint market between the two entities.[22] Following a string of appellations submitted between 2007 and 2010, the Court found that Art. IV.4 of the Constitution (competencies of the BiH Parliamentary Assembly) may be applied to regulate joint standards and bodies operating at the state level if such duties are essential for the country's process of European integrations.[23] This decision practically opened the doors for the strengthening of state-level competencies critical for the EU integration process.

However, the court's judicial activism had its limits and constraints. The Court did not support the changes that would bring the Constitution fully in line with the international human rights obligations, both those enshrined in the annexes to the Constitution and the protocols to the European Convention on Human Rights.[24] Equally, the Court, as Damir Banović aptly recognises in his contribution to this volume, stayed short of defining the elements of federalism present in BiH, opting instead to speak of a "complex state structure". The Court's decision in the so-called *Ljubić* case would give grounds to the principle of legitimate representation which would, as we will see later, be an important factor in the arguments for constitutional reform.[25] The Court did not shy away from declaring unconstitutional decisions of the High Rep-

21 Generally, see: https://www.venice.coe.int/webforms/documents/default.aspx?pdffile=CDL(2002)127-e.

22 Some commentators saw a seed of integration based on economic freedoms, such as the free movement of capital, goods, and persons between the two entities that would be on par with the four freedoms characterising the European Union. See: Ademović, Nedim, Marko, Joseph and Marković, Goran, *Ustavno pravo Bosne i Hercegovine*, (Sarajevo: Konrad Adenauer Stiftung, 2012), 93–97.

23 The Constitutional Court of BiH, Decision on Admissibility and Merits U-6/07, para 20 (deciding the appellation regarding public procurement regulation at the state level).

24 The Constitutional Court of BiH, Decision on Admissibility and Merits, AP-2578/06. See also: The Constitutional Court of BiH, Decision on Admissibility and Merits, U-18/05 (where the request to review the constitutionality of the entity name "Republika Srpska" was withdrawn).

25 The Constitutional Court of BiH, Decision on Admissibility and Merits, U-23/14.

resentative.[26] Still, the RS political representatives frequently criticised the Court's judicial activism and, in particular, its composition that includes three judges appointed by the President of the ECtHR as illegitimate. No doubt, what contributed to this perception was that in many of the key decisions, the three judges appointed by the ECtHR President voted *en bloc* with judges appointed from the FBiH, particularly the Bosniak ones.

4 International-Inspired Interventions to the Constitution

As we have seen, the two major drivers of institutional development, the OHR and the BiH Constitutional Court, were both heavily influenced by foreign presence. In that sense, they have limited the sovereignty of the state of Bosnia and Herzegovina. While the court's judicial activism created space for institutional reform, this institutional reform was driven primarily by external actors, who used the OHR as a vehicle for the imposition of solutions. However, even significant success stories, such as the creation of unified armed forces, the system of indirect taxation and the holding of elections,[27] did not change the overall paradigm of a dysfunctional state.

In the first decade of the 21st century, it was commonplace to invoke the necessity for constitutional reform, justifying it by a lack of local ownership in the existing governance structure and a lack of accountability of international actors who were de facto playing a key role in the governance of Bosnia and Herzegovina. The rather complex multi-level constitutional framework that stifles decision-making, economic development, and accountability and is incompatible with the European integrations was invoked as grounds for constitutional reform.[28] As the Constitution had been drafted primarily by an external power, that of the international community, which, during the 1990s held numerous talks and sessions regarding the constitutional future of the country, it does not surprise that this Internationalised *Pouvoir Constituant*[29] launched many initiatives that were to lead to constitutional reform.

---

26 The Constitutional Court of BiH, Decision on Admissibility and Merits, U-9/09 (declaring the OHR-imposed norms regarding the Statute of the City of Mostar unconstitutional for violation of electoral rights).

27 Until 2006, the elections were conducted by the OSCE Mission to Bosnia and Herzegovina.

28 Čengić, Rubina, "Ustav BiH treba mijenjati", *Nezavisne novine*, Feb 17, 2004.

29 For these reasons, the International Community has rightly been referred to as the "fourth constituent" element in Bosnia and Herzegovina, e.g. by Bose, Sumantra, *Bosnia*

In this period, much hope has been placed in the civil society in Bosnia and Herzegovina and its ability to bridge the (wide) gap between the ethno-territorial aspirations of the political parties and a modern liberal-democratic model of the citizen–state relationship. For example, Switzerland supported a cross-entity group of young lawyers who drafted and presented constitutional amendments to the BiH Parliamentary Assembly.[30] That same country sponsored the travel of the representatives of Bosnian NGOs and political parties to Switzerland and a series of public roundtable discussions concerning the constitutional reform.[31] Domestic actors, mainly NGOs, made several proposals but these were not introduced in the parliamentary procedure.[32] However, as the attention of the donors changed focus from constitutional reform to other questions, such as those of corruption and anti-discrimination, the number of proposals or advocacy activities related to constitutional reform dropped significantly. Despite its considerable capacities, civil society has failed to conduct a legal and political mobilisation that would lead to an advocacy for different constitutional solutions. Since 2010, only two significant proposals have been proposed: one focused on giving a stronger voice and role to the local governance structures and the other on gender equality aspects of constitutional reforms.[33] While both proposals have raised important questions about the deficiency of the constitutional framework (cf. also Nevenko Vranješ in this volume), neither of the two became significant in the political arena. It remains to be seen whether the direct democracy approaches, such as the ones organised through citizen assemblies that Iseric and Herenda aptly describe in their chapter, could be a way forward to a more inclusive democratic constitution.

The international actors themselves created two proposals for constitutional reform. According to one proposal, much discussed – at least in the

---

after Dayton: Nationalist Partition and International Intervention, Oxford: Oxford University Press, 2002. See also: Al-Ali, Zaid and Dann, Philipp, "The internationalized Pouvoir Constituant – constitution-making under external influence in Iraq, Sudan and East Timor", *Max Planck Yearbook of United Nations Law Online*, 10(1), 2006, 423–463.

30 Stanojlović, Dragan, Stručna lekcija političarima, *Oslobodjenje*, Feb 26, 2010.

31 E.g. see: Kovačević, S. "Najveći izazov države", *Nezavisne novine*, Jun 23, 2007.

32 There is even a Wikipedia page on "Constitutional reform in BiH" (https://en.wikipedia.org/wiki/Constitutional_reform_in_Bosnia_and_Herzegovina).

33 See: "Platforma ženskih prioriteta za ustavne promjene": Tri velika ZAŠTO, pet bitnih ZATO, https://zenskamreza.ba/platforma-zenskih-prioriteta-za-ustavne-promjene-tri-velika-zasto-pet-bitnih-zato-2/ and https://municipalizacija.ba/wp-content/uploads/2021/10/Model-Municipalizacije-Bosanski.pdf.

international bubble – by the think tank European Stability Initiative, BiH would remain an asymmetrical federation in which the competencies of cantons would become equal to those of the RS.[34] At the same time, the FBiH government would gradually be hollowed out and limited in competencies, while the BiH-level government would be strengthened by consolidation of competencies already conferred to it, primarily by the laws imposed by the High Representative. This proposal was never formally introduced, but rather proposed as a provocation, to stimulate further work on constitutional reform.

A much better-known proposal was the so-called April Package, which aimed at a comprehensive reform of the Dayton Constitution. Sponsored by the United States government and backed by most Western governments, the proposal would considerably strengthen the BiH-level institutions and reduce decision-making complexity. For example, the House of Peoples of the BiH PA would no longer be equal to the House of Representatives but reduced in its functions to vital national interest protection; also, the BiH Presidency would no longer be directly elected and much of its competences would be transferred to the Council of Ministers. Judicial institutions created through Transfer Agreements brokered by the OHR would be regulated by the constitution and three additional ministries would be created, while at the same time increasing the list of competences conferred to the state.

However, the proposal stayed short of redefining or questioning the territorial composition of the country, the principles of federalism on which it was constructed, as well as the concept of "constituent peoples" as the mechanism for collective rights protection. Such a stance provoked opposition from a certain number of Bosniak and Croat MP s. The former believed that the mechanism of entity voting[35] is the key obstacle to a more functioning country as it gives Serb MPs the key to stop the entire legislative process. The latter criticise(d) that, despite being one of the three "constituent peoples", Croats can be outvoted by Bosniaks in the Federation, Serbs in the RS, and at the BiH-level by Bosniaks and Serbs. Therefore, being the smallest group in number, Croats would deserve an entity of their own; otherwise, abolishing the entities should be an option. These two stances, represented primarily by two political parties, SBiH and HDZ 1990, led to the failure in the adoption of the April Package of constitutional amendments in the BiH PA by only two votes. The

34 See: Making Federalism Work – A Radical Proposal For Practical Reform, *European Stability Initiative*, 2005, https://www.esiweb.org/publications/making-federalism-work-radical-proposal-practical-reform.

35 Article IV.3.b of the Constitution.

US Embassy, as the proposal's main sponsor, blamed bribery of these two parties' representatives for that failure.[36]

Attempts to revive the April Package or some elements of this proposal continued between 2007 and 2010. Yet, the subsequent Butmir and Prud negotiations, despite being of much narrower scope, failed to bridge the gap among the political party representatives. The passing of the *Sejdić–Finci* judgment by the European Court of Human Rights in December of 2010 led to a renewed drive for constitutional reform. Paradoxically, despite the judgment declaring some important constitutional provisions as contravening the European Convention on Human Rights, specifically the election of the collective Presidency or House of Peoples members, the judgment actually strengthened the constitution. In fact, the negotiations, as well as the amendments created by the BiH political parties for the purpose of implementing the *Sejdić–Finci* judgment, did not lead to anything – despite the mediation of the EU enlargement commissioner – and have been discontinued after their failure in 2014.[37] Between 2014 and 2019, there have not been any initiatives to change the constitution. Instead, economic initiatives, such as the Reform Agenda, were launched by the EU, shifting the focus of the need to strengthen the country's economic system. A few institutions, such as the State Aid Council and the Coordination Mechanism for European Integrations created in this period, were highly decentralised with entity and ethnic voting principles embedded in their structure, leading some observers to ask if BiH is shifting towards confederation.[38] The EU gradually abandoned its stance that constitutional changes were the precondition for the Stabilisation and Association Agreement to enter into force, in 2015. Politically, this signalled a clear departure from the earlier stance that the EU integration would automatically lead to a stronger state level government.

In 2019, with the release of the so-called "fourteen priorities", the EU reintroduced the matter of constitutional reform in its Opinion on BiH's application for membership. It has done so by requesting that the country resolves two main problems in its constitutional system: the presence of foreign judges in the BiH Constitutional Court and that the BiH "thoroughly improve the institutional framework, including at the constitutional level, in order to

36 Srđan Blagovčanin and Boris Divjak, How Bosnia's political economy holds it back and what to do about it. *John Hopkins University Centre for Transatlantic Studies*, 2015, 6.

37 "Bosnia-Herzegovina - EU: Deep disappointment on Sejdić-Finci implementation", *European Commission*, 2014, ec.europa.eu/commission/presscorner/detail/en/MEMO_14_117.

38 Perry Valery, "Constitutional Reform in Bosnia and Herzegovina: Does the Road to Confederation go through the EU?" *International Peacekeeping*, 22(5), 2015, 490–510.

ensure legal certainty in terms of division of competences between levels of government."[39] Although from a federalist standpoint, the latter topic deserves more attention, the former, due to the high relevance of the BiH Constitutional Court, has seen numerous proposals, particularly those from Serb parties being introduced. Such an interest is not difficult to explain; although a complete statistical analysis does not exist, in many constitutional cases described earlier in this chapter, the foreign judges would vote together with the two Bosniak judges, thus forming a majority which has been decisive in some of the most important cases in the court's history.[40]

The latest rounds of negotiations regarding constitutional changes that took place in 2021 and 2022 demonstrate an absence of proximation. Taking place outside the governmental institutions in Neum, Bosnia and Herzegovina's only seaside resort, the negotiations focused on the implementation of the *Sejdić–Finci* judgment. However, the guarantee of rights of citizens not affiliated with the three constituent peoples had long disappeared from the focus of the negotiators. Instead, the negotiations focused on protecting the rights of Croats as a constituent people to elect a member to the BiH Presidency who may "legitimately represent" their interest, in line with the *Ljubić* judgment. The stances between the majority of Croat political representatives, who demanded the creation of a separate electoral unit for the direct election of Croat BiH Presidency member, and Bosniak representatives who advocated for considering other ECtHR judgments after *Sejdić–Finci* (cf. Balic in this volume) remain unresolved. Yet again, the EU abandoned its stance that the constitutional changes would be a precondition for candidate status, deciding, under strong geopolitical pressure triggered by the Russian invasion of Ukraine to confer candidate status to Bosnia and Herzegovina in 2022 (even if this does not automatically mean the opening of negotiations).

5 Missed Opportunities

The Dayton negotiations were on the brink of failure. Under immense pressure, the negotiating parties agreed to sign the agreement only on the

39 "Commission Opinion on Bosnia and Herzegovina's application for membership of the European Union", *European Commission*, COM, 2019, 261 final.

40 Which does not, however, hold true for all decisions. In many important cases the foreign judges would not vote *en bloc* with the two Bosniak judges, for example in the *Ljubić* case or the case deciding the scope of competences. See: Alex Schwartz, "International judges on constitutional courts: cautionary evidence from post-conflict Bosnia", *Law & Social Inquiry*, 44(1), 2019, 1–30.

final day. The dealbreaker was the resolution of the status of Brčko, a city of strategic importance that both entities wanted for themselves as it separates the eastern and western parts of the Republika Srpska (RS). Unable to reach an agreement, the sides agreed to future arbitration proceedings.[41] The FBiH representatives, arguing that only a quarter of the pre-war population was Serb, demanded Brčko's inclusion in the Federation. Serb representatives claimed that giving Brčko to the FBiH would prevent the RS's territorial continuity and change the territorial compromise between the two based upon a balance of 51:49 percent. The Final Arbitration Award (awarded in 1999) established Brčko District as a condominium, a joint property of the two entities.[42] However, Brčko is not governed by FBiH and RS representatives but is, in fact, a self-governing body ruled by its assembly and mayor.[43] The two entities exercise no governing prerogatives. There is only little cross-ethnic political organisation, but also little conflict. It is often noted that the district's education system is unified without segregation, unlike, for example, the education system in two cantons of the FBiH (characterised by the slogan "two schools under one roof").[44]

One would expect such a successful outcome of a very contentious issue to inspire lawmakers and the academic community to build on Brčko's example of integration and overcoming the legacy of war.[45] That is not the case; Brčko is rarely invoked in BiH in that context. Instead, the arbitration outcome is considered inspirational primarily by foreign experts.[46] Likewise, the creation of state institutions, instead of serving as an inspiration for creation of intergovernmental co-operation mechanisms remains underapplied despite its potential (analysed by Bojan Vlaški in his chapter).

---

41 Annex II Art. V to the Dayton Peace Accords.

42 Arbitral Tribunal for Dispute Over Inter-Entity Boundary in Brcko Area (The Federation of Bosnia and Herzegovina v. The Republika Srpska), Final Award of 5 March 1999, 38 ILM 534.

43 Bieber, Florian, "Local institutional engineering: A tale of two cities, Mostar and Brčko", *International Peacekeeping*, 12(3), 2005, 425–427.

44 Generally, see: Jones, Briony, "Exploring the politics of reconciliation through education reform: The case of Brčko district, Bosnia and Herzegovina", *International Journal of Transitional Justice*, 6(1), 2012, 126–148.

45 Zdeb, Aleksandra, "Accommodating Liberal Consociations: The District Brčko Case and the Role of Informal Institutions in the Consociational Model", *Ethnopolitics*, 21(5), 2022, 517–537 (explaining the success of Brčko through the lens of informal institutions, such as balanced ethnic-based budget spending).

46 E.g. see: DeLaney Strenski, Emma "The Brčko Arbitration: A Blueprint for Ending Current and Future Ethnic Territorial Conflicts", *Indiana Journal of Global Legal Studies*, 2022, 29, 181.

The legal status of the property formerly owned by the Socialist Republic of Bosnia and Herzegovina and by the Socialist Federal Republic of Yugoslavia, as legal predecessors of the current state of Bosnia and Herzegovina, best demonstrates the distant position of the political parties and the absence of any mediating role by its civil society. Failure to resolve this issue has allowed the OHR to remain in the country, as the resolution to the status of such property remains one of the key conditions to be met before the closure of the OHR, without which the country cannot join the EU.[47]

In 2005, the OHR banned both entities from freely using state property.[48] The OHR's argument, shared by many other international actors, is that the sole owner of this property is the state and that its status must be regulated by state-level legislation.[49] Contrary to this, representatives of the Republika Srpska claimed that the BiH Constitution never explicitly gave the state of BiH the authority to own property. In 2009, the OHR also created a list of immovable state property for all municipalities in BiH and published it on its webpage. Until 2012, a special commission existing with the Council of Ministers would award exceptions to the use of such properties, allowing the entities to use them.[50] During this period, the RS has repeatedly passed several pieces of legislation granting the exclusive right to manage such property.[51] All such efforts were thwarted either by the decisions of the Constitutional Court[52] that would annul such laws and the actions of the OHR that would suspend the application of these laws.

Failure to reach consensus on this issue often prevents the entity governments from granting building rights to domestic and foreign investors. Thus, state property became a contentious issue with important economic connotations.[53] Yet, the parties maintain irreconcilable positions. Bosniak parties argue that the former state property must become property of the state of

47 Office of the High Representative, Agenda 5+2, https://www.ohr.int/agenda-52/.

48 Office of the High Representative, "Decision Enacting the Law on a Temporary Prohibition of the of Disposal of State Property", Mar 18, 2005. https://www.ohr.int/decision-enacting-the-law-on-the-temporary-prohibition-of-disposal-of-state-property-of-bosnia-and-herzegovina/?print=pdf.

49 United States Embassy to Bosnia and Herzegovina, United States Position on State Property, 2022, https://ba.usembassy.gov/the-united-states-position-on-state-property/.

50 Čengić, Rubina, "Javni interes je rastegljiv pojam", *Start*, 2012.

51 Office of the High Representative, High Representative suspends application of the RS Law on Immovable Property, 2022, https://www.ohr.int/high-representative-suspends-application-of-the-rs-law-on-immovable-property/.

52 Constitutional Court of BiH, Decision on admissibility and Merits, U-1/11, 2013.

53 E.g. see: Mrkonjić, Anamarija, "Šarović porazio Dodika na Drini", *Dnevni list*, Sep 26, 2013.

Bosnia and Herzegovina and that this level of government should decide how to use such property by the entities. The Serb parties argue that state property is not an expressly mentioned prerogative of the state by the Dayton constitution.[54] Finally, just as it did not play any role in helping BiH acquire its independence from Yugoslavia, the state property and its legal status would play little, if any, role in the eventual secession of the Republika Srpska, as it is largely irrelevant to preventing or granting its claims to independence. Likewise, while state-level law might be an appropriate venue for regulating state property, the state-level government quite simply lacks the capacity to own or use most of it.[55] However, this does not prevent political party representatives from treating it symbolically and without much recourse to its functionality.

In so doing, the politicians, perhaps inadvertently and perhaps with intent, have increased the international institutionalised and informal presence. Thus, instead of a gradual dissipation of foreign presence in Bosnia and Herzegovina, the constant demands for foreign influence and interference that come from all prominent political actors consolidate it. These actors' different priorities make the constitutional reform appear important, as the changes demanded are only possible through constitutional amendments. Still, the diverse standpoints over the amendments make a consensus less likely.

6 Conclusion

Despite its hostile reception upon its adoption in 1995, the constitution of Bosnia and Herzegovina has demonstrated its longevity in the face of an almost permanent constitutional crisis. Several variables have determined its durability and resilience: the irreconcilable stances of domestic political leaders, the increasingly fragmented nature of international influence, the absence of a domestic constituency arguing for constitutional change, and the elasticity of interpretation of constitutional norms established by the Constitutional Court.

Constitutional development since adopting the Dayton constitution can be divided into three main periods. In the first decade after the war, the OHR and the BiH Constitutional Court were the key drivers of the constitutional reform

54 See: Constitutional Court of BiH, supra note 53.

55 Namely, the limited competences and budget constraints (Canton Sarajevo alone spends more money than the state-level government) leaves the state-level authorities little room to use the property.

developments. The extensive state-building in that period strengthened the contemporary Bosnian state. That period lasted until the fall of the April Package. It was succeeded by a second period in which the secessionist claims had arisen and the direct international intervention gradually ceased. Questioning the limits of the reforms enacted by the international actors and, in some instances, successful attempts to reclaim the authority transferred to the state level marked this period. Finally, the third period, beginning with the Constitutional Court's judgment in the *Ljubić* case, has returned constitutional reform to the spotlight within the European integration process. In a political sense, each of the three periods broadly corresponds to the demands stemming from one of the constituent peoples: first one to Bosniaks, second to Serbs, and the third to Croats.

Limited possibilities for reform exist, but the key elements of the Constitution, such as the primacy of the ethnic over the civic principle and the widely decentralised multi-level asymmetric system, will remain cornerstones of its existence.[56] Finally, despite all criticism, we must not forget that the frequent threats of secession and even violence lower the bar by which the Dayton Constitution is judged. Therefore, it might very well be that purely because of the absence of violence and secession, and a lack of alternatives, foreign diplomats and statesmen consider the Dayton constitution a success.[57] In the absence of constitutional amendments, the two main drivers of the constitutional change, the BiH Constitutional Court and the OHR, will remain key in preventing further constitutional erosion.

Bibliography

Ademović, Nedim, Marko, Joseph, Marković, Goran, *Ustavno pravo Bosne i Hercegovine*, (Sarajevo: Konrad Adenauer Stiftung, 2012), 93–97.

Al-Ali, Zaid and Dann, Philipp, "The internationalized Pouvoir Constituant – constitution-making under external influence in Iraq, Sudan and East Timor", *Max Planck Yearbook of United Nations Law Online, 10*(1), 2006, 423–463.

Annex I to the BiH Constitution.

Annex II Art. V to the Dayton Peace Accords.

56 Generally, see: Sahadžić, Maja, *Asymmetry, multinationalism and constitutional law: Managing legitimacy and stability in federalist states*, (London: Routledge, 2020).

57 Gilbert, Andrew, "The Limits of Foreign Authority: Publicity and the Political Logic of Ambivalence in Postwar Bosnia and Herzegovina", *Comparative Studies in Society and History, 59*(2), 2017, 415–417.

Annex X to the DPA, Article II d.

Arbitral Tribunal for Dispute Over Inter-Entity Boundary in Brcko Area (The Federation of Bosnia and Herzegovina v. The Republika Srpska), Final Award of 5 March 1999, 38 ILM 534.

Art. II Annex X to the Dayton Peace Agreement.Article IV.3.b of the Constitution.

Bakšić-Muftić, Jasna, Razumijevanje Dejtonskog ustava 10 godina kasnije. *Zbornik radova Pravnog fakulteta u Splitu*, *42*(1–2), 2005, 67–92.

Banning, Tim, "The Bonn Powers of the High Representative in Bosnia Herzegovina: Tracing a Legal Figment", *Goettingen J. Int'l L.*, 6, 2014, 259.

Bieber, Florian, "Local institutional engineering: A tale of two cities, Mostar and Brčko", *International Peacekeeping*, *12*(3), 2005, 425–427.

Blagovčanin, Srđan and Divjak, Boris, How Bosnia's political economy holds it back and what to do about it. *John Hopkins University Centre for Transatlantic Studies*, 2015, 6.

Bose, Sumantra, *Bosnia after Dayton: Nationalist Partition and International Intervention*, (Oxford: Oxford University Press, 2002).

"Bosnia-Herzegovina – EU: Deep disappointment on Sejdić-Finci implementation", *European Commission*, 2014, ec.europa.eu/commission/presscorner/detail/en/MEMO_14_117

"Commission Opinion on Bosnia and Herzegovina's application for membership of the European Union", *European Commission*, COM, 2019, 261 final.

Čengić, Rubina, "Javni interes je rastegljiv pojam", *Start*, 2012.

Čengić, Rubina, "Ustav BiH treba mijenjati", *Nezavisne novine*, Feb 17, 2004.

Constitutional Court of BiH, Decision on admissibility and Merits, U-1/11, 2013.

Dayton Peace Accords Side Letters, *Yale Law School*, (Lillian Goldman Library, The Avalon Project, 1995) https://avalon.law.yale.edu/20th_century/day23.asp#17.

DeLaney Strenski, Emma, "The Brcko Arbitration: A Blueprint for Ending Current and Future Ethnic Territorial Conflicts", *Indiana Journal of Global Legal Studies*, 2022, 29, 181.

Dijkstra, Gerrit S.A. and Raadschelders, Jos C.N. "The High Representative in Bosnia-Herzegovina: The Unusual Institutional Arrangement of a Non-Authoritarian, yet Controlled, Democracy", *World Affairs*, *185* (2), 2022, 285–311.

Gerard Toal, "Republika Srpska will have a referendum": the rhetorical politics of Milorad Dodik. *Nationalities Papers*, *41*(1), 2013, 166–204.

Gilbert, Andrew, "The Limits of Foreign Authority: Publicity and the Political Logic of Ambivalence in Postwar Bosnia and Herzegovina", *Comparative Studies in Society and History*, *59*(2), 2017, 415–417.

https://www.ohr.int/pic-bonn-conclusions/?print=pdf.

https://www.usip.org/sites/default/files/Framing%20the%20State/Chapter12_Framing.pdf

Jones, Briony, "Exploring the politics of reconciliation through education reform: The case of Brčko district, Bosnia and Herzegovina", *International Journal of Transitional Justice*, *6*(1), 2012, 126–148.

Karan, Siniša, "Form of Government in Bosnia and Herzegovina/Oblik državnog uređenja Bosne i Hercegovine" *Godišnjak fakulteta pravnih nauka*, *4*(4), 2014, 156–167.

Knaus, Gerald and Martin, Felix, "Travails of the European Raj", *Journal of democracy*, *14*(3), 2013.

Kovačević, S. "Najveći izazov države", *Nezavisne novine*, Jun 23, 2007.

Making Federalism Work – A Radical Proposal For Practical Reform,*European Stability Initiative*, 2005, https://www.esiweb.org/publications/making-federalism-work-radical-proposal-practical-reform.

Marko, Joseph, "Bosnia-Herzegovina: the role of the judiciary in a divided society," *Const. Rev.*, *5*, 2019, 194–196.

Marko, Joseph, 1–2 Sveske za javno pravo, 3, 2010.

Mrkonjić, Anamarija, "Šarović porazio Dodika na Drini", *Dnevni list*, Sep 26, 2013.

O'Brien, James C., "The Dayton Constitution of Bosnia and Herzegovina, in Framing the state in times of transition," 2010, 344–345.

Office of the High Representative, "Decision Enacting the Law on a Temporary Prohibition of the of Disposal of State Property", Mar 18, 2005. https://www.ohr.int/decision-enacting-the-law-on-the-temporary-prohibition-of-disposal-of-state-property-of-bosnia-and-herzegovina/?print=pdf.

Office of the High Representative, Agenda 5+2, https://www.ohr.int/agenda-52/.

Office of the High Representative, High Representative suspends application of the RS Law on Immovable Property, 2022, https://www.ohr.int/high-representative-suspends-application-of-the-rs-law-on-immovable-property/.

Peace Implementation Council (1998) Bonn Conclusions.

Perry, Valery, "Constitutional Reform in Bosnia and Herzegovina: Does the Road to Confederation go through the EU?" *International Peacekeeping*, 22(5), 2015, 490–510.

Perry, Valery, Constitutional Reform in Bosnia and Herzegovina: Does the Road to Confederation go through the EU? *International Peacekeeping*, 22(5), 2015, 490–510.

"Platforma ženskih prioriteta za ustavne promjene": Tri velika ZAŠTO, pet bitnih ZATO, https://zenskamreza.ba/platforma-zenskih-prioriteta-za-ustavne-promjene-tri-velika-zasto-pet-bitnih-zato-2/ and https://municipalizacija.ba/wp-content/uploads/2021/10/Model-Municipalizacije-Bosanski.pdf.

Sahadžić, Maja, *Asymmetry, multinationalism and constitutional law: Managing legitimacy and stability in federalist states*, (London: Routledge, 2020).

Schwartz, Alex, "International judges on constitutional courts: cautionary evidence from post-conflict Bosnia", *Law & Social Inquiry*, *44*(1), 2019, 1–30.

Sokol, Smiljko and Smerdel, Branko, *Ustavno pravo*, (Zagreb: Informator, 1998), 303–305.

Stanojlović, Dragan, Stručna lekcija političarima, *Oslobodjenje*, Feb 26, 2010.

Szasz, Paul C., The protection of human rights through the Dayton/Paris peace agreement on Bosnia. *American Journal of International Law*, 90(2), (April, 1996), 301–316.

The Constitutional Court of BiH, Decision od Admissibility and Merits, U-9/09.

The Constitutional Court of BiH, Decision on Admissibility and Merits, AP-2578/06.

The Constitutional Court of BiH, Decision on Admissibility and Merits, U-18/05.

The Constitutional Court of BiH, Decision on Admissibility and Merits, U-23/14.

Tirak, Goran, "The Bosnian Hiatus: A Story of Misinterpretations", *CEPS Policy Brief*, 2010, 219.

United States Embassy to Bosnia and Herzegovina, United States Position on State Property, 2022, https://ba.usembassy.gov/the-united-states-position-on-state-property/.

Vanjek, Dejan, "Bosnia and Herzegovina: A Country of Two Constituent Units and Three Peoples" in *The Forum of Federations Handbook of Federal Countries*, 2020, 65–82.

Waters, Timothy W. "The Naked Land: The Dayton Accords, Property Disputes, and Bosnia's Real Constitution," *40 Harvard Journal of International Law*, 1999, 68.

Woelk, Jens, "Bosnia-Herzegovina: Trying to build a federal state on paradoxes", *Constitutional Dynamics in Federal States–Sub-national Perspectives*, 2012, 109–139.

Zdeb, Aleksandra, "Accommodating Liberal Consociations: The District Brčko Case and the Role of Informal Institutions in the Consociational Model", *Ethnopolitics*, *21*(5), 2022, 517–537.

Tirak, Goran, "The Bosnian Hiatus: A Story of Misinterpretations", *CEPS Policy Brief*, 2010, 219.

United States Embassy to Bosnia and Herzegovina, United States Position on State Property, 2022, https://ba.usembassy.gov/the-united-states-position-on-state-property/.

Vanjek, Dejan, "Bosnia and Herzegovina: A Country of Two Constituent Units and Three Peoples" in *The Forum of Federations Handbook of Federal Countries*, 2020, 65–82.

Waters, Timothy W. "The Naked Land: The Dayton Accords, Property Disputes, and Bosnia's Real Constitution," *40 Harvard Journal of International Law*, 1999, 68.

Woelk, Jens, "Bosnia-Herzegovina: Trying to build a federal state on paradoxes", *Constitutional Dynamics in Federal States–Sub-national Perspectives*, 2012, 109–139.

Zdeb, Aleksandra, "Accommodating Liberal Consociations: The District Brčko Case and the Role of Informal Institutions in the Consociational Model", *Ethnopolitics*, *21*(5), 2022, 517–537.

CHAPTER 4

What Basic Values and Legal Principles Are Required for a Functional System of Multi-level Governance?

Damir Banović

1 Introduction

For the political and constitutional system of Bosnia and Herzegovina, conventional and normative recognition of basic values and legal principles is of particular importance to meet the collective demands of ethnic communities (constituent peoples and national minorities), as well as demands of individuals and individual rights, and to balance the system of functional state administration. In this light, we consider acknowledgement and recognition of (inherent) values and principles for a multinational society to be significant and necessary. These principles should not only be part of the normative sphere, but also of the constitutional and political practice of legislative and executive bodies. Furthermore, they should be effectively accepted in the broader political life of a multinational society. Guided by the above, the chapter starts from the basic conceptual frameworks of values and legal principles (which can be used interchangeably depending on whether they are part of the normative sphere, conventional practice, or are considered moral principles), it addresses comparative constitutional-legal analyses of multinational states, and then tackles the legal and the constitutional system of Bosnia and Herzegovina, which has already recognised certain values and principles. Finally, the chapter concludes with a proposal of missing values and legal principles that should become part of conventional practice, normative sphere, or goals that should be achieved.

2 On Basic Values and Legal Principles

Without embarking upon a thorough analysis of basic values and legal principles, it is necessary for the purposes of this chapter to at least describe the basic characteristics of the concepts used. In terms of the basic values of a legal and political system, we could discuss them as values conventionally

 | DOI:10.1163/9789004707887_005

recognised in a political and constitutional system; as the origins and foundations of the political and constitutional organisation of the state, which are not necessarily legally codified; as part of the normative sphere of a political and legal system, etc. We can also discuss them as the foundations and reasons for establishing a political community. These values can be constitutionally codified and transformed into legal principles or can only form part of moral principles. Furthermore, they can be expressed as constitutional conventions or as reasons for action and as deep conventions of a constitutional and political system. Knowledge about them is intuitive, but can be more clearly understood through empirical research into the value of a political and constitutional system. On the other hand, we can discuss legal principles as the most general legal norms; as generally accepted legal standards which recognise the status of a binding norm and which courts use in explaining their decisions; as generally accepted moral principles that primarily serve the interpretation of law.[1] Or, according to Robert Alexy, legal principles are norms that order something to be accomplished to the greatest extent, considering real and legal possibilities.[2] These are just some of the possible attitudes and understandings of the nature of legal principles. Looking at contemporary legal theory, the debate moves in two directions: (1) the difference between legal rules and legal principles is only in their *generality*, and (2) the difference between rules and legal principles is of *a structural* and *logical nature*.[3] Regardless of different understandings of the nature of legal principles, their instrumental use is undoubtedly significant. In this sense, defining legal principles, Raz lists five different purposes of their function in law, namely (1) as grounds for interpreting law; (2) as grounds for changing laws; (3) as grounds for particular exceptions to laws; (4) as grounds for making new rules; and (5) as the sole ground for action in particular cases.[4]

The theoretical consideration of principles for a (given) constitutional and political system is fundamentally an intuitive process characteristic of the methodology of philosophy of law. In its concrete analysis, the process is inspired by empirical facts, political processes, but also by comparative and

1 Spaić, Bojan, "Dva poimanja pravnih principa," *Anali Pravnog fakulteta Univerziteta u Beogradu* 65, 1, (2017), 114.

2 Spaić, "Dva poimanja pravnih principa," 116.

3 In his article *Legal Principles and the Limits of Law*, Joseph Raz claims that in law there is no single position on the distinction of what law is from what it is not. Raz, Joseph, "Legal Principles and the Limits of Law," *The Yale Law Journal* 81, (1972), 823; Spaić, "Dva poimanja pravnih principa," 110.

4 Raz, "Legal Principles and the Limits of Law," 839–841; Spaić, "Dva poimanja pravnih principa," 111.

national regulatory framework. In this regard, the chapter does not go beyond the proposal of basic values and constitutional principles. To present their value in a functional sense, several factors are relevant, of which their regulation in the constitutional system and conventional acceptance by the political sphere are one of the key elements. However, the philosophy of law with its methodology is not fit to provide more than what is proposed in this chapter.

A brief analysis of the analytical framework for understanding the concepts of values and legal principles helps us understand the significance and their position in society, but also in the legal and constitutional system. They are the legitimising reasons and the basis of establishing a social community, the foundations of the organisation of the political and legal system and the origin of legal norms. This is especially true for a society that needs to recognise new values and new legal principles, and further develop them in the context of a multinational state. In the context of a multinational state – Bosnia and Herzegovina, particularly significant are those that influence the development of the federal and consociational model; the development of principles for a plural society; the establishment of principles on the basis of which the criteria for a multinational state are developed; and the way to recognise them from the text and spirit of the Constitution – especially through case law of the Constitutional Court of Bosnia and Herzegovina. However, before embarking on an analysis of the development of legal principles in the constitutional-political system of Bosnia and Herzegovina, it is necessary to reflect on the comparative analysis of selected constitutional principles – the Swiss Confederation and Canada.

3 Comparative Analysis of Constitutional Values and Principles of Multicultural States

The methodology of comparative legal analysis implies a *comparison* of how certain legal matters have been regulated in two or several legal systems. The comparison can include the process of identifying and describing differences and similarities between two or several legal phenomena; understanding these differences and similarities; and explaining them. As it is a comparative legal analysis, we can compare (1) legislation; (2) case law; (3) specific legal thinking; and (4) the broader social context in which these legal systems operate. Legal and constitutional systems being compared are the same or similar in a certain important aspect, which constitutes the reason for their mutual analysis and comparison. The results have normative, as well as socio-contextual value. Guided by the thesis that the same or similar social system is correlated with the same or similar legal system and *vice versa*, comparison can provide an added value and insight into the understanding of one or more legal and constitutional systems. Considering the socio-contextual and normative similarities between Bosnia and Herzegovina, the Swiss Confederation and Canada, we believe that knowledge about the way mutual relations are regulated in these multinational states can be of relevance for resolving the internal relations of three ethnic groups, national minorities and persons who do not identify ethnically in the political and constitutional system of Bosnia and Herzegovina. Of course, without forgetting that the three states do have certain differences. Due to limited space, the analysis will focus only on the normative. Furthermore, this analysis can offer arguments for the claim that multinational states too can attain a significant degree of functionality and prosperity for their citizens.

The Swiss Confederation has a specific form of federal state in which there is formal and legal balancing between citizens, cantons, and the Confederation (Article 1 of the Constitution). Furthermore, it is a system of broad application of direct democracy in which laws are subject to fundamental confirmation by citizens. One of the values postulated by the Swiss Constitution in its preamble refers to the determination of the Swiss people and cantons to live together with mutual consideration and respect for their diversity. This supports the principle of solidarity and far-reaching inclusion of all segments of society. Article 2 of the Constitution stipulates its goals, including the promotion of common welfare, sustainable development, but especially the promotion and preservation of (1) internal cohesion and at the same time (2) cultural diversity of the country (Article 2, para 2 of the Constitution of the Swiss Confederation). Balancing the relationship between the collective and the individual, the Swiss Constitution introduces the concept of individual and collective responsibility, according to which all individuals should take responsibility for themselves and their own lives, but they also according to their abilities contribute to achieving the tasks of the state and society (Article 6 of the Constitution of the Swiss Confederation). Finally, the Swiss Constitution protects human dignity as a value that must be respected and protected (Article 7 of the Constitution of the Swiss Confederation). On the other hand, with the *Canadian Multiculturalism Act* (hereinafter: CMA), Canada more specifically introduces values and legal principles into the legal system, through which it protects the diversity, but also individualism of Canadian society. The CMA preamble, referring to the Canadian Constitution, balances between two values of Canadian society, providing that (1) every individual is equal before and under the law and has the right to the equal protection and benefit of the law without discrimination, and (2) recognising the importance of preserving and enhancing the multicultural heritage of Canadians, including particular rights of the aboriginal peoples of Canada and two official languages: French and English (preamble, CMA). The CMA obligates the Canadian government to fulfil certain objectives which are reflected in (1) recognising and promoting the understanding that multiculturalism reflects the cultural and racial diversity of Canadian society and acknowledges the freedom of all members of Canadian society to preserve, enhance and share their cultural heritage (3(1)a CMA); (2) recognising and promoting the understanding that multiculturalism is a fundamental characteristic of the Canadian heritage and identity and that it provides an invaluable resource in the shaping of Canada's future (3 (1)b CMA); (3) promoting the full and equitable participation of (1) individuals and (2) communities of all origins in the continuing evolution and shaping of all aspects of Canadian society and assisting them in the elimination of any barrier to that participation (3(1)c CMA); (4) recognising the existence of communities whose members share a common origin and their historic contribution to Canadian society, and enhancing their development (3(1)d CMA). Additionally, the Canadian government is obliged to ensure that all individuals receive equal treatment and equal protection under the law, while respecting and valuing their diversity (3(1)e CMA). In this way, there is a balance between the individual and their specific cultural context. Among other things, the government is committed to promote the understanding and creativity that arise from the interaction between individuals and communities of different origins (3(1)g CMA).

Both acts, through established values, goals and legal principles, balance between the individual and collective dimensions of personality within a federal framework and the desire to preserve the multicultural character of society. This is clearly seen in the protection of the individual, the prohibition of discrimination, the protection of human dignity, but also the protection of culture, language, and the multicultural character of both Canadian and Swiss society. The operationalisation of values and legal principles further depends on the specific social and legal context, and the inherent values of the societies. However, it is worth noting that neither of the two systems gives primacy to the collective and the community over the individual but emphasises the importance of both the individual as an abstract and the individual as a part of the collective, as well as the value of the collective dimension. Therefore, there is no exclusion, but rather balancing and inclusion of abstract and contextual dimensions of personality through values and legal principles.

4 Values, Constitutional and Legal Principles of Bosnia and Herzegovina's System

The constitutional and political system of Bosnia and Herzegovina is characterised by federal organisation and consociational democracy, which are partly the result of its multicultural character. It manifests itself through the prism of three constituent peoples, national minorities and people who do not identify ethnically. This multicultural character is also manifested in the values and principles expressed in the Preamble to the Constitution of Bosnia and Herzegovina according to which: Bosniaks, Croats and Serbs as constituent peoples (along with Others) and citizens of Bosnia and Herzegovina determine the Constitution of Bosnia and Herzegovina (hereinafter the Constitution of BiH). As parts of values and legal principles, the Constitution of BiH directly lists the principles of democratic organisation (Article I.2 of the Constitution of BiH), the basics of human rights and the prohibition of discrimination, and the direct application of the European Convention for the Protection of Human Rights and Fundamental Freedoms and its Protocols (Article II of the Constitution of BiH). However, the practice of the Constitutional Court of Bosnia and Herzegovina further developed the values and legal principles that, according to their interpretation, are inherent in the legal and constitutional system. What characterises most constitutional norms is a high degree of abstractness, and every constitution contains a significant number of legal principles. In addition, bearing in mind that it was a new constitution, constitutional and judicial activity and interpretation by the Constitutional Court of BiH was, and still is, significant for establishing the elements of the constitutional and legal structure.[5] However, the Constitutional Court of BiH, like the Constitution of BiH, refused to define the legal nature of the state, although its decisions referred to the comparative experience of federal states.[6] In its practice, the Constitutional Court used terms such as "the complex constitutional structure of BiH which indicates a *sui generis* system"; "complex constitutional structure"; "complex state structure."[7] The fact that neither the Constitution of BiH nor the Constitutional Court of BiH mentions federalism or a federal

5 Banović, Damir, Gavrić, Saša and Barreiro Mariño, Mariña, *The Political System of Bosnia and Herzegovina: Institutions – Actors – Processes*, (Cham: Springer Nature, 2021), 12.

6 Išerić, Harun, *Uloga Ustavnog suda BiH u profiliranju federalnog uređenja BiH* (Sarajevo: Fondacija Centar za javno pravo, 2019), 5; Banović, Gavrić, and Barreiro Mariño, *The Political System of Bosnia and Herzegovina*, 12.

7 Išerić, *Uloga Ustavnog suda BiH u profiliranju federalnog uređenja BiH*, 5; Banović, Gavrić, and Barreiro Mariño, *The Political System of Bosnia and Herzegovina*, 12.

structure does not mean that BiH is not a federal state.[8] The refusal of the Constitutional Court to define the legal nature and internal structure of BiH can be explained by its desire not to be instrumentalised in political debates.[9] Furthermore, it should be emphasised that there is still no consensus among political actors on the nature of the legal and political system, which significantly hinders its functioning and efficiency.[10] The judicial activity of the Constitutional Court is particularly visible in (1) defining constitutional principles; (2) the way in which they should be applied in the legal system; (3) defining the content of the exclusive jurisdiction of the state; (4) reference to the exclusive competences of the entity; (5) development of additional competencies of the state; (6) recognising the existence of a "common framework or competing competencies of the state and entities."[11] In its case law, the Constitutional Court recognised several constitutional and legal principles, namely: (1) the principle of the constituency of peoples; (2) rule of law; (3) democracy; (4) welfare states; (5) single market; (6) principles of human rights protection (especially prohibition of discrimination).[12] However, the following are of special importance for internal development: (1) the principle of multiethnicity; (2) the principle of collective equality of the constituent peoples and (3) the principle of prohibition of discrimination.[13] The three principles were developed based on the decisions of the Constitutional Court of BiH (U 5/98 from I to IV), which were to a large extent an expression of the extensive interpretation and development of the Constitution of BiH. As the Constitutional Court of BiH states, the elements of a democratic state and society and the assumptions in its background – pluralism, fair procedures and peaceful relations that stem from the Constitution – must serve as a guideline for further elaboration of the question of how BiH is organised as a democratic multinational state (see: especially U 5/98 – III, para 54). Based on the provisions of Article I/2 of the Constitution of BiH, stipulating that Bosnia and Herzegovina is a democratic state and point 3 of the Preamble, which defines a pluralistic society as a presumption of democratic government, the

8 Išerić, *Uloga Ustavnog suda BiH u profiliranju federalnog uređenja BiH,* 6; Banović, Gavrić, and Barreiro Mariño, *The Political System of Bosnia and Herzegovina,* 12.

9 Išerić, *Uloga Ustavnog suda BiH u profiliranju federalnog uređenja BiH,* 6; Banović, Gavrić, and Barreiro Mariño, *The Political System of Bosnia and Herzegovina,* 12.

10 Banović, Gavrić, and Barreiro Mariño, *The Political System of Bosnia and Herzegovina,* 12.

11 Išerić, *Uloga Ustavnog suda BiH u profiliranju federalnog uređenja BiH*; Banović, Gavrić, and Barreiro Mariño, *The Political System of Bosnia and Herzegovina,* 12.

12 Išerić, *Uloga Ustavnog suda BiH u profiliranju federalnog uređenja BiH,* 6–7; Banović, Gavrić, and Barreiro Mariño, *The Political System of Bosnia and Herzegovina,* 13.

13 Banović, Gavrić, and Barreiro Mariño, *The Political System of Bosnia and Herzegovina,* 13.

Constitutional Court of BiH derived the principle that Bosnia and Herzegovina – with its territorial division into two entities (Federation of BiH and the Republika Srpska), where the Federation of BiH is further divided into ten cantons – corresponds to the model of a multinational state, where territorial division must not lead to preservation of results of ethnic cleansing during the war and institutional segregation and national hegemonisation in state institutions (see: especially U 5/98 – III, para 61). The principle of collective equality of the constituent peoples implies the obligation of the entities to respect the principle of non-discrimination against any of the three constituent peoples, especially in those entities where they are in the position of a *de facto* minority (see: especially U 5/98 – III, para 59). The principle of collective equality also implies the prohibition of privileging any of the three constituent peoples in such a way that additional rights are recognised for members of one or two peoples (see: especially U 5/98 – III, para 60). According to the decisions of the Constitutional Court, the special rights of constituent peoples are recognised at the state level and as such cannot be transferred to lower levels of territorial-political organisation without special justification (see: especially U 5/98 – III, para 68). Bearing in mind the tension between collective and individual rights, the Constitutional Court of BiH established that the category of *Others* must be introduced into the system of representation to prevent the complete exclusion of individual rights (see: decision U – 5/98 – III). Finally, the Constitutional Court of BiH recognised the system of prohibition of discrimination in the following ways: (1) the prohibition of *de iure* discrimination; (2) prohibition of *de facto* discrimination (indirect discrimination) and (3) prohibition of retaining the results of earlier *de iure* discrimination (see: decision U – 5/98 – III).

The development of constitutional-legal principles through the practice of the Constitutional Court of Bosnia and Herzegovina has not significantly influenced the change in the constitutional practice of legislative bodies, executive bodies, or the practice of political entities. In other words, these principles, in general, have not been internalised as the *modus operandi* of the constitutional and political reality of Bosnia and Herzegovina. The dominant discourse is still collective, focusing on the dominance of the group with a de facto numerical superiority and disregarding national minorities and persons who do not identify ethnically. At a higher level of abstraction, one cannot speak of a more significant positioning of the *individual* in relation to the *collective*. Despite the normative constitutional law of Bosnia and Herzegovina recognising individual rights, they are either excluded or limited in the political sense. When the entities' constitutions recognise the political representation of the *Others*, they recognise them precisely as a group representing national minorities and persons who do not identify ethnically. Thus, as a very heterogeneous group without clearly defined common goals or identity characteristics. Furthermore, as the matter at hand is the social context, collective identification is still dominant in the political sense and the individual has not yet been clearly profiled.

5 From Values to Constitutional Goals and Legal Principles

The development of the constitutional system of Bosnia and Herzegovina, especially under the influence of the Constitutional Court of BiH, recognised the values and developed significant legal principles for a multinational state. However, this development lacks, in my understanding, certain values, goals, and principles that can be part of the normative sphere, but not necessarily. They are much more significant as recognised values in the relations of the political sphere and developed as parts of conventional practice. Intuitively, among them, we consider the following important:[14]

(1) the minimum content of a common identity that goes beyond the identities of the segments (constituent peoples and national minorities) that would have legitimising significance. This includes the development of a supra-ethnic identity of constituent peoples, national minorities and persons who do not identify ethnically through mapping of common identity elements, values, and interests that would have the legitimising power of the political and constitutional system. As we have stated below, this could be the value of "unity in diversity", "value of multiethnicity and multi-confessionalism", but also "value of constitutional patriotism", etc.

(2) cooperation between social segments, either at the political level or within the civil society or interest groups, but also at the individual level in fields of common interest. This implies cooperation between individuals, informal groups, formalised organisations, business entities, etc. in areas of common interest, either through joint projects, activities, and platforms. This would strengthen internal integration and mutual trust between the segments;

(3) development of trust and mutual respect between social segments. This value is of particular importance in relations between political entities

14 For more, see: Banović, Damir, "Parlamentarni sistem Bosne i Hercegovine kao primjena multikulturalnog koncepta političke predstavljenosti kolektiva," *Godišnjak Pravnog fakulteta u Sarajevu* 58, (2015), 245–278.

and elites representing segments through which mutual value of the collective and the individuals within the collective, the sense of self-worth, would be acknowledged, and would attain not only symbolic, but substantive significance for the collectives and the individuals within them. Furthermore, in addition to mutual collective acknowledgement, the recognition of the individual as part of, but also distinct from, the collective is also notable;

(4) values of consensus and the legitimacy of political representation of social segments in relations between the political elites. This value is controversial, but we deem it important for stabilisation and democratic consolidation. Consociational democracy, whatever the number of its shortcomings, implies the need for legitimate representation of the collective. This condition would lead to stabilisation as a prerequisite for the possibility of involving others in the process of reforming the constitutional and political system of Bosnia and Herzegovina and its transformation towards a liberal type of consociational democracy;

(5) democratic education that encourages the development of values within segments, but also common values within segments, through formal education in primary and secondary schools, symbolic acknowledgement at universities, informal forms of education, etc. as a substantive basis for an efficient and functional system of consociational democracy in the multicultural society of Bosnia and Herzegovina;

(6) consensus on the nature of the political system is one of the prerequisites for a functional political and legal system of Bosnia and Herzegovina. Disagreements about the nature of the political system often lead to blockages in its functioning, where a common agreement would eliminate this possibility, at least in some segments.[15]

The establishment of values and principles should also take into account comparative solutions and balancing between the collective and the individual, and the value of individual human dignity. Of course, the dimension of the collective's dignity as a value that gives a context of meaning to the individuals should not be ignored here either. Nor should the value and principle of "unity in diversity" through which a shared umbrella identity is achieved, but also the uniqueness maintained of either the collective or the individual along with the values and principles of mutual recognition, the policy of inclusion, the principle of subsidiarity and, finally, the value, goal, principle, but also the fact of multiculturalism. The values and principles presented in this chapter

15 Banović, "Parlamentarni sistem Bosne i Hercegovine kao primjena multikulturalnog koncepta političke predstavljenosti kolektiva," 272–273.

should become part of the political and constitutional system of Bosnia and Herzegovina, either through their normative inclusion in the Constitution or through a separate Charter on the Values and Principles of Multiculturalism of Bosnia and Herzegovina, which would serve as normative instructions for political entities. Furthermore, and perhaps more importantly, these values and principles should be internalised and become part of political and constitutional practice in the social context of Bosnia and Herzegovina.

Bibliography

Banović, Damir, "Parlamentarni sistem Bosne i Hercegovine kao primjena multikulturalnog koncepta političke predstavljenosti kolektiva." *Godišnjak Pravnog fakulteta u Sarajevu* 58, (2015), 245–278.

Banović, Damir, Gavrić, Saša and Barreiro Mariño, Mariña. *The Political System of Bosnia and Herzegovina: Institutions – Actors – Processes*. Cham: Springer Nature, 2021.

Canadian Multiculturalism Act. Accessed October 25, 2023. https://laws-lois.justice.gc.ca/eng/acts/C-18.7/page-1.html#h-73115.

Constitution of Bosnia and Herzegovina. Accessed October 25, 2023. https://www.ustavnisud.ba/public/down/USTAV_BOSNE_I_HERCEGOVINE_engl.pdf.

Federal Constitution of the Swiss Confederation. Accessed October 25, 2023. https://www.fedlex.admin.ch/eli/cc/1999/404/en#tit_4.

Išerić, Harun, *Uloga Ustavnog suda BiH u profiliranju federalnog uređenja BiH*, (Sveske za javno pravo | Blätter für öffentliches Recht, 38 (2019): 44-69.

Partial decision U – 5/98 – III of the Constitutional Court of Bosnia and Herzegovina. Accessed October 26, 2023. https://www.ohr.int/ohr-dept/legal/const/pdf/Djelomicna-odluka-3.pdf.

Partial decision U – 5/98 of the Constitutional Court of Bosnia and Herzegovina. Accessed October 26, 2023. https://www.ustavnisud.ba/hr/djelimicne-odluke-u-598.

Raz, Joseph, "Legal Principles and the Limits of Law." *The Yale Law Journal* 81, (1972), 823–854, accessed October 25, 2023. https://scholarship.law.columbia.edu/faculty_scholarship/569.

Spaić, Bojan, "Dva poimanja pravnih principa." *Anali Pravnog fakulteta Univerziteta u Beogradu* 65, 1, (2017): 109–130, accessed October 24, 2023. https://anali.rs/dva-poimanja-pravnih-principa/.

CHAPTER 5

Relationship between Consociation and Federalism in Bosnia and Herzegovina

Goran Marković

1 Introduction

Serious differences exist among authors on the nature of the political regime and the form of government of Bosnia and Herzegovina. Their roots lie exclusively in the ideological and political attitudes of the political and legal scientists who wish to wrap them up into scientific attitudes. This kind of approach of scientists (mostly from Bosnia and Herzegovina) leads to great misunderstandings of the basics of the constitutional system of Bosnia and Herzegovina. Although it is very often described as a "complex state" or a "complex state community", these terms have been employed only for the purpose of avoiding clear answers to some basic questions, such as about the type of the political regime or the form of government.

One could not easily neglect the fact that Bosnia and Herzegovina is a consociational democracy. Whether one advocates this type of political regime or not is another issue. It is more complex to define Bosnia and Herzegovina as a federal state,[1] although we find that federal principles have been rather clearly defined in its constitution.

Bosnia and Herzegovina is one of the rare states which combines consociational democracy and federalism.[2,3] This fact makes it additionally difficult to

1 Some authors differentiate among territorial and multiethnic federal states (Boucher, François, *Deep Diversity and Multinational Federalism in Canada,* (Fribourg, Paper Prepared for the Institute of Federalism, Summer 2008, 8–9).

According to this division, Bosnia and Herzegovina would be a multiethnic federation.

2 Arend Lijphart thought that the theory on the principles of federalism could be understood as a limited and particular type of theory on the principles of consociation for two reasons: overrepresentation of less numerous subjects, and the autonomy of the units of a state. Lijphart, Arend, *Demokracija u pluralnim društvima* (Zagreb: Globus – Školska knjiga, 1992), 49.

3 Although many federations are at the same time consociational regimes, it is not a rule without exception. Lijphart, Arend, "Non-Majoritarian Democracy: A Comparison of Federal and Consociational Theories", *Publius: The Journal of Federalism*, 15, 85, 4. In the same

 | DOI:10.1163/9789004707887_006

understand the nature of the constitutional system of Bosnia and Herzegovina.[4] There is no "clear" situation.[5] The state is composed of two entities, which we describe as federal units, while the society is divided along ethnic lines into three societal segments. This very fact ("two entities and three constituent peoples" as the political elites would say) greatly influences the research of the constitutional system. It would be much easier if each constituent people had its own territorial unit. It would also be relatively easy if both entities have been territorial units of all three constituent peoples from the very beginning. But, the fact that one entity was monoethnic, while the other was "bi-ethnic" determined the constitutional solutions for the structure of the institutions of Bosnia and Herzegovina and the decision-making in them.

2 The Main Principles

The main principles of both consociational democracy and federalism have been constitutionalised in Bosnia and Herzegovina.[6] Following Lijphart, we enumerate the principles of consociation relevant for this paper: (1) grand coalition; (2) mutual veto; (3) equal or proportional representation of societal segments; and (4) segmental autonomy.[7]

2.1 *Grand Coalition*

The notion of grand coalition[8] is of essential importance for the very concept of consociational democracy since it guarantees that societal segments will be

work, Lijphart defined conditions under which consociational democracy fits in with federal state.

4 Some authors rightly point that in some cases (such as segmented societies), it is necessary to combine federalism and consociation. Juhász, József, "Ethno-Federalism: Challenges and Opportunities", *Međunarodni problemi*, 3, 2005, 258.

5 Marković, Goran, *Bosanskohercegovački federalizam* (Beograd – Sarajevo: Službeni glasnik – University Press, 2012), 249.

6 *Ibid.*, 237.

7 Lijphart, Arend, *Democracy in Plural Societies. A Comparative Exploration* (New Haven and London: Yale University Press, 1977), 25.

For an expanded list of the features of consociation, see: Lijphart, Arend, *The Politics of Accommodation: Pluralism and Democracy in the Netherlands* (Berkeley: University of California Press, 1968).

8 Lijphart, *Democracy in Plural Societies. A Comparative Exploration*, 25–31.

legitimately represented in political institutions.[9] It is obvious that this is in contradiction with the principles of liberal democracy, but to some extent also with the very nature of society. Namely, liberal democracy is based on the notion that the parliament is a citizens' representation regardless of their belonging to different social groups, and that the coalitions are the result of political negotiations and compromises. Coalitions exist both in the parliament and in the government. A ruling coalition has to have support of the majority in the parliament. It is less important whose interests it represents and protects as long as it has the majority of parliamentary seats, which are the result of the majority or plurality of votes in the elections.

It is different in consociational democracy since societal segments (ethnic groups, religious communities, linguistic communities, etc.) are political subjects[10] as well, and as such they have to be represented by their political elites in political institutions.

The question of legitimacy arises at this point. Namely, the dilemma is whether members of political institutions have to belong only to different societal segments or do they have to be their legitimate representatives? Two approaches clash here. According to one, if a constitution does not prescribe anything explicitly, a member of a political institution does not necessarily represent his/her societal group but only needs to belong to it. This approach includes the elements of liberal democracy into consociational democracy, since it enables a member of an institution to claim that he/she represents all citizens, if it is not possible to explicitly prove that he/she has been elected by voters of one societal group or if it has not been explicitly prescribed that he/she represents only one societal group.

This is a formal approach with the background in the constitutional text itself. However, the other approach, which we advocate here, takes into consideration the nature and purpose of the political regime of consociational democracy. If a constitution prescribes, for example, that an institution has to be composed of members who belong to different societal groups either equally or proportionally, the fundamental question is why such a provision has been enacted. In other words, what was the intention of the Constitution-

9 This very concept is not without limitations and deficiencies. Lijphart wrote about them examining the Belgian case (Lijphart, Arend, "Constitutional Design for Divided Societies", *Journal of Democracy* Vol. 15, No. 2/2004, 103).

Some of them are discrimination of the groups which are not represented in the government and the second is the overrepresentation of the smaller societal segments.

10 Marković, Goran, *Ustavni lavirint. Aporije ustavnog sistema Bosne i Hercegovine* (Beograd: Službeni glasnik, 2021), 110–111.

maker? In a segmented society, the purpose could only be to guarantee participation of societal groups in political institutions with the primary aim to guarantee fulfilment and protection of their equal rights. Equal rights mean the protection of all constitutionally guaranteed rights, which the societal groups exercise as collectives, but first and foremost the right to effectively participate in the process of decision-making. The absence of such a right could have as its consequence the decisions which will not be approved by legitimate representatives of one of the constituent peoples. While it could be acceptable for some less important decisions, constitutionally defined as such, to be made without consensus, some other, also constitutionally defined decisions, should not be made without the approval of legitimate representatives of all constituent peoples.

Another question could be posed: if this was the intention of the Constitution-maker, why not explicitly prescribe it in the constitution? Did the Constitution-maker think that it would be sufficient to have members of different societal groups in political institutions? If so, does that mean that the Constitution-maker thought that such members would unavoidably represent the interests of their respective societal groups? Maybe the Constitution-maker thought precisely that. However, members of political institutions who have to belong to societal groups have to be legitimate representatives of the latter. Otherwise, it would be meaningless to have political institutions composed of members of societal groups.

The answers to these dilemmas have to be found in the interpretation of the constitutional provisions in the context of understanding the political regime of the country, as well as the aims which the Constitution-maker had in mind during the drafting of the constitutional text. However, the constitutional text itself does not give a usual answer. Therefore, two opposite concepts exist from the very beginning of the constitutional system, with no possible consensus on the horizon. If one adopts a literal interpretation of the constitutional provisions, one can easily conclude that only the ethnic belonging of members of political institutions is relevant, since it is the only necessary requisite. This interpretation, however, does not take into consideration the nature of the political regime and the purposes of the construction of such a constitutional system. One can argue, on the other hand, that it is not quite clear what the nature of the constitutional system is. However, this literal interpretation does not take into consideration the nature of the constitutional system at all. It is based exclusively on the words in the constitutional provisions.

Both consociational and federal principles are present in the composition of the institutions of Bosnia and Herzegovina. Political institutions are composed according to the principle of parity representation of the constituent peoples, while the entities are represented according to the "2:1" formula. However, it seems that the consociational principles prevail. This is visible in the fact that the constituent peoples are represented equally in the institutions, which is not the case with the entities as federal units.

It is true that comparative federalism registers cases in which federal units are not equally represented in federal parliaments, i.e. their upper houses. The most notable cases are those of Germany, Austria, and Canada. However, this should not be the case in Bosnia and Herzegovina, considering the fact that it is quite a weak federation, as well as the historical conditions which caused its federal structure. However, this has been exactly what was prescribed in the Constitution of Bosnia and Herzegovina – there are twice more deputies in the House of Peoples of the Parliamentary Assembly of Bosnia and Herzegovina from the Federation of Bosnia and Herzegovina than from the Republika Srpska. The reason for this lies in the fact that consociation prevailed over federalism in the structure of the House of Peoples.

On the other side, one can agree or disagree with the reason for the establishment of the "2:1" formula, but the very reason is quite obvious and is embedded in the consociational arrangements themselves. Namely, at the time of Dayton, only the Serbs were constituent in the Republika Srpska, while only the Bosniacs and the Croats were constituent in the Federation. Therefore, the "2:1" formula had to express this fact. It did not have anything to do with the fact that the Federation was twice as numerous or twice as economically or politically stronger than the Republika Srpska (since this was not the case), but only with the fact that consociational arrangements had to express not only the structure of the population of both entities at the moment, but also the fact that only one (or two) of the peoples was politically dominant in them.

The roots of grand coalition have to be found not only in the constitutional provisions but also in the political practice, i.e., in the relationship of political forces. That was the case already in the first elections. Therefore, the principles of consociation and federalism converged. The explicit constitutional provisions were not even necessary for the constitutionalisation of the principle of grand coalition. Its presence and necessity were almost self-evident.[11]

However, things started to change only five years after Dayton when the splits happened in the strongest ethnic parties. Different party combinations in the Parliamentary Assembly, as well as on the polls, caused uncertainty in

11 On grand coalitions in Bosnia and Herzegovina, see: Marković, Goran, *Ustavni lavirint*, 113–115.

the composition of grand coalitions and sometimes even in the possibility of their creation.

Although the Constitution explicitly guarantees the federal principle in the composition of the Council of Ministers,[12] for example, it does not necessarily guarantee it when it comes to consociation, precisely the grand coalition. The very fact that the Council of Ministers is composed of political parties representing three constituent peoples does not in itself mean that it has a character of a grand coalition. That is because the meaning of "representation" has to be understood correctly. An ethnic political party can represent only a small portion of a constituent people. The vast majority of the population which belongs to a constituent people can vote for other political parties which would not be included in the Council of Ministers. If this were the case, the grand coalition would not exist and one of the basic features of consociational democracy would be missing.[13]

The dilemma arises whether the grand coalition has to be formed in all cases or only in those when it converges with the notion that a parliamentary majority has the right to form a government, regardless of the party or ethnic composition of a majority. The political will of the majority is already limited by the constitutional provision stipulating that a certain number of ministers has to come from each entity. This fact limits the programmatic character of a grand coalition since the Council of Ministers has to include political parties from both entities regardless of their real political strength. However, it is necessary and justified to constitutionalise such a limitation because it is a guarantee of relative stability of a weak and fragile federal state.

On the other hand, the Constitution-maker did not find it opportune to provide for the same kind of limitation with respect to representation of the constituent peoples in the Council of Ministers. If a parliamentary majority is required to include ministers from both entities in the Council of Ministers, would the same be required for inclusion of ministers from all three constituent peoples, provided that they are legitimate representatives of their respective constituent peoples?

The answer of the Constitution-maker is obviously negative. The only reason which we can see is that the Constitution-maker has intended to provide

12 Article v 4b explicitly prescribes that no more than two-thirds of all ministers may be appointed from the territory of the Federation.

13 This is precisely what happened with the government led by the Alliance for Changes which included two very small Croat political parties. While the Croat societal segment was represented in the Council of Ministers, it was represented by a very small minority, which meant that the grand coalition was non-existent.

for the principle of efficacy in the formation of the Council of Ministers. The election of the Council of Ministers by both parliamentary chambers (which has not been prescribed in the Constitution) would be in accordance with the principles of consociation, but it can also be dangerous because it could linger or even disenable the election of this institution. The fact that the Council of Ministers is responsible to both parliamentary chambers is not a result of the Constitution-maker's desire to promote the principles of consociation but rather of the desire to stabilise the political position of the Council of Ministers since the vote of no confidence would be less probable if both parliamentary chambers would have to agree on it.

2.2 *Mutual Veto*

The constitutionalisation of mutual veto is very wide and it shows the importance of consociational democracy in the very process of decision-making. Veto is well-known in the theory and practice of federalism, but not as a feature of the federal state but of the confederation as a union of sovereign states. Therefore, veto either points to the confederal character of Bosnia and Herzegovina or it has been constitutionalised for some other reason. Some authors argued that veto is a feature of Bosnia and Herzegovina as a confederation or a union. Such a conclusion is reductive and proves that there is a misunderstanding regarding the legal nature of Bosnia and Herzegovina. The veto which has been widely recognised in the Constitution of Bosnia and Herzegovina is not a proof that it is a confederation or a union, but rather that it is a consociational democracy. In other words, veto has nothing to do with the form of government but with the type of the political regime.

The mechanisms of consensus, mutual veto, or even qualified majorities (except for the adoption or revision of a constitution) are not typical for a federal state. Here we mean the usage of these mechanisms by federal units in a federal state. These mechanisms are typical for consociational democracies[14] and they have nothing in common with the constitutional position of territorial units (federal units or others), but with that of societal segments. These segments can be territorially concentrated, but not necessarily.

In Bosnia and Herzegovina, some mechanisms of mutual veto are used not only by societal segments but by federal units as well. "Entity voting" is an example. Since at least one-third of deputies (in the House of Representatives)

14 Take, for example, the alarm bell mechanism in Belgium, or, to some extent, the mechanisms of decision-making in the Northern Ireland Assembly or the Assembly of North Macedonia.

or delegates (in the House of Peoples) from the territory of each entity have to vote for a decision, it is obvious that interests of the federal units have to be protected in this way. Even in the House of Peoples, whose main purpose is the protection of vital interests of the constituent peoples, the belonging of one-third (or any other third) of delegates to societal segments is not important.

The composition of the House of Representatives leads to the conclusion that this kind of mutual veto cannot even be used by all societal segments individually. The electoral results are such that there are usually six or around six deputies from the Croat people. Even if all of them belong to the same political party, they still cannot use entity voting without support of the deputies who belong to other constituent peoples. One could say that this is quite adequate since the deputies in the House of Representatives do not represent their constituent peoples. This is true, and it shows that the veto principle sometimes has nothing to do with consociation, but with the federal structure of the state.

One could say that mutual veto is contrary to the very nature of the federal state, and this is correct. However, each federal state is a *sui generis* federation. It is possible that one or few confederal features are present in the constitutional system of a federal state, which still does not terminate its federal legal nature if most elements of a federal state are present and if they prevail.

It is obvious that this form of mutual veto is necessary even in the House of Representatives, although it does not look appropriate or justified at first sight. The arguments against mutual veto (entity voting) in the House of Representatives go as follows. Firstly, since the House of Representatives is, at least formally, a representation of the citizens, mutual veto is against the very nature of this parliamentary chamber and the nature of representation in it. Secondly, in some cases, mutual veto in the form of entity voting complicates the functioning of the House since deputies use this mechanism of decision-making relatively often to obstruct its work.

The opposite arguments are also very important and significant. Firstly, the entities have a different number of deputies in the House of Representatives. If a decision would be made by a simple majority, it could be made with no votes from the Republika Srpska or with a minimum number of votes from it. In a weak federation and a segmented society, such a method of decision-making could potentially be very dangerous in the sense that it could cause a constant political crisis. Secondly, if entity voting would be deleted from the Constitution, it would strongly jeopardise the possibility for protection of equality both of the federal units and of the constituent peoples. The federal units would not be able to protect their interests in any way except indirectly through the mechanism of vital national interests which serves for the protection not of the federal units but of the societal segments. However, even the use of the mechanism of vital national interests is not guaranteed, since the Constitutional Court of Bosnia and Herzegovina, which includes foreign judges and decides by majority votes, can decide, whenever it finds it appropriate, that a matter is not an issue of vital national interest.

Mutual veto in the strict sense, namely veto as a mechanism for protection of societal segments, has been constitutionalised very broadly. Its existence means that qualified majorities have been prescribed quite often, which influences some authors to wrongly conclude that Bosnia and Herzegovina is a confederation or a union. The conclusion of these authors is wrong because they do not see the difference between the veto by political-territorial units and the veto by societal segments. Veto in Bosnia and Herzegovina essentially belongs to representatives of the constituent peoples and it is therefore in most cases the feature of consociational democracy.

A specific case is veto which belongs to members of the Presidency of Bosnia and Herzegovina. In my opinion, it is also a feature of consociational democracy and not the right which belongs to federal units (although through members of the Presidency elected in the entities). The issue with the nature of this veto is tightly connected with the question as to whose representatives the members of the Presidency are. Do they represent the entities as federal units, all citizens, or their respective constituent peoples?

The answer to this question is important to understand the nature of the collective head of state of Bosnia and Herzegovina, as well as the relationship between consociation and federalism. It would not be contrary to the nature of a federal state if members of the Presidency represent their respective entities. The principle of participation of federal units in federal institutions is a legitimate and usual one. Since the Presidency is a collective federal institution, it is quite natural that the entities have their representatives in it. The idea of representation of federal units in federal institutions, however, encounters difficulties since party affiliation of the deputies, as well as the party discipline, greatly diminishes the very notion of representation of federal units since the question arises as to how the deputies can avoid dominance of their political parties over their political actions.

In Bosnia and Herzegovina, there are some traces of the idea that members of the Presidency represent their respective entities. These traces can be found in the fact that members of the Presidency can veto its decisions if they find that they are harmful for vital entity interests (not for vital national interests or vital interests of the citizens).[15] Therefore, if members of the Presidency protect vital interests of the entities, they must be the representatives of their entities. This conclusion is only strengthened by the fact that in the Republika Srpska the National Assembly decides on veto, while in the Federation it is the competence of a part of delegates in the House of Peoples.

These arguments are firm only at first sight. Their weakness is proven already when one wonders how it is possible that only one member of the Presidency vetoes its decision harmful for vital entity interests, while the other member of the Presidency from the same entity finds that the same decision is not harmful and therefore does not want to veto it. It is understandable that each member of the Presidency has his/her own opinion whether a vital entity interest is damaged by a decision of the Presidency. However, if two members of the Presidency from the same entity have opposing opinions, the dilemma arises whether a vital interest is really damaged.

This dilemma is, in our opinion, of secondary importance since each member of the Presidency should be given the right to assess if a decision of this institution is harmful. What happens after the veto is more important. The veto of the member of the Presidency from the Republika Srpska could even confirm the hypothesis that members of this institution represent their respective federal units since the parliament as a whole decides on a veto. In my opinion, this is not so because the Constitution-maker wanted to create a constitutional solution according to which a member of the Presidency would be a representative of the entity. The existing solution is simply the only possible one, having in mind the fact that at the moment of drafting the Constitution the National Assembly was the only legislative and representative political institution in the Republika Srpska. The correctness of this attitude could be proven also by the fact that it is not the Parliament of the Federation (or at least its House of Representatives) which decides on a veto of the members of the Presidency from this entity. A decision has to be made by the delegates of only one constituent people in the House of Peoples in the Federation which clearly shows who the members of the Presidency represent.

The protection of vital interests of the constituent peoples is a specific case of mutual veto. Its potential is, however, quite limited. Firstly, although the House of Peoples has equal competences as the House of Representatives (except for one issue), in many cases its legislative function has been prevented by the House of Representatives, whose members used entity voting.

---

15 Some authors see it as a mechanism for protection of the federal relations state – entities. Ademović, Nedim, Marko, Joseph and Marković, Goran, *Ustavno pravo Bosne i Hercegovine* (Sarajevo: Konrad Adenauer Stiftung, 2012), 133.

Secondly, the role of the Constitutional Court, with foreign judges in its composition, limits the use of the mechanism of vital national interests in particular cases. The constitutional procedure allows for the annulment of veto used by delegates of one of the constituent peoples if the Constitutional Court finds that an issue is not harmful for vital national interests. This in itself would not be unacceptable if the Constitutional Court would be composed entirely of domestic judges and if a constitutional provision would be explicitly defined in this way. On the other side, such role of the Constitutional Court limits the role of the delegates. Their role as representatives and protectors of the vital interests is limited since the Constitutional Court may decide that an issue is not of vital interest for a constituent people.

The veto of delegates of one constituent people should not have an absolute character in the sense that it could be used to block the process of decision-making. This aim has been fulfilled. However, the balance has been disturbed in the other extreme. Namely, while the delegates certainly cannot block the decision-making process on their own, their intention to protect vital national interests could be prevented by the Constitutional Court. Namely, the Constitutional Court of Bosnia and Herzegovina decides under constitutionally defined conditions[16] on the regularity of the procedure for protection of vital national interests. Although the constitutional provision only prescribes the role of the Constitutional Court in guaranteeing the procedural regularity, it nevertheless developed the practice of deciding on the content of vital national interests, i.e., on the violation of vital national interests by the decisions of the Parliamentary Assembly. This includes the authority of the Court to decide if a decision regulates at all the issues which are of vital interest for the constituent peoples. It further means that it is possible that the deputies of one of the constituent peoples differ from the Court when it comes to the interpretation of compatibility of a decision with vital national interests. In any case, the opinion of the Court prevails over the opinion of the deputies of a constituent people.

2.3 *Representation in the Institutions*

Equal and proportional representation can be features of both federalism and consociation. The fact that the entities are represented according to the "2:1" formula is a feature of federalism since they are represented as federal units. At the same time, the constituent peoples are represented equally, on the parity principle in all the main institutions. It is the case even in those institu-

16 Article IV 3f.

tions for which the Constitution did not explicitly prescribe such a representation. Some authors argue that the parity principle in the Constitutional Court is a *contra constitutionem* custom while others find it a *secundum constitutionem*.[17] On the other side, the Council of Ministers Act explicitly prescribed the parity composition of this institution,[18] although it has not been prescribed by the Constitution. These two examples confirm the importance of the parity principle. While proportional representation of the entities has been explicitly prescribed (since it is of fundamental importance for the constitutional system), the parity representation of the constituent peoples in these two institutions has been prescribed by a custom or a law again since it is of fundamental importance for the constitutional system, although the Constitution-makers did not think so or they maybe were not able to reach a consensus on this issue.

The representation of federal units and societal segments has been combined so to satisfy the need of both federal units and constituent peoples. It was not possible to reach the parity representation of both since during the peace negotiations in Dayton only Serbs were constituent in the Republika Srpska, while only Bosniacs and Croats were constituent in the Federation. Therefore, if the constituent peoples had to be equally represented in the institutions, the entities could not be.

Principally, in weak federations, created in fragile political circumstances, it would be more appropriate to prescribe equal representation of federal units, particularly in federal parliament. In the case of Bosnia and Herzegovina, it was not necessary for two reasons. Firstly, the parity principle in the representation of the constituent peoples has been even more important. Secondly, since the Constitution has prescribed specific mechanisms for decision-making, such as entity voting, the entities could protect themselves.[19] Therefore, it is not their primary concern to be equally represented in the institutions.

In modern federal states, it is most important for federal units to achieve effective equality when it comes to the exercise of powers of federal parliaments and protection of their own constitutional position and interests. Al-

17 On different opinions, see: Marković, Goran, *Ustavni lavirint*, 360; Balić, Lejla, "Ustavni običaj u BiH – osvrt na izbor sudija Ustavnog suda BiH", *Godišnjak Pravnog fakulteta u Sarajevu* LII/2009, 22.

18 See Article 6 of the Council of Ministers of Bosnia and Herzegovina Act, *Official Gazette of Bosnia and Herzegovina*, Nos. 38/02, 30/03, 42/03, 81/06, 76/07, 81/07, 24/08.

19 The same: Ademović, Nedim, Marko, Joseph and Marković, Goran, *Ustavno pravo Bosne i Hercegovine*, 131.

though federal units participate in other institutions as well, usually there are no firm provisions on their equal representation in the latter. It is usually considered that it is necessary and, at the same time, enough for federal units to be represented in a way, at least proportionally. On the other side, consociational democracy usually requires an adequate representation of societal segments in other (at least political) institutions too. In Bosnia and Herzegovina, federal units are represented in all political institutions (as well as in the Constitutional Court)[20] on the same principle which strengthens the federal principle. Nothing strange or wrong could be found in this solution. On the other side, the representation of the constituent peoples is also constitutionalised in the same institutions, and it is even stronger since parity representation is guaranteed to the latter.

2.4 *Segmental Autonomy*

The societal segments in Bosnia and Herzegovina have their own organisations and institutions, but none of them exercises political power. Their functions are political, economic, cultural, etc. The state and local powers, however, belong to the institutions which, in some cases at least, represent the constituent peoples, but which are not the institutions of these respective constituent peoples. For example, the House of Peoples represents the constituent peoples, but it is not an institution of any particular constituent people or of all of them. It is a state institution, moreover, a segment of a wider state institution (the Parliamentary Assembly).

Segmental autonomy,[21] if understood as the exercise of political power, has to be found in the political-territorial organisation of the state and the existence of two entities which are federal units by their legal nature.[22] Therefore, federalism and consociation are interconnected even in this sense. The entities have a double character. They are at the same time territorial organisations of all citizens who at least formally are bearers of state power, while at

20 This representation is visible in the facts that domestic judges come from the entities, and that they are elected by the entity parliaments rather than by the state parliament.

21 Lijphart found the segmental autonomy in some other federal states as well. He thought, for example, that the segmental autonomy in the Canadian federalism is at the same time its most important consociational feature (Lijpahrt, Arend, *Demokracija u pluralnim društvima* 127).

22 Lijphart thought that federalism was an excellent choice for divided societies with geographically concentrated groups. Lijphart, Arend, *Thinking about Democracy. Power sharing and majority rule in theory and practice* (London and New York: Routledge, 2008), 83.

the same time they are the territorial-political expression of the segmented society and the constituent peoples as its basic elements.

However, segmental autonomy has not been constitutionalised to its final consequences. Firstly, in Dayton, Serbs got their federal unit since the Republika Srpska has been defined as a state of the Serb people and other citizens. The Federation was defined as an entity of Bosniacs and Croats, who had to share power. In practice, most of the cantons were dominated by one constituent people numerically and its political elites politically. This was not the segmental autonomy in the proper sense, since both Bosniacs and Croats had more than one of its own "segmental autonomies" in each canton, which their political elites controlled. These segmental autonomies were not connected politically or institutionally, since each canton existed as a separate federal unit.

Secondly, the decision of the Constitutional Court in the case U-5/98 changed the constitutional system to some extent. Formally, it could influence the possibility for realisation of segmental autonomy since both the entities and the cantons became multiethnic. The constituent peoples became constituent in all of them. Although consociational mechanisms were strengthened and widened, all these political-territorial units were not the units of any particular constituent people anymore, and therefore the principle of segmental autonomy weakened.

This would be the conclusion if one would analyse only the constitutional provisions. In practice, but to some considerable extent even in the constitutional provisions, these political-territorial units remained the area of segmental autonomy. This was so because the practical political dominance of the political elites of one constituent people remained, but also because the consociational mechanisms were not as developed as they were in the Constitution of Bosnia and Herzegovina.

3 Conclusion

Some authors deny the federal nature of the constitutional system of Bosnia and Herzegovina for ideological and political reasons. For the same reasons, they deny the need for consociational arrangements in the constitutional system. Despite that, even a superficial, let alone a serious analysis shows that almost all features both of federalism and consociation are present in the constitutional system.

The thing is not whether one desires one or both of these systems since their existence or absence does not depend on one's wishes or political programmes. It depends on the nature of the society which is objectively given, and on the historical and political circumstances under which the Constitution was drafted.

Bosnia and Herzegovina belongs to few states which combine federalism and consociation. It is quite complicated to draft such a constitutional system since it is possible that particular features either of federalism or consociation would be missing. However, the fact that a constitutional system does not perfectly match all the features does not in itself mean that either federalism or consociation is missing.

It is hard to achieve that features of both federalism and consociation are equally constitutionalised in a constitutional system. The same is true for Bosnia and Herzegovina. It seems that the features of consociational democracy prevail.[23] That is the reason why it sometimes seems that Bosnia and Herzegovina is a confederation rather than a federal state. This conclusion is a consequence of a wrong understanding of the functioning of the constitutional system of Bosnia and Herzegovina. For example, the principles of parity and consensus could not be understood as features of confederation since they point to consociation rather than federation or confederation.

Given the ongoing political crisis, the prospects for constitutional reforms are highly limited, and they are not feasible in the short term. However, in the near future, the discussion on eliminating discrimination in the Constitution of Bosnia and Herzegovina must be reintroduced. This means that the Others should be allowed to be elected to the Presidency and the House of Peoples of the Parliamentary Assembly. This reform is important, although it will not lead to changes in the federal structure of the state and the nature of its consociative political regime. In our view, this reform should address the issue of the Presidency's competences, reducing them from their current scope. Another important issue is the adoption of the law on the Constitutional Court of Bosnia and Herzegovina. With it, the Parliamentary Assembly would regulate the issues related to the organisation and work of this institution, and partly to the election of its members. The idea that there should be no foreign judges in the Constitutional Court, in our opinion, should be accepted and incorporated into the new constitutional solutions. As an interim solution, the Law on the Constitutional Court may prescribe that foreign judges, while still in this body, be elected by the entity parliaments or the Parliamentary Assembly, with equal participation of both houses. This solution would not have a significant impact on the federal system and the consociational regime, but it could be

23 Marković, Goran, *Bosanskohercegovački federalizam*, 249.

effective for political stability and shifting the centre of gravity of political responsibility to domestic elites. So far, they have often successfully avoided this responsibility, because some of them hoped that foreign judges, together with some domestic judges, would make decisions in their favour. Other elites, by contrast, have used such outcomes to bolster their legitimacy. In any case, the existing model of the Constitutional Court did not meet the expectations of those who hoped that the presence of foreign judges would contribute to the stabilisation of the situation, although it is true that the Constitutional Court, through a series of decisions, significantly influenced the shaping of the constitutional system.

Bibliography

Ademović, Nedim, Marko, Joseph, Marković, Goran, *Ustavno pravo Bosne i Hercegovine* (Sarajevo: Konrad Adenauer Stiftung, 2012).

Balić, Lejla, "Ustavni običaj u BiH – osvrt na izbor sudija Ustavnog suda BiH", *Godišnjak Pravnog fakulteta u Sarajevu* LII /2009.

Boucher, François, *Deep Diversity and Multinational Federalism in Canada*, Paper Prepared for the Institute of Federalism, Fribourg, Summer 2008.

Juhász, József, "Ethno-Federalism: Challenges and Opportunities", *Međunarodni problemi*, 3, 2005.

Lijphart, Arend, "Constitutional Design for Divided Societies", *Journal of Democracy* Vol. 15, No. 2/2004.

Lijphart, Arend, "Non-Majoritarian Democracy: A Comparison of Federal and Consociational Theories", *Publius: The Journal of Federalism*, 15, 85.

Lijphart, Arend, *Democracy in Plural Societies. A Comparative Exploration* (New Haven and London: Yale University Press, 1977).

Lijphart, Arend, *Demokracija u pluralnim društvima* (Zagreb: Globus – Školska knjiga, 1992).

Lijphart, Arend, *The Politics of Accommodation: Pluralism and Democracy in the Netherlands* (Berkeley: University of California Press, 1968).

Lijphart, Arend, *Thinking about Democracy. Power sharing and majority rule in theory and practice* (London and New York: Routledge, 2008).

Marković, Goran, *Bosanskohercegovački federalizam* (Beograd – Sarajevo: Službeni glasnik – University Press, 2012).

Marković, Goran, *Ustavni lavirint. Aporije ustavnog sistema Bosne i Hercegovine* (Beograd: Službeni glasnik, 2021).

CHAPTER 6

The False Dilemma of Bosnian and Herzegovinian Constitutionalism

Dražen Barbarić

1 Introductory Remarks: Diagnosis of the Condition

In its modern history, Bosnia and Herzegovina (BiH) is in an imminent crisis of the political system, which is generated, among other things, by a fundamental disagreement over the basis of BiH's constitutionalism. This chapter does not aim to provide a review of past attempts of constitutional reform, to provide a critical analysis of them, nor does it aim to analyse potential scenarios for constitutional change. Without going into details about the discussion on this topic, it is necessary to make a constitutional diagnosis of the situation in BiH in order to better understand the problems of the functioning of the political system that arises from it. The basic methodological assumption of this chapter is that BiH constitutionalism is not of a civic nature where equally worth citizens embedded their shares of sovereignty into a common state framework. Probably the closest attempt to that model was the referendum in 1992, but one national community completely ignored it and did not perceive it as legitimate.[1] This thesis is supported by the contextualisation of that time. On the first day of the referendum, February 29, *Oslobođenje* wrote, "preparation for the referendum of BiH citizens has been successfully accomplished and what remains now is simply to express the political will for an independent and indivisible BiH of it sovereign peoples."[2] From the above quote, it is possible to infer that the most read and most influential print media of that time, in its public narrative, used the term

1 The Serb population consciously and deliberately boycotted or at least obstructed the referendum, while the Croats were denied the so-called Livno issue, which demanded a differently worded referendum question, which would incorporate the sovereignty of the three peoples and reject the unitary state system.

2 "Kako su mediji 1992. godine izvještavali o referendumu za nezavisnost BiH," *Klix.ba*, March 1, 2020, https://www.klix.ba/vijesti/bih/kako-su-mediji-1992-godine-izvjestavali-o-referendumu-za-nezavisnost-bih/200228132.

 | DOI:10.1163/9789004707887_007

“sovereign peoples” in the period before the war. Thus, public opinion at the time recognised the term “sovereign peoples” as a label for political collectives that were to build a common demos.

In the traumatic period of the conflict, the above-mentioned sovereign nations transformed their temporary organisational form into three “war nations,”[3] mutually conflicting and aimed at creating their own national territories over which they will have absolute power. Although in a state of emergency and in the absence of a constitutional framework that could be considered any form, or at least a feeling, of a common statehood, the three war nations had unquestionable sovereignty over the territory they controlled.[4] In other words, they controlled it in a zero-sum model, where the gain of one is the absolute loss of the other parties, and so in all directions. The end of war conflicts and peace processes led to the necessity to transfer the three war sovereignties into a certain form of common statehood. Therefore, it is only through the Dayton Peace Accords (DPA) that a tripartite sovereignty was created from the transferred stocks of sovereignties of three war communities and their ownership over the territory.[5] The transfer of sovereignty was an act of political will, aided by exhaustion by a relentless war, while the key question remained of how to translate this potentially accumulated state sovereignty into a sustainable constitutional order with a stable political system, without the possibility of slipping back into the abyss of war.

Creators of the constitution were fully aware that classical model of liberal representative democracy will not be sufficient for the preservation of liberal civic regime in a multinational society thorn by war trauma. That kind of a model would later produce domination of three nations on the territory or administrative levels where each holds a demographic majority of population. Without any democratic tradition and with deep war wounds, there is no guarantee that it will not be abused and turned into a mechanism of legitimate hegemony over the minority population. Neven Andjelic described this

3 Vlaisavljević, Ugo, “Tri nacije kao tri ratne naracije,” *Status – magazin za (političku) kulturu i društvena pitanja*, 14 (2010), 152–160.

4 Vlaisavljević, Ugo, “Ustav i zemljišni posjed,” *Status – magazin za (političku) kulturu i društvena pitanja*, 9 (2006), 166–176.

5 Constitutional Court in case U-5/98 confirmed that the principle of the constituency of peoples “is the overarching principle of the Constitution of BiH with which the entities must fully comply.” Barbarić, Dražen and Forić, Samir, “Constituent Peoples,” in: Sahadžić, Maja et. al. (eds.), *Citizens, Constitution, Europe: Glossary of essential constitutional concepts in BiH*, Pravni fakultet Univerziteta u Sarajevu, 2023.

problem as a "majority dictatorship,"[6] a situation where the majority national community grabs a hegemonic position and automatically excludes others from real political authority. It is a pure zero-sum game where politics is perceived as a continuity of war by other means. Constitutional creators tried to avoid this trap by implementing the consociational part of the political system as prevention of hegemonies or majority domination at different levels of state government. The original Dayton, besides stopping the war conflict, had another crucial function – creating a common political framework. The main problem with DPA is that it was imagined as a provisional solution, where no one had any idea what will come after and in which direction will the political system evolve. This provided a huge space for different interpretations of the "Dayton," as well as its evolutionary trajectories.

All three national communities developed and still have their own conceptions of how to upgrade or change the Dayton constitutional framework. Bosniaks have a tendency for unitarisation of the state with the regional structure, which basically means the concept of a state nation with a connected sense of patriotism of all citizens. This would position Bosniaks as a titular ethnicity of the civic political community. Serbs plea for further disintegration toward secession or a confederate structure, in which the Republic of Srpska would *de facto* gain the features of a state. This is a concept of a second Serb national state. After they abandoned the secessionist tendencies, Croats were advocating for further federalisation with the final goal of creating their own entity to include the biggest possible number of Croats in BiH. Basically, this is a concept of sub-state nationalism with a federal autonomy of all three national communities. The paradox of this situation is the fact that "Dayton" remains a golden calf, an irreplaceable reference to modern BiH statehood, but without real integration power. The problem is that no one has sincere confidence in the Dayton structure. All three national political elites swear deeply in Dayton but none of them trust in it honestly. For Bosniaks, it is a necessary evil, a temporary obstacle for the creation of a unitary state, but at the same time it is a guarantee of the sovereignty and territorial integrity of BiH. For Serbs, it became a test of how far political Sarajevo is ready to go in the process of disempowering the RS. For Croats, it was also a temporary obstacle for creating a Croatian federal entity but now it serves as a final goal. Contemporary demands of the Croatian political elite integrated under the umbrella of the Croatian National Assembly (HNS), when we sum them up, are to reset the

6 "Andjelic, Neven: Rezultati izbora iz nekih ljudi oslobodili najgore što u njima postoji," *N1.ba*, September 2, 2020, https://ba.n1info.com/vijesti/a459139-andjelic-rezultati-izbora-iz-nekih-ljudi-oslobodili-najgore-sto-u-njima-postoji/.

current political system to the Dayton basic principles and mechanisms. One of the crucial problems of the Dayton political system is that it does not function in its original structure, it has been disrupted by unilateral decisions of the OHR without any democratic legitimacy.[7] At the moment, we have one original DPA – the constitution – versus three "Daytons" – national visions and interpretations of the future of our country.

Mirjana Kasapović emphasises three major reasons for the failure of the Dayton constitution: (1) nonexistence of consensus about minimum sense of common statehood; (2) nonexistence of consensus about political system; (3) inconsistent strategy of International Community for the democratisation of BiH.[8] Starting with the first point, it is possible to conclude that the absence of a long-term evolutionary vision of the Dayton system has resulted in its temporary expiration date having passed, while in the meantime the International Community has not found a new model for the upgrade. This in no way excuses domestic political actors and their lack of political will to achieve political compromises that would lead to improving the functionality of the political system, and thus to upgrading the Dayton system. Apparently, domestic actors believed that the responsibility for improving the latter lay with the OHR, which consequently reduced their sense of political responsibility and maintenance of the *status quo*. Therefore, every crisis of the political system is in fact a certain form of improvisation that no one has counted on, and there are neither institutional capacities nor democratic traditions or the political will to modify within oneself. As for the lack of consensus on the nature or modifications of the political system, these are in fact symptoms of the first

7 It is worth noting the amendments of Robert Barry (former Head of the OSCE Mission) from 2000. He created the new election law for the House of Peoples based on the principle "everyone elects everyone," meaning that all members of the cantonal assembly, irrespective of nationality, are electing every candidate for the House of Peoples (HoP). The consequence was that Bosniaks in the cantons in which they are demographically predominant could elect Croatian delegates to the HoP without votes or support of Croatian members. Second are amendments of Wolfgang Petrich (former High Representative) from the same year. He changed the procedures of electing President and Vice-President of the Federation of BiH, as well as the election of the federal government – list of candidates needs to get 1/3 of votes from each national club in House of Peoples. The consequence was visible in 2011 when two dominant Bosniak parties, SDA and SDP, created, with the help of two minor Croatian parties, an illegal government with support of only 6 Croatian MP s who were elected by Bosniaks in cantonal assemblies, not 7 which is 1/3 in the HoP. The Central Election Commission decided that this procedure was illegal, but the High Representative Valentin Inzko suspended it and legitimised the illegally elected government.

8 Kasapović, Mirjana, "Bosnia and Herzegovina: Consociational or Liberal Democracy?", *Politička misao 42*, 5 (2005), 9.

point. Political elites remain trapped within an unplanned system and they, in the process of constant improvisation, completely paralyse the functionality of the system. At the moment, we have three different political forces: centripetal, centrifugal, and federalist, which are incommensurable with each other and remain unquestionable political vectors of each national community. The responsibility of the International Community is more than obvious, in a system in which the OHR has become the fourth constitutive subject and where multitude of modifications have come precisely through the political force of the International Community. It is problematic that they tried to enforce a transitional model which did not count on the specificity of the nationally divided post-conflict societies. In doing so, they have created idealistic criteria of development that BiH will never be able to reach, and compared to them, any progress towards democratisation and the functioning of the political system will seem insignificant or insufficient. Thus, BiH will remain in the status of a permanent state of emergency which needs a foreign factor to compensate for the lack of a common vision of statehood and functionality of the political system.

2 Normative Dimension: A Diversive Approach to Diversity

The ambition of this chapter is not to offer concrete solutions for the constitutional and legal problems that burden the political system of BiH, but to point out the normative principles on which potential solutions should be based. The constitutional legal framework and constitutionalism that BiH inherits, which draw their roots from the three stakes of sovereignty in a common political framework, cannot become a stable and functional state if consociational mechanisms turn into means of obstruction and paralysis of the political system. The latter always occurs when political actors have a chronic lack of mutual mistrust, which is often transmitted in an interethnic intolerance within society. The fundamental problem of that situation is the absence of "politics of recognition,"[9] which basically means prescription of equal value to different cultural segments of society and their neutral and equal treatment from the state. Our problem in BiH is the neglect of political outcomes of those recognitions. In BiH, the fact of multiculturalism is almost indisputable, "the fact" is equally proud of everyone as the greatest possible wealth that a modern society can have. The diversity of Bosnia and Herzegovina is almost sacral-

9 Taylor, Charles, "The Politics of Recognition," in *Multiculturalism: Examining the Politics of Recognition*, ed. Amy Gutmann (Princeton: Princeton University Press, 1994), 25–73.

ised and naturalised as a genuine determinant of the centuries-old history of these areas and peoples, while their coexistence has become an ideological reference of an almost utopian nature. In a somewhat reduced version, Rusmir Mahmutćehajić emphasised that "Bosnian political philosophy" is, in its essence, a revelation of the plurality of society as most valuable property.[10] However, the problem is that the fact of diversity, sacralised in the cultural sphere, is not recognised in the political. Simply through the idea of a "civic state," the cultural differences of the three national identities are levelled as an atavism of some past times without use value in the contemporary context.[11] The forces of diversity are not recognised or acknowledged when they are transferred from the socio-cultural to the political sphere, where the outlines of diversity are defamed into premodern forms of politics, as imperfect forms of ethno-politics. No one can sacralise or take pride in the cultural diversity as an essence of our society and at the same time refuse to accept that diversity in the political system. Non-recognition produces a sense of weakness, marginalisation, and frustration for all those citizens who want to be represented in the political sphere through their national identity. A system that is based on mutual distrust in every direction is conducted to failure and will never be able to produce a sustainable political system. Using a scene from The Watchmen, a whole tangle of mistrust relationships is mirrored that permanently blocks any form of progress: after Roarshack is imprisoned he tells the other inmates, "I am not imprisoned with you, but you are imprisoned with me."[12] This scene is a cold but most precise description of our current situation. In a way, a value stream has been created that raises civic identity, cleansed of contamination of national particulars, to the level of *zoe*, i.e. an equal political being to all other citizens, while national uniqueness and cultural diversity is left to our *bios* of existence, the non-political sphere as cultural appendage to the civic state.[13]

---

10 Fukelj, Selma, "Mahmutćehajić o sjećanju na referendum '92.," *N1.ba*, March 1, 2019, https://ba.n1info.com/video/info/a319295-rusmir-mahmutcehajic-o-sjecanju-na-referendum-and3992/.

11 An open example of the denial of differences in the public sphere is the thesis that in BiH there are not three cultural communities but one – Bosnian. Lavić, Senadin, "U Bosni se ne radi o multikulturnom društvu. "U Bosni je riječ o jednoj kulturi!", *Slobodna Bosna*, November 4, 2020, https://www.slobodna-bosna.ba/vijest/175506/profesor_senadin_lavic_u_bosni_se_ne_radi_o_multikulturnom_drustvu_u_bosni_je_rijech_o_jednoj_kulturi.html.

12 Snyder, Zack (director), *Watchmen*, 2009, https://www.imdb.com/title/tt0409459/.

13 Agamben, Giorgio, *Homo Sacer: Sovereign Power and Bare Life*, (Stanford, Stanford University Press, 1998).

BiH needs honest politics of recognition, national specificities and tripartite composition of our state sovereignty, in other words, we need a painful diagnosis so we can begin recovery. In a prescriptive sense, this means a reference to Western democracies that have had a similar problem of interethnic intolerance and constant tension in the functioning of the political system. Charles Taylor offers a normative framework for the aforementioned recovery process: "we have to recognize we cannot all share the same historical identity; our growing nation-state is going to need to accept and work with a plurality of historical identities ... But we can develop viable multinational societies in which the citizens' common identity includes a set of basic principles that recognize that we all want to work with each other to preserve these historical identities with their differences intact."[14] His "diverse approach to diversity" is a recipe for removing mistrust, even if we start from a different understanding of the genuine multiculturalism of society and its overflow into the political. No kind of arrogant civic *a priori* superiority will force people to give up their national habitus, which at this moment is the most important generator of political attitudes and commitments among the citizens of BiH. After all, was it not that approach that produced Canada as one of the most prosperous and open societies in the world; why is the same principle problematic in the context of BiH? The point is that a civic state cannot be created without civic society and civic society cannot be enforced, it can only be created by consent of citizens and their support to such politics. Currently in BiH, there are no indications of a strong transgressive civil society, but three fragmented civic frameworks that again stem from a dominant attachment to one of the three national communities. Civic society can only be created through transgression, in our case with patient and long-term work, and by no means by trans-aggression like we have in BiH. The degradation of political forces that flow from national identities to the level of the *bios* cultural sphere that the civil state will be proud of is a form of cultural violence that creates a sense of humiliation and devaluation among citizens. Summarised, BiH can function only as a product of the so-called "differentiated citizenship,"[15] which will respect its own multinational composition and, at the same time, enable the creation of transgressive civic society. The political sphere must necessarily respect and maintain both dimensions of our socio-identity dynamics.

---

14 Taylor, Charles, "Globalization and the Future of Canada," *Queen's Quarterly* 105, 3 (1998), 341.

15 Kymlicka, Will, *Multicultural Citizenship: A Liberal Theory of Minority Rights*, (Oxford, Oxford University Press, 1995).

3 Institutional Dimension: Hybrid Political System

In the public and political spheres of Bosnia and Herzegovina, a narrative is often imposed about two models of political organisation that are mutually exclusive. On the one hand, there is the existing Dayton system, which is characterised by ethnic division and constant obstruction, while it is opposed by a civic model that turns all individuals into equal citizens without any possibility of discrimination and with an important outcome of the disappearance of ethno-political actors. These two ideal-type models presented as separate realities are in a relationship of exclusivity and cannot coexist. However, the Dayton constitutional framework incorporated parts of both models into the existing political system. This is clearly seen in the construction of a symmetrical bicameral legislative model in which one house is composed exclusively according to the classical civic model of representation while the other is reserved for the formation of national veto subjects, i.e. reflects the will of the constituent peoples.[16] The fundamental problem of such a system that combines classical liberal and consociational elements is the absence of a common normative foundation that would legitimise the system and, in a certain way, drive its dynamics. In other words, the software of such system has completely failed, which means that in the absence of a common vision of statehood, a common understanding of the evolution of the political system and an enormous degree of mutual distrust, it becomes a vehicle for paralysing parts or even the whole system. We already have a hybrid political system, so it has to be supported with normative core of "overlapping consensus"[17] filled with common values and a sense of common state. For a start, it implies the political frame of free existence of national identity without transaggression of the civic identity that can undermine their affection towards a common state. A hybrid system cannot succeed if one segment of multinational society has mechanisms for the establishment of hegemony or domination.[18] It can succeed only "if no opposing national community seeks to assimilate others and establish its own national state or force others to accept a new artificial national identity that it is developing."[19] The overlapping con-

16 See: Balić, Lejla in this volume.

17 Rawls, John, *Political Liberalism*, (New York, Columbia University Press, 1993).

18 Kasapović, Mirjana, "Lijphart and Horowitz in Bosnia and Herzegovina: Institutional Design for Conflict Resolution or Conflict Reproduction?" *Politička misao 53*, 4 (2016), 176.

19 Kasapović, Mirjana, "Popis stanovništva u BiH jasno pokazuje: Federaciji prijeti ciprizacija", *Globus*, July 15 2016, https://www.jutarnji.hr/globus/politika/popis-stanovnistva-u-bih-jasno-pokazuje-federaciji-prijeti-ciprizacija-4533272.

sensus, which must necessarily contain a minimal sense of a common statehood, will not be legitimised through the idea of abstract citizens, but by the expression of the political will of the constituent peoples who have woven fragments of their sovereignty into that same state. Only then it will be possible to develop a subtler normative software that will drive a hybrid political system and transform it from a set of obstruction mechanisms to a set of cooperation mechanisms. This overlapping consensus would generate elements that would enable the transgressive development of civil society and the spill over of their interest into the political system, without any institutional imposition, but by the power of the democratic will of the citizens. BiH as a *sui generis* political hybrid system should not reinvent the wheel, but use existing models and mechanisms developed by Western democracies for the purpose of their own management of national and ethnic differences.

There are models in Western democracies which successfully balance between state stability and territorial integrity. Those models provide specific group differentiated rights to minor national communities within the state.[20] This does not mean that level of democracy or protection of individual rights decreased, and the best example is again Canada that we mentioned before. Across Europe, there are models of division of sovereignty, territorial autonomies, and consociational mechanisms that just create a balance between the demands for collective national rights and individual liberal rights in combination with a stable central state. In BiH, the concept of constituency of peoples is often defamed as a "Soviet model"[21] that does not befit modern democratic societies. If we start from the fact that constituency is only a linguistic mark of the essentially constitutional and political fact of national segmentation of BiH society and their desire for political articulation of that segmentation, in fact, constituency of peoples is a linguistic derivative for a certain set of group-differentiated rights on which modern BiH was constituted. Are not many European countries based on similar principles, such as Spain with the concept of autonomous communities, the autonomy of the Åland Islands in the constitutional framework of Finland or South Tyrol in Italy, not to mention the consociational models of Switzerland or Belgium that completely dispelled interethnic disputes and created stable political systems with the inviolable protection of both individual and cultural rights

20 Kymlicka, *Multicultural Citizenship*, 34–48.

21 This position is propagated by the member of the Presidency of BiH, Željko Komšić. "Komšić: BiH se može urediti bez konstitutivnosti, taj je pojam uveo Sovjetski Savez," *Faktor.ba*, September 1, 2021, https://faktor.ba/vijest/komsic-bih-se-moze-urediti-bez-konstitutivnosti-taj-je-pojam-uveo-sovjetski-savez/136524.

of communities? It is really difficult in the above examples to recognise the handwriting of the soviet constitutionalists in those systems. After all, has not the EU itself been based on multilayer governance, subsidiarity, decentralisation, recognition and respect of national differences and federalism? From that perspective, it is hard to see the reasons for them to be discredited in BiH as pre-modern atavisms.

4 Concluding Remarks

On the basis of what has been said, it is clear that the combination of classical models of liberal representation and consociational and federalist elements does not necessarily cause paralysis of the system or its dysfunction.[22] On the contrary, the examples of these democracies show that hybridity of the system can also contribute to the democratisation of society, building a system of rule of law and human rights, while politically recognising multicultural differences within society. Named constituency of peoples or something else, the constitutional subjectivity of national segments in BiH must remain embedded in the political system if we want to have a functional state and a stable society. The thesis on abandoning the principle of constituency of peoples as a sort of transformation into a civic state regime is completely wrong and sometimes extremely malicious. The reason is obvious – the abolition of the constituency principle will not automatically melt the three national communities into one civic society; on the contrary, it would create: a titular nation (major Bosniaks), one minority nation (Serbs), and one national minority (Croats). In that situation, the major nation would definitely increase the suppression mechanism because the other two communities will drastically decrease their loyalty towards the state. The International Community and the titular nation will not be able to ignore the dissatisfaction and requests of those communities. The key question remains – why would Serbs and Croats give up the status of constituent peoples and reduce their subjectivity to a minority position, unless it is an imposition – from this arises the question of whether this undermines the fundamental constitutive act of investment of the three sovereignties codified in the Dayton Agreement?

To avoid that scenario, the concept of constituency of peoples must be integrated into the hybrid political system without any kind of discrimination of those who do not declare themselves in the dominant national matrix.

22 See: Marković, Goran in this volume.

Three main reasons why BiH should maintain the consociational mechanism and the protection of group differentiated rights are: (1) it is the most divided society in Europe; (2) historical circumstances – every political regime recognised the fact of political identity diversity and included them into the political system, except the Kingdom of Yugoslavia and the NDH; (3) war traumas deepened discrepancies between nations and made them territorially more compact.[23] National segmentation did not originate in the 1990s, but has deep historical roots that have been inscribed in various forms in the political frameworks of different regimes. The experiences of war have deepened intolerance and created stocks of mistrust that do not go away just like that. Any radical constitutional cut that would remove group-differentiated rights would create strong distrust and fear of minority nations towards a common state and would open the space for the establishment of a majority dictatorship. If we have three ethno-national forces, two of which would be passivated in a civic state by the fact that they would be reduced to minority positions, it is illusory to expect that majority ethno-nationalism would be transformed into a civic one, or that it would not use political levers to establish its own hegemony. Respect of every *demos*, national and civic, and reconfiguration of the political system, including the electoral law through implementation of every judgment of the European Court for Human rights and the Constitutional Court of BiH, as well as honest application of the existing constitutional principles, is the way towards a functional state and stable society. That will increase inter-national trust and reduce the need for veto mechanisms. Otherwise, we will have double division, *de facto* statehood of the Republic of Srpska and unfortunate Cypriotisation of the Federation.[24] In order to prevent such an outcome, BiH really needs a true politics of recognition.

Considering the political situation in BiH, there is no doubt that institutional modifications will necessarily occur, and they will include certain constitutional changes. The extent of these changes, of course, depends on the expressed political will and willingness to compromise in the current political constellation. Demands or wishes that the International Community will cut the Gordian Knot of BiH politics and impose constitutional changes do not seem realistic and could cause a bigger problem than the preservation of the *status quo*. As indicated in the introduction, this chapter does not have the

---

23 Kasapović, Mirjana, "Bosnia and Herzegovina: Consociational or Liberal Democracy?", *Politička misao* 42, 5 (2005), 7.

24 Kasapović, Mirjana, "Popis stanovništva u BiH jasno pokazuje: Federaciji prijeti ciprizacija", *Globus*, July 15, 2016.

ambition to review previous attempts of constitutional reform, nor to provide a critical analysis of them. Its modest attempt is merely to show that constitutional reform is very unlikely in the current constellation, but that it is nevertheless conceivable to reconstruct three situational moments that would open up such a possibility of constitutional reform as a real option. These moments serve as theoretical elements for contemplating the future of BiH constitutionalism. Therefore, these are analytical scenarios that serve as a framework for understanding in which hypothetical situations constitutional changes would be feasible, and by no means predications about the forms or content of potential constitutional reforms. All three scenarios include some sort of extraordinary situations.

The first option is a new state of war and a repetition of the extraordinary situation that we had in Dayton. This would mean a retrograde disintegration of an already fragile social structure, into three initial war sovereignties and ownership of a controlled territory. The situation would be followed by negotiations between the leaders of the three war communities and the recomposition of a common statehood like the one in Dayton. It goes without saying that this option is the least certain one and absolutely unacceptable, but it would certainly create the most radical conditions of extraordinary state in which a compromise would be much more likely than at present. Another option is a mass public expression of citizens' dissatisfaction that would necessarily have to cross the boundaries of national identities. Thus, it would be a matter of mass civil unrest within all three national communities with a common guiding thread. This situation can be caused by the economic and demographic collapse of BiH, something like the Spanish Indignados who unequivocally accused the existing political elite of the bad socio-economic situation with the slogan "these people do not represent us." This would create an emergency situation that would necessarily require some reset of the political system, presumably led by some new political actors. The experience of recent civil protests in BiH does not speak in favour of the certainty of this situation, because citizens mostly expressed their rebellion within the framework of their own national communities and without mass transgression on other national communities. Also, the goals of the protests were often abused, and after a while they lost their political edge and were reduced to a very narrow circle of interested people, while the current government relatively effectively absorbed the unfavourable outcomes and mass support. The third scenario can be anticipated only in the phase when BiH becomes a formal candidate on the path to membership in the European Union. This means, first of all, that the internalisation of European issues must take place in the BiH political sphere and public opinion. The negotiation process will do its part, constantly putting demands before the domestic actors, the fulfilment of which will show their readiness for difficult adjustment and the institutional capacity of these adjustments. The accession process will be under public scrutiny and many problems in its implementation will become existentially important for citizens. When the fulfilment or non-fulfilment becomes the main component of our internal political process, the politicians will consequently start to win or lose elections on those topics. Declarative support or bluffing will be punished, because accession will be within a hand's reach and citizens will perceive it as panacea for all our problems. That situation will bring key actors to a state of exception where the International Community, especially the EU representatives, will regain a strong pressure mechanism and domestic politicians will be forced to leave maximalist goals and make compromises. "Thus, if constitutional reform shall happen, the International Community and the EU will have to become involved in the process leading to proposals by creating safe spaces for public debate, guaranteeing the procedures, and facilitating the process – without imposing the outcome."[25] This is a potential situation when the accession process reaches an advanced stage, and the citizens exert real pressure on domestic politicians to bring it to an end. The most difficult issues that will be left for last, including the constitutional changes, will become possible because the stakes will be too high – full membership in the EU. This is the most likely situation that will create a state of emergency and a willingness to compromise on the fundamental issues of the state and the political system. The only problem is that it requires a tremendous amount of patience.

Bibliography

Agamben, Giorgio, *Homo Sacer: Sovereign Power and Bare Life*, (Stanford, Stanford University Press, 1998).

Andjelic, Neven, "Rezultati izbora iz nekih ljudi oslobodili najgore što u njima postoji," *N1.ba*, September 2, 2020, https://ba.n1info.com/vijesti/a459139-andjelic-rezultati-izbora-iz-nekih-ljudi-oslobodili-najgore-sto-u-njima-postoji/.

Barbarić, Dražen and Forić, Samir, "Constituent Peoples," in: Maja Sahadžić et. al. (eds.), *Citizens, Constitution, Europe: Glossary of essential constitutional concepts in BiH*, Pravni fakultet Univerziteta u Sarajevu, 2023.

25 See: Woelk, Jens in this volume (Chapter 15).

Fukelj, Selma, "Mahmutćehajić o sjećanju na referendum '92.," *N1.ba*, March 1, 2019, https://ba.n1info.com/video/info/a319295-rusmir-mahmutcehajic-o-sjecanju-na-referendum-and3992/.

Kasapović, Mirjana, "Bosnia and Herzegovina: Consociational or Liberal Democracy?", *Politička misao 42*, 5 (2005), 3–30.

Kasapović, Mirjana, "Lijphart and Horowitz in Bosnia and Herzegovina: Institutional Design for Conflict Resolution or Conflict Reproduction?" *Politička misao 53*, 4 (2016), 174–190.

Kasapović, Mirjana, "Popis stanovništva u BiH jasno pokazuje: Federaciji prijeti ciprizacija," *Globus*, July 15, 2016, https://www.jutarnji.hr/globus/politika/popis-stanovnistva-u-bih-jasno-pokazuje-federaciji-prijeti-ciprizacija-4533272.

Komšić, Željko, "BiH se može urediti bez konstitutivnosti, taj je pojam uveo Sovjetski Savez," *Faktor.ba*, September 1, 2021,https://faktor.ba/vijest/komsic-bih-se-moze-urediti-bez-konstitutivnosti-taj-je-pojam-uveo-sovjetski-savez/136524.

Kymlicka, Will, *Multicultural Citizenship: A Liberal Theory of Minority Rights*, (Oxford, Oxford University Press, 1995).

Lavić, Senadin, "U Bosni se ne radi o multikulturnom društvu. U Bosni je riječ o jednoj kulturi!", *Slobodna Bosna*, November 4, 2020, https://www.slobodnabosna.ba/vijest/175506/profesor_senadin_lavic_u_bosni_se_ne_radi_o_multikulturnom_drustvu_u_bosni_je_rijech_o_jednoj_kulturi.html.

Rawls, John, *Political Liberalism*, (New York, Columbia University Press, 1993). S.H.P., "Kako su mediji 1992. godine izvještavali o referendumu za nezavisnost BiH," *Klix.ba*, March 1, 2020, https://www.klix.ba/vijesti/bih/kako-su-mediji-1992-godine-izvjestavali-o-referendumu-za-nezavisnost-bih/200228132.

Taylor, Charles, "Globalization and the Future of Canada," *Queen's Quarterly 105*, 3 (1998), 331–342.

Taylor, Charles, "The Politics of Recognition," in *Multiculturalism: Examining the Politics of Recognition*, ed. Amy Gutmann (Princeton: Princeton University Press, 1994), 25–73.

Vlaisavljević, Ugo, "Tri nacije kao tri ratne naracije," *Status – magazin za (političku) kulturu i društvena pitanja*, 14 (2010), 152–160.

Vlaisavljević, Ugo, "Ustav i zemljišni posjed," *Status – magazin za (političku) kulturu i društvena pitanja*, 9 (2006), 166–176.

Taylor, Charles, "The Politics of Recognition," in *Multiculturalism: Examining the Politics of Recognition*, ed. Amy Gutmann (Princeton: Princeton University Press, 1994), 25–73.

Vlaisavljević, Ugo, "Tri nacije kao tri ratne naracije," *Status – magazin za (političku) kulturu i društvena pitanja*, 14 (2010), 152–160.

Vlaisavljević, Ugo, "Ustav i zemljišni posjed," *Status – magazin za (političku) kulturu i društvena pitanja*, 9 (2006), 166–176.

CHAPTER 7

Political Equality in the Case Law of the BiH Constitutional Court in "Dialogue" with the European Court of Human Rights

Joseph Marko

1 The Political and Legal Discourse Thirty Years after Dayton

To this day, any public debate about the political situation by the people – here in the meaning of everyday language as you and me – in Bosnia and Herzegovina (BiH) is firmly grounded in the reference to the so-called "Dayton constitution" and its legal institutionalisation of ethnic keys for the constitutional category of "constituent peoples", on the one hand, and its internal territorial delimitation into two so-called "Entities", the Federation of BiH (FBiH) and the Republika Srpska (RS), on the other. According to the text of its preamble, "Bosniacs, Croats, and Serbs, as constituent peoples (along with Others), and citizens of Bosnia and Herzegovina" shall have "determined" the content of the "Constitution of Bosnia and Herzegovina." This part of the constitution has to be seen in conjunction with the provisions of Articles IV and V of the constitution providing for *ethnic* representation and participation of *Bosniacs, Croats, and Serbs* – but not the "Others" also mentioned in the text of the preamble – in the composition of the three-member Presidency of the country and the second chamber of Parliament, the House of Peoples (HoP), on the basis of the parity principle with five delegates from each of these three by name determined constituent peoples. In addition, the Dayton constitution provides for *political* representation and participation of the mentioned Entities as *territorial units,* as can be seen from the fact that they form the electoral units in the ratio of 2 (from FBiH): 1 (from RS) for the election of members of the Presidency and the HoP and, thus, the democratic legitimation also of the Council of Ministers, as well as the Constitutional Court. Finally, similar ethnic keys for posts in the legislature, executive, and judiciary are foreseen also by the constitutions of the Entities.

All these constitutionally entrenched ethnic keys therefore raise the central constitutional and political question discussed since the conclusion of the Dayton Peace Agreement in December 1995: How *shall* we understand the fact that the Dayton constitution provides for political representation in the

 | DOI:10.1163/9789004707887_008

form of ethnic keys for the composition of legislative, executive, and judicial bodies, *as well as* through territorial delimitation into two Entities and, in addition, according to the FBiH constitution, also into cantons? *Must* these legal categories – derived from the personality and territoriality principle – be considered as "legal subjects" being guaranteed by the respective constitutional provisions legal *and thus* political equality like all citizens of BiH as this follows without ambiguity from Article II.4. of the Dayton constitution? Or does the text of the Dayton constitution through this combination of individual equality of "abstract" citizens and territorial delimitation, as well as differentiation into the legal categories of constituent peoples and Others, express a model of "ethnocracy" instead of liberal democracy based on individual human rights, as the applicant in a recent case before the European Court of Human Rights has complained?[1] Shall we understand the "complex" governmental structure foreseen in the Dayton constitution as an *irreconcilable mix* of political science models of power-sharing and federalism with human rights, as many academics in and outside of BiH claim? And if so, "shall" this mean that the Dayton constitution "is" firmly based on the combination or even "identification" of ethnic identity and territorial delimitation for political representation and participation?[2] Such an *identification of territory and ethnicity* would, legally speaking, transform not only "Others" and citizens, but also Serbs, Bosniacs and Croats into a *de facto* ethnic "minority" at the Entity level. But is there any evidence that this was the infamous "will of the parties" when concluding the Dayton Peace Agreement in 1995?

However, for lawyers, "names" of peoples or theoretical models of power-sharing or federalism cannot or shall not define the *normative* meaning of specific constitutional provisions. Lawyers must, first and above all, *interpret the text* of legal and constitutional provisions in line with the generally accepted methods of legal interpretation foreseen in democratic countries with a functioning system of judicial review.[3] Thus, our topic of political

1 ECtHR, Kovačević v. Bosnia and Herzegovina, 29 August 2023, para 44. This case will be discussed in detail in Section 4.

2 See: McCrudden, Christopher and O'Leary, Brendan, *Courts and Consociations. Human Rights and Power-Sharing* (Oxford (Oxford University Press) 2013); Kasapović, Mirjana, *Bosna i Hercegovina: podijeljeno društvo i nestabilna država* (Zagreb (Politička kultura) 2005); Mujkić, Asim, "Bosna i Hercegovina i izazovi konsocijacije", *Odjek, 1* (2007), 6–12; Marković, Goran, *Bosanskohercegovački federalizam* (University press, Službeni glasnik, 2012), and his chapter in this volume. See also the chapters by Dražen Barbarić, Lejla Balić, and Maja Sahadžić referring to power-sharing and federalism.

3 See, above all, Kischel, Uwe, *Comparative Law* (Oxford (Oxford University Press) 2019), 301–343, for common law countries and 392–408 and 512–516 for civil law countries.

equality in BiH crystallises in the question what the *specific legal status* of the political subjects mentioned above *shall be*. This "status" question, including their mutual relationships, must be analysed through the case law of national and international apex courts.[4]

In order to comply with the implicit promise in the title of this chapter, I will discuss the meaning of the *legal concept* of political equality in terms of political representation and participation in decision-making processes, as this was developed in the case law of the European Court of Human Rights (ECtHR) and the Constitutional Court of Bosnia (BiHCC) – the institutions mandated to decide with legally binding force. I will thereby focus on the analysis of the intimate relationship between the (active) right to vote and the right to stand as candidate in general elections. Only this way can we understand the underlying concept of political "representation" in any form of "representative democracy" and why the constitutional system of BiH is in no way unique or more "complex" than several other countries or regions such as Belgium, Cyprus, Northern Ireland or South Tyrol. The following Section 2 shall thus summarise the conceptual and doctrinal standards of the general legal term "equality" in human and minority rights law following from the jurisprudence of the ECtHR. Section 3 will then deal with the case-law of the ECtHR concerning electoral rights in combination with the prohibition of discrimination from a comparative perspective. Section 4 provides an analysis of the so-called "constituent peoples" case of the BiHCC handed down in 2000, having set the normative standards in the interpretation of the concept of constituent peoples in relation to Others and citizens. Section 5 deals with the subsequent case law of the BiHCC and its argumentation in refusing to follow the reasoning of the ECtHR case law in electoral matters. The final Section 6 provides summary conclusions with regard to the normative standards in electoral matters.

2 "Equality": An Empty Shell?

From the perspective of comparative constitutional jurisprudence of liberal democratic states, the conundrums of the conceptualisation of the normative concept of equality were best explained by the judges of the ECtHR through their interpretation of the wording of Article 14 ECHR in the so-called "Belgian Linguistics" case in 1968:

4 From a comparative perspective see, in particular, Graziadei, Stefan, *Courts and the Consociation: Judicial Review of Founding Political Agreements in Multi-National Democracies* (Universiteit Antwerpen (PhD Thesis), 2017).

> … In spite of the very general wording of the French version (sans distinction aucune), Article 14 (art. 14) does not forbid every difference in treatment in the exercise of rights recognised. This version must be read in the light of the more restrictive text of the English version ('without discrimination'). In addition, and in particular, one would reach absurd results were one to give Article 14 (art.14) an interpretation as wide as that which the French version seems to imply. One would, in effect, be led to judge as contrary to the Convention every one of the many legal or administrative provisions which do not secure to everyone complete equality of treatment in the enjoyment of the rights and freedoms recognised. The competent national authorities are frequently confronted with situations and problems which, on account of differences inherent therein, call for different legal solutions; moreover, certain legal inequalities tend to correct factual inequalities....[5]

Hence, any debate about the normative rules which shall follow from the abstract normative principle of equality under the legal regime of the ECHR has to take into account the categorical distinction between *legal* and *factual* (in)equalities and the guideline expressed by the judges that factual inequalities can be corrected by "legal inequalities", what is then termed in law and academic literature "positive measures" in European and "affirmative action" in American legal language. As a consequence of this conceptualisation of the term equality, two specific normative concepts and rules follow in legal-dogmatic terminology from the case law of supranational human rights courts such as the ECtHR and the European Court of Justice (ECJ). First, the so-called "formal" equality *before* the law and, second, the "substantive" equality *through* law in order to correct factual inequalities.

The first concept is specified by the prohibition of "direct" and "indirect" *discrimination* of individuals with the latter defined as prohibition of discrimination when on the face "neutral" legal language has a disproportionate effect – of particular relevance for our topic – on persons "of a racial or ethnic origin … compared with other persons" and cannot be justified by a legitimate aim and means that are appropriate and necessary.[6] Insofar as the required comparison can only be made between persons who claim to be

5 ECtHR, Case 'Relating to certain aspects of the use of laws on the use of languages in education in Belgium' v. Belgium, 23 July 1968, section B, § 10.

6 This quotation follows the definition from the text of Article 2 of the EU "Race Directive" (Council Directive 2000/43/EC), which is also the standard of judicial review in the jurisprudence of the ECtHR.

discriminated against on the basis of the characteristics enumerated as legal categories in anti-discrimination provisions, even the concept of formal equality, requiring state bodies and private persons to refrain from both forms of discrimination, makes sense only for what I have termed elsewhere "group-related" rights.[7] Positive action measures as political possibility for the national legislator or even required as constitutional duty in order to "correct factual inequalities" following from the conception of "substantive equality" will even more so require to take their "group-relatedness" into account in all legislative, administrative or judicial activities in order to be "effective" as "group rights" in the narrow sense guaranteeing the exercise of corporate forms of self-government.

In conclusion: For the analysis of the meaning of the concept of political equality in the overall Dayton "constitutional system",[8] these legal-dogmatic text-book specifications of the abstract principle of equality *crystallise in the problem* of their relationship. Do individual rights of "abstract" citizens, such as the right to vote and to stand as candidate in elections, *and* group-related or even so-called "collective" rights, in the form of political representation and participation in state bodies, necessarily exclude each other or can they be combined and how? Is it possible to identify normative guidelines from the

---

7 Even if women or citizens are not a "group" in the sociological sense, but usually only aggregated by statistical numbers for the purpose of comparison. See, above all, the matrix for the three types of rights, namely individual, group-related, and group or "collective" rights, to be distinguished from a comparative analysis of constitutional law and jurisprudence in Marko, Joseph, "Law and sociology: the constructivist and interpretative turn", in Marko, Joseph and Constantin Sergiu (eds.), *Human and Minority Rights Protection by Multiple Diversity Governance* (London-New York (Routledge), 2019), 166.

8 Although Annex IV of the Dayton Peace Agreement is called "the Constitution" in the text of this Annex itself, the BiHCC had to clarify early on what constitutional rank the other 10 Annexes, as well as the annexes to "the Constitution" and to Annex VI, shall have due to existing normative inconsistencies or even contradictions in their texts. In conclusion, the BiHCC ruled in a series of cases that the Dayton Peace Agreement itself with all the Annexes have the same constitutional rank as can be seen from the fact that the BiHCC consistently used the other mentioned annexes as legal standards for the review of all sub-constitutional law. See, in particular, Marko, Joseph, "Constitutional Jurisprudence in Bosnia and Herzegovina: Experiences form the First Mandate of the Constitutional Court from 1997–2002", *European Autonomy and Diversity Papers* (EDAP), European Academy Bozen/Bolzano, 2004 at www.eurac.edu/edap and Marko, Joseph and Vranješ, Nevenko, "Amendments to the Constitution of Bosnia and Herzegovina", in: Sahadžić, Maja et al. (eds.), *Citizens. Constitution. Europe. Glossary of Essential Constitutional Concepts in BiH* (Sarajevo (University of Sarajevo, Faculty of Law) 2023), 471. It goes without saying that also the constitutions of the Entities and the cantons of FBiH are part of the entire constitutional system subjected however to the entire Dayton Peace Agreement due to the supremacy clause of Article III.3.b. of Annex 4 as the BiHCC ruled in cases U 5/99 and U 39/00.

analysis of the case law of the BiHCC in "dialogue" with the judgments of the ECtHR regarding the interrelationship of the ECHR and the Dayton constitution as to how different elements of (ethnic) power-sharing and (territorial) federalism laid down in the Dayton constitutional system might be combined in order to satisfy the standards of judicial review by the ECtHR which are a pre-condition for further EU integration?[9]

As I will try to demonstrate in the following sections, in particular this "third way" follows from the jurisprudence of the ECtHR and the "landmark" decision[10] of the BiHCC in case U-5/98, 2000, whose Third Partial Decision is colloquially called the "constituent peoples case" discussed in Section 4 in detail.

3 The Case Law of the ECtHR in Developing the Normative Standards of Equality against Ethnic Discrimination

Let us start with the most recent judgment of the ECtHR in the case *Kovačević v. Bosnia* and Herzegovina, 2023,[11] in particular with the dissenting opinion of Judge Kucsko-Stadlmayer. She raised the most far-reaching questions in terms of our problematique of political equality. The applicant had claimed that due to the combination of territorial and ethnic requirements of the Dayton constitution "he had been unable to vote for the candidates of his choice in those elections", that is, "that the candidates best representing his political views were not from the 'right' Entity and/or of the 'right' ethnic origin" (para 8). In criticising the majority opinion which had declared that the ethnic keys for the BiH Presidency and the House of Peoples in the Dayton constitution violate Article 1 of Protocol No.12 ECHR,[12] she, however, finds it a "paradox" that the active right to vote should be "automatically" restricted by these constitutional provisions, since there would be "a deep structural difference" between these rights in the case law of the ECtHR. She justifies this conclusion with a question in the form of a rhetorical *argumentum ad absurdum*: "Has every single voter with an active voting right also a right 'to be represented' in a parliamentary body, even more so if this body is not directly elected? Does

9 See: Vranješ, Nevenko in this volume and Woelk Jens in this volume (Chapter 15).

10 See this characterisation by the ECtHR in the case Kovačević v. Bosnia and Herzegovina, 2023, para 15.

11 See above However, after finishing this chapter for publication, the Grand Chamber of the ECtHR has decided on 25 July 2025 to declare the application inadmissible and thereby revoked the judgment of the Chamber. The reasoning for this decision had not been published during the process of corrections of this article.

12 Which has been ratified by BiH.

every voter in a democracy have a right to a party or a candidate 'of his choice'? Must constitutional provisions governing the right to stand for election ... ensure that every single voter and/or every group of voters is 'represented' in a democratic body?" In conclusion, she rejects the normative concepts of a "right to vote for a candidate of one's choice" (para 17 diss. op) and the concept of "vote dilution" (para 20 diss. op). Nor would there be a positive obligation of the Contracting States of the ECHR to take positive measures to ensure the representation of all social, religious, economic, or other groups. This would change the concept of parliamentary, representative democracy as such (paras 19–20 diss. op).

However, a detailed analysis of the development of the case-law of the ECtHR[13] since the first landmark judgment *Mathieu-Mohin and Clerfayt v. Belgium*, 1987,[14] demonstrates that one *cannot* deduce a "deep structural difference" between active and passive electoral rights from this and the following ECtHR cases.

In the said case, the ECtHR established the elementary *doctrinal rules* for the interpretation of Article 3 Protocol No. 1 in conjunction with Article 14 ECHR In the wording of the Court, the phrase "conditions which will ensure the free expression of the opinion of the people in the choice of the legislature ... implies essentially ... the principle of equality of treatment of all citizens in the exercise of their right to vote *and* the right to stand for election" (para 54, emph. JM). Hence, *without any differentiation* between these two electoral rights, the Court argues from the very beginning that the wording of Article 3 expresses with this phrase a *conceptually coherent concept* which has to be guaranteed equally.

Nonetheless, these rights are not absolute. The Contracting States have "a wide margin of appreciation" so that any electoral system must be assessed in light of the political evolution of the country concerned. But in order to guarantee the "very essence" and "effectiveness" of these rights, the Court reviews the respective national electoral system with the proportionality test, namely that the interferences "are imposed in pursuit of a legitimate aim, and that the means employed are not disproportionate" (para 52). Finally, by taking into account the conceptually essential *mutual interrelationship* of the *active right to vote* and the *composition* of the *parliamentary bodies along linguistic lines* in the Belgian constitution, the Court came to the conclusion that the require-

13 Some of the following paragraphs concerning the case law of the ECtHR have already been published as Marko, Joseph, "The ECtHR Grand Chamber May De-Block the Constitutional Impasse in Bosnia and Herzegovina", *verfassungsblog.de*, 28 March 2024.

14 ECtHR, Mathieu-Mohin and Clerfayt v. Belgium, 2 March 1987.

ment to use an official language other than the mother tongue in public office was not a "disproportionate limitation" (para. 57) for *minority* language speakers of what could be called a "right to vote for a candidate of one's choice" from a comparative constitutional law perspective.[15]

However, public international law in the European context has dramatically changed at the beginning of the 1990s, not the least with the adoption of legal instruments for the protection of national minorities within the framework of the Council of Europe and institutions on minorities within the OSCE.[16] Accordingly, the case-law of the ECtHR has taken ethnic discrimination more seriously and has developed *normative standards* concerning more detailed *positive obligations* of Contracting States to ensure the *effectiveness* of protection in a series of cases in the 2000s.[17]

In the case of *Aziz v. Cyprus*,[18] the ECtHR for the first time ruled on the *complete exclusion* from the (active) right to vote. The Cypriot Supreme Court had upheld the political situation after the military invasion and occupation of the northern part of the country by Turkey in and after 1974 by allowing that the parliamentary elections were carried out on the basis of electoral lists only for citizens declaring to be members of the Greek-Cypriot community. The applicant, a Turkish-Cypriot citizen, was therefore "completely deprived of any opportunity to express his opinion in the choice of the members of the House of Representatives of the country of which he is a national and where he has always lived" so that "the very essence of the applicant's right to vote, as guaranteed by Article 3 of Protocol No. 1 ECHR was

15 See Sect 2, US Voting Rights Act 1965. "Vote dilution" amounts to a violation of the equal effect of votes, if members of racial or ethnic minorities have less chances than other members of the electorate to participate in the electoral process and to elect "candidates of their choice".

16 These are the Council of Europe's Framework Convention for the Protection of National Minorities (FCNM) and the European Charter of Regional and Minority Languages with their supervisory mechanisms, as well as the OSCE High Commissioner on National Minorities as conflict prevention mechanism.

17 First, a "duty to protect minorities' identities" was established by the ECtHR case Chapman v. United Kingdom, 18 January 2001; second, "institutional segregation" in educational systems was prohibited as form of direct discrimination which can never be justified in ECtHR Grand Chamber, D.H. and Others v. Czech Republic", 13 November 2007; third, a "duty to take measures of affirmative action" was adopted in the ECtHR case Oršuš v. Croatia, 16 March 2010. For a systematic analysis see: Marko, Joseph, "Against discrimination: the right to equality and the dilemma of difference", in Marko and Constantin (eds.), *Human and Minority Rights Protection*, 307–339.

18 ECtHR, Aziz v. Cyprus, 22 June 2004 and the Resolution CM/ResDH (2007)77 on the execution of the judgment.

impaired" (para 30). Moreover, the Court ruled that there was a "*double violation*" in relation to Article 14 ECHR since the difference in treatment had resulted "from the very fact that the applicant was a Turkish Cypriot" preventing him from "voting at any parliamentary election" (paras 36–7).

These two criteria, the exclusion from the substantive right and ethnic discrimination and their link, were *expressis verbis* confirmed and further specified in two more recent cases. In the case *Riza and Others v. Bulgaria*, 2016,[19] the Court, confirming its case law, ruled that "the active electoral right as guaranteed by Article 3 of Protocol No. 1 is not confined exclusively to the acts of choosing one's favourite candidates in the secrecy of the polling booth and slipping one's favourite candidates into the box. It also involves each voter being able to see his or her *vote influencing the make-up of the legislature*, subject to compliance with the rules laid down in electoral legislation. To allow the contrary would be tantamount to rendering the right to vote, the election and ultimately the democratic system itself meaningless" (para 148, emph. JM).

With reference to minority rights, this was recently confirmed in the case of *Bakirdzi and E.C. v. Hungary*, 2023.[20] Concerning the prohibition of ethnic discrimination, the Court held that "no difference in treatment which is based exclusively or to a decisive extent on a person's ethnic origin is capable of being objectively justified in a contemporary democratic society built on the principles of pluralism and respect for differing cultures" (para 50). Moreover, the Court also affirmed its case-law concerning the *effectiveness* of positive obligations on behalf of minorities and its members by declaring the following: "[T]o express and promote its identity it may be instrumental in helping a minority to preserve and uphold its rights" (para 54). Thus, the Court finally ruled: "[T]he national legislator needs to assess whether the statutory scheme creates a disparity in the *voting power* of members of national minorities, as the applicants, in order to avoid that the potential value of votes that might be cast for national minority lists becomes *diluted*" (para 59, emph. JM) and concluded: "[R]ather than perpetuating the exclusion of minority representatives from political decision-making at a national level ... the system that was put in place limited the opportunity of national minority voters to enhance their political effectiveness as a group and threat-

---

19 ECtHR, Riza and Others v. Bulgaria, 13 January 2016.

20 ECtHR, Bakirdzi and E.C. v. Hungary, 3 April 2023. See the seminal commentary by Sándor-Szalay, Elisabeth, and Kiss, Balázs, "An Odd Solution – Comments on the Margins of a Recent Debate on National Minority Suffrage: ECtHR judgement in Case Bakirdzi and E.C. v. Hungary", *Pécs Journal of International and European Law, 2022/II*, 55–79.

ened to reduce, rather than enhance, diversity and participation of minorities in political decision-making" (para 73).

When we come to the rulings in the case law of the ECtHR concerning the ethnic keys in the Dayton constitution, we can see how these normative standards are applied in the constitutional and political context of BiH.

Mr. Jakob Finci and Mr. Dervo Sejdić, prominent members of the Jewish and Roma communities, respectively, and not willing to self-classify as members of any of the constituent peoples,[21] had directly submitted an application to the ECtHR on 3 July and 18 August 2006 without, however, the exhaustion of possible domestic remedies, usually a requirement to lodge such an individual application.

The ECtHR accepted their application and the Grand Chamber delivered its judgment on 22 December 2009, declaring the contested provisions in violation of Article 3 Protocol No. 1 ECHR. In essence, the Court, applying its proportionality test, agreed with the Government in the justificatory reasoning of its judgment that the exclusion of others "pursued at least one aim which is broadly compatible with the general objectives of the Convention, as reflected in the Preamble to the Convention, namely the restoration of peace" (para 45) and that "there is *no requirement* under the Convention *to abandon totally the power-sharing mechanisms* peculiar to Bosnia and Herzegovina and that the time may still not be ripe for a political system which would be a simple reflection of majority rule…" (para 48, emph. JM). However, as had been demonstrated by the Opinions of the Venice Commission, the Court finally concluded, "there exist mechanisms of power-sharing which do not *automatically* lead to the *total exclusion* of representatives of the other communities" (para 48, emph. JM) so that "the possibility of alternative means achieving the same end" was seen as decisive factor for finding the contested provisions in violation of the ECHR.

In several other cases concerning the claims of "citizens"[22] or members of legally recognised "minorities"[23] against the violation of their electoral rights through ethnic discrimination, the ECtHR confirmed these normative standards of review in finding a violation of Article 3 Protocol No. 1 ECHR, Article 14 ECHR and/or Article 1 Protocol No. 12, but also specified the reasons for its findings.

---

21 Like Mrs. Azra Zornić who had lodged an application with the ECtHR already on 19 December 2005. Her case was, however, delivered by the Court only on 15 December 2014.

22 See: ECtHR, Zornić v. BiH, 15 July 2014; Kovačević v. BiH, 29 August 2023.

23 See: ECtHR, Šlaku v. BiH, 26 May 2016.

In line with the rule expressed in *Mathieu-Mohin*, 1987, that the "electoral system must be assessed in light of the political evolution of the country concerned", the ECtHR argued in *Zornić v. BiH*, 2014, that "...now, *more than eighteen years after the end of the tragic conflict*, there could no longer be any reason for the maintenance of the contested constitutional provisions. The Court expects that democratic arrangements will be made without further delay ... to ensure *effective* political democracy ... without discrimination based on ethnic affiliation and *without granting special rights* for constituent people to the exclusion of minorities or citizens of Bosnia and Herzegovina" (para 43, emph. JM).

In the following two cases, we can see that the question of a possible identification of territory and ethnic identity, based on an "essentialist" interpretation of legal categories[24] and in consequence leading to further ethnic homogenisation of the population and institutions, is explicitly rejected.

In the ECtHR case *Pilav v. Bosnia and Herzegovina*, 2016,[25] the applicant, self-classifying as a Bosniac member of the National Assembly of the RS, claimed a violation of his "right to stand for elections *or to vote* for a member of his community", that is, both the passive and active right to vote in the Presidential elections according to Article 1 of Protocol No. 12 ECHR. He rejected the governmental submission that the exclusion was the consequence of his subjective choice of residence arguing that "... by limiting the pool of candidates in a multi-ethnic territorial unit to members of a certain ethnic group or groups, the right in question is deprived of its effectiveness" since freedom of movement would thereby be turned into a compulsory measure. And indirectly hinting at the *intent* and *consequence* of *ethnic homogenisation through territorial delimitation,* he argues: "All non-Serb residents of the Republika Srpska would in effect be told that they had to move if they wanted to exercise that right" (paras 8, 9, and 29).

The ECtHR indeed rejects the Government's *formalistic interpretation* of the equality principle that, following from the BiH constitutionally and legally

24 See the critique of such an approach that every individual has "a singular, integral, harmonised and unproblematic identity" by Banović, Damir, "Individual Identity, Collective Identity and Human Dignity. What are the Best Models to Accommodate Different Identities?", in *Ethnic Diversity, Plural Democracy and Human Dignity*, Krešič, Mario et al (eds.). Challenges to the European Union and Western Balkans, Springer Nature 2022, 92–3. See also: Mujkić, Asim, "We, the Citizens of Ethnopolis," *Constellations*, Vol. 14, No. 1, 2007, 117–8 criticising the international community's "key errors" that "it accepts such an essentialist view" of the existence of constituent peoples as "three self-enclosed, homogenous particularities."

25 ECtHR, Pilav v. Bosnia and Herzegovina, 9 June 2016.

established electoral system, he is treated in the same way in the same situation like all other members of constituent peoples living in the "wrong territory" and comes to the conclusion that "unlike the applicants Sejdić and Finci, the present applicant is theoretically eligible to stand for election to the Presidency, in reality, as long as he lives in the Republika Srpska he cannot use this right." Thus, the Court rules, since this "exclusion is based on the combination of ethnic origin and place of residence", this fact "as such amounts to a discriminatory treatment in breach of Article 1 of Protocol No. 12" (paras 43 and 48). And in the following ECtHR case, *Pudarić v. Bosnia and Herzegovina*, 2020,[26] with the applicant who had self-identified as Serb living in the FBiH, whose candidacy was however rejected on appeal by the BiHCC, the Court "by way of observation" noted "that the Constitution itself does not expressly make the exercise of the electoral rights conditional on residency requirements..." (para 27).

Finally, in the ECtHR case *Kovačević v. Bosnia and Herzegovina*, 2023,[27] the Court found Bosnia and Herzegovina again in violation of Article 1 of Protocol No. 12 ECHR because of discriminatory treatment on grounds of ethnicity and place of residence, as mentioned at the beginning of this section.

The Government invoked that the individual right to vote "for a candidate of one's choice" had been denied by the ECtHR in the case *Mathieu-Mohin and Clerfayt v. Belgium*, 1987, but the ECtHR referred to case U 5/98 of the BiHCC, in particular its Partial decision III of July 2000, in which the Court had distinguished the Bosnian electoral system from the Belgian case. The ECtHR found "no reason to disagree with the finding of that Court" (para 60). By quoting from the BiHCC's reasoning, the decisive difference must be seen in the fact that "[T]he Belgian system does not exclude *per se* the right to stand as a candidate *solely* on grounds of language. ... whereas provisions of the Constitution of the Federation of Bosnia and Herzegovina provide for *a priori* ethnically defined Bosniac and Croat delegates, caucuses and veto powers for them" (para 15, emph. in the original).

Hence the conclusion of the ECtHR that this system also interferes and amounts to a violation of the active right to vote for two reasons. Firstly, "the applicant must vote for persons who declare affiliation with Bosniacs and Croats in elections for his cantonal assembly, because only the Bosniac and Croat caucuses of that assembly elect Bosniac and Croat delegates to the House of Peoples of the Federation, who, in turn, elect Bosniac and Croat

26 ECtHR, Pudarić v. Bosnia and Herzegovina, 8 December 2020.

27 ECtHR, Kovačević v. Bosnia and Herzegovina, 29 August 2023. See, however, also the text at Fn 11.

delegates to the House of Peoples of the Parliamentary Assembly of Bosnia and Herzegovina" (para 54). "Secondly, it follows from the combination of the relevant territorial and ethnic requirements that the applicant, as a resident of the Federation, cannot participate in the election of the Serb delegates to the House of Peoples" at state level (para 54). In conclusion, the applicant may *formally* cast a *vote* in the general elections *along pre-determined ethnic lines*, but he is thereby substantially unable "to see his or her *vote influencing the make-up of the legislature*, subject to compliance with the rules laid down in electoral legislation" as the Court had argued in *Riza v. Bulgaria*.

Concerning the right to vote in elections to the Presidency, the ECtHR draws the same conclusions. The combination of territorial and ethnic requirements amounts to discriminatory treatment in violation of Article 1 of Protocol No. 12 because the applicant did not have the option of voting for candidates who did not declare affiliation with any of the "constituent peoples". Thus, "the applicant is not genuinely represented in the collective Presidency" (para 73). And as normative rule to prevent ethnic discrimination, the ECtHR establishes as standard: "No one should be forced to vote only according to prescribed ethnic lines, irrespective of their political viewpoint ... Even if a system of ethnic representation is maintained in some form, it should be secondary to political representation, should not discriminate against 'Others and citizens of Bosnia and Herzegovina' and should include ethnic representation from the entire territory of the State" (para 74).

The ECtHR thus draws the following conclusions in terms of rights not only of explicitly by law and constitution recognised members of minorities, but *for all citizens* irrespective of any ethnic self-classification:

- "The current *constitutional* and *electoral arrangements* render ethnic considerations and/or representation more relevant than political, economic, social, philosophical and other considerations and/or representation and thus *amplify ethnic divisions* in the country and undermine the democratic character of elections."
- However, "Article 3 of Protocol No. 1 taken in conjunction with Article 14 of the Convention means that the right to vote encompasses the *opportunity* for voters to choose *candidates* or party lists which *best reflect their political views*, and that election regulations should not require voters to espouse political positions that they did not support" (para 56).
- "*None* of the 'constituent peoples' is in the *factual position* of an *endangered minority* which must preserve its existence. On the contrary, the 'constituent' peoples clearly enjoy a privileged position in the current political system" (para 61). And by quoting from its own reasoning in the case *Zornić*, the ECtHR repeats: "In view of the need to ensure effective political

democracy, the Court considers that time has come for a political system … without discrimination based on ethnic affiliation and without granting special rights for constituent peoples to the exclusion of minorities or citizens of Bosnia and Herzegovina" (para 58, all emph. JM).

This way, the ECtHR case law has come full circle with normative standards which the constituent peoples case of the BiHCC had already developed in 2000.

4 The "Constituent Peoples Case" of the BiHCC

After a terrible war with ethnic cleansing of almost the entire territory going hand in hand with ethnic homogenisation of all legislative, executive and judicial institutions of the so-called Entities as territorial units, named as such only later by the Dayton constitution,[28] it will come as no surprise that the most "existential" issue, predetermining like an ideological "frame" all political debates about constitution- and institution-engineering to this day, is the question of state-formation and nation-building in and for a post-conflict society. Does this mean that "the deep ethnic division" of BiH society has to be taken for "granted"[29] so that the territorial delimitation along ethnic lines into

28 See the comparison of population figures and the ethnic make-up of police and judiciary following from figures of the 1991 census before the beginning of the war and the figures provided by the UNHCR representation in BiH for the year 1997 established as factual evidence in the BiH Constitutional Court case U-5/98, Third Partial decision, 1 July 2000, colloquially referred to as "constituent peoples case", paras 86–7, 92–3, 130–1, and 136.

29 See, for instance Marković, Goran, "Kovačević v. Bosnia and Herzegovina: Do Federalism and Consociation Matter?," NBP *Journal of Criminalistics and Law*, 2023, Vol. 28, Issue 3, 2–18 who argues that the ECtHR had to take into account "the fact that the society in Bosnia and Herzegovina has been a fragmented or a segmented one…" Insofar, the contested ethnic keys "stemmed from the historical and political circumstances (civil war in Bosnia and Herzegovina 1992–1995), the nature of society (fragmented society), the relationship of political forces (balance of power of ethnic political elites which tended to and were able to check each other" (at p. 8) so that the Court is criticised of neglecting important features of the constitutional system. In a similar vein, by giving preference to the ethnic division of institutions and society over territorial elements and human rights by invoking the constituent peoples case as evidence, Vanjek, Dejan, "Federal Equality in Multinational Bosnia and Herzegovina," in *The Principle of Equality in Diverse States. Reconciling Autonomy with Equal Rights and Opportunities*, Belser, Eva Maria et al (eds.) (Leiden-Boston 2021), 361- 393. At p. 371 he argues, that "the hierarchy of principles outlined in the Constitution imply that the 'constituent' status of Serbs, Croats, and Bosniaks is superior to the administrative-political organisation and as such it precedes organisational principles of the State. Namely, the case is that the

Entities and cantons (in the FBiH) and the ethnic keys in their institutions resemble a quasi "historic compromise" which must not be put into question, as this was argued by some of the parties in the "constituent peoples" case before the BiH Constitutional Court in 2000?[30] And does the judgment of the Grand Chamber of the ECtHR in *Sejdić and Finci v. BiH*, 2009, endanger the corporate power-sharing institutional system and, thus, a precarious peace as internationally renowned lawyers and political scientists argued at book-length?[31]

However, the vantage point for any debate on political equality must be Article II of the Dayton-constitution, if the *normative* principles that BiH shall be a "democratic state, operating under the rule of law" are taken seriously. This article provides a catalogue of human rights and fundamental freedoms "to be secured to all persons in Bosnia and Herzegovina without discrimination" such as, *inter alia*, "sex, language, religion, … national or social origin, association with a national minority, …" thereby following the language of Article 14 of the ECHR. Moreover, Article II. 2. prescribes that the rights and freedoms set forth in the ECHR and its Protocols "shall apply directly" in BiH and "[T]hese shall have priority over all other law."

The first conclusion which thus follows from a textual interpretation of the Dayton-constitution – and which was indeed drawn by the BiHCC in its "landmark" case U-5/98, Third Partial Decision – is the differentiation of the following constitutional categories to answer the question "who" shall be equal, as already raised in the introductory section.

These are "persons" and "citizens", whether they declare to be "in association" with a "national minority" or "constituent people" or not, as well as "constituent peoples" and "Others". Of course, this "who is who" of the text of the Dayton-constitution raised more legal questions than answers already in this case in 2000, in particular when seen in light of the different *political* "visions" of political parties and their leaders for the country coming to the fore in the arguments of the parties in the case: Does the RS have a constitutionally guaranteed right to national self-determination including secession? Are Croats as a constituent people discriminated against because of not hav-

substance and nature of BiH as a multinational federation is not of territorial, but corporative-communitarian character" and asserts that this is the result of the BiHCC constituent peoples judgment where the category of constituent peoples "was elaborated as an overarching constitutional category superimposed to all constitutional principles, laws, and regulations." As can be seen from the text of this chapter, I try to demonstrate exactly the opposite conclusions.

30 See: 3rd Partial Decision, case U-5/98, 2000, paras 31, 40, and 46.

31 McCrudden and O'Leary, *Courts and Consociations*, fn 2.

ing been constitutionally granted their own territorial autonomy in 1995 as "third Entity"? And later on, as we will discuss in the next section, because the candidate of the HDZ, the biggest Croat party, had been "outvoted" in the presidential elections several times by the candidate of the SDP, the Social-Democratic Party, who declared himself "Croat", but got many votes from Bosniac voters? Does the electoral system with the subjective right and choice of candidates standing for elections to declare their ethnic affiliation or not, but not guaranteeing a closed system of ethnic representation so that voters and their elected representatives must "belong"[32] to the same ethnic group, violate the principle of equality of constituent peoples and thereby violate the "equal" constitutional status of Croats in a discriminatory way, as this was claimed before the Constitutional Court in the BiHCC case U-23/14 (Ljubić) in 2016?[33]

First, and above all, the Court has rejected already in its Third Partial Decision in U-5/98, 2000, the reading of the Dayton constitutional framework as *coming-together federalism* composed of former sovereign states as this is insinuated in academic literature by arguing that BiH is a "state union" or "confederal system" established by the Dayton Agreement. The Court rendered all references to "sovereignty", "state independence", "a democratic right of the Serb people from Republika Srpska to link its State completely and closely with other States of the Serb people", in short, a right to *national* self-determination including secession laid down in the original Constitution of RS 1992, unconstitutional by arguing with legally "binding force" according to Article VI.4. Dayton constitution:

> 29. Article I.1 of the Constitution of BiH undoubtedly establishes the fact that only Bosnia and Herzegovina continues 'its legal existence under international law as a state, with its internal structures modified

32 This could technically be achieved only through an official voters' register and the ensuing problems how to "control" subjective declarations against fraud as can be seen from the judicial disputes in the Habsburg monarchy or in Finland for the elections of the Sami parliament and in New Zealand for the Maori seats in Parliament. For the problems created in dealing with "subjective" declarations of "belonging" for administrative and judicial bodies see, in particular Bernatzik, Edmund, *Nationale Matriken*, Wien 1910 (Manzsche K.u.K. Hof-Verlags- und Universitätsbuchhandlung). For the Sami parliament and Maori seats see: Marko, Joseph, "Comparative Jurisprudence from Five Continents: Concluding Observations" in *Search for Meaning through Intercultural Understanding*, de Villiers, Bertus et al. (eds.) Litigating the Rights of Minorities and Indigenous Peoples in Domestic and International Courts, Leiden-Boston 2021 (Brill), 245 and 249–250.

33 BiHCC U-23/14 (Ljubić), 1 December 2016, which will be discussed in detail in the next section.

as provided herein'. In consequence, Article I.3 establishes two Entities, the Federation of Bosnia and Herzegovina and the Republika Srpska as component parts of the state of Bosnia and Herzegovina. In addition, as seen from Article III.2 (a) of the Constitution of BiH for instance, the Entities are subject to the sovereignty of Bosnia and Herzegovina. Despite examples of component units of federal states, which are also called states themselves, in the case of Bosnia and Herzegovina it is thus clear that the Constitution of BiH did not recognise the Republika Srpska and the Federation of Bosnia and Herzegovina as 'states' but instead refers to them as 'Entities'.

30. Hence, contrary to the assertions of the representatives of the People's Assembly of the Republika Srpska, the Constitution of BiH does not leave room for any 'sovereignty' of the Entities or a right to 'self-organization' based on the idea of 'territorial separation'. Citizenship of the Entities is thus granted by Article I.7 of the Constitution of BiH and is not proof of their 'sovereign' statehood. In the same manner, 'governmental functions', according to Article III.3 (a) of the Constitution of BiH, are thereby allocated either to the joint institutions or to the Entities so that their powers are in no way an expression of their statehood, but are derived from this allocation of powers through the Constitution of BiH."

The Dayton constitutional system can thus not be interpreted as a "historic compromise" in terms of *coming-together* federalism and the establishment of a system of necessarily *permanent* corporate power-sharing as argued by some of the parties of the case and academic scholarship.

Against the parties' agonistic method of cherry-picking from parts of the text and thus partial interpretations of the Dayton constitution in pursuing their politically motivated views and interests, the reasoning of the Constitutional Court is based on a *systematic* interpretation *of the entire text* of the "constitutional system" and leads to the identification of *all* those normative elements which can be perceived as legally coherent whole.[34] This approach

34 This method follows from Hans Kelsen's axiomatic point of his positivist legal theory that a "state" is nothing but "the unity of the legal system." Moreover, any reader of the reasoning of the case will recognise that the structure of the argumentation is based on the use of all of the four generally accepted methods of interpretation *before* drawing the conclusion from a comparison of the results of interpretation which of them is normatively most convincing. Thereby it is made clear that the majority opinion is not based on a result which had already existed in the minds of judges *before* deliberation when they

reveals an obvious, rather different "political compromise" in the negotiations before and in Dayton-Ohio:

First, all the ethnic keys and veto mechanisms for constituent peoples in the Dayton constitution express the legal concept of their "collective equality" which is, however, *not* based on a *uniform model of ethnic representation,* as advocates of the ethno-federal model would claim. As the Court argues in differentiation of representation mechanisms of constituent peoples on the one hand, and the Entities as federal units and its citizens on the other:[35]

> 65. A strict identification of territory and certain ethnically defined members of joint institutions of BiH in order to represent certain constituent peoples is not even accurate with respect to the rules of the composition of the Presidency as laid down in Article V, first paragraph...It must not be forgotten that the Serb Member of the Presidency, for instance, is not elected by voters of the Serb ethnic origin, but by all citizens of the Republika Srpska with or without specific ethnic affiliation. ... The same also holds for the Bosniac and Croat Members to be elected from the Federation.

Moreover, not even the "Entity veto" rights of the single members of the Presidency according to Article V.2. (d) can be invoked for the argument that they represent *only* constituent peoples. A veto of the Member elected from the territory of the RS shall be referred to the National Assembly as such, including also non-Serb representatives, for deliberation and voting.

The same conclusion is drawn also for the composition of the House of Peoples:

> 66... the Court finds it striking that the Serb Delegates shall be elected by the Peoples' Assembly, as such, without any differentiation along ethnic lines. Therefore, this provision [Article IV.1. Dayton constitution] includes a constitutional guarantee that non-Serb Members of the Peoples' Assembly have the same right as the Serb Members to take part in the election of the five Serb Delegates to the House of Peoples of BiH. Hence, there is no strict uniform model of ethnic representation

try to hide their pre-determined decision by using simply this method of interpretation which will lead to the favoured result.

35 See: Marković, Goran in this volume who criticises the confusion of institutional mechanisms foreseen in the Dayton constitution for the representation of the Entities or constituent peoples.

> underlying these provisions of the Constitution of BiH. Had this been the intent of the framers of the Constitution, they would not have regulated these election processes differently.[36]

Second, there is *no dichotomisation* of *individual* versus *group rights* as the Court argues in differentiation of a majority or minority position in actual fact, let alone a general precedence of collective rights over individual rights:

> 59. Even if the constituent peoples are, in actual fact, in a majority or minority position in the Entities, the express *recognition* of Bosniacs, Croats, and Serbs as *constituent peoples* by the Constitution of BiH can *only mean* that none of them is constitutionally recognized as a majority or, in other words, that they enjoy *equality as groups*. It must therefore be concluded, in the same way that the Swiss Supreme Court derived from the recognition of the national languages an obligation of the Cantons not to suppress these language groups, that the recognition of the constituent peoples and its underlying constitutional principle of collective equality poses an *obligation* on the Entities *not to discriminate* in particular against these constituent peoples which are, in *actual fact*, in a *minority position* in the respective Entity. Hence, there is not only a clear constitutional obligation not to violate individual rights in a discriminatory manner which obviously follows from Article II.3 and 4 of the Constitution of BiH, but also a constitutional obligation of non-discrimination in terms of a group right if, for instance, one or two of the constituent peoples are given special preferential treatment through the legal system of the Entities.
>
> (EMPH. JM)

Group rights, therefore, *do not* have *priority* over individual rights *per se*, but quite the other way round, the Court argues. Ethnic keys and veto mechanisms must not be exported to Entity level in light of the Court's specific warning:

> 68. … insofar as these special collective rights might violate the non-discrimination provisions, … they are legitimised solely by their constitu-

36 See: Third Partial Decision, paras 65–6. The same argumentation is outlined for the composition of the Council of Ministers which "certainly does not represent one, two, or even all of the three constituent peoples only, but all citizens of BiH regardless of their national origin" (para 67).

> tional rank and therefore, have to be narrowly construed. In particular, it cannot be concluded that the Constitution of BiH provides for a general institutional model, which could be transferred to the Entity level or that similar, ethnically-defined institutional structures on an Entity level … need not meet the overall binding standard of non-discrimination in accordance with Article II.4. of the Constitution of BiH …[37]

Third, and most important for the transformation of the deep ethnic divisions of society, the right to return of refugees and displaced persons including their *absolute* right to property restitution[38] is further specified by the provisions of Annex VII to the Framework Agreement as follows from the reference in Article II.5. Dayton constitution.[39] In particular, the text of Article I.3 (a) of Annex 7 imposes a legislative obligation or "state duty", in legal-dogmatic terminology, to repeal "all legislation and administrative practices with discriminatory intent or effect." Based on this language, which is in substance identical with the concepts of direct and indirect, group-related discrimination (see Section 2), the Constitutional Court then includes as standard of review also the obligation to counteract the "effects of past de jure discrimination": all the measures of ethnic cleansing during the war through legislative, administra-

37 See: Third Partial Decision, para 68.

38 This follows from the text of Article II.5. of the Dayton constitution: "…to have restored to them property of which they were deprived in the course of hostilities since 1991 and to be compensated for any such property which cannot be restored to them. Any commitments or statements relating to such property made under duress are null and void."

39 This is totally put into question by Palermo, Francesco and Woelk, Jens, *Diritto Costituzionale Comparato Dei Gruppi E Delle Minoranze* (Milano; Ceram, Terza editione, 2021) (Wolters Kluwer), 367: "Interpretando la ricostituzione della società multietnica come un obbligo positivo, le disposizioni dell' allegato 7 dell' Accordo di Dayton sul ritorno dei profughi vengono utilizatte dai guidici costituzionali come un grimaldello per scardinare la Costituzione stessa: il sistema multietnico viene imposto sopratutto dalla prevalenza dei diritti internazionali dell' uomo e non dalla Costituzione, e la prescrittività della Costituzione deriva da principi super- (e in questo caso anche extra-)costituzionali." This critique overlooks, however, two important elements: first the reference in the text of Article II.5. of Annex IV, "the Constitution", itself concerning refugees and displaced persons: "They have the right, in accordance with Annex VII to the General Framework Agreement, to have restored to them property of which they were deprived in the course of the hostilities since 1991…" What else shall this specific constitutional rule and not abstract principle mean in systematic interpretation with Article I.3. (a) of Annex VII but the constitutional obligation to restore the multi-ethnic society which had existed before the war and was then destroyed by ethnic cleansing as a war goal? Second, as outlined above in fn 8, the authors completely overlooked that Annex VII also has the rank of constitutional law and cannot, therefore, be declared to include "super-" or "extra-constitutional principles".

tive, and judicial actions must not be upheld by the "respective public authorities at all state levels, not only by their actions but also through their inaction." This rule follows from the text of Article I of Annex VII – "[t]he early return of refugees and displaced persons is an important objective of the settlement of the conflict in Bosnia and Herzegovina" – because, in the wording of the Court's reasoning, "it is an overall objective of the settlement of the Dayton Peace Agreement … thereby … to re-establish the multi-ethnic society that had existed prior to the war without any territorial separation that would bear ethnic inclinations."[40]

Based on this *textual and systematic interpretation*, the Court then develops what is called "directive principles" (German: "Staatsziele") in legal-dogmatic terminology for future legislative measures and constitutional amendments of both the Dayton constitution and the Entity constitutions by arguing:

- "55. … Democratic decision-making would be transformed into ethnic domination of one or even more groups if, for instance, absolute and/or unlimited veto-power would be granted to them, thereby enabling a numerical minority represented in governmental institutions to forever enforce its will on the majority"; and
- "57. … in the context of a multi-ethnic state such as BiH, the accommodation of cultures and ethnic groups prohibits not only their assimilation but also their segregation. Thus, segregation is, in principle, an illegitimate aim in a democratic society. There is no question therefore that ethnic separation through territorial delimitation does not meet the standards of a democratic state and pluralist society."[41]

In conclusion, the constituent peoples case of the Constitutional Court does *not read* either the civic state-nation model into the entire constitutional system of BiH nor does it agree with the reading of Dayton as ethno-federal and power-dividing system, what is frequently dubbed a "multi-national federation" in academic literature.[42] This can be seen from the different terminology the Court *intentionally* uses with the term "multi-*ethnic*" instead of "multi-national" state and society. Hence, the Court rejects the "static" interpretation of Dayton as historic compromise having for ever "frozen" the territorial delimitation of the country along ethno-national lines and clearly dem-

40 See the detailed argumentation in Third Partial Decision, paras 78 through 80.

41 Third Partial Decision, paras 55 and 57.

42 See my critical literature review in Marko, Joseph, "What is Wrong with the Concept of Multinational Federalism? Some Thoughts about the Interrelationship between the Concepts of (Multi-)Nationalism, Federalism, Power Sharing and Conflict Resolution", *Ethnopolitics*, 19:4: 2020, 416–432.

onstrates the necessary "dynamic" interpretation of Dayton for the post-conflict re-construction of state *and* society.

5 The BiCC's Case Law on the Constitutionality of Ethnic Keys

These "directive principles" and the amendments of the constitutions of both Entities and the Election Law in 2002 were, however, more and more put into question by the majority of the judges of the BiHCC. In two cases in 2006, both of them on the basis of abstract review procedures requested by then President Sulejman Tihić,[43] the BiHCC rejected to review the ethnic keys in the Dayton constitution and the Election Law against the standards of the ECtHR despite the clear and unambiguous wording of Article II.2. of the Dayton constitution that the ECtHR is "superior to all other law" of BiH and shall be "directly applicable." In anticipating later judgments of the ECtHR, Judge Grewe identified in her dissenting opinion in the second case the discriminatory effect of the ethnic keys by arguing:

> ... the distribution of posts in the State organs between the constituent peoples was a central element of the Dayton Agreement *making* the *peace* in BiH *possible*. ... [h]owever, in the light of *developments in Bosnia and Herzegovina* since the Constitution entered into force ... the country has therefore to be assessed according to the yardstick of common European standards.

Thus, the ethnic keys for constituent peoples should be seen as "*transitional arrangement* until the realisation of the principles of the civil state. This can, however, be achieved without entering into conflict with international standards. It is not the system of consensual democracy as such which raises problems but the *mixing of territorial and ethnic criteria* and the *apparent exclusion* from certain political rights..."[44] (EMPH. JM).

However, in reaction to the ECtHR cases Sejdić and Finci, 2009, and Zornić, 2014, the BiHCC in case U 14/12,[45] in which then President Komšić had requested the Court to review the ethnic keys in the constitutions of the Entities, the Court no longer refused to decide on the merits, but simply

43 See: BiHCC U 5/04 (Tihić I), 31 March 2006, para 14 and BiHCC, U 13/05 (Tihić II), 26 May 2006, para 10.

44 U 13/05, pages 7, 10 and 11.

45 Case U 14/12 (Komšić), 26 March 2015, paras 74–75.

declared in *obvious contradiction* to its reasoning in the first part of the decision[46] that the contested provisions are *not* discriminatory in light of the standards of Article II.4. of the Dayton constitution and Article 1 of the Protocol No.12 ECHR by arguing with reference to *future* constitutional amendments:171F

> However, it is impossible to foresee the scope of these changes in this moment. The Constitutional Court *will not quash the aforementioned provisions of the Constitutions of the Entities and the Election Law*, it *will not order the Parliamentary Assembly of BiH*, National Assembly and Parliaments of the Federation *to harmonise* the aforementioned provisions until the adoption, in the national legal system, of constitutional and legislative measures removing the current inconsistency of the Constitution of Bosnia and Herzegovina and the Election Law with the European Convention...
> para 74, (EMPH. JM)

This is all the more remarkable, since the BiHCC is obviously competent to review the constitutions of the Entities and to abrogate their unconstitutional provisions as follows from the supremacy of the Dayton constitution and the Court's settled case law in such conflicts. There was thus no need to "wait" for amendments of the Dayton constitution or to decide on the question whether the ECHR "shall have priority over all other law" of BiH according to Article II.2. of the Dayton constitution.

All the decisions of the ECtHR were again completely ignored by the BiH Constitutional Court in 2018 in case AP-3464/18 (Pudarić II), by declaring the appeal of Svetozar Pudarić against his exclusion from the right to stand as candidate in the presidential elections inadmissible by arguing: "[F]or the courts and other competent bodies to apply the European Convention directly to this matter, as the appellant requests, it is necessary to end the current incompatibility of the Constitution of Bosnia and Herzegovina with the European Convention as found by the European Court in the judgments of Sejdić and Finci, Zornić and Pilav. ... Otherwise ...", the Court holds, it would act *ultra vires*: "..., the Constitutional Court, but also the Court of Bosnia and Herzegov-

46 See: U 14/12, paras 65, 70, and 72 in particular: "Namely, in exercising the right guaranteed by law, the mentioned provisions of the Entitie's Constitutions and the Election Law establish the differential treatment of 'Others' which is based on ethnic affiliation and result in the discrimination in contravention of Article II (4) of the Constitution of BiH and Article 1 of Protocol No. 12 to the European Convention."

ina and the Central Election Commission of Bosnia and Herzegovina would be acting outside their prescribed competences …" (paras 21–22) ignoring again the explicit text of Article II.2. Dayton constitution and examples from other jurisdictions such as Austria which do not find the concept of "unconstitutional constitutional law" a paradox.

The political and constitutional debate about the right to "collective equality" of the constituent peoples got a twist with the claim to strengthen collective rights against discrimination with the case U-23/14.[47] This time, the BiHCC had to decide on a request of Dr Božo Ljubić, then Chairman of the House of Representatives of the Parliamentary Assembly of BiH, to review the provisions of the Election Law, because the method of elections of delegates to the FBiH House of Peoples would deviate from the principle of proportionality, in violation of the guarantees of political representation of constituent peoples: " … [T]he mentioned right is abused in a manner in which 'the members of another people/s ensure the election of the delegates from the peoples who do not live in adequate number in the area of some cantons'." And with reference to statistical figures, he tries to prove "the absurdity of the election system", since it would be clear that "more Croat delegates are elected from the cantons with Bosniac people majority than from the cantons with the Croat people majority" (paras 10, 13, 19–20).

The quoted allegations of the applicant then led to the claim that only a system of "legitimate representation" – requiring that candidates of constituent peoples must be elected by voters of the same ethnicity – can prevent the discrimination of the collective right to equality (of Croats). This raised, in fact, two legal problems to be decided by the BiHCC.

In deciding on the admissibility and merits of the request, the Court was, first, indirectly confirming, at first sight, indeed, the "paradox" claim of the applicant that the collective equality *of one and the same* constituent people shall already be violated if the equal weight of votes for Croat representatives elected in cantons with Croat majority population is different from those of Croat candidates elected in Cantons where the Croat population is in a de facto minority position. Second, the Court then declares that the contested provisions make it, moreover, possible "for the representatives of one of the constituent people to afford legitimacy to the representatives of another constituent people in the cantonal legislative body…" This declarative statement is then followed by the legally binding ruling of the BiHCC that the initially contested provision of the Election Law is in violation of Article I.(2) of the

47 BiHCC U-23/14 (Ljubić), 1 December 2016.

Constitution of BiH – which does, however, say nothing about the underlying claim for "legitimate representation."[48]

The constantly repeated claim of the HDZ political leadership for "implementation" of the Ljubić judgment in the following years[49] makes the political motivation of the "paradox" visible. This has to be taken into account for the analysis of the proposal for the "reform of the BiH Election Law" by parliamentary representatives of the HDZ on 5 July 2021 in the form of a draft law.

The proposed Article 8.1 concerned the electoral process for the election of the three members of the BiH Presidency. The proposed provision foresaw the creation of three "ad hoc electoral districts A, B and C" for the election of the Bosniac and Croat member of the BiH Presidency on the territory of the BiH Federation. District A was then characterised as territory with at least a two thirds majority of Bosniac population and district B was to comprise the territory with at least a two thirds majority of Croat population. The following rules according to the proposed Article 8.1, paragraph 3 made this effort of election engineering a *clear case of ethnic gerrymandering* in the end, because they would have favoured the biggest parties, namely the Bosniac SDA and the Croat HDZ, as can be seen from this provision drafted: "The Bosniac member of the BiH Presidency shall be the candidate who got most votes among the Bosniac candidates under the condition that he won more votes from the territory of districts A and C than districts B and C." And the same rule was then foreseen for the Croat member of the Presidency under the condition that he wins more votes from districts B and C than from districts A and C. This draft law did not, however, get the necessary majorities in parliament.

2021 was, moreover, a year of continued political and economic crisis. The outgoing High Representative (HRep), Valentin Inzko, had imposed amendments to the BiH Criminal Code to sanction the denial of genocide, stirring up strong reactions from the RS. The then Serb member of the Presidency, Milorad Dodik, threatened not only with the suspension of Serb representatives in state-level institutions, but also with secession. This again caused strong reactions by the new HRep, Christian Schmidt, and the BiHCC declaring resolutions of the RS National Assembly unconstitutional. In the FBiH, the dysfunctionality of its institutions had lasted since the general elections in 2018, with a caretaker government in power since political parties were unwilling to form a coalition government.

48 All quotations from para 52.

49 Through legislative amendments which would not require an amendment of the Dayton constitution as a pre-condition for giving up its blockade for the election of a new FBiH government after the general elections 2018.

Thus, HRep Christian Schmidt decided to make a renewed effort to "deblock" the political stalemate in FBiH with a "functionality package" to amend the Election Law through a decision of his Office the following year, only a few months before the general elections, scheduled for 2 October 2022.[50]

Article 9, paragraph 3 of the draft law, leaked to the press several months before this date, did prescribe: "…[I]f the Bosniak, Croat and/or Serb population of a Canton according to the last census constitute less than 3 percent of the total population of the same constituent people in the Federation, no seat shall be allocated from that Canton to that constituent people." This provision raised not only the constitutional, but also the political question: What is the purpose of this provision? Who shall be favoured?[51]

Such a 3 percent threshold would have constitutionally privileged again the candidates of those parties in the BiH Federation cantons who win most votes in general elections so that, for instance, the HDZ which wins most votes in cantons with a majority Croat population would then gain more seats for the House of Peoples than before, with the effect that it can possibly prevent the nomination and thus election of candidates for the position of Presidents and Prime Minister of the BiH Federation if no other party or coalition achieves the necessary number of six seats in the Croat ethnic caucus of the House of Peoples. Against the case law of the ECtHR on electoral rights, also voters of constituent peoples in a de facto minority position would thereby have been made a completely neglectable "minority", depriving them of the "effectivity" of their active right to vote when the weight of their votes were in practice reduced to zero. In line with the Venice Commission's "Report on Constituency Delineation and Seat Allocation",[52] this proposal would also have been a clear case of ethnic gerrymandering through "packing" of electoral districts with mandates favouring one party, but HRep Schmidt then dropped this

50 See: Woelk, Jens and Sahadžić, Maja, "Cutting the Gordian Knot in Bosnia and Herzegovina", *VerfBlog*, 2022/10/07, https://verfassungsblog.de/cutting-the-gordian-knot-in-bosnia-and-herzegovina/.

51 See also: Marko, Joseph, "Is Ethnic Gerrymandering a Solution for the Constitutional Impasse?", *VerfBlog*, 2022/8/23, https://verfassungsblog.de/is-ethnic-gerrymandering-a-solution-for-the-constitutional-impasse/.

52 Venice Commission, "Report on Constituency Delineation and Seat Allocation", 12 December 2017 (CDL-AD (2017)034, 4–5: "The equality of voting power is a crucial standard of the concept of electoral integrity … it is important to avoid the danger of drawing ethnic seats in such a way that it could lead to a form of electoral apartheid."

provision in the finally imposed amendments to the Election Law in terms of a "technical mandate" to stop electoral fraud.[53]

Finally, all normative standards developed by the ECtHR were again ignored by the BiH Constitutional Court in case U-27/22, in 2023.[54] Presidents Željko Komšić and Šefik Džeferović had submitted a request for review of the imposed Amendments of the High Representative to the Constitution of the Federation of BiH and the Law on Amendments to the Election Law of Bosnia and Herzegovina on the very evening of the general elections in October 2022.[55] Important for our analysis is the fact that these constitutional impositions had increased the number of delegates in the FBiH House of Peoples from 17 to 23 for each of the constituent peoples and from 7 to 11 for Others.

The first applicant argued that these amendments violated Articles I through III of the Dayton constitution and Article 1 of Protocol No. 12 ECHR, because the challenged provisions guarantee in practice that delegates of constituent peoples "are elected from the territories [within FBiH] where they are the majority." If the High Representative intended to protect "possibly endangered members of constituent peoples" (that is, in the terminology of the constituent peoples case, constituent peoples in a de facto minority position), "then it would be logical that the majority of those representatives are elected from the areas where they are in a relatively 'minority' position. Thus, through their position in the FBiH House of Peoples they could protect their rights, which is actually the purpose of that body." Hence, "the only thing that matters" now in the election process through the HReps amendments "is securing a majority in the respective caucus in the House of Peoples" so that "this leads to the possibility that a political party does not have a single representative in the House of Representatives, but could win, within the cantonal assemblies, a sufficient number of mandates for the House of Peoples and manage political processes in the entire FBiH, and thus also at the state level" (para 31).

---

53 Decision Enacting the Law on Amendments to the Election Law of Bosnia and Herzegovina, 07/27,2022 OHR, https://www.ohr.int/decision-enacting-the-law-on-amendments-to-the-election-law-of-bosnia-and-herzegovina-7.

54 BiHCC, U-27/22 (Komšić and Džaferović), 23 March 2023.

55 Decision Enacting Amendments to the Constitution of the Federation of Bosnia and Herzegovina, 10/02/2022 OHR, https://www.ohr.int/decision-enacting-amendments-to-the-constitution-of-the-federation-of-bosnia-and-herzegovina-3/, and Decision Enacting the Law on Amendments to the Election Law of Bosnia and Herzegovina, 10/02/2022 OHR, https://www.ohr.int/decision-enacting-the-law-on-amendments-to-the-election-law-of-bosnia-and-herzegovina-8.

The Court, this time, declared the request admissible again, but rejected it on the merits by arguing in the opinion of the majority that the applicant could not prove his request "beyond the abstract level … on how the imposed amendments to the FBiH Constitution and the Election law could affect the free expression of the voters' opinion", because "there is [no] sufficiently close causal connection between the right of voters to directly elected representatives to the cantonal legislators and changes in the number of delegates to the FBiH House of Peoples, who are elected in indirect elections" (para 98). For the differentiation thereby made in the system of representation for the legitimation of the members of the House of Peoples, the majority opinion referred to case AP-35/03, 2005, against the appeal of the Social Democratic Party of BiH against the decision of the Central Election Commission and the Court of BiH.[56] In this decision, the majority of the BiHCC had upheld the interpretation of the Election Commission concerning Amendment XXXIV to the FBiH Constitution that the election results of the direct elections to the cantonal assemblies in terms of seats won by political parties shall not serve as pre-condition for the indirect elections to the House of Peoples, but that every member in the respective caucus of constituent peoples can vote for any candidate nominated by one of the parties of the constituent peoples. The majority opinion in 2005, taken over by the majority opinion in 2023, justified its interpretation with the rhetorical question: "If the composition of the House of Peoples of the Parliament of the Federation were to be proportionate to the election results accomplished by parties in the direct elections … the question what is the point of holding indirect elections … could rightfully be posed" (para 98).

However, the majority opinion in 2022 simply ignored (again) the dissenting opinion of Judge Grewe in the 2005 case. She had convincingly argued that the majority in this case did not correctly interpret and apply Amendment XXXIV to the FBiH Constitution. In particular, its paragraph (4) regulating the indirect election and legally valid to this day reads: "Bosniac delegates, Croat delegates and Serb delegates from each Canton shall be elected by their respective representatives, *in accordance with the election results in the legislative body of the Canton,* and the election of delegates from among the Others shall be regulated by law" (EMPH. JM). Judge Grewe therefore concluded that the wording of this provision – which had not been taken into account by the Central Election Commission and also the majority of the

56 BiHCC, AP-35/03, 28 January 2005.

BiHCC in its reasoning – requires "that the delegates to the HoP have to be elected from the political party that has won the majority of votes on the immediate elections for the cantonal legislative bodies" (page 20) so that the interpretation of the Election Commission and the Court of BiH were in violation of this provision of the FBiH Constitution. And she makes the political logic behind the majority decision visible: "This sort of interpretation gives much more discretional power to the representatives in the different caucuses; in particular, it permits these representatives to give *preference to the ethnic membership over political membership* and vote therefore for the party which is not their own. The risk of such discordance is as higher as the political parties are only composed of one of the constituent peoples or are present only in some Cantons but are not represented everywhere and do not represent all peoples" (EMPH. JM).

However, in this recent BiHCC case, the majority opinion was heavily criticised. The three dissenting judges obviously take up this political context as starting point of their argumentation when declaring "it is obvious that 'strategic voting' is a characteristic element of direct elections followed by indirect elections" (page 89, fn 12). Hence, the dissenting judges argue that the "right to know in advance ... how the votes will be used in the follow-up process, especially, ... how many representatives from which caucus will be sent to the House of Peoples on the basis of the election of the cantonal legislators ... is not only denied to the voters, but also the political parties although they necessarily have to develop strategies for direct elections followed by indirect elections and have to take into account the whole election process in order to be successful." In conclusion, they deny the differentiation in the democratic legitimation process and thus the strict separation between a civic and an ethnic representation through direct elections on the one hand, and indirect elections on the other: "Direct and indirect elections have to be seen together as a whole. The democratic legitimacy of the representatives of the House of Peoples as well as the President and Vice-President of the Federation of Bosnia and Herzegovina is conferred on them on the basis of a chain of elections; one depends on the other; direct and indirect elections are inextricably linked" (page 89) so that – in my reading – the ethnic component of elections shall not de facto get superiority over the civic elements following as normative standard of political equality from the ECtHR case law and the original constituent peoples case.

6 Conclusion: Normative Standards of Political Equality

Graphically representing the political visions of political parties in BiH on a theoretical continuum between the two possible extreme poles, the question is raised: Shall BiH be a *confederation*, territorially and institutionally *strictly divided along ethno-national lines*, as Serb political leaders and academics argue and what I will call ethnic power-dividing instead of power-sharing?[57] Or, in stark contrast, a *"civic" state* more or less decentralised or *regionalised along geographic and economic terms* without any ethnic keys for public offices, as some Bosniak parties maintain? However, as our analysis of the case law of the ECtHR and the BiHCC has exemplified, these two alternatives do not necessarily form a dichotomy, but can and must be combined in legislative and constitutional reforms for further EU integration.

In conclusion, we can thus summarise the following normative standards to be implemented for future reform efforts:

- The ECtHR case law does not require giving up a power-sharing system as such, but a "flexibilisation" of the strict ethnic keys if and where they are constitutionally entrenched for constituent peoples only. In particular, the identification of territorial and ethnic identities is thereby seen as one of the causes for unjustified ethnic discrimination.
- The phrase "... conditions which will ensure the free expression of the opinion of the people in the choice of the legislature... " according to Article 3 Protocol No. 1 ECHR is based on what is called the formal principle of "one person, one vote" for not only the right to literally cast "one" vote, but also requires that the votes cast have equal weight to be considered "effective." Thus, the normative principle of free and equal elections comprises both the right to vote *and* to stand for elections as coherent conceptual unity, only thereby guaranteeing the right "of each voter to see his or her vote influencing the make-up of the legislature" as follows from ECtHR, *Riza v. Bulgaria*.

---

57 This follows from my analysis of the BiH party system as ethno-national "cartel of power" based on the principle of divide and rule instead of Lijphart's assumption of elite cooperation as mechanism of power sharing. See: Marko, Joseph, "Defective Democracy in a Failed State? Bridging Constitutional Design, Politics and Ethnic Division in Bosnia-Herzegovina", in *Practising Self- Government: A Comparative Study of Autonomous Regions*, Ghai, Yash and Woodman, Sophia (eds.) (Cambridge: Cambridge University Press 2013), 281–314 and Mujkić, Asim, "We the Citizens of Ethnopolis", *Constellations*, Volume 14, No. 1, 2007, 113 who speaks of a "democracy of ethnic oligarchies rather than a democracy of citizens".

- The conclusion of the ECtHR in *Mathieu-Mohin and Clerfayt v. Belgium* which rejected the claim to interpret Article 3 Protocol No. 1 as a minority "right to vote for a candidate of one's choice" is overruled by the ECtHR judgments on behalf of minority protection quoted in the sections above.
- This does not, however, lead to an "affirmative duty" to introduce measures of minority protection in the national legal system. If, however, the member states have legally institutionalised the political representation and participation of minorities or other ethnically defined communities and ratified Protocol No. 12 ECHR, the ECtHR is competent to review legal and/or constitutional mechanisms based on ethnic keys against ethnic discrimination. This follows, in particular, from the intimate connection made in the legal reasoning of the ECtHR with the prohibition of ethnic discrimination according to Article 14 ECHR and/or Article 1 Protocol No. 12 which is, to repeat, not restricted to a prohibition of discrimination of members of only legally recognised ethnic minorities.
- Thus, with the *Kovačević* case, not only minority representatives have a right to vote for a candidate of their choice, but also all citizens whose active right to vote would otherwise be diluted if the ethnic keys foreseen for public offices "totally or to a decisive extent" exclude them in the wording of ECtHR, *Bakirdzi v. Hungary*. In other words, ethnic keys for members of constituent peoples must then be considered as "special privileges" of those ethnic communities, who are de facto in a dominant majority position, in particular, at the Entity level. Efforts of ethnic gerrymandering on behalf of political parties to (re-)gain their political monopoly to be able to decide who is a "real" member of the respective ethnic community against the "subjective" decision of single candidates of other political parties will certainly be found discriminatory as the quoted report of the Venice commission explains.

Hence, parts of the electorate composed of voters who identify with one of the constituent peoples or even voters of the same constituent people, can also be in a de facto minority position and must effectively be protected against *ethnic discrimination*, which is carried out with the *intention* or the *effect* of leading to *further ethnic homogenisation* through separation of territories and segregation of people. As could be seen from the case law of the ECtHR, as well as the BiHCC constituent peoples case, all forms of segregation, including to uphold the so-called "past de jure discrimination", are strictly prohibited and can never be justified through a reference of thereby preserving "peace" in the country.

Bibliography

Banović, Damir, "Individual Identity, Collective Identity and Human Dignity. What are the Best Models to Accommodate Different Identities?", in *Ethnic Diversity, Plural Democracy and Human Dignity. Challenges to the European Union and Western Balkans*, Mario Krešič et al (eds.) (Springer Nature 2022), 91–109.

Graziadei, Stefan, *Courts and the Consociation: Judicial Review of Founding Political Agreements in Multi-National Democracies* (Universiteit Antwerpen (PhD Thesis), 2017).

Kasapović, Mirjana, *Bosna i Hercegovina: podijeljeno društvo i nestabilna država* (Zagreb: Politička kultura, 2005).

Kischel, Uwe, *Comparative Law* (Oxford: Oxford University Press, 2019).

Marko, Joseph and Vranješ, Nevenko, "Amendments to the Constitution of Bosnia and Herzegovina," in *Citizens. Constitution. Europe. Glossary of Essential Constitutional Concepts in BiH*, Maja Sahadžić et al. (eds.) (Sarajevo: University of Sarajevo, Faculty of Law, 2023), 471–476.

Marko, Joseph, "Comparative Jurisprudence from Five Continents: Concluding Observations in Search for Meaning through Intercultural Understanding," in: *Litigating the Rights of Minorities and Indigenous Peoples in Domestic and International Courts*, Bertus de Villiers et al. (eds.) (Leiden-Boston: Brill, 2021), 239–263.

Marko, Joseph, "Constitutional Jurisprudence in Bosnia and Herzegovina: Experiences form the First Mandate of the Constitutional Court from 1997–2002", *European Autonomy and Diversity Papers* (EDAP), European Academy Bozen/Bolzano, 2004 at www.eurac.edu/edap.

Marko, Joseph, "Defective Democracy in a Failed State? Bridging Constitutional Design, Politics and Ethnic Division in Bosnia-Herzegovina," in *Practising Self-Government: A Comparative Study of Autonomous Regions*, Yash Ghai/Sophia Woodman (eds.) (Cambridge University Press 2013), 281–314.

Marko, Joseph, "Is Ethnic Gerrymandering a Solution for the Constitutional Impasse?" *VerfBlog*, August 23, 2022, https://verfassungsblog.de/is-ethnic-gerrymandering-a-solution-for-the-constitutional-impasse/.

Marko, Joseph, "Law and sociology: the constructivist and interpretative turn," in *Human and Minority Rights Protection by Multiple Diversity Governance*, Joseph Marko and Sergiu Constantin (eds.) (London-New York (Routledge), 2019), 138–177.

Marko, Joseph, "The Kovačević Case Revisited: The ECtHR Grand Chamber May De-Block the Constitutional Impasse in Bosnia and Herzegovina", *VerfBlog*, March 28, 2024, https://verfassungsblog.de/the-kovacevic-case-revisited/.

Marko, Joseph, "What is Wrong with the Concept of Multinational Federalism? Some Thoughts about the Interrelationship between the Concepts of (Multi-)Nationalism, Federalism, Power Sharing and Conflict Resolution", *Ethnopolitics*, 19:4: 2020, 416–432.

Marković, Goran, "Kovačević v. Bosnia and Herzegovina: Do Federalism and Consociation Matter?", NBP *Journal of Criminalistics and Law*, 2023, Vol. 28, Issue 3, 2–18.

Marković, Goran, *Bosanskohercegovački federalizam* (University press, Službeni glasnik RS, 2012).

McCrudden, Christopher and O'Leary, Brendan, *Courts and Consociations. Human Rights versus Power-Sharing* (Oxford; Oxford University Press, 2013).

Mujkić, Asim, "Bosna i Herzegovina i izazovi konsocijacije," *Odjek*, 1 (2007), 6–12.

Mujkić, Asim, "We, the Citizens of Ethnopolis," *Constellations*, Vol. 14, No. 1, 2007, 112–128.

Sándor-Szalay, Elisabeth and Kiss, Balázs, "An Odd Solution – Comments on the Margins of a Recent Debate on National Minority Suffrage: ECtHR judgement in Case Bakirdzi and E.C. v. Hungary," *Pécs Journal of International and European Law*, *2022/II*, 55–79.

Vanjek, Dejan, "Federal Equality in Multinational Bosnia and Herzegovina" in *The Principle of Equality in Diverse States. Reconciling Autonomy with Equal Rights and Opportunities*, Belser, Eva Maria et al (eds.) (Leiden-Boston: Brill, 2021), 361–393.

Venice Commission, "Report on Constituency Delineation and Seat Allocation", 12 December 2017 (CDL-AD (2017)034.

Woelk, Jens and Sahadžić, Maja, "Cutting the Gordian Knot in Bosnia and Herzegovina," *VerfBlog*, July 10, 2022, https://verfassungsblog.de/cutting-the-gordian-knot-in-bosnia-and-herzegovina/.

CHAPTER 8

Bicameralism in Bosnia and Herzegovina: Problems and Perspectives

Lejla Balić

1 Introduction

Annex IV to the Dayton Peace Agreement (hereinafter: the Constitution of Bosnia and Herzegovina), fundamentally changed the state organisation and form of the political regime of the former Republic of Bosnia and Herzegovina. The modification of the internal structure of Bosnia and Herzegovina (hereinafter: BiH) and designating the constituent peoples as bearers of democratic legitimacy also entailed reforms in the organisation of all state institutions. The bicameral organisation of the state legislative body is one of the instruments of constitutional policy, with which BiH profiled itself as a democratic, federal, and consociational state. In comparative law, the principles of federalism and consociation often play the role of a corrector of majority democracy as a model of government organisation, with the aim of protecting the special interests of social elements (ethnic, linguistic, territorial). The problem of bicameralism in BiH is precisely the deficit of the democratic principle with respect to the House of Peoples, which, in addition to legal theory, has also been detected in a series of judgments of the European Court of Human Rights (hereinafter: ECtHR) rendered in cases initiated against BiH by its citizens. In the most recent judgments, *Kovačević v. BiH*, the ECtHR, apart from repeatedly confirming the systemic constitutional discrimination of citizens based on ethnicity and place of residence, clearly stated that consociation solutions undermine democratic elections, and gave primacy to political instead of ethnic representation.[1] For 20 years now, the institutions of the Council of Europe have clearly been asking the authorities in BiH to harmonise its constitutional

1 The judgment in the case Kovačević v. BiH was passed on 29 August 2023. On 5 October 2023, BiH filed an appeal. On 25 June 2025, the Grand Jury upheld the objection to the admissibility of the application on the grounds that the applicant had abused the right of application and that he lacked victim status. The decision of the Grand Chamber has not yet been published.

 | DOI:10.1163/9789004707887_009

mechanism with international legal standards. This implies, as a minimum, the respect for the principles of the rule of law and institutional assurance that human rights will not be violated by the Constitution, which, viewed from the perspective of ECtHR judgments, means a completely new concept of bicameralism. In its 14 key priorities, the European Commission clearly indicated that without a revision of the Constitution to guarantee equal rights to all citizens throughout the entire territory, the European path to BiH remains closed. In addition to the democratic deficit, the Parliamentary Assembly of BiH is characterized by pronounced asymmetric bicameralism, which is reflected in the disproportion between the lack of direct electoral legitimacy of the House of Peoples and its extensive powers. The constitutional provisions regulating the House of Peoples of BiH are primarily aimed at protecting the position of the constituent peoples, but they also serve as instruments through which three indirectly elected delegates can, by not attending sessions, completely and for an extended period, halt the work of the Parliamentary Assembly of BiH.

Thus, the imbalance in proportionality can be identified as a problem in the relationship between the goal of protecting the interests of the constituent peoples and the multiple veto mechanisms available to delegates in the House of Peoples. This jeopardizes the functioning of the entire state.

Two aforementioned issues of bicameralism in BiH are interconnected and their resolution should be part of a reform package to meet the conditions for Bosnia and Herzegovina's accession to the European Union. Specifically, alongside eliminating systemic constitutional discrimination regarding the election of delegates to the House of Peoples of BiH, it is important to find mechanisms that will fulfil the primary function of this body, namely the protection of the vital interests of the constituent peoples, but without the possibility of completely blocking all legislative processes.

2 Bosnia and Herzegovina: A Democratic, Complex, and/or Consociational State?

BiH is a democratic state. Article I/2 of the Constitution specifies: "Bosnia and Herzegovina shall be a democratic state, which shall operate under the rule of law and with free and democratic elections," while Article II guarantees the highest level of protection of fundamental rights and freedoms, as well as the direct application and supra-legal force of the European Convention on Human Rights (hereinafter: the ECHR). By joining the Council of Europe, Bosnia and Herzegovina undertook to meet the standards of the so-called European-type legal states,[2] which are: an abstract citizen as a procedural and legitimacy basis for decision-making, rule of law, democratic elections and the protection of human rights and freedoms.[3]

The Constitution of Bosnia and Herzegovina does not define the form of state organisation, however, the provisions on entity-based organisation, the principle of supremacy of the state constitution, division of competences, and organisation of state institutions, point to a complex federal type of state organisation. This is now supported by the opinions of numerous scholars,[4] but also the positions of the Human Rights Commission within the BiH Constitutional Court[5] and of the BiH Constitutional Court.[6]

On the other hand, federalism is not the only feature of the state system of Bosnia and Herzegovina, it is certainly also characterised by (ethno) consociation as a form of political regime.[7] In this sense, state power is based on collective representation and reserved seats for members of constituent peoples in state institutions. Governing is based on power-sharing, a large coalition and a mechanism for protecting the vital interests of the constituent peoples. The consociational principle is most pronounced in relation to the composition and powers of the House of Peoples of BiH.[8]

Each of the substrates of BiH statehood – a democratic state, a complex federal-type state, a consociation – implies certain basic principles from which state power and the organisation of all institutions of BiH are derived and shaped.[9] These principles sometimes overlap and complement each

2 For more on the European-type legal state, see: Edin Šarčević, *Dejtonski ustav: Karakteristike i karakteristični problemi* (Sarajevo: Konrad Adenauer Stiftung, 2009), 73, 77–78.

3 Parliamentary Assembly, Resolution of the Parliamentary Assembly 1383 (2004) Honouring of obligations and commitments by Bosnia and Herzegovina, June 23, 2004, para. 1.

4 See more in Marković, Goran, *Bosanskohercegovački federalizam* (Sarajevo: University Press, Službeni glasnik, 2012); Šarčević, Edin, *Dejtonski ustav*; Ibrahimagić, Omer, *Supremacija Bosne i Hercegovine nad entitetima* (Sarajevo: Vijeće Kongresa bošnjačkih intelektualaca, 1998); Soeren, Keil, *Multinational Federalism in Bosnia and Herzegovina* (London: Ashgate, 2013); Šarčević, Edin ed., *Bosanskohercegovački federalizam* (Sarajevo: Fondacija Centar za javno pravo, 2020).

5 Cases no. CH702/12468 and CH/03/15129.

6 Constitutional Court, Decision U-1/11, July 13, 2012, para. 64.

7 The organisation of the state, which is based on mechanical participation in state bodies without an organic connection to the BiH state is called "participatory ethnocracy." Šarčević, Edin, *Ustav iz nužde* (Sarajevo: Rabic, 2010), 311.

8 Balić, Lejla and Izmirlija, Midhat, "Consociation in Bosnia and Herzegovina: Practical Implementation of the Theoretical Principles," *South-East European Journal of Political Science* 1, 3 (2013), 121–134.

9 See: Marković Goran in this volume for a detailed relationship between consociation and federalism in Bosnia and Herzegovina.

other; however, the problem lies in constitutional antinomies and the collision of principles that determine the status and rights of the citizen and the role of the constituent peoples in relation to the organisation and operation of the highest legislative body in the country.[10]

3 Characteristics of the Bicameral Structure of the BiH Parliamentary Assembly State of Affairs

The problem of achieving a balance between democratic, federal and consociational principles characterises almost every segment of BiH state organisation, and it is especially visible in the case of the Parliamentary Assembly of BiH (hereinafter: the PABiH).

The structure of the PABiH reflects the complex socio-political circumstances in which the Constitution of BiH was created and constitutes a compromise of the representatives of the three BiH constituent peoples on the future state organisation.[11] BiH had a bicameral legislative body before,[12] but of a different legal nature and without continuity with the existing solutions.

The PABiH consists of the House of Representatives as the lower house (hereinafter: the HoR) and the House of Peoples as the upper house (hereinafter: the HoP), while their names already indicate that they were created with different goals.

The HoR,[13] as the lower house of a federal state, should fulfil the role of the institution of people's representation.[14] However, some scholars believe that it

10 Article II/4 of the Constitution of BiH guarantees the enjoyment of all rights and freedoms provided for by the Constitution, including passive suffrage, to all persons without discrimination on any ground, which includes ethnic origin. On the other hand, Article IV/1 of the Constitution and Article V contain discriminatory provisions limiting the passive suffrage on the ground of ethnic origin and place of residence.

For more on constitutional antinomies in the constitutional system of BiH, see: Šarčević, Edin, *Dejtonski ustav*, 77–78.

11 Šarčević, *Ustav iz nužde*, 336–337.

12 With the 1991 amendments to the 1974 Constitution of the SR BiH, the former Assembly of the Socialist Republic of Bosnia and Herzegovina was reorganised into two councils: the Council of Citizens, for which 130 representatives were directly elected, and the Council of Municipalities, to which each municipality and city elected one representative.

13 The PABiH House of Representatives has 42 members who are directly elected by citizens – 28 from the territory of the Federation of BiH and 14 from the territory of the RS (Article IV/2 of the Constitution of BiH).

14 Modern democratic constitutions proclaim the principle of popular sovereignty as the foundation of representative democracy and the idea that state power derives from the

is primarily a federal house, and not a democratic house of a bicameral system. Namely, the composition of the house in a proportional ratio of 2:1 in "favour" of the Federation of BiH minimises its role as a general representative of all citizens of BiH and makes it "a sum of entity delegations."[15] In addition to the method of its formation, the federal nature of the HoR is also reflected in the decision-making, which deviates from the civil-procedural type of democracy and majority decision-making.[16] Decisions are made by the so-called entity voting,[17] where two-thirds of the representatives from one of the entities can block the adoption of any act. Therefore, it is a kind of mechanism for the protection of territorial interests[18] which has been proven throughout the 28

people. In this sense, the term people refers to all citizens, i.e. citizens of the state, regardless of their national (ethnic) and other differences; the term political people is also often used. Parliament, as the sovereign and highest body in a democratic state, is elected in democratic elections and is constituted as a representative of all citizens, the political people. One of the characteristics of most federal states is a bicameral parliament, where the first or lower house is elected based on one man – one vote. It is a democratic house that represents the citizens/political people as a whole and has full legislative powers. For more, see: Jovičić, Miodrag, *Savremeni federalizam* (Beograd: Službeni glasnik, 2006), 116; Palermo, Francesco and Kössler, Karl, *Comparative Federalism: Constitutional Arrangements and Case Law* (Oxford – Portland: Bloomsbery, 2017); Friedrich, Carl J. *Konstitucionalna demokratija* (Podgorica: CID, 2015), 261–312; Smerdel, Branko and Sokol, Smiljko, *Ustavno pravo* (Zagreb, Pravni fakultet, 2006), 209–210.

15 Pobrić, Nurko, *Ustavno pravo* (Mostar: Slovo, 2000), 449.

16 Comparative law shows that in federal states decisions in the lower house are adopted by a majority vote of all members, while the upper – the so-called federal house – serves to protect interests of the federal units (this is the case in Germany, Switzerland, the USA, Belgium, Canada, Australia). Belgium is a different example with peculiarities in the organisation of the legislative branch. Namely, the House of Representatives represents all citizens, while the Senate represents federal units (regions), as well as language communities. However, in the procedure for the adoption of certain (special laws), the members of both houses are grouped by language, and a double majority (a two-thirds majority of the total number of members and a simple majority within two language groups) is required in both houses for special laws to be adopted. Therefore, this is a deviation of sort from the majority vote in relation to certain matters as determined by the Constitution. For more, see: Stanković, Marko, "*Belgijski federalizam*" (Beograd: Pravni fakultet Univerziteta, 2009), 182.

17 Constitution of BiH, Article IV/3.d.

18 Entity voting as a guarantor of the preservation and a protection mechanism of the Republika Srpska in the constitutional system of BiH and a form of "collective voting" is often highlighted by scholars of constitutional law and politicians from the RS.

Available at: https://srpskainfo.com/bez-prava-na-veto-srpska-bi-brzo-nestala-entitetsko-glasanje-nema-veze-sa-stranim-sudijama/

years to be as an absolute entity veto[19] whose frequent use slows down legislative processes and makes Parliament ineffective.[20] The HoP BiH is the upper house of the PABiH, but unlike federal states in comparative law, its primary role is not the representation of entities as federal units, but of constituent

19 The analysis of the reasons for the non-adoption of laws in the period 1997–2007 showed that 59.9% of the laws were rejected because they did not get the needed support entity MP s. Kasim Trnka et al., *Procesi odlučivanja u Parlamentarnoj skupštini BiH* (Sarajevo KAS, 2009), 89–90. After 2007, there have been no similar studies, but the trend of non-adoption of laws due to failure to achieve the entity majority continued, especially in relation to laws that were to strengthen BiH institutions. Over the years, the following laws, among others, did not get support: Proposal of the Law Banning Denial of the Holocaust, Crimes of Genocide and Crimes Against Humanity (2008), Proposal of the Law on the Supreme Court of BiH (2012), and Proposal of the Law on the Disposal of Immovable Military Property (2013). Due to the absence of entity majority, the Amendments to the Law on the Flag of BiH were not adopted either, the aim of which was to amend the provisions declared unconstitutional by the Constitutional Court of BiH. In 2023, due to the so-called entity vote, the Proposal of the Law on Foreign Affairs of BiH and the Proposal of the Law on Conclusion and Implementation of International Treaties were not adopted, which, although not on the list of 14 priorities for accession, are important for European integration and international activities of BiH. When it comes to BiH's European path, the entity voting mechanism proved to be the main obstacle to meeting the criteria set by the European Commission. Political leaders from the RS often point out that, regardless of the significance and content, no law will be adopted until the Law on the Constitutional Court of BiH is enacted, which would replace foreign judges in the Constitutional Court of BiH with local judges; a statement of the BiH House of Peoples notes to that end: "It is the political position of the Republika Srpska that no law shall be adopted until the Law on the Constitutional Court of BiH is enacted, and that for that reason alone they will not adopt laws." Available at: https://djaka-city.info/2023/10/05/nije-usvojen-zakon-kojim-se-dize-prag-za-ulazak-u-pdv-sustav/#google_vignette; https://istinomjer.ba/nema-kvoruma-nema-sjednice-nema-odluke-nema-ni-odgovornosti/; https://radiosarajevo.ba/vijesti/bosna-i-hercegovina/milorad-dodik-najavio-nove-blokade-nema-europskih-zakona-sa-strancima-u-ustavnom-sudu/53210M; https://www.klix.ba/vijesti/bih/milorad-dodik-danas-naglasio-da-se-nijedan-zakon-nece-usvojiti-prije zakona-o-ustavnom-sudu/230929113; https://www.dw.com/hr/nema-dogovora-o-ustavnom-sudu-i-sudovima-u-bih/a-67280229, https://radiosarajevo.ba/vijesti/bosna-i-hercegovina/dodik-uoci-dana-d-vrijeda-i-postavlja-uslove-evo-kad-ce-zakon-o-sudovima-biti-usvojen/536609

20 In its Opinion on BiH's application for EU membership, the European Commission clearly emphasised that entity voting affects the effectiveness of the legislative procedure, but it did not include it among the conditions for BiH's accession to the EU. European Commission, "Opinion on Bosnia and Herzegovina's application for membership of the European Union," COM (2019) 261 Final, May 29, 2019, 7.

In Resolutions 1513 (2006) para. 18 and 1626 (2008) para. 4, Parliamentary Assembly of the Council of Europe points to the problem of entity voting that makes the legislative body ineffective and calls for reform.

peoples.[21] It comprises only Bosniaks, Serbs, and Croats, by the parity formula, delegated from the respective ethnic bases.[22] Therefore, the equality of the constituent peoples is ensured, not of the entities as federal units. In addition to the full legislative powers it shares with the HoR, the HoP is also responsible for the protection of the vital interest of the constituent peoples, which is linked to the veto right. The only characteristic of the HoP as a federal house is entity voting,[23] which protects entity interests in the same way as in the HoR.

4 The Problem

According to the competences, the method of election and the mutual relationship of the houses, bicameralism in Bosnia and Herzegovina can be defined as strong[24] and asymmetric bicameralism.[25]

---

21 Marković, Goran, *Bosanskohercegovački federalizam*, 97; Pobrić, Nurko, *Ustavno pravo*, 262.

22 The House of Peoples of the PABiH consists of 15 delegates, of which two thirds (5 Bosniaks and 5 Croats) are elected from the Federation of BiH, and 5 delegates from the Republika Srpska – all of whom are members of the Serb people. Croat and Bosniak delegates from FBiH are elected by the Croat and the Bosniak delegates, respectively, in the House of Peoples of the FBiH Parliament (HoP PFBiH). The Federation of BiH is an entity with a federal organisation, which is composed of 10 cantons. The HoP PFBiH is the upper house of the FBiH Parliament, which is composed of 23 delegates from the three constituent peoples and 11 delegates from the Others (Amendment CXI to the Constitution of the FBIH). Bosniak, Croat, Serb, and the Others delegates in the HoP PFBiH are elected by representatives in the cantonal assemblies from among the respective constituent peoples. Although Federation of BiH consists of cantons as federal units, HoP PFBiH is primarily the House of Constituent Peoples, which has also been emphasised in the Decision of the Constitutional Court of BiH (U-23/14, para 50). It is determined as such by its composition, method of election and competence to protect the vital national interest of the constituent peoples. Serb delegates to HoP PABiH are elected by the National Assembly of the RS – not representatives from the ranks of the Serb people exclusively. However, since 1996 and the first democratic elections, until today, the absolute parliamentary majority has been held by Serb national parties, which are the *de facto* the electoral base. For more, see: Marković, Goran, *Bosanskohercegovački federalizam*, 99–100.

23 Constitution of BiH, Article IV/3(d).

24 For more on the distribution of competences between the Houses, see: Tsebelis, George and Money, Jeannette, *Bicameralism* (Cambridge: Cambridge University Press, 2003); Jovičić, Miodrag, *Savremeni federalizam*, 116–142; Petrov, Vladan, *Parlamentarno pravo* (Beograd: Pravni fakultet Univerziteta, 2010), 58–65; Stanković, Marko, *Preobražaj federalne države* (Beograd: Pravni fakultet Univerziteta, 2020), 261–283.

For strong bicameralism, it is sufficient to have the constitutional equality of both chambers in all stages of the legislative procedure (right of legislative initiative, right to propose amendments and decision-making),[26] as the fundamental competence of legislative bodies. In addition to full equality in legislative competence,[27] both houses of the PABiH are equal in other fundamental competences[28] (constitutional, budgetary, ratification of international treaties), and it is necessary for both houses to adopt all decisions in an identical text for them to enter into force. Differences in competences relate to the appointment procedure of the BiH Council of Ministers, in which only the HoR participates along with the Presidency of BiH.[29] However, the HoP and the HoR are equal in the oversight function, and both houses need to pass a vote of no confidence for the removal of the BiH Council of Ministers. Therefore, given the fact that most of the basic functions are under the common competence of both houses and that they are equal in the performance of those functions, bicameralism in BiH has all the characteristics of a strong bicameralism.

Asymmetric bicameralism is a feature of bicameral legislatures, where there are significant inequalities between the constitutional powers and the democratic legitimacy of the two chambers. In the case of the PABiH, the asymmetry of bicameralism is a consequence of the disproportion between the equal constitutional powers of both chambers and the deficit of democratic legitimacy of the HoP. Namely, the representatives in the HoR have direct electoral legitimacy, they are elected in general and direct elections, by the citizens of BiH registered in the Central Register of Voters. On the other hand, members of the HoP, whose decisions directly affect the creation of all state policies and the lives of all citizens of BiH, not only in relation to matters that are relevant to the special interests of the constituent peoples, are delegated by a relatively small number of representatives in the entity legislatures, especially the Bosniak and Croat delegates. The provisions of the Constitution of BiH stipulate that nine members of the House of Peoples constitute a quorum, provided that three delegates from each constituent people are present.[30] Along with the ethnic veto and entity voting, such a quorum repre-

25 For more on asymmetric federalism, see: Lijphart, Arend, *Modeli demokratije* (Podgorica: Službeni list SCG i CID, 2003), 212–218.

26 Vladan Petrov, *Parlamentarno pravo*, 59.

27 Constitution of BiH, Article IV/3.

28 Constitution of BiH, Articles IV/3, IV/4c and X/1.

29 Constitution of BiH, Article V/4.

30 Constitution of BiH, Article IV/1.b.

sents an additional, de facto mechanism for blocking the Parliamentary Assembly of Bosnia and Herzegovina, which delegates have repeatedly abused by failing to attend sessions of the House of Peoples when proposals they did not want to be adopted were on the agenda.[31]

The composition and method of decision-making in the HoP are a specific combination of ethnic and territorial representation based on the implementation of consociational principles, with a complete deficit of the democratic principle. This deficit is primarily reflected in the fact that citizens identifying as Others and members of constituent peoples from the "wrong"[32] entity are completely deprived of passive suffrage in relation to the HoP.

The collision of democratic and consociational principles in the constitutional system of BiH is not only a theoretical problem of bicameralism and a constitutional antinomy. It is a proven[33] constitutional discrimination of citizens on the ground of ethnicity and place of residence, which is an obstacle to

31 The longest period during which the HoP failed to hold regular sessions due to a lack of quorum occurred in 2024. Namely, during the 14th regular session of the HoP on 18 March 2024, an item was added to the agenda proposing an expedited consideration of the Draft Law on the Constitutional Court. Delegates from the Bosniak caucus walked out of the session, thereby breaking the quorum. Among other provisions, the draft law proposed replacing foreign judges with domestic ones, which is one of the 14 conditions for EU accession. However, it also introduced so-called entity-based and ethnic decision-making within the Constitutional Court, which Bosniak delegates considered unconstitutional and unacceptable. They returned to the parliamentary benches only after receiving guarantees from the Chair of the HoP and after the proposer withdrew the law, marking the end of an almost eight-month stalemate. The most recent example of obstruction occurred on 18 February 2025, during the 9th emergency session, where the agenda included the dismissal of Nikola Špirić, the First Deputy Chair of the HoP, from the Serbian caucus. At the time, Špirić's party, the SNSD, was in coalition with the HDZ BiH, whose leaders publicly opposed Špirić's dismissal. The session began and included a debate partly focused on Špirić's removal. However, after a break was announced, delegates from the Croatian caucus did not return, thereby breaking the quorum and causing the session to be interrupted.

32 Serbs who live in FBiH cannot be elected to the HoP BiH, nor do they have the possibility to influence the election of delegates from the Serb people to the HoP, whose competence is to protect the vital interest of the Serb people; this is the same with Croats and Bosniaks in the RS.

33 Judgments of the European Court of Human Rights in cases: *Sejdić and Finci v. BiH*, Applications nos. 27996/06 and 34836/06, December 22, 2009; *Zornić v. BiH*, Application no. 3681/06, July 15, 2014, *Šlaku v. BiH*, Application no. 56666/12, May 26, 2016; *Pilav v. BiH*, Application no. 41939/07, June 09, 2016, *Pudarić v. BiH*, Application no. 55799/18, December 8, 2020. See also: Marko, Joseph in this volume.

the European path of BiH[34] the elimination of which would entail a change in the nature of bicameralism.

No constitutional system is static – it is conditioned by the dynamics of changes in political forces, the development of economic flows, as well as the international obligations that the state undertakes, which means that the balance between certain principles changes over time. It is therefore important to recall the circumstances under which the Constitution of Bosnia and Herzegovina was created. The primary goal at that time was to stop the war suffering, genocide, and ethnic cleansing, and the precondition for signing the peace agreement was the "acceptance of ethnically based rules," which justifies the legal equality of the principles of consociation and democracy.[35] Where two principles of the same legal rank are opposed to each other, the rule applies that none of the principles may be applied in such a way to annul the requirement of validity of the other principle.[36] Therefore, the provisions of Article II of the Constitution of BiH represent a ballast to the constitutional privileges of the constituent peoples, but also a legal basis and guideline for further development of the constitutional system of BiH.[37]

5 Perspectives: From the Viewpoint of the Council of Europe

As early as 20 years ago, relevant international bodies took a dynamic approach in assessing the justification of constitutional solutions in BiH, with an objective distance from the period and circumstances under which the Constitution entered into force. The message that the European institutions have been sending to the authorities in BiH since 2002 is that the rule of law

34 By signing the Stabilisation and Association Agreement with the European Union in 2008, Bosnia and Herzegovina assumed an international obligation to harmonise the controversial provisions of the Constitution with international standards.

Among the 14 key priorities for EU accession, under the Democracy/Functionality heading, equality and non-discrimination of citizens is listed in relation to the ECtHR judgment in the case *Sejdić and Finci v. BiH* (European Commission, "Opinion on Bosnia and Herzegovina's application for membership of the European Union," 4. 4(f), 15).

35 Venice Commission, "Opinion on the constitutional situation in Bosnia and Herzegovina and the powers of the high representative," CDL-AD (2005) 004, March 11, 2005, para. 74; Nysten, Gro, *Achieving Peace or Protecting Human Rights? Conflicts between norms regarding ethnic discrimination in the Dayton Peace Agreement* (Leiden/Boston: Martinus Nijhoff Publishers, 2005), 240–241; *Sejdić and Finci v. BiH*, para. 45; *Zornić v. BiH*, para. 43.

36 Šarčević, *Ustav iz nužde*, 116.

37 Gro, *Achieving Peace or Protecting Human Rights? Conflicts between norms regarding ethnic discrimination in the Dayton Peace Agreement*, 100.

and the protection of human rights are not of the same legal rank as the principle of consociational rule, but that they have priority,[38] and that a gradual but essential democratisation of the political regime in BiH is needed.

In this sense, the European Commission for Democracy through Law (hereinafter: the Venice Commission) stated in as early as 2005: "It would certainly not be realistic to expect that BiH move quickly from a system based on ethnic representation to a system based on representation of citizens. This will certainly be a long-term process. Nevertheless the Commission wishes to encourage people and politicians in BiH to start examining the extent to which the mechanisms of ethnic representation are really required and to replace them progressively by representation based on the civic principle."[39]

The Parliamentary Assembly of the Council of Europe in Resolution 1513 (2006) (para 20.1.) urges to replace the mechanisms of ethnic representation by representation based on the civic principle. Resolution 1626 (2008) reads that "the entity voting system in the House of Representatives and the excessively broad scope of the "vital national interests" clause, together with the related veto mechanism in the House of Peoples, must be reformed for Bosnia and Herzegovina to become a genuine civic state for all those living in it. Members of Parliament should act as free and democratically elected representatives of all the citizens of Bosnia and Herzegovina and not as defenders of purely ethnic interests."[40] Building on the views of the Venice Commission, in the case *Sejdić and Finci v. BiH,* the ECtHR notes that "there is no requirement (...) to abandon totally the power-sharing mechanisms peculiar to Bosnia and

38 As far back as 2002, the Parliamentary Assembly of the Council of Europe pointed out the need to eliminate discrimination on the ground on ethnicity in the constitutional system of BiH. Parliamentary Assembly, "Opinion 234(2002) Bosnia and Herzegovina's application for membership of the Council of Europe," January 22, 2002, para. 5 (i(b)).

Venice Commission, "Opinion on the constitutional situation in Bosnia and Herzegovina and the powers of the high representative," t. 75 and 76.

In the judgment *Sejdić and Finci v. BiH* passed 14 years after the end of the war, the ECtHR observed in para. 47 the positive development of the political situation in BiH (reform in the field of defence, the creation of single armed forces of BiH, the signing of the EU Stabilisation and Association Agreement, the fact that BiH became a member of the Council of Europe and unreservedly ratified the Convention and its protocols...), and reiterated the position of the Venice Commission that that there exist mechanisms of power-sharing which do not lead to the exclusion of representatives of the other communities (para. 48).

39 Venice Commission, "Opinion on the constitutional situation in Bosnia and Herzegovina and the powers of the high representative," para. 44.

40 Parliamentary Assembly, Resolution of the Parliamentary Assembly 1383 (2004), paras. 4 and 11.8.4.

Herzegovina and that the time may still not be ripe for a political system which would be a simple reflection of majority rule (...) there exist mechanisms of power-sharing which do not automatically lead to the total exclusion of representatives of the other communities."[41]

In the cases that followed[42] the ECtHR repeated the positions it expressed in the case *Sejdić Finci v. BiH*, and particularly emphasised that undemocratic and discriminatory constitutional solutions can no longer be considered justified, bearing in mind the time that has passed since the end of the war. In the *Zornić* case, the Court observes: "...The nature of the conflict was such that the approval of the "constituent peoples" was necessary to ensure peace ... However, now, more than eighteen years after the end of the tragic conflict, there could no longer be any reason for the maintenance of the contested constitutional provisions. ... In view of the need to ensure effective political democracy, the Court considers that the time has come for a political system which will provide every citizen of Bosnia and Herzegovina with the right to stand for elections to the Presidency and the House of Peoples of Bosnia and Herzegovina..."[43]

In the case *Šlaku v. BiH*, the Court resolutely stated that it "expects that democratic arrangements will be made without further delay" and emphasised that one of the goals of abolishing discriminatory provisions is "...the need to ensure effective political democracy."[44]

However, the biggest leap so far was made in the judgment *Kovačević v. BiH*.[45] In a way, it is an expected and logical continuation of earlier judgments[46] – the obverse – while this judgment is the reverse of the established violation of human rights. Previous judgments established systemic discrimination with respect to passive suffrage, while the *Kovačević* case established systemic discrimination of all BiH citizens related to active suffrage with respect to the election of the HoP PABiH and the BiH Presidency.[47]

However, in the *Kovačević* case, the ECtHR very strongly commented on the effect of power-sharing mechanisms on democratic processes in BiH: "(...) in addition to excluding certain citizens from the House of Peoples on the grounds of their ethnicity, the current arrangements render ethnic con-

41 *Sejdić and Finci v. BiH*, para. 48.

42 See: footnote 28.

43 *Zornić v. BiH*, para. 43.

44 *Šlaku v. BiH*, para. 40.

45 *Kovačević v. BiH*, Application no. 43651/22, ECHR, August 29, 2023.

46 See: footnote 29.

47 *Kovačević v. BiH*, paras. 62 and 75.

siderations and/or representation more relevant than political, economic, social, philosophical and other considerations and/or representation and thus amplify ethnic divisions in the country and undermine the democratic character of elections..."[48] To the objection by the BiH's Agent that the existing system is justified to maintain peace and to facilitate dialogue between different ethnic groups, the Court responded that: "it considers that peace and dialogue are best maintained by an effective political democracy (...) of which the ability to freely exercise one's right to vote is a pillar. Therefore, no one should be forced to vote only according to prescribed ethnic lines, irrespective of their political viewpoint (...) Even if a system of ethnic representation is maintained in some form, it should be secondary to political representation, should not discriminate against "Others and citizens of Bosnia and Herzegovina" and should include ethnic representation from the entire territory of the State."[49]

6 Instead of a Conclusion

After the *Kovačević v. BiH* judgment, the European Court of Human Rights established that the concept of exclusive ethnic representation is contrary to democracy, and rejected the argument that it ensures dialogue between the constituent peoples. On the contrary, the Court assessed that after 28 years, consociational solutions only deepen the divisions and destabilise political processes, indicating the need for a radical constitutional reform. With this, the Court unequivocally gave priority to political representation as an absolute democratic standard, and reduced the ethnic representation that dominates the constitutional system of BiH to the ultimate corrective measure of political democracy. The Court in fact confirmed the positions of the CoE Parliamentary Assembly 1626 (2008) on the necessity of the constitutional transition of BiH from a consociation to "a genuine civic state for all those living in it" and placed the individual rights of citizens above the rights of the collective.

In the formal legal sense, there should be no obstacles to the implementation of these judgments because there is enough space in the provisions of the BiH Constitution to legally justify and strengthen the change of the political regime. Apart from the cited Articles I/2 and II of the Constitution, there is also the 3rd indent of the Preamble of the Constitution of BiH, indicating that "democratic governmental institutions and fair procedures best produce

48 *Kovačević v. BiH*, para. 56.

49 *Kovačević v. BiH*, para. 74.

peaceful relations within a pluralist society," as well as Decision U 5/98 – III of the Constitutional Court of BiH, declaring the concept of territorial divisions of the constituent peoples at the entity level unconstitutional.[50] The standard of the European legal state in BiH can hardly be achieved without being modified in relation to the constitutional status of the constituent peoples. Most scholars and political elites agree with this, however, the ECtHR, the Venice Commission, and even the European Commission, in assessing the fulfilment of the conditions for BiH's accession to the European Union, never emphasised the requirements to completely abandon the power-sharing mechanisms specific to BiH.

However, will the *Kovačević* judgment really change the constitutional system of BiH, will the political elites be accountable and act in accordance with the principle of the rule of law and the international obligations that BiH has undertaken? Soon it will be 15 years since the *Sejdić and Finci v. BiH* judgment and no serious steps have been taken to implement it – there is no reason to believe that the even more demanding requirements from the *Kovačević* case will be met. But, if the reform is to start in accordance with all previous judgments regarding the method of election and composition of the HoP PABiH, with the elimination of discriminatory provisions, mechanisms to protect the special interests of the constituent peoples should be foreseen.

From the angle of consociational principles, a legislative body in which social groups are represented with autonomous decision-making powers and the right of veto in connection with special internal issues is not in itself contrary to the democratic governing principle. The fact that the representatives are delegated from the respective ethnic groups should also be the starting point for determining the issues to which the ethnic veto can be applied (identity, culture, language, etc.), but not in relation to issues that reflect on all members of the political community.[51]

The ECtHR reasoned in this direction in the *Sejdić and Finci* case and emphasised that a "legislature" under Article 3 of Protocol 1 ECHR should be interpreted in the light of each state's constitutional structure, traditions, and specificities, and that it refers to directly elected houses of parliament. The delegation system, following this logic, may be subject to a different regime and states may have greater freedom in determining the modalities of its implementation. Despite this, the Court found discrimination against "non-

50 Constitutional Court of BiH, Decision U 5/98 – III, paras. 60. and 69.

51 See also: Haverić, Tarik, "Bosanskohercegovačko uređenje i većinsko odlučivanje", *Sveske za javno pravo br.29*, (Sarajevo Fondacija Centar za javno pravo, 2017), 55–56.

constituents" in the case of the election of delegates to the HoP PABiH, referring to broad legislative powers.[52] Therefore, the reform can go in the direction of reducing the powers of the House of Peoples of BiH with the inclusion of representatives of all three peoples from the territory of both entities.[53]

The reform would primarily mean adopting solutions that clearly distinguish the competencies of the two houses of the PABiH. Thus, the HoR, with its direct electoral legitimacy, would remain the house with full legislative authority. However, the HoP would be reformed into a body whose primary task is to protect the vital interests of the constituent peoples, specifically in enumerated areas such as the right of constituent peoples to equal representation in legislative and executive bodies, issues of identity, tradition, cultural heritage, and language. To ensure the inclusion of delegates from all constituent peoples and Others from both entities, it is necessary to increase the total number of delegates from each constituent people. The decision on the distribution of the number of delegates from each entity should be subject to a specialized expert study, which would take into account the results of the 1991 and 2013 censuses. Considering that the competencies of the House of Peoples of BiH would be significantly reduced and specified, the selection of delegates should be indirect in both entities. For example, the selection of delegates from the Federation of BiH would remain the same: Bosniak and Croat delegates in the HoP PFBiH would be elected by the Bosniak and Croat caucuses, respectively. A new provision would be that Serb delegates are elected by the Serb caucus in the HoP FBiH. When it comes to representatives from the Republika Srpska, they would no longer be elected by the National Assembly but rather by the corresponding caucus in the Council of Peoples of the RS. As for representatives of Others in the HoP PABiH, it is challenging to propose a straightforward solution for such a complex issue in a brief format. There is neither a political nor an academic consensus on which category of BiH citizens falls under the term "Others." This is a very fluid and heterogeneous concept, influenced by the understanding of the position of constituent peoples within the constitutional system of BiH. Nonetheless, the minimum requirement regarding the position of Others is the inclusion of representatives of national minorities in the House of Peoples of BiH, who would be delegated by the Council of National Minorities and would have a special mechanism for protecting minority rights.

52 *Sejdić and Finci v. BiH*, para. 41.

53 Similar solutions, which may serve as a starting point for new reforms, were part of the so-called April Package of constitutional amendments from 2006 (Amandmani na Ustav Bosne i Hercegovine (Aprilski paket ustavnih promjena), March 25, 2006).

Another possible option is to keep the current powers of the House of Peoples, but open it up to representatives of the Others and representatives of constituent peoples delegated from both entities.[54] Since the House of Peoples is not perceived as a federal house, and in the event that the representatives of the constituent peoples have the ethnic veto at their disposal, there is no reason to retain the entity voting mechanism.

So far, the European Court of Human Rights has not considered any matter in relation to the House of Representatives of PABiH, although the model in which 2/3 of representatives are elected from the territory of the FBiH and 1/3 from the territory of the RS can be questioned from the perspective of equal voting rights.[55] However, the Venice Commission and the Parliamentary Assembly of the Council of Europe clearly indicated the problem of blockage and inefficiency of the HoR PABiH because of the entity vote. The House of Representatives of the PABiH has, above all, the role to represent all citizens of BiH, and accordingly, decisions should be made by the majority of votes of all representatives, without the possibility of entity veto. This mechanism is particularly questionable, bearing in mind that the HoP makes decisions in the same way, so entity interests can be protected at that level as well. However, it is not realistic to expect that political elites will support the abolition of the so-called entity vote because it was retained in the April Package, which so far received most substantive support from political parties and the public.

Bibliography

"Amandmani na Ustav Bosne i Hercegovine (Aprilski paket ustavnih promjena)." March 25, 2006, accessed October 22, 2023,https://fcjp.ba/templates/ja_avian_ii_d/images/green/Aprilski_paket1.pdf.

Balić, Lejla and Izmirlija, Midhat, "Consociation in Bosnia and Herzegovina: Practical Implementation of the Theoretical Principles," *South-East European Journal of Political Science* 1, 3 (2013), 121–134.

Bieber, Florian, "Reforming the House of Peoples of the Parliamentary Assembly of Bosnia and Herzegovina" Sarajevo: Analitika, 2012, accessed October 19, 2023,

54 For more on the possible reform of the House of Peoples in line with the *Sejdić and Finci v. BiH* judgment, see: Hodžić, Edin and Stojanović, Nenad, *Kako reformirati dom naroda Parlamentarne skupštine BiH? Izazovi izvršenja presude u predmetu Sejdić i Finci protiv BiH* (Sarajevo: Analitika, 2011); Bieber, Florian, *Reforming the House of Peoples of the Parliamentary Assembly of Bosnia and Herzegovina* (Sarajevo: Analitika, 2012).

55 Goran Marković, *Bosanskohercegovački federalizam*, 90.

https://www.analitika.ba/sites/default/files/publikacije/bieberf_-_reforming_the_house_of_peoples_bih_25april2012_final.pdf.

"Constitution of BiH" accessed October 20, 2023, https://www.ustavnisud.ba/public/down/USTAV_BOSNE_I_HERCEGOVINE_engl.pdf.

European Commission. "Opinion on Bosnia and Herzegovina's application for membership of the European Union," *COM* (2019) 261 Final, May 29, 2019.

Friedrich, Carl J. *Konstitucionalna demokratija*. (Podgorica: CID, 2015).

Haverić, Tarik, *Bosanskohercegovačko uređenje i većinsko odlučivanje*, (Sarajevo, Sveske za javno pravo 2017).

Hodžić, Edin and Stojanović, Nenad, "Kako reformirati dom naroda Parlamentarne skupštine BiH? Izazovi izvršenja presude u predmetu Sejdić i Finci protiv BiH." Sarajevo: Analitika, 2011, accessed October 16, 2023, https://www.analitika.ba/bs/publikacije/policy-brief-kako-reformirati-dom-naroda-ps-bih.

Ibrahimagić, Omer, *Supremacija Bosne i Hercegovine nad entitetima*, (Sarajevo: Vijeće Kongresa bošnjačkih intelektualaca, 1998).

Jovičić, Miodrag, *Savremeni federalizam*. (Beograd: Službeni glasnik, 2006).

Keil, Soeren, *Multinational Federalism in Bosnia and Herzegovina*. (London: Ashgate, 2013).

Marković, Goran, *Bosanskohercegovački federalizam*. (Sarajevo: University press, Službeni glasnik, 2012).

Nysten, Gro, *Achieving Peace or Protecting Human Rights? Conflicts between norms regarding ethnic discrimination in the Dayton Peace Agreement*. (Leiden/Boston: Martinus Nijhoff Publishers, 2005).

Palermo, Francesco and Kössler, Karl, *Comparative Federalism: Constitutional Arrangements and Case Law*. (Oxford – Portland: Bloomsbury, 2017).

Parliamentary Assembly, "Opinion 234(2002) Bosnia and Herzegovina's application for membership of the Council of Europe," January 22, 2002.

Parliamentary Assembly, "Resolution 1513 (2006) Constitutional reform in Bosnia and Herzegovina," June 27, 2006, accessed October 22, 2023, https://assembly.coe.int/nw/xml/XRef/X2H-Xref-ViewHTML.asp?FileID=11406&lang=EN.

Parliamentary Assembly, "Resolution 1626 (2008) Honouring of obligations and commitments by Bosnia and Herzegovina," September 30, 2008.

Parliamentary Assembly, "Resolution of the Parliamentary Assembly 1383 (2004) Honouring of obligations and commitments by Bosnia and Herzegovina," June 23, 2004, accessed October 22, 2023, https://www.esiweb.org/pdf/bridges/bosnia/CoE_Resolution_1383.pdf.

Petrov, Vladan, *Parlamentarno pravo*. (Beograd: Pravni fakultet Univerziteta, 2010).

Pobrić, Nurko, *Ustavno pravo*. (Mostar: Slovo, 2000).

Šarčević, Edin, *Dejtonski ustav: karakteristike i karakteristični problemi*. (Sarajevo: Fondacija "Konrad Adenauer," 2009).

Šarčević, Edin, ed., *Bosanskohercegovački federalizam.* (Sarajevo: Fondacija Centar za javno pravo, 2020).

Šarčević, Edin, *Ustav iz nužde.* (Sarajevo: Rabic, 2010).

Smerdel, Branko and Sokol, Smiljko *Ustavno pravo.* (Zagreb, Pravni fakultet Univerziteta, 2006).

Stanković, Marko, *Belgijski federalizam.* (Beograd: Pravni fakultet Univerziteta, 2009).

Stanković, Marko, *Preobražaj federalne države.* (Beograd: Pravni fakultet Univerziteta, 2020).

Trnka, Kasim et al. "Procesi odlučivanja u Parlamentarnoj skupštini BiH." *Sarajevo KAS, 2009,* accessed October 17, 2023, https://www.kas.de/c/document_library/get_file?uuid=b0549a34-e453-ab40-063f-f3b42dd5279d&groupId=252038.

Tsebelis, George and Money, Jeannette, *Bicameralism.* (Cambridge: Cambridge University Press, 2003).

Venice Commission. "Opinion on the constitutional situation in Bosnia and Herzegovina and the powers of the high representative," *CDL-AD* (2005) 004, March 11, 2005, accessed October 21, 2023, https://www.venice.coe.int/webforms/documents/CDL-AD(2005)004-e.aspx.

Trnka, Kasim et al. "Procesi odlučivanja u Parlamentarnoj skupštini BiH." *Sarajevo KAS, 2009,* accessed October 17, 2023, https://www.kas.de/c/document_library/get_file?uuid=b0549a34-e453-ab40-063f-f3b42dd5279d&groupId=252038.

Tsebelis, George and Money, Jeannette, *Bicameralism.* (Cambridge: Cambridge University Press, 2003).

Venice Commission. "Opinion on the constitutional situation in Bosnia and Herzegovina and the powers of the high representative," *CDL-AD* (2005) 004, March 11, 2005, accessed October 21, 2023, https://www.venice.coe.int/webforms/documents/CDL-AD(2005)004-e.aspx.

Case Law

Decision 5/98. – III Constitutional Court of BiH BiH, July 1, 2000.

Decision U-1/11. Constitutional Court of BiH, July 13, 2012.

Decision U-23/14. Constitutional Court of BiH BiH, December 1, 2016.

Kovačević v. BiH. Application no. 43651/22, ECHR, August 29, 2023.

Pilav v. BiH. Application no. 41939/07, ECHR, June 9, 2016.

Pudarić v. BiH. Application no. 55799/18, ECHR, December 08, 2020.

Sejdić and Finci v. BiH. Application no. 27996/06 and 34836/06, ECHR, December 22, 2009.

Šlaku v. BiH. Application no. 56666/12, ECHR, May 26, 2016.

Zornić v. BiH. Application no. 3681/06, ECHR, July 15, 2014.

CHAPTER 9

A Few Constitutional and Legal Problems of the Executive Power in Bosnia and Herzegovina

Marko Romić

1 The Concept of Executive Power in the Constitutional System of Bosnia and Herzegovina

In modern constitutional law, executive power is exercised by the head of state and the government. When we say "government", we mean the collective body of the executive as the highest, constitutional body of government, but also the body of administration, if we adhere to the quadrialist conception of the division of power, as the author of this paper does.[1] The preliminary question here refers to the role of the head of state and government in different systems of the organisation of state power, implying that executive power is manifested differently in presidential and parliamentary systems (irrespective of whether the government or the head of state has supremacy), while historical relics point to a completely peculiar form of executive power in the so-called assembly systems (for example, the Soviet or Yugoslav type).[2]

Defining the executive power in Bosnia and Herzegovina is an easy task, given the complexity of the state system and the genesis of the relationship between different levels of government within Bosnia and Herzegovina.[3] At the beginning, we would define Bosnia and Herzegovina as a specific federally organised state with admixtures of confederal elements.[4] This unusual consti-

1 Among the first to advocate for such a conception in the legal theory of the so-called Yugoslav peoples (primarily Serbian and Croatian legal authors) was Professor Jovan Đorđević, who believed that the political-executive function and the administrative function should be distinguished, claiming that these are two completely separate activities, which cannot be performed simultaneously or by the same authority. See: Đorđević, Jovan, *Politički sistem – prilog nauci o čoveku i samoupravljanju* (Beograd: Udruženje pravnika Jugoslavije, 1967), 602.

2 Marković, Ratko, *Izvršna vlast* (Beograd: Savremena administracija, 1980), 115.

3 See: Vlaški, Bojan in this volume for more about the relationship between different levels of government and their modes of cooperation.

4 For a more detailed substantiation of the position on the confederal-federal form of government, see: Kuzmanović, Rajko, "Narušavanje podjele nadležnosti između entiteta i Bosne i Hercegovine," in *Podjela nadležnosti između institucija Bosne i Hercegovine i entiteta*, ed.

 | DOI:10.1163/9789004707887_010

tutional and legal amalgam is framed by the General Framework Agreement for Peace in Bosnia and Herzegovina, i.e., the Dayton Agreement, which outlines the scheme of its executive power. In accordance with the Dayton Agreement, Bosnia and Herzegovina is composed of two entities; therefore, the executive power is exercised at two, i.e., three different levels. First, at the joint level, we have the Presidency of Bosnia and Herzegovina, as well as the Council of Ministers, while at the entity level, executive power in the Republika Srpska belongs to the Government of the Republika Srpska and the President of the Republika Srpska. In the Federation of BiH, executive power is exercised at the federal level and at the level of ten cantons – there is the Government of the Federation of Bosnia and Herzegovina and ten cantonal governments. The intricate "constitutional labyrinth" is further complicated by Amendment I to the Constitution of BiH, implementing the Arbitral Decision for the Brčko District, by which the executive power is inseparable from the organisation of the Brčko District as a unit of local self-government, and power in the District is exercised by the Government of the Brčko District headed by the Mayor. One could not compare BiH with the French Fifth Republic, where the president of the republic and the prime minister are the first among the ministers to form *un tandem original*.[5] Although the Council of Ministers is constitutionally defined within the framework defined by the BiH Presidency, unlike in the French example, there are no formal prerequisites for direct participation of the Presidency in the work of the Council of Ministers. This is best illustrated by the fact that members of the Presidency never preside or directly participate in the sessions of the Council of Ministers (whereas it is common in the French environment for the president to preside over government sessions, while the prime minister is only *primus inter pares*). At the same time, in the Republika Srpska, it is possible for the RS President to convene a session of the Government of the Republika Srpska, and to include in the agenda matters under the government's competence.[6]

Kuzmanović, Rajko, (Banja Luka: Akademija nauka i umjetnosti Republike Srpske, 2000), 28 and further; Also see: Savić, Snežana, *Republika Srpska poslije Dejtona* (Banja Luka: Pravni fakultet Univerziteta u Banjoj Luci, 1999), 21–32. Namely, these authors base their views on the following argumentation line: (1) the way in which BiH came into being, which was an international treaty, as confederations are usually created; (2) parity representation of entities in the institutions of Bosnia and Herzegovina; (3) decisions made by consensus in the institutions of Bosnia and Herzegovina; (4) the competences assigned to BiH according to the Constitution are significantly below the level that would be expected in a federal state system.

5 Porteli, Hugues and Ehrhard, Thomas, *Droit constitutionnel* (Paris: DALLOZ, 2021), 233.

6 Constitution of the Republika Srpska, Art. 82.

2 Executive Power and the Question of Competence in Bosnia and Herzegovina

As stated above, the problem of theoretical understanding of the executive power in Bosnia and Herzegovina is manifold, and the initial impulse comes from the still complicated system of competences, both the one entrusted to the joint federal level and those competences assigned to the entities by the constitution. Using a system of positive enumeration, the constitution-maker pursued simplicity, designating departments that should be handled by ministries and administrative bodies at the level of Bosnia and Herzegovina, and leaving all other matters to governments (i.e., ministries) and the administrative apparatus of the Republika Srpska and the Federation of BiH. The constitution did not remain silent on the possibility of transferring competences, when there is a consensus between the entities to which such competences initially belong. However, theory rightly raised the question of whether competences from the level of Bosnia and Herzegovina can be transferred to entity executive authorities, while at the same time the previously transferred competences from the level of Bosnia and Herzegovina can be returned to the entities, where the manner of their returning depends on the very competences.[7] With regard to the original competences of BiH, only a change of the Constitution of BiH would enable the transfer of competences to the entities, while in the case of constitutionally transferred competences (e.g., indirect taxation and the army) the procedure is carried out by the Parliamentary Assembly of BiH, which must pass laws repealing laws on the transfer of competences (e.g. the Law on Defence of BiH and the Law on Service in the Armed Forces of BiH); if the entities' legislative bodies were to aspire to the armed forces in this situation, they would have to amend their constitutions along with the adoption of the relevant legal framework. With respect to unconstitutionally transferred competences (through decisions of the high representatives for BiH or decisions of the Constitutional Court of BiH), any return of competences could happen in two ways – by corresponding decisions of the Constitutional Court, establishing a violation of the principle of constitutionality (by cassation decisions on the unconstitutionality of laws) or by new laws of the Parliamentary Assembly of BiH that would have a repealing effect for such laws which transferred the competences. In literal adherence to

---

7 See more: Dmičić, Mile, "Podjela nadležnosti između institucija BiH i entiteta" in *Zbornik radova "Pravo, tradicija i promjene"* (Istočno Sarajevo: Pravni fakultet Univerziteta u Istočnom Sarajevu, 2020), 86–116.

the federal principle of the organisation of government, we do not see a problem here, if there was political readiness by both entities to reach an agreement regarding the tasks or competences that should eventually be realised at the BiH level. The competence discussion constitutes a preliminary constitutional matter in the constellation of relations between bodies that exercise executive power, therefore, we present here a set of considerations to facilitate the understanding of challenges to the organisation of the executive in BiH. The basic competences of Bosnia and Herzegovina[8] listed in Article III/1a, could be divided into four basic categories: (1) foreign affairs: foreign policy, foreign trade policy, international assistance in criminal matters, including relations with Interpol; (2) cash flows and customs: customs policy, monetary policy, financing of the institutions and for the international obligations of Bosnia and Herzegovina; (3) communications: regulation of inter-entity transportation, air traffic control, facilitation of common and international communications; (4) movement of people: refugee and migration policy and asylum. Some authors see this distribution of competences not as exclusive, since such a type of competences is abandoned in complex states; the conclusion here emerges by itself – the entities have a dimension of competence in these affairs as well.[9] An example is the possibility for entities to establish special and parallel relations with neighbouring countries, and to conclude agreements with countries and international organisations, with the consent of the BiH Parliamentary Assembly.[10] This kind of agreement exists between the Republic of Serbia and the Republic of Srpska from 2007. In contemporary federations, the still fluid academic concept of "power sharing" is gaining importance – the sharing or division of power between different levels exercising state power (in the Bosnia and Herzegovina example, these would be the BiH level, the entity level and the cantonal level, but also the Brčko District level). This form is especially important in multinational federations with constitutional asymmetry, because it forces, in a way, the different levels of government to be interested in fields of common interest and to participate in mutual communication in achieving the set goals (e.g., harmonisation of BiH

8 The General Framework Agreement for Peace in Bosnia and Herzegovina, Annex IV – Constitution of Bosnia and Herzegovina, Art. 3 (1).

9 Mijanović, Gašo, "Sistem zaštite ustavnosti i zakonitosti u Republici Srpskoj," in: *Izgradnja i funkcionisanje pravnog sistema Republike Srpske* (Banja Luka: Pravni fakultet, 1997), 32–33.

10 The General Framework Agreement for Peace in Bosnia and Herzegovina, Annex IV – Constitution of Bosnia and Herzegovina, Art. III.2.a and d.

law with EU standards during the accession negotiations[11]).[12] Furthermore, the Constitution linguistically defines the competences of BiH as "policies"[13] in certain areas, which led some authors to draw the conclusion that the intention of the constitution-maker was not to comprehensively regulate and secure relations, but to leave room for the bodies of the entities' executive power to participate in the implementation of those competences.[14] The best example is the implementation of foreign and monetary policy. Namely, foreign policy is dictated by the BiH Presidency with the participation of ambassadors and other diplomatic and consular representatives elected on the basis of equal representation of the constituent peoples from the two entities, with a possibility for both entities to conclude international agreements with other states (sic!) and international organisations (either with prior consent of the Parliamentary Assembly or in accordance with a special law that allows the conclusion of contracts without such consent). Monetary policy is implemented through the Central Bank of BiH, managed by the Governing Board, whose five members are appointed from the Republika Srpska and the Federation of BiH, ensuring representation of all constituent peoples – thus, the entities directly participate in the constitution of the Central Bank's governing body, which appoints the governor and vice-governors of the bank.[15]

In addition to the competences of the institutions of BiH and the competences of the entities, there is the question of the so-called joint or parallel competences. Answers should be sought not only in the Constitution of BiH, but also in other annexes to the Dayton Agreement, which reveal, when carefully read, that BiH and the entities jointly ensure the realisation of human rights and freedoms (Article II of the Constitution of BiH), the electoral system (there are electoral laws at the joint and entity level), tax policy (indirect

11 See: Woelk, Jens in this volume (Chapter 15) on what are the expected constitutional reforms or which ones may seem possible.

12 Vanjek, Dejan and Forić, Samir, "Dijeljenje moći/podjela moći," in: *Građani, ustav, Europa, Rječnik osnovnih ustavnih pojmova u BiH* (Sarajevo: Pravni fakultet Univerziteta u Sarajevu, 2023), 158.

13 In the signed and finalised version of the Dayton Agreement, the term "responsibilities" is used in the part pertaining to competences. Although this term is often translated as "nadležnost" in the local language in the meaning of competence, there are other words in the English language, such as "jurisdiction" or "competence" that provide a more direct and closer meaning. Article III 2 a) perhaps offers a guideline in this regard, as it describes "responsibility" as "functions and powers".

14 Dmičić, Mile, *Ustavno pravo, dopuna osnovnoj literaturi* (Banja Luka: Pravni fakultet Univerziteta Banja Luka, 2011), 155.

15 Law on the Central Bank of Bosnia and Herzegovina (Official Gazette of, 1/1997, 29/2002, 8/2003, 13/2003, 14/2003 – corr. 9/2005, 76/2006, 32/2007), Art. 8.

taxes at the BiH level and direct taxes at the entity level), regulations on privatisation, foreign direct investment policy, etc. One can find also other types of joint competences, and illustrative examples to this end are framework laws at the level of BiH, regulating fundamental principles that are further specified and more closely regulated in entity level laws. Finally, in light of comparative law, it should be emphasised that this type of distribution of competences in federal states is not unusual – we can find it in the texts of German, Swiss, Russian, Brazilian, and Argentine constitutions.[16] The above competences are implemented by the BiH Presidency and the Council of Ministers, but also by the executive authorities at the level of the entities, District, cantons, and local self-government units; therefore, we now turn to these matters.

3 Presidency of BiH

The Presidency is the collective head of state. It emerged as the only possible solution in extremely heterogeneous and divided, post-war Bosnia and Herzegovina. The Presidency consists of three members: a Serb, a Croat, and a Bosniak. This structure reflects the essence of a tri-nation state (in the context of the constituent peoples), because only a Serb from the Republika Srpska, and a Bosniak and a Croat from the Federation of BiH can be elected as members. The intention of the constitution-maker is clear – each of the constituent peoples elects their own member to this collegial body. The members of the Presidency are elected directly by the citizens – the member from the Republika Srpska is elected by the citizens in the Republika Srpska, and two members from the Federation, one Croat and one Bosniak, are elected directly by the citizens in the Federation of BiH. The members of the Presidency are elected for a term of 4 years, with one possible re-election. There is an acute issue in the BiH society regarding the method and procedure of electing members of the Presidency. The challenges are internal and international in nature. Namely, a voter registered in the Central Voters Register from the territory of the Federation of BiH can vote for a Bosniak or a Croat, but not for both. Bosniak or Croat candidate who receives the highest number of votes among candidates from the same constituent people is elected. There is no mechanism to ensure that, for example, voters who identify as Bosniaks exclusively vote for Bosniak candidates – a voter can vote for one of the candidates from the Croat or Bosniak list, regardless of their own ethnic affiliation. This created

16 Marković, Goran, *Ustavni lavirint, Aporije ustavnog sistema Bosne i Hercegovine* (Beograd: Službeni glasnik, 2021), 465.

the current crisis surrounding the electoral legislation and the objections of illegitimate representatives of certain constituent peoples. The key question that needs to be answered is who the members of the Presidency represent, because if the members of one constituent people vote for the candidate of another constituent people, this calls into question the legitimacy of the elected Presidency member. This happened in 2006, 2010, 2018, and 2022 elections, when a Croat member of the Presidency was elected by votes of the Bosniak electorate.[17] It is an intriguing question of what kind of legitimacy does a member of the Presidency have when elected from among one people but thanks to the votes of another constituent people. Namely, the secrecy of voting and the absence of a constitutional norm stipulating that a member of the Presidency from a constituent people is elected only by members of that constituent people raises a dilemma – how can someone, in this case, represent the interests of the Croatian people when they owe their electoral legitimacy to the Bosniak electorate. At the same time, we know that the Presidency rests on the principle of consociational democracy and that the view according to which Presidency members represent all citizens cannot be accepted (they do represent them, but as a community of constituent peoples reflected in the three-member Presidency). In the future, and as *de lege ferenda*, we can advise changing the Election Law of BiH in the way to preserve the constitutional rights of Croats to elect their member of the Presidency, in order to find a proper module of how that constitutional right can be implemented.

The aforementioned international aspect further complicates the situation with the judgments of the Strasbourg-based European Court of Human Rights, which contested in its many judgments the impossibility of a citizen of Bosnia and Herzegovina who does not identify with any of the three constituent peoples to be elected as a member of the Presidency.[18] Raising this issue, as of the famous *Sejdić-Finci v. Bosnia and Herzegovina* case, would imply the amendment of the Constitution and the change of the Dayton structure,[19]

---

17 Vukoja, Ivan and Sitarski, Milan, "Ustavno-pravno-politološki algoritam reforme izbornog zakonodavstva BiH" in: *Mostariensia: časopis za društvene i humanističke znanosti*, Vol. 22 No. 1 (Mostar: Institut društvenih znanosti Ivo Pilar Sveučilište u Mostaru, 2018), 508–510.

18 For more on this topic, see: Krišto, Borjana and Čolak, Bariša, "Utjecaj odluka Europskog suda za ljudska prava na Ustav Bosne i Hercegovine," in: *Mostariensia: časopis za društvene i humanističke znanosti*, Vol. 22 No. 1, (Mostar: Institut društvenih znanosti Ivo Pilar Sveučilište u Mostaru, 2018), 241–248.

19 See: Marko, Joseph in this volume on a detail analysis about relationship between the Constitutional Court of BiH and the European Court of Human Rights.

which the European Union has recently been insisting on in the accession negotiations.[20] Building on this decision of the European Court of Human Rights, the decision of the Constitutional Court of BiH in the *Ljubić* case confirmed that the House of Peoples of the Parliament of the Federation is the house of the constituent peoples[21] and not of the federal units, abolishing the disputed provisions of the Election Law that were not in accordance with the Constitution of BiH.[22] Following the international intervention in 2022, only a part of the requests regarding the protection of the constitutionality of Croats in the Federation of BiH has been implemented, in contrast to increasingly loud political aspirations to abolish the House of Peoples of the Federation Parliament as discriminatory.[23] It seems almost impossible in nowadays BiH and its Dayton structure to implement the *Sejdić-Finci* verdict because it is not just incompatible with the Constitution and it would imply constitutional reform but it is contrary to the constitutional values on which BiH federalisms founded.

The powers of the Presidency are relatively broad within the overall competence of the institutions of BiH. The Constitution established the following: (1) Conducting the foreign policy of BiH, (2) Appointing ambassadors and other international representative of BiH, (3) Negotiating, denouncing, and, with the consent of the Parliamentary Assembly of BiH, ratifying treaties of BiH, (4) Executing decision of the Parliamentary Assembly of BiH, (5) Proposing, upon the recommendation of the Council of Ministers, an annual budget to the Parliamentary Assembly of BiH, (6) Reporting to the Parliamentary Assembly of BiH on expenditures of the Presidency, (7) Performing such other functions as may be necessary to carry out its duties. The problem with the competences set in this way by the constitution is their overly extensive formulation, which in practice can create many issues. Namely, it is unusual for a head of state, even a collective one, to conduct foreign policy completely independently or to submit a budget proposal of BiH to the Parliamentary Assembly for approval. It is reasonable to doubt the ability and capacity of the three-member Presidency to independently prepare a complex

20 See the European Commission Bosnia and Herzegovina Report 2023, adopted on 8 November 2023.

21 See: Balić, Lejla in this volume on the problem of parliamentary bicameralism.

22 U-23/14 of 1 December 2016.

23 On the use of Bonn Powers and the international intervention that solved the blockage of the executive and constitutional judicial authorities in the Federation, see: Sahadžić, Maja, "The Bonn Powers in Bosnia and Herzegovina: Between a rock and a hard place", *ConstitutionNet*, International IDEA, 29 November 2022, https://constitutionnet.org/news/bonn-powers-bosnia-and-herzegovina-between-rock-and-hard-place.

document such as the BiH budget, despite the fact that the draft is prepared by the competent ministry of the Council of Ministers. On the other hand, it is important to underline that not all the duties of the Presidency are prescribed by the constitutional provision. By transferring competences in the field of defence, the legislative framework granted certain powers over the Armed Forces of BiH (for example, in appointing the general corps). However, the provision of the Rules of Procedure of the BiH Presidency from Art. 1 stipulating that the Presidency is the highest collective body of the executive power is unconstitutional because the list of competences neither explicitly states this position of the Presidency nor can it be assumed considering its relationship to other institutions at the BiH level. Nevertheless, proof of importance of the Presidency's powers can be seen from the way it operates and makes decisions.

The method of the Presidency's work is determined by the Constitution and the Rules of Procedure. The members of the Presidency elect a chair from among themselves, who rotates at equal intervals, so that all three members serve as chair during a mandate. The Presidency adopts all decisions within its competence by consensus, with the proviso that in the event of a failed attempt to reach a unanimous decision, the decision can be made by two members. However, if one member of the Presidency opposes a decision adopted by the other two members, he/she can declare it destructive to vital national interest. Such a decision is immediately submitted to the parliament of the entity (the National Assembly of the Republika Srpska or the Parliament of the Federation of BiH) from which the member of the Presidency comes, for assessment of vital national interest. If the objection is upheld, the contested decision cannot enter into force.[24] This type of voting, with the principle of consensus and the right of veto of each member of the Presidency, is a deviation from the federal principle, because all decisions, except for those of minor importance (e.g. submission of the report on Presidency expenses), must be made by consensus, with the protection of the right of veto.[25] There is disagreement in theory as to whether this type of decision-making affects the form of state organisation in the sense of it leaning towards confederal elements, or whether this is just one of the deviations from the federal principle in BiH.

---

24 Rules of Procedure of the Presidency of Bosnia and Herzegovina (Official Gazette of BiH, 10/13, 32/13), Arts. 1–2.

25 Marković, Goran, *Bosanskohercegovački federalizam*, (Beograd, Sarajevo: Službeni glasnik, University Press. Izdanja Magistrat, 2012), 116–117.

4 Council of Ministers

The executive power at the BiH level is, in addition to the Presidency, exercised by the Council of Ministers. The method of election and appointment of the chair of the Council, the ministers and deputy ministers are defined by the Constitution. The Presidency of BiH appoints the chair, whereas the chair appoints ministers and deputy ministers. Ministers and their deputies take office only once they are confirmed by the House of Representatives of the Parliamentary Assembly. In political life, ministers are appointed by agreement of the parliamentary majority, with the confirmation of the entity vote in the House of Representatives. The Constitution provided for the existence of a Minister of Foreign Affairs and a Minister of Foreign Trade,[26] leaving the possibility of subsequent organisation of more ministries as needed. Interestingly, the Constitution does not recognise ministries as administrative bodies but only ministers as officials, and that leaves open space for legal contemplation if maybe the original Dayton makers did not think that the Council of Ministers need ministries but only ministers and that some special secretary of the Council of Ministers can provide backup for activities of those ministers. Today, nine ministries operate within the Council of Ministers; in addition to the aforementioned two, these are ministries of justice, security, defence, finance and treasury, communications and transport, human rights and refugees, and civil affairs.[27] Over time, by the transfer of competences from the entities to Bosnia and Herzegovina a nine-member Council of Ministers was established, with the chair as tenth member.

Historically, the first convocation had two chairs and one vice-chair, from the three constituent peoples, along with three ministers, each of whom had two deputies. While the number of deputy ministers could, according to the Constitution, be interpreted differently (a plural form not specified by the constitution – "deputies" could mean a deputy of each of the aforementioned three ministers or two deputies of all ministers), this number of co-chairs was *prima facie* unconstitutional, and reforms were launched. Until 2003, the chair also headed one of the ministries.[28] The powers of the chair of the Council of

26 The General Framework Agreement for Peace in Bosnia and Herzegovina, Annex IV – Constitution of BiH, Art. V 5.1.

27 Law on Ministries and Other Bodies of Administration of Bosnia and Herzegovina (Official Gazette of BiH, 5/2003, 42/2003, 26/2004, 42/2004, 45/2006, 88/2007, 35/2009, 59/2009, 103/2009, 87/2012, 6/2013, 19/2016, 83/2017), Art. 7.

28 Nešković, Radomir, *Nedovršena država, Politički sistem Bosne i Hercegovine* (Sarajevo: Fondacija Fridrih Ebert-Stiftung, 2013), 275–286.

Ministers are the following: (1) coordinating the work of the Council of Ministers; (2) harmonising the constitutional relations of the Council of Ministers with the work of the Presidency of BiH, the Parliamentary Assembly of BiH, as well as with the entities and Brčko District of BiH; (3) ensuring cooperation between the Council of Ministers and governments of the entities and lower levels; (4) convening sessions of the Council of Ministers; (5) chairing sessions of the Council of Ministers; (6) proposing agendas for sessions of the Council of Ministers; (7) implementing the decisions of the Council of Ministers, and (8) being responsible for the work of the Directorate for EU Integration.[29] For the sake of ensuring full conduct of its activities, the Council of Ministers can establish working bodies, of permanent or temporary nature; today, the following permanent working bodies operate in its composition: Directorate for European Integration of BiH, General Secretariat, Legislative Office, Internal Policy Committee, Economy Board, Civil Service Appeals Board, and the Office of the Coordinator of Brčko District of Bosnia and Herzegovina.

The constitutional nature of the Council of Ministers as a peculiar kind of government is interesting. Neither the Constitution of BiH nor the Law on the Council of Ministers explicitly states that this body represents the "government", and the problem is of a more complex, not purely linguistic nature. The Constitution of BiH provides that the Council of Ministers will implement the policy and decisions of Bosnia and Herzegovina, and the Law on the Council of Ministers stipulates that it is an executive body, which will exercise its rights and duties as "government functions". Thus, not as "government" but as government functions. What is determined implicitly by the constitutional text and explicitly by the Law is an indisputable fact – the Council of Ministers is the body of the executive. Namely, we know that the Constitution of BiH is of Anglo-American provenance, not only in terms of its place of origin and legislative drafting style, but also in terms of its content. The US Constitution does not recognise the government as an executive body; therefore, there is no prime minister, and all executive power is concentrated in the hands of the US president. Above listed are the competences of the Presidency of BiH, indicating that it has the competences of a classic executive body, such as conducting foreign policy, commanding the military, proposing the budget of BiH, representing BiH in international organisations and institutions, negotiating and signing international treaties, executing the decisions of the Parliamentary Assembly. The Constitution of BiH did not foresee these competencies for

---

29 Law on the Council of Ministers of Bosnia and Herzegovina (Official Gazette of BiH, 38/02, 30/03, 42/03, 81/06, 76/07, 81/07, 24/08), Art. 8.

the Council of Ministers, but quite consciously placed them under the competences of the Presidency.

Furthermore, it is noteworthy that the Council of Ministers, unlike other constitutional institutions (Presidency of BiH, Constitutional Court of BiH, Central Bank of BiH), does not have the designation "Bosnia and Herzegovina" (i.e., "BiH") in its official name; in addition, in terms of the legal drafting, the constitutional architecture of the BiH Constitution, does not stipulate a separate article pertaining to the Council of Ministers – it is encompassed by the article laying down the provisions on the Presidency of BiH. Given the above, some scholars concluded that it is not a separate government body of Bosnia and Herzegovina, but an auxiliary body of the Presidency,[30] and even those who do not see the Council of Ministers as an auxiliary body, accept that in such a constellation, there is a prominent supremacy of the Presidency as "the main body of the BiH executive".[31] Also, one of the arguments that stand out in support of this is that the Constitution of BiH did not foresee a president of the Council of Ministers, but a "chair", providing a linguistic corroboration for the claims.

No more than two-thirds of the members of the Council of Ministers are appointed from the Federation of BiH, while one-third comes from the Republika Srpska. The formulation "no more than" is important because it indicates the possibility of appointing less than two-thirds of the composition, although constitutional practice shows otherwise. In addition, the composition of the Council of Ministers reflects an ethnic key applied in the formation of constitutional bodies, given that three ministers are appointed each from among the Serb, Croat and Bosniak people, but it is visible also in the ministry structure, as civil servants must reflect the national structure according to the latest census in Bosnia and Herzegovina.[32] Differing views exist that rely on the decision of the Constitutional Court of BiH, designating the Council of Ministers as an expert, operational and executive body, and not an ethnic government that protects ethnic interests.[33] It is not out of place to note that this constitutional court decision never mentions the Council of Ministers as a "government", but exclusively as an executive body, which has never been disputed either in terms of its constitutional or its legal physiognomy. The

30 Kuzmanović, Rajko, *Ustavno pravo* (Banja Luka: Centar za publikacije Pravnog fakulteta, 2000), 385.

31 Steiner, Christian and Ademović, Nedim, *Ustav Bosne i Hercegovine*, (Sarajevo: Konrad Adenauer Stiftung, 2010), 599.

32 Law on Ministries and Other Bodies of Administration of BiH, Art. 3.

33 Decision of the Constitutional Court of Bosnia and Herzegovina U 12/12, para 31.

decision of the Constitutional Court is disputable in another aspect – its part referring to the ethnic principle in the appointment and work of ministers.[34] Namely, the arguments of the Constitutional Court moved along the line that the selection of members of the Council of Ministers begins and ends in the House of Representatives, not in the House of Peoples, which indirectly means that the constituency of the peoples is not the focus in the formation of this body. Furthermore, the decision reads that consensus in decision-making, characteristic of other highest bodies of state power (Presidency, Parliamentary Assembly), is not foreseen for the work of the Council of Ministers. Some authors note, critically viewing the cited constitutional court decision, that it failed to take into account that the work of the ministerial council must follow the rule stipulating that in certain cases determined by law, the vote of at least one minister from among the constituent peoples is required as necessary.[35] This is one of the illustrative examples of the constituency of the peoples principle in the constitutional system of BiH.

If at least three representatives of one of the constituent peoples take part in the Council of Ministers, one of the three suffices to satisfy the constitutionality requirement, although not a consensus, however, this can be justified by the fact that the Council of Ministers does not make the most important decisions, which fall under the competences of the Presidency and the Parliamentary Assembly, and by the fact that consensus being required for their decision-making would only constitute an obstacle to effective operation.[36] Furthermore, the non-participation of the House of Peoples in the election procedure is possibly a consequence of the constitution-makers desire to simplify the process of electing ministers for the purpose of contributing to faster and more productive operation of this body. The House of Peoples participates in perhaps the most important control mechanism for the Council of Ministers, which is the motion of no confidence. Finally, the constitutional

34 See: Sekulić, Tatjana in this volume.

35 Marković, Goran, *Ustavni lavirint, Aporije ustavnog sistema Bosne i Hercegovini*, 224.

36 The law differentiates between final decisions of the Council of Ministries, i.e., decisions made and executed exclusively by the Council of Ministers, and decisions the final adoption of which falls under the competence of another institution (e.g., the Presidency or the Parliamentary Assembly). The first group of decisions includes such decisions that must be made in consensus; where this is not possible, then by majority vote with at least one vote from each constituent people. The authentic interpretation goes further, although perhaps interpreting this legal situation somewhat too broadly – if a consensus cannot be reached, the decision will be considered rejected if the chair or his deputy voted against. For the second group of decisions, a simple majority of the members of the Council of Ministers present is sufficient.

court's assessment of the Council of Ministers as an expert body is incorrect, demonstrated by the simple fact that it can be composed (and the practice supports this) of political figures who do not have to be experts in the department for which they are proposed. Any kind of expertise had to first be mentioned in the constitution, and later elaborated by law; however, there is no trace of it either in the constitutional or the legal text. It could be useful that Council of ministers have experts as a ministers and not the political figures, that would be much more adequately to its constitutional role, as a "council" and as an "executive body".

The aforementioned legal obligation for the internal structure to reflect the ethnic composition of the most recent official census is, one should add, also an aggravating circumstance because there has been no agreement on a single population census in BiH for a long time, while in practice not a single ministry has complied with this legal obligation. With regard to the chair, there is a constitutional custom that foresees that he/she is selected each time from a different constituent people, although such a rotation system is not explicitly provided for in the text of the constitution. The maturing of such a constitutional convention speaks of the power of constituency that has penetrated all the pores of the BiH political system, even those that are not defined by a written (constitutional) legal norm. The competences of the Council of Ministers refer to implementing the policies of Bosnia and Herzegovina, particularly foreign policy, foreign trade policy, customs and monetary policy, financing of institutions and international obligations, enforcement of criminal laws on the international level, domestic and interstate communications, regulation of inter-entity transportation and air traffic control.[37] In addition, by order of the Presidency, certain coordination tasks between the entities are carried out if the entities agree thereon. The Council of Ministers also carries out other tasks if they arise and establish additional institutions if necessary and if the entities accept them. In performing its duties, the ministerial council enters into regular legal and factual relations with the administrative bodies at the level of Bosnia and Herzegovina. There is no room to claim that the Council of Ministers heads the administrative structure of joint institutions – this assertion stems from two arguments. The first – one of a constitutional nature – is that nowhere in the Constitution is the hierarchy of administrative organisations envisaged, which is a regular *materia constituens* in comparative law, nor are the institutions of Bosnia and Herzegovina directly connected with the

---

37 Krtalić, Ines, "Savjet/Vijeće ministara Bosne i Hercegovine" in: *Država, politika i društvo u Bosni i Hercegovini*, prir. Banović, Dragan i Gavrić, Saša (Sarajevo: IKD University Press Magistrat Izdanja, 2011), 289–291.

Council of Ministers in terms of a hierarchical relationship, even in the normative function (e.g., administrative organisations at the BiH level can pass bylaws independently, and in most cases the Council of Ministers does not interfere in these normative affairs). The second is that the mutual relationship between the Presidency of BiH and the Council of Ministers with the bodies of the BiH administration is legally established, indicating the subordination of bodies of administration to executive authorities; however, there is no indication of a pyramid of the BiH administration headed by the Council of Ministers. The mentioned executive authorities have the legal possibility to: (1) define instructions and guidelines for the implementation of laws and other regulations; (2) order that regulations be adopted or measures taken for which they are authorised and impose deadlines for the execution of certain tasks; (3) order the administrative bodies to examine the situation in certain areas within their competence and to submit a report with relevant proposals to the Presidency or the Council of Ministers.[38] Furthermore, the Council of Ministers (as well as the Presidency) have the authority to initiate a dismissal procedure in case of misconduct of the head or deputy head of an administrative body at the BiH level, but before doing that they must initiate a discussion on the operation and responsibility of the administrative body in a certain area. The reciprocal relationship of the administrative authorities to the executive authorities is that they can ask for guidance and instructions and, when needed, to inform, submit documentation, data or files if that is necessary for the work of the Presidency or the Council of Ministers. Interestingly, in cases where the administrative bodies request guidelines or instructions, the Presidency or the Council of Ministers must respond to such a request.

At this point, the acts adopted by the Council of Ministers are noteworthy. These include general and individual legal acts. The first group are classic general normative acts of administration: regulations, instructions, decisions, as well as drafts/proposals of laws, but also acts such as analyses, information, programmes, agreements, protocols, and others.[39] The most important document that the Council passes, intended to explain more closely the functioning of this collegial body of government, is the Rules of Procedure of the Council of Ministers. In addition to the above, they make decisions, conclusions, or other administrative acts in the first instance or, exceptionally the second instance administrative procedure, manifesting the administrative work of

38 Law on Administration (Official Gazette of BiH, 32/02, 102/09, 72/17), Art. 28.

39 Rules of Procedure of the Council of Ministers BiH (Official Gazette of BiH, 22/03), Art. 54.

this executive authority. Acts of the Council of Ministers, depending on whether they are general or individual, can be controlled by the Constitutional Court of Bosnia and Herzegovina in case of compliance of general acts with the constitutional norm, or the Court of Bosnia and Herzegovina on two grounds – the legality of general acts of the Council of Ministers in a procedure of unusual normative control (this competence of the Court of Bosnia and Herzegovina is the subject of a dispute with the Constitutional Court), in this case, carried out by an ordinary court, and in an administrative dispute in case of acts that have acquired finality.[40] The problem of abstract normative control, which should be carried out exclusively by the Constitutional Court of BiH for bylaws of both bodies – the Presidency of BiH and the Council of Ministers – was transferred inappropriately and unfoundedly to the Court of BiH. Referring to competences determined by the constitution,[41] the Constitutional Court of Bosnia and Herzegovina states that it is not competent to assess constitutionality or legality of general acts of the two bodies exercising executive power. In such a situation, the administrative department of the Court of BiH emerged as a necessary enforcer of this type of control, although such action would make sense for general normative acts of administrative bodies at the level of BiH, but not for the highest bodies envisaged by the constitution – such as the Presidency and the Council of Ministers.[42] Future reform processes *de constitutione ferenda* should envisage in the Rules of the Constitutional Court of Bosnia and Herzegovina this type of normative control that is only natural for the constitutional court, referring to the provision of the constitution stipulating that the Constitutional Court is not limited only to the cases in which it exercises control.

5 Conclusions

The relationship between the Presidency and the Council of Ministers rests on their constitutionally established links and positions. We mentioned above that the close connection between these two bodies has been demonstrated nomotechnically; in the daily functioning, it is reflected in the fact that the Council of Ministers can: (1) propose an item on the agenda of the Presidency; (2) prepare and recommend the draft budget of BiH institutions; (3) imple-

40 Krtalić, Ines, *Savjet/Vijeće ministara Bosne i Hercegovine*, 297–299.

41 Constitution of Bosnia and Herzegovina, Article VI 3.

42 Romić, Marko, *Neustavnost zakona i upravni akti* (Beograd: Institut za uporedno pravo, 2023), 23–24.

ment foreign policy, in cooperation and according to the guidelines of the BiH Presidency; (4) report to the Presidency on its decisions and other activities; (5) participate in sessions at the invitation of the Presidency; (6) at the invitation of the Standing Committee for Military Affairs, participate in the sessions of that body; (7) convene a session of the Council of Ministers at the request of the Presidency; (8) other tasks in accordance with the Constitution, laws and rules of procedure of the two bodies.[43] Given this overview of the mutual relationship, the pendulum seems to tilt slightly in favour of the BiH Presidency, which could reaffirm the thesis about the Council of Ministers being an auxiliary body of the Presidency, strongly deriving from the authority of the Presidency to convene a session of the Council of Ministers and the obligation of the Council of Ministers to regularly report to the Presidency on its activities. The intertwining and dependence of the two bodies is visible in the field of foreign policy, defence, and budget. Foreign policy falls under the competence of the Presidency but is inextricably linked to the Ministry of Foreign Affairs; in matters of defence, the Presidency can only decide on the use of the BiH Armed Forces, but operational command and other activities are carried out through the Ministry of Defence. Finally, the budget for BiH institutions is proposed to the Parliamentary Assembly by the Presidency, but the preparation of the budget is managed by the Ministry of Finance and Treasury.

The governing structure in the ministry follows the monocratic principle. Ministry is headed by a minister who manages the entire ministry and is assisted by the deputy and the secretary of the ministry.[44] Deputy ministers (each minister has one, except the minister of defence who has two deputies) are appointed in the same procedure as the ministers, and they cannot be members of the same people as the minister. As a rule, deputies should replace the minister when the minister is absent or prevented from performing his/her duties.[45] In the event that the minister is prevented *ex constitutione*, there is no mention of the deputy minister's role, but the law obliges the deputy to be present at the session only with the authorisation of the minister, and even then he/she is under the positive obligation to vote the way his/her minister would vote. The intention was to prevent possible abuse of the deputy's position (first by explicit authorisation and then by mandatory voting) – this is particularly reflected in the number of deputies in the defence department. With the transfer of competence from the Republika Srpska and the Federation of Bosnia and Herzegovina, under difficult political circumstances

43 Rules of Procedure of the Council of Ministers of BiH, Art. 82.

44 Law on Ministries and Other Bodies of Administration of BiH, Art. 3.

45 Law on the Council of Ministers of BiH, Article 7 (3).

and with protests from all parties, defence was included in the Council of Ministers. It is known that high representatives for BiH have on several occasions transferred competences from the entity level to the level of BiH by their decisions, most often abolishing institutions in the Republika Srpska and/or the Federation of BiH, while at the same time constituting bodies at the level of BiH. This manner of transferring competences was in gross violation of the constitutional mechanisms of competence transfer, but also in absence of elementary democratic legitimacy – all in violation of the mandate of the High Representative as defined in Annex x to the Dayton Agreement.[46] The changed circumstances dictated the organisational oddity of appointing two deputies of the minister, who must come from different constituent peoples. This, at least ostensibly, provided for managing a common military force to all peoples that previously had separate national military structures.

The work of the Council of Ministers can be influenced the most by the Parliamentary Assembly, which makes sense if we bear in mind that the chair and ministers are confirmed by members of the House of Representatives. In their work, they can ask parliamentary questions, depending on whether they are asked in the House of Representatives or the House of Peoples, and they can submit an interpellation or propose a motion of no confidence. Interpellation is stronger than parliamentary question, which mainly has a political character and cannot significantly affect the work of the Council of Ministers. It is submitted by at least eight deputies of the House of Representatives or three delegates of the House of Peoples, and it can have serious consequences for the work of the Council of Ministers, because interpellation must be discussed in the chambers, which consequently ends with the chamber's position on the interpellation. Such a position may consist of suggestions for the work of the Council of Ministers, proposed measures, or even establishing responsibility of the Council of Ministers.[47] The motion of no confidence is a serious instrument of control and influence of the Parliament over the Council of Ministers. In practice, two such initiatives have been submitted so far. They happened in 2017 and 2021;

---

46 Vlaški, Bojan and Romić, Marko, "Pravna priroda akata Visokog predstavnika – (u) pravna i(li) politička" in *Uporednopravni izazovi u savremenom pravu – in memoriam dr Stefan Andonović*, ed. Rajić Ćalić, Jovana, (Beograd: Institut za uporedno pravo i Pravni fakultet Univerziteta u Kragujevcu, 2023), 99–100.

47 Rules of Procedure of the House of Representatives of the Parliamentary Assembly of Bosnia and Herzegovina (Official Gazette of BiH, 79/14, 81/15, 97/15), Arts. 178–181; Rules of Procedure of the House of Peoples of the Parliamentary Assembly of Bosnia and Herzegovina (Official Gazette of BiH, 58/14, 88/15, 96/15, 53/16), Arts. 162–165.

the first initiative was submitted by the Union of Independent Social Democrats (SNSD) and the second by a group of political parties (Naša stranka, Independent Bloc and Social Democratic Party) – both unsuccessful, i.e., they did not end in vote of no confidence.[48] However, the Constitution of BiH does not stipulate the procedure or who submits a motion of no confidence in the Council of Ministers; some authors have rightly criticised that such an important procedure should not be left to the rules of procedure.[49] However, the consequence of such regulation would be to make the procedure of initiating a motion of no confidence too difficult or too easy, while its constitutional norming would make both of these extremes impossible. The procedure can be initiated by at least eight members of the House of Representatives, i.e., at least three delegates of the House of Peoples (regardless of the constituent peoples), while the BiH Presidency may propose the dismissal of the chair.[50] The procedure continues at the sessions of the chambers, where the motion is discussed and the decision is made by a majority, which is generally required for other decisions under the competence of parliamentary chambers. A doubt has rightly been raised as to why both chambers participate in the no confidence motion with respect to the Council of Ministers, while only the House of Representatives participates in the process of confirming the chair and the ministers. The lighter election procedure, compared to the dismissal of the Council of Ministers, may have been inspired by the constitution-maker's desire to strengthen the executive power – due to complex structure and difficult procedures in complex states, this reason seems more acceptable.

Finally, both bodies of the executive power in Bosnia and Herzegovina – the Presidency of Bosnia and Herzegovina and the Council of Ministers, together with the governments of the Republika Srpska, the Federation of Bosnia and Herzegovina and the Brčko District, close the construction of the executive of a complex state in which there would be no conflict of competences of the above-mentioned levels if the constitutional division of competences is respected, adhering at the same time to the principles of mutual cooperation, assistance and informing. However, these are challenges also faced by other federal states (even confederate ones), which Bosnia and Her-

48 https://srpskainfo.com/video-foto-sve-njihove-smjene-rekonstrukcija-savjeta-ministara-bih-je-rijetka-pojava-cak-i-kada-postoje-cvrsti-razlozi-za-to/.

49 Marković, Goran, *Ustavni lavirint, Aporije ustavnog sistema Bosne i Hercegovine*, 232.

50 Rules of Procedure of the House of Representatives of the Parliamentary Assembly of Bosnia and Herzegovina Art. 153; Rules of Procedure of the House of Peoples of the Parliamentary Assembly of Bosnia and Herzegovina, Art. 141.

zegovina is not deprived of either. The future, especially the European integration, brings with it demands and challenges in the functioning of the core political institutions of Bosnia and Herzegovina, that can be most succinctly expressed in the dilemma of whether the Dayton Constitution and the distribution of competences between the different levels of government will be followed literally or whether they will be overly broadly and unconstitutionally interpreted in the application of law, creating a completely new concept of executive power that was not foreseen by the original Dayton solutions.

Bibliography

Constitution of Bosnia and Herzegovina, Article VI 3.

Constitution of the Republika Srpska, Art. 82.

Decision of the Constitutional Court of Bosnia and Herzegovina U 12/12, para 31.

Dmičić, Mile, "Podjela nadležnosti između institucija BiH i entiteta" in Zbornik radova "Pravo, tradicija i promjene" (Istočno Sarajevo: Pravni fakultet Univerziteta u Istočnom Sarajevu, 2020), 86–116.

Dmičić, Mile, Ustavno pravo, dopuna osnovnoj literaturi (Banja Luka: Pravni fakultet Univerziteta Banja Luka, 2011), 155.

Đorđević, Jovan, Politički sistem – prilog nauci o čoveku i samoupravljanju (Beograd: Udruženje pravnika Jugoslavije, 1967), 602.

European Commission Bosnia and Herzegovina Report 2023, adopted on 8 November 2023.

Krišto, Borjana and Čolak, Bariša, "Utjecaj odluka Europskog suda za ljudska prava na Ustav Bosne i Hercegovine," in: Mostariensia: časopis za društvene i humanističke znanosti, Vol. 22 No. 1, (Mostar: Institut društvenih znanosti Ivo Pilar Sveučilište u Mostaru, 2018), 241–248.

Krtalić, Ines, "Savjet/Vijeće ministara Bosne i Hercegovine" in: Država, politika i društvo u Bosni i Hercegovini, prir. Dragan Banović i Saša Gavrić, (Sarajevo: IKD Universtiy Press Magistrat Izdanja, 2011), 289–291.

Krtalić, Ines, Savjet/Vijeće ministara Bosne i Hercegovine, 297–299.

Kuzmanović, Rajko, "Narušavanje podjele nadležnosti između entiteta i Bosne i Hercegovine," in Podjela nadležnosti između institucija Bosne i Hercegovine i entiteta, ed. Rajko Kuzmanović (Banja Luka: Akademija nauka i umjetnosti Republike Srpske, 2000).

Kuzmanović, Rajko, Ustavno pravo (Banja Luka: Centar za publikacije Pravnog fakulteta, 2000), 385.

Law on Administration (Official Gazette of BiH, 32/02, 102/09, 72/17), Art. 28.

Law on Ministries and Other Bodies of Administration of BiH, Art. 3.

Law on Ministries and Other Bodies of Administration of BiH, Art. 3.
Law on Ministries and Other Bodies of Administration of Bosnia and Herzegovina (Official Gazette of BiH, 5/2003, 42/2003, 26/2004, 42/2004, 45/2006, 88/2007, 35/2009, 59/2009, 103/2009, 87/2012, 6/2013, 19/2016, 83/2017), Art. 7.
Law on the Central Bank of Bosnia and Herzegovina (Official Gazette of, 1/1997, 29/2002, 8/2003, 13/2003, 14/2003 – corr. 9/2005, 76/2006, 32/2007), Art. 8.
Law on the Council of Ministers of BiH, Article 7 (3).
Law on the Council of Ministers of Bosnia and Herzegovina (Official Gazette of BiH, 38/02, 30/03, 42/03, 81/06, 76/07, 81/07, 24/08), Art. 8.
Marković, Goran, Bosanskohercegovački federalizam, (Beograd, Sarajevo: Službeni glasnik, University Press. Izdanja Magistrat, 2012), 116–117.
Marković, Goran, Ustavni lavirint, Aporije ustavnog sistema Bosne i Hercegovine (Beograd: Službeni glasnik, 2021), 465.
Marković, Goran, Ustavni lavirint, Aporije ustavnog sistema Bosne i Hercegovini, 224.
Marković, Goran, Ustavni lavirint, Aporije ustavnog sistema Bosne i Hercegovine, 232.
Marković, Ratko, Izvršna vlast (Beograd: Savremena administracija, 1980), 115.
Mijanović, Gašo, "Sistem zaštite ustavnosti i zakonitosti u Republici Srpskoj," in: Izgradnja i funkcionisanje pravnog sistema Republike Srpske (Banja Luka: Pravni fakultet, 1997), 32–33.
Nešković, Radomir, Nedovršena država, Politički sistem Bosne i Hercegovine (Sarajevo: Fondacija Fridrih Ebert-Stiftung, 2013), 275–286.
Porteli, Hugues, Ehrhard, Thomas, Droit constitutionnel (Paris: DALLOZ, 2021), 233.
Romić, Marko, Neustavnost zakona i upravni akti (Beograd: Institut za uporedno pravo, 2023), 23–24.
Rules of Procedure of the Council of Ministers BiH (Official Gazette of BiH, 22/03), Art. 54.
Rules of Procedure of the Council of Ministers of BiH, Art. 82.
Rules of Procedure of the House of Peoples of the Parliamentary Assembly of Bosnia and Herzegovina (Official Gazette of BiH, 58/14, 88/15, 96/15, 53/16), Arts. 162–165.
Rules of Procedure of the House of Peoples of the Parliamentary Assembly of Bosnia and Herzegovina, Art. 141.
Rules of Procedure of the House of Representatives of the Parliamentary Assembly of Bosnia and Herzegovina (Official Gazette of BiH, 79/14, 81/15, 97/15), Arts. 178–181.
Rules of Procedure of the House of Representatives of the Parliamentary Assembly of Bosnia and Herzegovina Art. 153.
Rules of Procedure of the Presidency of Bosnia and Herzegovina (Official Gazette of BiH, 10/13, 32/13), Arts. 1–2.
Sahadžić, Maja, "The Bonn Powers in Bosnia and Herzegovina: Between a rock and a hard place", ConstitutionNet, International IDEA, 29 November 2022, https://con

stitutionnet.org/news/bonn-powers-bosnia-and-herzegovina-between-rock-and-hard-place.

Savić, Snežana, Republika Srpska poslije Dejtona (Banja Luka: Pravni fakultet Univerziteta u Banjoj Luci, 1999), 21–32.

Steiner, Christian and Ademović, Nedim, Ustav Bosne i Hercegovine, (Sarajevo: Konrad Adenauer Stiftung, 2010), 599.

The General Framework Agreement for Peace in Bosnia and Herzegovina, Annex IV – Constitution of Bosnia and Herzegovina, Art. 3 (1).The General Framework Agreement for Peace in Bosnia and Herzegovina, Annex IV – Constitution of Bosnia and Herzegovina, Art. III.2.a and d.

The General Framework Agreement for Peace in Bosnia and Herzegovina, Annex IV – Constitution of BiH, Art. V 5.1.

Vanjek, Dejan and Forić, Samir, "Dijeljenje moći/podjela moći," in: Građani, ustav, Europa, Rječnik osnovnih ustavnih pojmova u BiH (Sarajevo: Pravni fakultet Univerziteta u Sarajevu, 2023), 158.

Vlaški, Bojan and Romić, Marko, "Pravna priroda akata Visokog predstavnika – (u)pravna i(li) politička" in Uporednopravni izazovi u savremenom pravu – in memoriam dr Stefan Andonović, ed. Jovana Rajić Ćalić, (Beograd: Institut za uporedno pravo i Pravni fakultet Univerziteta u Kragujevcu, 2023), 99–100.

Vukoja, Ivan and Sitarski, Milan, "Ustavno-pravno-politološki algoritam reforme izbornog zakonodavstva BiH" in: Mostariensia: časopis za društvene i humanističke znanosti, Vol. 22 No. 1 (Mostar: Institut društvenih znanosti Ivo Pilar Sveučilište u Mostaru, 2018), 508–510.

Vukoja, Ivan and Sitarski, Milan, "Ustavno-pravno-politološki algoritam reforme izbornog zakonodavstva BiH" in: Mostariensia: časopis za društvene i humanističke znanosti, Vol. 22 No. 1 (Mostar: Institut društvenih znanosti Ivo Pilar Sveučilište u Mostaru, 2018), 508–510.

CHAPTER 10

Rule of Law, the Judiciary, and Necessary Constitutional Reforms

Jens Woelk

1 "One Country, Four Systems?": The Decentralised Organisation of the Judicial Sector

The separation of powers into three branches – legislative, executive, and judicial – is the institutional precondition for the Rule of Law which requires independent institutions for deciding controversies based on pre-established rules, in both substance and procedures. This is the function of the judiciary.

This chapter explores the difficulties with judicial reforms in Bosnia and Herzegovina. Though framed as essential for EU accession, reform efforts have consistently failed to bring substantial change due to elite resistance and the ambiguous impact of international support. The chapter argues that EU conditionality in the judiciary, while normatively strong, remains constitutionally far-reaching and thus politically sensitive. After an overview of the judicial system and the EU's conditionality requirements, the analysis focuses on three unresolved and constitutionally significant areas with regard to EU-conditionality: (1) the independence and self-governance of the judiciary; (2) the role of international judges at the Constitutional Court and the enforcement of its decisions; and (3) the necessity to guarantee legal certainty through consistent judicial interpretation across the country.

In Bosnia and Herzegovina, the judiciary consists of four judicial systems that reflect the complex administrative-territorial organisation of the country: there are distinct systems at the state level, in the two Entities, the Republika Srpska (RS) and the Federation of BiH (FBiH), as well as in the Brčko District (BD). As the text of the Dayton Constitution does not provide for any judicial institution at the state level (except for the Constitutional Court of BiH), the competences for the organisation and operation remain with the Entities. Some institutions and their functions are regulated in the Entity constitutions.

The judiciary of the RS consists of the Supreme Court and courts of general and specialised jurisdiction, the Constitutional Court of RS, the Republic and District Public Prosecutor's Offices, the Attorney General's Office of RS, the Bar Association, the Notary Chamber and the Ministry of Justice of RS. In the RS, 6

 | DOI:10.1163/9789004707887_011

specialised commercial courts (and the Higher Commercial Court) also exist, in addition to 28 basic courts (first instance jurisdiction in civil and criminal matters) and 7 district courts (first instance in specific matters as well as appeal jurisdiction).[1] The Supreme Court of RS has the task of ensuring the uniform application of the law (Article 123 of the Constitution of RS). The organisation of the Public Prosecutor's Office, established by the Constitution of RS, consists of the hierarchically superior Republic Public Prosecutor's Office and six district public prosecutor's offices.[2] The jurisdiction, composition, and legal nature of decisions of the Constitutional Court of RS are regulated in Article 69 of the Constitution of RS.[3]

The FBiH's judicial system consists of 34 municipal courts, 10 cantonal courts, and the Supreme Court of FBiH as the highest appellate court of FBiH,[4] as well as of Federal and Cantonal Prosecutor's Offices. The Federal Prosecutor's Office supervises the work of the cantonal offices ensuring legality and efficiency in proceedings. There is also the Constitutional Court of FBiH, the Federal General Attorney's Office, the Bar Association, the Notary Chamber, and the Federal Ministry of Justice. The Constitutional Court of FBiH is listed among the courts in the FBiH Constitution, which also regulates its composition, jurisdiction, procedure, and the legal nature of its decisions. Its main function is to resolve disputes between different levels of government and institutions or within the institutions of the federal government (FBiH Constitution, IV. C. 3. Article 10).[5]

The judiciary of the BD consists of the basic court with universal jurisdiction, and the appellate court as an appeal court (the latter also functions as an equivalent to a constitutional court).[6] The Prosecutor's Office of the BD is defined as an autonomous and independent body that undertakes measures and actions in the detection and prosecution of perpetrators of criminal offences and economic offences and performs other tasks specified by law.[7]

---

1 The organisation and jurisdiction of courts is regulated by the Law on Courts of the RS (Official Gazette of the RS, no. 37/12, 14/14, 44/15, 39/16, and 100/17).

2 The Law on Public Prosecutor's Offices of RS (Official Gazette of the RS, no. 69/16).

3 Further aspects are regulated by the Law on the Constitutional Court of the RS (Official Gazette of the RS, no. 104/11 and 92/12) and the Rules of Procedure (Official Gazette of the RS, no. 104/11 and 92/12).

4 Law on Courts of the FBiH (Official Gazette of the FBiH, no. 8/05, 22/06, 63/10, 72/10, 7/13, 52/14, and 85/21).

5 See in addition: The Law on Procedure before the FBiH Constitutional Court (Official Gazette of the FBiH, no. 6/95 and 37/03) and the Rules of Procedure of the Constitutional Court of the FBiH Court (Official Gazette of the FBiH, no. 40/10 and 18/16).

6 See: The Law on Courts of the BD (Official Gazette of the BD, no. 18/20).

7 Statute of the BD (Official Gazette of the BDV, no. 2/10) and Law on the Prosecutor's Office of the BD, (Official Gazette of the BD, no. 19/07).

Regarding the judiciary at the state level, the Dayton Constitution only foresees the Constitutional Court of BiH. Article VI of the Constitution of BiH regulates its composition and the election of judges, the decision-making procedure, the competence to adopt the Rules of the Court, the competences of the Constitutional Court, and the legal nature of its decisions. Interestingly, the Constitution does not provide for the adoption of a law on the Constitutional Court, as this would allow the legislator at the state level to regulate its functioning in detail. Even such limited power for the state level was to be avoided. Thus, the Constitutional Court adopts its own Rules of Procedure (Article VI/2 b) of the Constitution of BiH) which strengthens its independence vis-à-vis politics.[8] Within the judiciary of BiH, the Constitutional Court of BiH has appellate jurisdiction over issues under the BiH Constitution arising out of a judgment of any other court in BiH, which means that the final judgment of all courts may be reviewed in case of an alleged violation of any provision of the Constitution of BiH (human rights, as well as Rule of Law guarantees). The non-existence of a Supreme Court at the state level seems to make it necessary for the Constitutional Court of BiH, sometimes, to expand its jurisdiction regarding decisions of regular courts and their application of substantive law.[9] The need to establish a Supreme Court of BiH was underlined by the Constitutional Court of BiH, as harmonisation of all courts in BiH with regard to the case-law in war crimes requires coordination and a final say.[10]

2 Internationally Induced Reforms Create Further Judicial Institutions at the State Level

Two judicial institutions at the state level were established in 2000 and 2003 as part of the judicial reform-package carried out by the international community from 2000 to 2004: the Court of BiH and the Prosecutor's Office of BiH.[11]

8 The work of the Constitutional Court is regulated by Amendment No. I to the Constitution of BiH (Official Gazette of BiH, no. 25/09) and the Rules of the Constitutional Court (text available in the Official Gazette of BiH, no. 94/14).

9 For instance, in case no. AP-775/08, in which the Constitutional Court decided on the way the courts interpreted and applied the laws. Otherwise, in appeals procedures, the Constitutional Court would be forced to apply unconstitutional laws which violate human rights, in Steiner/Ademović, 744–748, with references to case-law.

10 Decision on admissibility and merits in case no. AP-1785/06 (para. 90).

11 Both institutions were established by Decisions of the High Representative, in 2000 and 2003, respectively.

The Court of BiH is an ordinary specialised court with narrowly defined criminal, administrative, and appellate jurisdictions and three corresponding divisions. While it is not superior to the entity courts, in cases of war crimes, the latter need to respect and follow its case law according to the Constitutional Court of BiH, in order to guarantee the principle of legal certainty and the Rule of Law.[12] There is also an Appellate Division, which is further structured in three sections and decides on legal remedies, as well as a Joint Secretariat and Registry Office. The Prosecutor's Office of BiH has two special divisions for war crimes and for organised crime and corruption. As is with the Court of BiH, the Prosecutor's Office of BiH is not superior to the entity prosecutors' offices and therefore cannot control the legality of their work or issue binding instructions. As the Court of BiH is not foreseen in the original text of the Dayton Constitution, its legitimacy was challenged. However, the Constitutional Court of BiH confirmed the constitutionality of its establishment (case no. 26/01) and of its jurisdiction (case no. 16/08).

The four judicial systems operate with considerable autonomy in their respective territories, and essentially without hierarchical relations between them.[13] Since 2004, they are coordinated and governed by a state institution, the High Judicial and Prosecutorial Council (HJPC/Council), which was also established as part of the judicial reform carried out by the international community from 2000 to 2004.[14] The Law on the HJPC of BiH is the result of the Agreement on the transfer of certain competencies of the Entities to the state level,[15] by which the Entities (FBiH and RS) gave their consent to establish HJPC BiH as a state institution.[16]

Following the "Council of Europe-model" for institutional guarantees of judicial independence,[17] the High Judicial and Prosecutorial Council has been created as the central body of "judicial self-management" in the country.

---

12 Decision on admissibility and merits in case no. AP-1785/06, para. 89.

13 Apart from the general supremacy clause, Article III.3. b) Constitution of BiH. The powers of the Court of BiH and the Prosecutor's Office of BiH are mainly founded on specific functions and/or subject matters.

14 The HJPC (*Visoko sudsko i tužilačko vijeće* – VSTV) was established in 2004, by a law adopted by the Parliamentary Assembly of BiH (Law on the HJPC of BiH, Official Gazette of BiH, no. 25/04).

15 Agreement on the establishment of the HJPC of BiH (Official Gazette of the FBiH, no. 16/04).

16 These Agreements on the transfer of entity competences are expressly foreseen by Article III 5.b) of the Constitution of BiH.

17 See, for instance: Bobek, Michal and Kosar, David, Global Solutions, Local Damages: A Critical Study in *Judicial Councils in Central and Eastern Europe* (November 7, 2013). In 15 (7) German Law Journal 171 (2014), Available at: (https://ssrn.com/abstract=2351299).

The HJPC's competences comprise the appointment of judges, prosecutors and legal associates, disciplinary responsibility, judicial administration and statistics, budgets of judicial institutions, supervision over professional development of officeholders, the introduction and maintenance of ICT systems, as well as taking a leading role in the implementation and coordination of reform activities in the BiH justice sector. The HJPC is also a state-level regulatory body establishing the standards of ethics and professional conduct for the entire judicial community of the country. The Council is composed of representatives of the BiH legal community (judges, prosecutors and lawyers), and the executive and legislature (Article 4 HJPC Law). The same article also provides that the ethnic and gender composition of the Council shall reflect the structure of the population according to the 1991 census, so that the Council so formed shall be composed of six Bosniaks, five Serbs, three Croats, and one member from the rank of Others.[18]

3 The European Union's Conditionality in the Judicial Sector

Judicial reforms are an essential element of democratic transformation. They shall entrench the principle of the Rule of Law in the reality of the states in the Western Balkans and thus contribute to the process of preparing them for EU membership. Rule of Law is the fundamental systemic principle on which the Union itself is based: 'integration through law'. In fact, after this had been clarified by the European Court of Justice, it is now generally recognised as a general principle of EU law, in the rank of primary law.[19]

For judicial reforms, in (potential) candidate countries, the starting points are the key requirements for EU membership, laid down in the so-called Copenhagen criteria.[20] These criteria for accession require that a state's institutions are fit to guarantee democratic governance and protect human rights, that it has a functioning market economy, and accepts the obligations and aims of the European Union. They include the capacity to effectively implement all rules, standards and policies which make up the body of EU law (the

18 See the institutional website of the HJPC/VSTV (https://vstv.pravosudje.ba/vstvfo/E/141).

19 Von Bogdandy, Armin, 1. Founding Principles, in *Principles of European Constitutional Law*, Von Bogdandy, Armin and Bast, Jürgen eds., (Hart/C.H. Beck/Nomos, 2009), 11–53.

20 The Treaty on European Union sets out the values (Article 2), conditions (Article 49), and principles (Article 6.1) to which any country wishing to become a member of the European Union (EU) must conform. The accession criteria were established by the Copenhagen European Council in 1993 and strengthened by the Madrid European Council in 1995.

'acquis'). Thus, all countries that want to join the EU must respect the fundamental rights and obligations enshrined in the European Convention on Human Rights (ECHR), and the Charter of Fundamental Rights of the European Union. The guarantee of a reasonable duration of trials (Art. 6 ECHR) is particularly important for judicial reforms.

In the EU, over the years, a consensus has developed on the core (legal) meaning of the Rule of Law. According to the European Commission, this concept entails compliance with six constitutional principles:[21] (1) legality; (2) legal certainty; (3) prohibition of arbitrariness of the executive powers; (4) independent and impartial courts; (5) effective judicial review, including respect for fundamental rights; and (6) equality before the law. It is accepted that the precise content of these principles and of standards related to the Rule of Law 'may vary at national level, depending on each Member State's constitutional system'.[22] However, the above six principles are part of the constitutional traditions common to most European legal systems and thus define the core content of the Rule of Law within the context of the EU legal order. The Rule of Law must be understood as a 'constitutional principle with both formal and substantive components', which 'is intrinsically linked to respect for democracy and for fundamental rights.'[23]

For giving concrete meaning to these principles and abstract criteria in the accession process, the European Commission determines the degree of preparedness of each country based on a feasibility study.[24] This overall assessment becomes the frame within which the European Commission assists the country in drawing up strategies for the necessary reforms in the judiciary. Those strategies become concrete through specific action plans for different sectors which are realised in projects. Implementation and progress are monitored and evaluated. This 'dialogue' between the European Commission and national authorities usually starts well before the formal opening of accession negotiations, i.e., based on the Stabilisation and Association Agreements (SAAs).[25] Once the negotiations are opened, two of the 35 thematic negotiating chapters are specifically devoted to the topics of the Rule of Law

---

21 Pech, Laurent, "The Rule of Law as a Well-Established and Well-Defined Principle of EU Law", *Hague J Rule Law* 14, (2022), 107–138.

22 European Commission, "A new EU Framework to strengthen the Rule of Law", COM (2014), 158 final/2, 4.

23 Ibid., 4.

24 In the case of BiH, the Opinion on Bosnia and Herzegovina's application for EU membership of May 29, 2019.

25 Phinnemore, David, "The Stabilisation and Association Process. A Framework for European Union Enlargement?" in *European Integration and Transformation in the Western Balkans*, Arolda Elbasani ed., (London: Routledge 2013).

and justice;[26] however, these two key chapters are also being considered from the outset regarding states that have not started negotiations, i.e., BiH, which is a candidate only since December 2022. The Rule of Law is also one of the nine priority areas of the Instrument for Pre-Accession Assistance (IPA II, i.e., the EU's financial programme to support the pre-accession process), supported by a specific budget allocation for each country.[27]

The justice systems in all Western Balkan countries face serious challenges due to deep-rooted corruption and organised crime, which are often closely intertwined with the political elites. This connection stems from the wars in the 1990s, where nationalist leaders and armed groups gained influence, embedding themselves in political structures. In countries like Bosnia and Herzegovina and Kosovo, the complexity is heightened by ethnic divisions, with ethno-nationalist parties maintaining control over resources and institutions through patronage systems.[28] These groups, while seemingly at odds, often collaborate to maintain power, further complicating efforts to address these issues. The pervasiveness of political elites and organised crime in seeking to intimidate and influence the justice system, including through the media, is widespread and a source of great concern.[29]

Therefore, in the past and today, reforms and technical and financial assistance concentrate on the strengthening of judicial independence, as well as on the fight against corruption (at all levels).[30] Despite years of reforms and significant investments aimed at enhancing judicial independence and tackling corruption, progress has been moderate. Reports from the European Commission and others highlight ongoing problems,[31] including in Bosnia, where in

---

26 Chapter 23, Judiciary and Fundamental Rights, and Chapter 24, Justice, Freedom and Security.

27 In the period 2014–2020, around EUR 0.7 billion was allocated to the Western Balkans for the Rule of Law and fundamental rights, representing around 16% of all EU bilateral assistance to these countries, European Court of Auditors, EU support for the Rule of Law in the Western Balkans. Special Report EN 2022 (ECA Report 2022).

28 Grewe, Constance and Riegner, Michael, "Internationalized Constitutionalism in Ethnically Divided Societies: Bosnia-Herzegovina and Kosovo Compared", in *Max Planck Yearbook of United Nations Law*, Volume 15, 2011, 1–64, Bogdandy, Armin Von and Wolfrum, Rüdiger (eds.), (https://www.mpil.de/files/pdf3/mpunyb_01_Riegner_152.pdf).

29 See, e.g.: Expert Report on Rule of Law issues in Bosnia and Herzegovina, Brussels, 5 December 2019 (Priebe report 2019), in particular paras 53–62.

30 Woelk, Jens, "Conditional or Sustainable? The Rule of Law and Judiciary Reforms in the Western Balkans", in *The Rule of Law in the EU. Challenges, Actors and Strategies*, Ruzza, Carlo and Antoniolli, Luisa (eds.), (Springer, Cham, 2024), 245–262.

31 European Court of Auditors, EU support for the rule of law in the Western Balkans. Special Report EN 2022.

2019 an Expert Report on the Rule of Law, commissioned by the European Commission detailed significant judicial shortcomings despite two decades of efforts. However, the report did not lead to major changes, which demonstrates the resistance of elites to reform and suggests that judicial independence, when not paired with accountability, hinders meaningful change.[32] On the contrary, generous international assistance has facilitated domestic political and judicial elites' engagement in practices of rent-seeking and state capture.[33]

However, it cannot be overlooked that EU conditionality is particularly sensitive in the judiciary. Usually, it demands reforms that do not automatically or concretely result from the broad and abstract formulation of the Copenhagen accession criteria. These broad principles need to be made concrete and adapted to the respective context. In addition, specific conditions regularly affect different dimensions of sovereignty and, in some cases, touch the core of what constitutes a state and how political authority is organised within it. An example are the judicial institutions created at the state level in Bosnia and Herzegovina (Court of BiH and Prosecutor's Office of BiH, as well as the High Judicial and Prosecutorial Council), but not yet provided for in the country's constitution. The establishment of those institutions in the first international phase, and their consolidation based upon EU conditionality, is actually a constitutional transformation without an explicit constitutional amendment.[34]

4 Priority Conditions in the EC Opinion regarding the Judiciary

In June 2022, the European Council called on the political leaders of BiH to urgently finalise pending constitutional reforms. Key priority 4 of the Euro-

32 See for the experience in Central and Eastern European countries, Moliterno, James E. et al., "Independence without accountability: The harmful consequences of EU Policy toward Central and Eastern European Entrants", *Fordham International Law Journal*, vol. 42, issue 2, 481 (2018), and Mendelski, Martin "The Limits of the European Union's Transformative Power: Pathologies of Europeanisation and Rule of Law Reform in Central and Eastern Europe", *SSRN Electronic Journal*, (September 18, 2014).

33 Bartlett, Will, International assistance, donor interests, and state capture in the Western Balkans, in Journal of Contemporary European Studies (Special Issue: EU enlargement to the Western Balkans: The geopolitical turn or another postponement?), 2022, 184–200.

34 Kulenović, Nedim, "Faktična ustavna promjena u teoriji i praksi ustavnog prava, sa posebnom osvrtom na Ustav Bosne i Hercegovine", (Doktorska disertacija, Univerzitet u Sarajevu-Pravni Fakultet), Sarajevo 2019.

pean Commission's Opinion requires substantial reforms to "fundamentally improve the institutional framework, including at constitutional level". Regarding the judicial sector, this priority demands to "a) ensure legal certainty on the distribution of competences across levels of government; b) ...; c) guarantee the independence of the judiciary, including its self-governance institution (HJPC); d) reform the Constitutional Court, including the issue of international judges, and ensure enforcement of its decisions; e) guarantee legal certainty, including by establishing a judicial body entrusted with ensuring the consistent interpretation of the law throughout Bosnia and Herzegovina; f) ensure equality and non-discrimination of citizens, notably by addressing the *Sejdić-Finci* ECtHR case law; ...". Besides only partial fulfilment through some amendments to the Law on the HJPC,[35] not a single serious matter, such as regarding the status of international judges in the Constitutional Court of BiH, the amendment of the Constitution of BiH, or the implementation of the *Sejdić-Finci* judgments has been addressed by the political elites.

Nevertheless, in November 2023, BiH received conditional green light for the opening of accession negotiations with the European Union. In March 2024, the European Commission proposed the start of negotiations, and, on 21 March 2024, the European Council voted in favour of opening negotiations with Bosnia and Herzegovina. However, the European Council invited the Commission to prepare the negotiating framework with a view to its adoption by the Council "the moment *all relevant steps* set out in the Commission's recommendation of 12 October 2022 *are taken*". This refers to the above priorities related to the judicial system.

Among the European Commission's priorities, three major issues of constitutional relevance can be distinguished regarding judiciary reforms and the Rule of Law:[36]

a) Guarantee of the independence of the judiciary, including its self-governance institution (HJPC),
b) Reform of the Constitutional Court, including the issue of international judges and the enforcement of its decisions, and
c) Guarantee of legal certainty, including by establishing a judicial body entrusted with ensuring the consistent interpretation of the law throughout Bosnia and Herzegovina.

35 These limited "integrity" amendments, adopted in September 2023, regard the asset declarations of judges and prosecutors and the relative procedure and verification as well as guarantees for judges and prosecutors.

36 *Rule of Law* Key Priority no. 6, in: EC Opinion (2019), 15.

The following analysis will concentrate on these three issues, which are still open, not least because all of them have constitutional impact and thus require constitutional change for their implementation.

5 Guarantee of the Independence of the Judiciary, Including Its Self-Governance Institution (HJPC)

Judicial independence is a constitutional principle which follows from the overarching construction principle of the separation of powers and the need for control to guarantee the effective implementation of the constitution as the 'supreme law of the land'. In fact, as there must not be unlimited power, a system of checks and balances is established in constitutional democracies which guarantee oversight and effective remedies. Judicial review is the well-established means, above all for individual citizens.[37] At the European level, the right to a fair trial, Article 6 of the European Convention on Human Rights (ECHR), and the right to an effective remedy, Article 47 of the Charter of Fundamental Rights of the European Union, make this connection and contain the respective guarantees for individuals.

Judicial independence comprises an institutional as well as an individual dimension.[38] Institutionally, it refers to the judiciary's freedom from interference by the legislative or executive branches, known as external institutional independence. It also involves relationships between courts within the same system, which is internal institutional independence. Key criteria for institutional independence are *decision-making autonomy* (judicial decisions should not be reviewed by non-judicial bodies); *administrative independence* (the judiciary must manage its administration autonomously, without outside interference); *financial independence* (the judiciary should have control over its funding and how it is allocated, ensuring it has adequate resources to fulfil its role).

---

37 With his decision in *Marbury v. Madison* (5 U.S. 137 (1803), Chief Justice John Marshall established the principle of judicial review as an important addition to the system of "checks and balances" created to prevent any one branch of the federal government from becoming too powerful.

38 See for the single aspects European Commission for Democracy through Law (Venice Commission), Compilation of Venice Commission Opinions and Reports concerning Judges, CDL-PI (2023)019, Strasbourg, 18 July 2023 (https://www.venice.coe.int/webforms/documents/?pdf=CDL-PI(2023)019-e), and Opinion on Legal Certainty and the Independence of the Judiciary in Bosnia and Herzegovina, CDL-AD (2012)014.

The Constitution of BiH does not expressly contain principles regarding the judiciary and its independence. However, these principles apply via reference to the ECHR (Article II.2 of the Constitution of BiH, in combination with Article 6 ECHR), which is used as a standard of review in abstract and concrete review procedures by the Constitutional Court of BiH; the right to a fair hearing is also guaranteed by the Constitution of BiH (Article II.3 e). As the Dayton compromise assigned all judicial powers to the Entities, except for the Constitutional Court of BiH, the Entity Constitutions ensure judicial independence through several provisions. The Constitution of FBiH reads that the judiciary is independent and autonomous, Article IV.C.3.1., and Article IV.C.3.2 outlines the establishment of the courts and ensures that no interference from the executive or legislative branches is permitted in judicial matters. The Constitution of the Republika Srpska contains similar provisions: Article 121 declares the independence of the judiciary, stipulating that judges shall be independent in performing their judicial duties and free from any influence from the legislative or executive branches. Article 128 further ensures that the judiciary is protected from external pressure and that decisions made by courts are final and cannot be influenced by political entities.

These constitutional provisions are part of a broader legal framework that seeks to guarantee judicial independence across BiH, aligning with international standards such as those set by the European Convention on Human Rights (ECHR). Courts in BiH have full internal institutional independence; the only form of external institutional dependence is financial, because judicial institutions are funded by the budgets of the respective territorial units. As part of its competences, the High Judicial and Prosecutorial Council, at its own discretion, makes proposals for the annual budget proposed by authorities and/or governments for courts and prosecutor's offices.

According to the Venice Commission, the establishment of a judicial council as a self-governance institution for the judiciary is appropriate for guaranteeing judicial independence. In the context of the "complex state" of BiH and its four distinct judicial systems, having one institution responsible for judicial self-governance is a huge advantage in terms of economies of scale (as it becomes immediately clear when looking at the HJPC secretariat which guarantees and coordinates *inter alia* the management of projects with foreign donors and, above all, the IT management for all judicial authorities in BiH). However, constitutional guarantees for the HJPC, its composition, powers, and autonomy appear necessary.[39] Thus, the recommendations for the HJPC to

39 Venice Commission, Opinion on legal certainty and the independence of the judiciary in Bosnia and Herzegovina, CDL-AD (2012)014, Strasbourg, 18 June, Opinion No. 648/2011,

receive an explicit constitutional basis aim at certainty. This would clarify its role as a guarantor of judicial independence in Bosnia and Herzegovina and facilitate its active functions of coordination across the four distinct legal systems.

An explicit constitutional basis and the related legal certainty appear even more important, as there have been repeated attempts to challenge the legitimacy of the HJPC's establishment. Politically, this is in line with the slogan of "going back to the 'original' Dayton", as in the original text such an institution was not foreseen. The aim is to re-establish judicial councils in the Entities before the creation of the HJPC. The Entity Judicial Councils were part of the post-war judicial reforms in Bosnia and Herzegovina, aimed at decentralising judicial power and ensuring judicial independence at the entity level and thus responsible for judicial appointments, discipline, and management within their respective Entities. However, the two councils were later dissolved following the establishment of the HJPC at the state level in 2004, which consolidated judicial oversight and ensured that judicial independence would be maintained across the country under a unified system. The attempt to regain these functions is part of the wider picture of weakening the state level and putting the judiciary under entity control.

The current constitutional basis of the HJPC is a competence-transfer, foreseen as an option in Article III.5.a) of the Constitution of BiH, formalised in 2004 with the Agreement on the Transfer of Competencies from the Entities to the state level, as part of the judicial reform process led by the international community. While, theoretically, any agreement can be revisited, the undoing of the transfer agreement that established the HJPC would face significant legal, political, and institutional obstacles. Legally, reversing it requires unanimity (in the same way as for its stipulation), as well as considerable amendments to the legal framework. Thus, politically, it would require political consensus between both the Entities' and the state-level institutions. Given the sensitivity of judicial independence and the vested interests of various political groups, achieving such a consensus would already be challenging enough. But the HJPC was part of internationally driven reforms to ensure judicial independence and strengthen the Rule of Law. Reversing its establishment is contrary to all recommendations for progress on Rule of Law, as part of the

and Venice Commission, Opinion on the Draft Law on the High Judicial and Prosecutorial Council of Bosnia and Herzegovina, CDL-AD (2014)008, Strasbourg, 24 March 2014, Opinion no. 712/2013. The adoption of a new Law on HJPC is also part of the Recommendations in the EC Opinion (2019) and the Analytical Report.

accession process, and would inevitably lead to strong negative reactions from the international community, particularly from the European Union.[40] There might even be institutional resistance as the HJPC has been in operation for two decades, and dismantling or transferring its functions back to the Entities would disrupt the judiciary and create institutional instability.

Currently, political elites have not yet discussed constitutional changes in favour of anchoring the HJPC and its functions in the Constitution of BiH. However, the work on amendments to the Law on the HJPC has begun, but the process is very slow. After the limited amendments to that law which regard the judicial integrity (with the introduction of a new system of asset declarations), the requirement of the Opinion's 14 priorities, i.e., to adopt a new law, remains an open political challenge. Such a new law should also introduce some innovations, such as a division of the HJPC into two sub-councils – one for judges and one for prosecutors – for deciding issues which regard either of these two separate groups. The Venice Commission first introduced this proposal in 2011.[41] This recommendation aims to ensure the separation of the judicial and prosecutorial functions, promoting greater independence and accountability within each body and preventing outvoting by the other category. The division into two sub-councils has been a recurring suggestion in later reports and recommendations concerning judicial reforms in BiH.

Constitutional amendments should also include formally recognising the Court of BiH, the Prosecutor's Office of BiH, together with the HJPC, as judicial bodies at the state level in the constitutional text. These judicial institutions were originally established by decisions of the High Representative due to the failure of local political elites to reach a consensus on their formation (through agreement on the "transfer of competence"). Later, their existence was validated through the adoption of relevant laws by the Parliamentary Assembly of BiH. However, despite these legal foundations, they have not yet been included in the Constitution of BiH. The Venice Commission, in its Opinions, has highlighted this issue, recommending that these institutions be explicitly recognised in the Constitution of Bosnia and Herzegovina to solidify their constitutional status.[42]

40 See, in this sense: Expert Report on Rule of Law issues in Bosnia and Herzegovina (Priebe report), Brussels, 5 December 2019 (para. 67).

41 Venice Commission, Opinion no. 712/2013.

42 For the Venice Commission, the legal basis for the formation and functioning of the judicial institutions at state level can be found in "general constitutional rules"; Opinion no. 648/2011, para 32.

6 Reform of the Constitutional Court, Including the Issue of International Judges

The Constitutional Court of BiH is well established in Article VI of the Constitution of BiH, but frequently subject of controversy regarding its composition. It is composed of nine constitutional judges, four of which are elected by the House of Representatives of FBiH, and two by the Assembly of the RS. The remaining three judges are foreigners, who must not hold the citizenship of neighbouring countries and are appointed by the President of the European Court of Human Rights after consultation with the BiH Presidency. Although "international" judges can be found in other jurisdictions,[43] the presence of three foreigners is a specific feature which embodies the firm international guarantee for the unity of the state of Bosnia and Herzegovina and the Constitution of BiH. By consequence, the term of the first judges appointed was only five years, not eligible for reappointment. This reveals the transitional character of the arrangement. In fact, the Constitution provides that after the initial appointment of judges (for a five-year term), the Parliamentary Assembly of BiH (PA BiH) may introduce, by law, a different method of selection of foreign judges (Article VI.1 d).

Foreign judges were included in the Constitutional Court of BiH for *knowledge-sharing* (of comparative law, human rights law, expertise in constitutional law, experience and additional perspective), *countering the rigid ethnic representation and ethnic division* within the Court, *preventing blockage* of the Court, *avoiding division* within the Court along ethnic lines and *domination of ethnic interests* in decision making process, as well as *mediating* between domestic judges from different constituent peoples. In summary, foreign judges were supposed to preserve the Court's independence and integrity, and embody values, principles, and standards of international law, thus contributing to the public trust in the institution.[44]

---

43 Dziedzic, Anna and Young, Simon N.M. eds., *The Cambridge Handbook of Foreign Judges on Domestic Courts*, (Cambridge: Cambridge University Press 2023). See also: Nedžad Smailagić, Entry "Constitutional Court of Bosnia and Herzegovina (Ustavni sud Bosne i Hercegovine)", *Max Planck Encyclopedia of Comparative Constitutional Law* [MPECCoL], June 2023 (D. Foreign Judges..., 26–28) (https://oxcon.ouplaw.com/display/10.1093/law-mpeccol/law-mpeccol-e804#law-mpeccol-e804-div1–5), and Marko, Joseph, "Foreign Judges: a European Perspective", in *Hong Kong's Final Court of Appeal. The Development of the Law in China's Hong Kong*, Young, Simon N. M. and Ghai, Yash (eds.), (Cambridge University Press, 2014), 637–665.

44 Kulenović, Nedim, "Court as a Policy-Maker?: The Role and Effects of the Constitutional Court of Bosnia and Herzegovina in Democratic Transition and Consolidation", *Analitika*, Working Paper 5/2016, Sarajevo, 2016.

In recent years, the political elites from the Republika Srpska, with the support of HDZ, have vocally claimed that the time has come for the departure of "international" judges.[45] While also the European Commission's Opinion (2019) underlines the need to address the question,[46] the EU Expert Report on the Rule of Law (2019) states more prudently that "the system has not yet achieved the level of maturity needed to allow it to dispense with the need for international judges, but this must remain the ultimate objective".[47]

After several failed attempts to adopt a law on the foreign judges (2007, 2010, and 2020), in 2023, a Draft Law on the Constitutional Court of BiH has been introduced by a Serb delegate to the House of Peoples of the PA BiH.[48] The Draft Law does not only address the status of foreign judges but also the composition and selection of judges, organisation, competencies, decision-making process, and other issues relevant to the work of the Court. As a piece of ordinary legislation, the Draft Law itself is not of constitutional rank. The Constitution provides for the Constitutional Court to adopt its own rules to regulate all the above issues. Thus, it is not up to the PA BiH to adopt constitutional, organic, or regular laws on those matters, except for the expressly mentioned case of a new selection method of foreign judges. On the contrary, taking into account the special position and role of the Constitutional Court, the framers of the Constitution, by Article VI.2 b) of the Constitution of BiH, gave the Constitutional Court the authority to adopt its own rules of procedure in order to ensure its independence and thereby prevent any interference with the exercise of the powers conferred upon it.[49]

The Draft Law also eliminates the foreign judges from the Court's composition and terminates the tenure of the current foreign judges by prescribing that their mandate shall end as soon as their replacement gets elected by the FBiH Parliament and National Assembly of the RS. It also provides a deadline in which Entity parliaments must select the replacement judges. However, the

45 In 2023, the Republika Srpska also adopted the Law on Non-application of Decisions of the Constitutional Court BiH, which was supposed to be temporarily enforced, as long as the PA BiH did not adopt a Law on the Constitutional Court of BiH, without foreign judges. See also: Išerić Harun and Sahadžić Maja, "Perils from Within and Without: The Constitutional Court of BiH Under Pressure", *VerfBlog*, 2023/7/27 (https://verfassungsblog.de/perils-from-within-and-without/).

46 EC, Opinion on Membership of BiH (2019), 7.

47 Priebe report (2019), para 27.

48 Draft Law (in Bosnian) available at (https://www.parlament.ba/olaw/OLawDetails?lawId=108099).

49 Constitutional Court of BiH, Decision on Admissibility and Merits in case no. U-11/21 (para. 14).

mandate of foreign judges shall end in any case with the deadline. The Court will continue to work without foreign judges (eventually even without their replacement). Such provisions contrast with the Constitution, as the Constitution allows the PA BiH only to change the selection method of foreign judges, but not the composition of the Court or the status of judges, which are matters reserved for the Constitution. Judicial tenure of judges is an important guarantee of judicial independence.[50]

The Draft Law has not been discussed yet in the PA BiH; in March 2024, it should have been put on the agenda of the House of Peoples of BiH PA, but there was no quorum. Already in July 2023, BiH's Ministry of Justice had formed a working group with the aim to develop legislation regarding the position of the foreign judges at the Constitutional Court of BiH. Again, the chosen title – "Law on the Status of International Judges" – suggests that the law shall address more than just the new method of selection, which contrasts with the formulation in the Constitution. The presence of the three judges selected by the President of the European Court of Human Rights can only be ended or their status changed by an amendment to the Constitution of BiH, not by an ordinary law (as wrongly stated by several politicians, e.g., Minister of Justice of BiH, Davor Bunoza).

However, it remains to be seen, whether legislative intervention limited to changing the method of selection of international judges will be considered sufficient to meet the requirements of the European Commission for the reform of the Constitutional Court (Priority 4). As the selection of foreign judges has so far happened in the shadows and far away from the public eye, as well as without effective involvement of domestic authorities in the selection procedure, the procedure needs be changed, to preserve the integrity of the Constitutional Court of BiH, as well as the public trust in foreign judges. In the end, this seems to be the ratio of the European Commission's request (rather than the citizenship of constitutional judges).

If foreign judges are to remain at the CC BiH, as they probably should at least for the foreseeable future, the selection procedure needs to become more transparent and inclusive of domestic institutions (e.g., a two stage-process with pre-selection at international level guaranteeing the merit and the experience of foreign candidates and the appointment by the democratically legitimated House of Representatives of BiH). At the same time, the selection process should reflect the fact that foreign judges do not decide human rights

50 Judicial tenure is protected by Article VI.1 c) of Constitution BiH: "Judges subsequently appointed shall serve until age 70, unless they resign or are removed for cause upon consensus of the other judges."

cases anymore (since December 2003, these cases are the competence of the Grand Chamber, composed exclusively of domestic judges). The primary involvement of foreign judges now pertains to significant constitutional review cases, which often lead to divisions within the CC BiH along ethnic lines and frequently result in ethnic interests dominating the decision-making process. As EU law will play an increasingly vital role in the country's legal framework, the selection process of foreign judges should reflect the need for future foreign judges to have proven experience and knowledge in comparative constitutional law, especially federalism, and EU law.[51]

Improving the selection criteria and method would be beneficial in general. The criteria for becoming a constitutional judge are quite broad and the procedure is not really transparent. The fact that it is not regulated by any legal act leaves room for a practice of selection dominated by political criteria. Drawing from comparative experience, the trend is the increasingly public nature of the (s)election process. In the U.S., since 1955, almost all Supreme Court nominees have testified formally before the Senate Judiciary Committee.[52] The procedures used by the Senate in considering nominations can affect the likelihood of confirmation for a Supreme Court Justice.

In comparative terms, it is quite rare that the legislative bodies of federal units appoint judges to the Constitutional Court of the federal level (in BiH: state level); usually the appointing authority for the federal Constitutional or Supreme Court is a legislative body of the federal state – often the body in which the states are represented. In the U.S., the Appointments Clause provides that the President shall appoint, subject to Senate confirmation, judges of the Supreme Court, and all other officers of the United States (U.S. Const. art. II, § 2, cl. 2). In Germany, the representative body of the *Länder* (executives) at federal level, the *Bundesrat*, elects half of the constitutional judges at the Federal Constitutional Court (Article 94.1 Basic Law).[53] By contrast, in Bosnia and Herzegovina, all judges of the Constitutional Court of BiH (except

51 See in more depth: Woelk Jens and Išerić Harun, "Don't throw out the baby with the water: How not to misread an EU request about foreign judges at the Constitutional Court of Bosnia and Herzegovina", in *50 Shades of Federalism* (https://shorturl.at/ElZdj).

52 Those hearings have been televised since 1981. Collins, Paul M. and Ringhand, Lori A., *Supreme Court Confirmation Hearings and Constitutional Change*, (Cambridge: Cambridge University Press 35, 2013).

53 The Belgian Constitutional Court is composed of 12 judges, appointed for life by the King from a list of two candidates proposed alternately by the House of Representatives and the Senate by a majority of at least two-thirds of the members present. Six judges belong to the Dutch language group, six to the French language group. (Article 32 of the Special Law on the Constitutional Court).

for "foreign" judges) are appointed by the Parliament of FBiH and the National Assembly of the RS.

Recently, the Constitutional Court has come under political pressure.[54] The President of the RS, Milorad Dodik, announced that the Republika Srpska would not appoint any judge until the resolution of the question of 'international judges' in the Constitutional Court.[55] Delays in appointment risked to seriously hamper its functioning as two judges were permanently missing. In this regard, the Venice Commission adopted two important opinions on the Constitutional Court of BiH, with immediate consequences for the current situation.

In March 2024, it noted that the Constitutional Court can determine in its own rules that a judge who has reached the age of 70 can remain in office until the appointment of a judge to replace him/her. Although contrary to the express 70 years age limit in Article VI.1 c) of the Constitution of BiH, for the Venice Commission, a literal interpretation must yield to the overarching constitutional principle of guaranteeing a functioning Constitutional Court, to safeguard the fundamental right of access to a court.[56] The Constitutional Court of BiH supplemented its Rules accordingly and the current president of the Court, already close to the age limit, will remain in office until a new judge is elected. If that change had not happened, the Court would soon lack three judges, compromising its functioning, especially in appellate jurisdiction. Although an "Opinion" is not legally "binding", the authority of the Venice Commission is increasingly used by the European Commission to frame (or confirm) conditionality obligations in detail. A final legal evaluation of the constitutionality of the Constitutional Court's amendments to its own Rules is only possible by the Court itself.

In its second Opinion on the Constitutional Court,[57] the Venice Commission criticised the ethnicisation of the Constitutional Court, considering the

---

54 Išerić, Harun and Sahadžić, Maja, "Perils from Within and Without: The Constitutional Court of BiH Under Pressure", *VerfBlog*, 2023/7/27 (https://verfassungsblog.de/perils-from-within-and-without/).

55 The RS National Assembly failed to appoint a judge after Judge Knežević retired, while the position of Judge Simović has been vacant already earlier on.

56 Venice Commission, Opinion on certain questions relating to the functioning of the Constitutional Court of Bosnia and Herzegovina, CDL-AD(2024)002-e, Strasbourg, 18 March 2024, para 25: "Too strict an interpretation of the clause "judges (…) shall serve until age 70" would lead to the strange conclusion that the drafters of the Constitution would prefer a complete paralysis of an essential constitutional organ to temporary prolongation of the term in office of legitimately appointed judges."

57 Venice Commission, Opinion on the method of electing judges to the Constitutional Court, CDL-AD (2024)015-e, Strasbourg, 24 June 2024.

established practice of combining the election of two judges by the RS National Assembly and four by the Parliament of FBiH with ethnic criteria (two judges from each constituent people) discriminatory. For the Venice Commission, ethnic affiliation must not be a prerequisite for the election of constitutional judges: "strict ethnic requirements or quotas are not consistent with the distinctive role and responsibility of the Constitutional Court as a federal institution reflecting and serving the rule of law".[58] The practice of ethnic-territorial appointment of judges of the Constitutional Court had started early on and was continued by ethno-nationalist parties from all three "constituent peoples". Is this only a political custom or has considering a candidate's ethnicity already become a constitutional convention?[59] However, the parties of the coalition currently in power are in no way obliged to continue this political practice.[60] Instead, the parties in power always had, and still have, the opportunity to amend the Constitution of BiH and establish stricter criteria and objective parameters for the appointment of judges of the Constitutional Court.[61]

Some political representatives even demand a law that would introduce entity voting in the Constitutional Court (which means a specific veto-option against over-ruling).[62] However, such proposals contrast with the competence of the Constitutional Court to autonomously regulate its own decision-making, voting, sessions, etc. with its own rules (Article VI.2 b) of the Constitution of BiH). Thus, not the legislator but only the Constitutional Court can decide on its organisation, operation and functioning. Introducing new consociational mechanisms would not only mean serious risks of paralysing the institution; it would also infringe upon the individual independence of the judges, as well as contrast with all international recommendations regarding the role of the Constitutional Court in a democratic society.

58 Idem (para 35). In its Opinion on Membership (2019), the European Commission has expressed the same position regarding administrative bodies and ethnic veto rights, 7.

59 Balić, Lejla, "Ustavni običaj u Bosni i Hercegovini – osvrt na izbor sudija Ustavnog suda Bosne i Hercegovine." *Godišnjak Pravnog fakulteta u Sarajevu* (2009), 13–23. See, on this important question, also Maja Sahadzic's chapter on subnational constitutionalism in this volume.

60 The appointments of Sead Palavrić and Mirsad Ćeman (previously members of the Democratic Action Party) by the previous coalition does not oblige the parties in power to nominate a Croat and/or a prior HDZ candidate for the House of Peoples of the BiH PA.

61 Article VI.1. b) of the Constitution of BiH simply provides: "Judges shall be distinguished jurists of high moral standing. Any eligible voter so qualified may serve as a judge of the Constitutional Court".

62 A suspensive "ethnic" veto already exists. See: Article 39 Rules of Procedure.

In sum, no major reform of the Constitutional Court is possible without amending the Constitution of BiH as the latter does not contain any basis for the adoption of either a constitutional or an ordinary law to regulate any matter related to the Constitutional Court (except for the selection method of the three foreign judges). That the Constitutional Court itself "shall adopt its own rules of court by a majority of all members" is a clear indication of the intention of the constitution-drafters to ensure its independence by preventing the interference of other state bodies. And this should be well preserved.

7 Guarantee of Legal Certainty, Including by Establishing a Judicial Body for Consistent Interpretation of the Law throughout Bosnia and Herzegovina

Judicial power in federal countries is strongly interconnected even when it is divided between two levels of government (e.g., in the U.S. and Germany). "There is more interdependence of courts in federations than there is of other institutions of government" (Saunders). This is due to factors such as, among others, uniformity in interpretation, centripetal tendencies, legal and political culture.[63] In several federal systems, the judiciary is not even divided between the national and the subnational level, e.g., in Austria and Belgium.

In federations, "one highest, supreme court, (...) must have as one of its core tasks the harmonisation of the judicial practice of courts within the federal units (through its appellate or revision jurisdiction), because otherwise significant differences may emerge in the understanding of justice in that federation".[64] Even where judicial competences are divided between the national and the subnational levels, at the former level there needs to be at least a supreme court as it ensures "the ultimate authority of the federation and its legal order on the one hand, and meets the demand for uniformity of judicial practice in interpreting and applying the legal order of the federation, on the other".[65] However, each federation is *sui generis*, there is no generally accepted model of judicial organisation in comparative federalism.

There is no Supreme Court of BiH in the constitutional system of Bosnia and Herzegovina, only two Entity Supreme Courts (mentioned in the respect-

63 Palermo, Francesco and Kössler, Karl, *Comparative Federalism. Constitutional Arrangements and Case Law*, (London, Bloomsbury Publishing, 2017), 159 and 160.

64 Jovičić, Miodrag, *Savremeni federalizam* (Beograd: Savremena administracija, 1973), 140.

65 Marković, Ratko, *Ustavno pravo* (Beograd: Službeni glasnik, 2009), 395.

ive Entity Constitutions).[66] Currently, the harmonisation of judicial practice in Bosnia and Herzegovina is carried out in meetings of a "panel for the harmonisation of judicial practice", organised by the Court Documentation Centre of the HJPC BiH, with the support of the Council of Europe, and with participation of judges of all highest ordinary courts in the country. Working within the framework of the Council of Europe project "Reinforcing the capacity of the judiciary as regards the implementation of the European Convention on Human Rights in Bosnia and Herzegovina", the panel discussed cases of different treatment by the courts and tried to agree upon uniform solutions. The meetings resulted in conclusions that serve as orientation for judges of lower courts but are not legally binding. This is a limit of "voluntary panels" adopting "guidelines" for unifying judicial practice. It explains why the Venice Commission insists on the formation of a state judicial body that will have a similar function. In Germany, where federal apex courts exist, there is an interesting institutional solution: The Constitution foresees a panel composed of apex courts of different jurisdictions (ordinary, administrative, labour, financial, social) which need to coordinate in case of divergent views on issues concerning more than one of them (Article 95.3 GC).[67]

From the beginning of the implementation of the Dayton constitutional system, the leading legal authorities indicated that a judicial coordination body is necessary for the functioning of the Rule of Law.[68] Since 2012, also

66 The original text of Annex 4 does not contain provisions on the army, police and judiciary at state level, which are the three levers on which every state rests. Milićević, Neđo, "Bosna i Hercegovina poslije Dejtona-nepodnošljivo skupa država", *Revija slobodne misli* (1996) br. 4, 4.

67 *Gemeinsamer Senat der Obersten Bundesgerichte.* All details are regulated by federal statute. See: https://shorturl.at/39AEi.

68 Krneta, Slavica, "Prilog raspravi o potrebi uvođenja vrhovnog suda države BiH," *Ljudska prava* (2000), br. 2. god. 1, 96–97. – In Bosnia and Herzegovina, there are four systems of judiciary, four prosecutor's offices, four substantive and four procedural laws. The criminal law reform carried out in 2003 by imposing the Criminal Code of Bosnia and Herzegovina and the Law on Criminal Procedure of Bosnia and Herzegovina as framework and systemic laws intended to harmonise criminal law regulations in the Entities and the Brčko District. Today, the Republika Srpska differs the most (a kind of legal separation in criminal law), after the adoption of the RS Criminal Code, contrary to the High Representative' approach in the imposed framework and systemic legislation. Protection chapters, criminal offences, and essential elements of offences are regulated differently. There is no system of coordination or any other mechanism to overcome differences, and analogy in criminal law is prohibited. Also, there are major differences between the RS Criminal Procedure Code (CPC) and the Criminal Procedure Codes of BiH, FBiH, and BD. The RS CPC grants greater rights to victims in criminal proceedings and the legal framework of *ex officio* defence is arranged differently.

the Council of Europe's Venice Commission recommends the formation of the Supreme Court of BiH,[69] at least in the long term perspective.[70] The creation of such a body is considered important both from the perspective of the judiciary, for which it would provide useful guidelines on how to proceed with the interpretation and application of certain legal provisions, as well as from the perspective of BiH citizens, for whom it would guarantee legal certainty, foreseeability, and uniformity in the interpretation and application of the law in the country. In the short term, the creation of a special Court of Appeal of BiH is recommended as a second-instance court for reviewing decisions of the Court of BiH, by transforming the internal Appellate Division of this Court and using the financial resources of the Court of BiH.[71]

The difference between the proposed Appeals Court of BiH and a Supreme Court is important: the former is only competent for appeals against the decisions of the Court of BiH; the latter is competent for appeals against decisions of both Entity Supreme Courts, as well as the Court of BiH. One could raise the question whether the supremacy clause of the Constitution of BiH (Article III.3) could serve as constitutional basis for the establishment of a Supreme Court of BiH, even through an ordinary law. However, the practice so far, as well as the political situation, suggests placing such an important institution with far-reaching powers, both vis-à-vis citizens as well as Entity institutions, on safe legal grounds by creating a proper constitutional basis.

In fact, there are several options for creating the supreme judicial instance. One would probably best form a Court of Appeal at the state level first, and only after that the Supreme Court, since many changes in organisational, substantive and procedural regulations are needed to form a new apex court for encompassing the Entities' legal and judicial systems, including their supreme courts, the State Court (with its Appeal Division), and the Appellate Court of the Brčko District. It may also be an option to establish the Court of Appeal of BiH (for regular and extraordinary legal remedies against the decisions of the Court of BiH) and the Supreme Court of BiH to exist in parallel.[72] While the organisation and functioning of the Court of Appeal of BiH could either be regulated in a special law establishing this court or – more common in the

69 Venice Commission, Opinion on legal certainty and independence of the judiciary in Bosnia and Herzegovina, Strasbourg, 18 June 2012, CDL-AD (2012)014, Opinion No. 648/2011.

70 Ibid., para. 102.

71 Ibid. paras 63 and 102.

72 The Court of Appeal could also relieve the Constitutional Court of BiH from its appellate jurisdiction (which makes up the overwhelming majority of its cases) allowing the latter to focus on judicial review; of course, this would require a constitutional amendment.

Western Balkan countries – in a law on the courts of Bosnia and Herzegovina. By contrast, for the establishment of a Supreme Court, a constitutional amendment is necessary, due its position and powers of coordination vis-à-vis the four judicial systems.

The state needs to ensure the establishment of a single economic system in BiH (Article I.4 of the Constitution BiH), whose uniform application is necessary for EU accession. Without a single Supreme Court, it will hardly be possible to ensure the efficient and uniform application of state regulations that will serve the transposition of EU regulations into national legislation. The approximation clause in Article 70 of the Stabilisation and Association Agreement demands the harmonisation of Entity regulations, as the first step towards gradual fulfilment of compliance with EU law.[73] Procedurally, a single body also appears necessary with a view to the EU's preliminary reference procedure (Article 267 TFEU).

8 The Importance of a Rule of Law Culture

At the constitutional level, the HJPC (and the judicial authorities at the state level) would benefit from an explicit base in the text of the Constitution of BiH; some issues regarding the Constitutional Court could be clarified by amendment; an institution for ensuring consistent interpretation of the law, i.e., the equivalent of a Supreme Court at the state level, can only be established by constitutional amendment. In addition, further measures are required at the level of ordinary legislation, such as the adoption of a new Law on the HJPC, as well as of a new Law on Courts.

Although Bosnia and Herzegovina is characterised by a complex constitutional framework, as well as by a difficult political situation, according to the Expert Report on the Rule of Law (2019), also known as "'Priebe Report", these circumstances are not the only reasons for the weakness of the Rule of Law. One of the main reasons for dysfunctional public institutions is the lack of will on the part of key stakeholders to reform the judiciary. Bosnian and Herzegovinian institutions lack a culture of accountability and transparency. It is pointed out that the problem is not so much the laws (despite the political difficulties with the Law on the HJPC BiH, most of them have already been adapted to EU standards), but the gulf between laws and the everyday prac-

73 Meškić, Zlatan, "Osnivanje Vrhovnog suda Bosne i Hercegovine kao uslov za članstvo u Evropskoj uniji," in *Jedan Vrhovni sud za BiH?* Edin Šarčević (ed.), (*Fondacija Centar za javno pravo*, Sarajevo 2011), 109–140.

tice of their (non-)application. "The positivist and formalistic behavior of many officeholders at all levels often appears as a real obstacle to proper implementation."[74]

Therefore, the main problem in implementing the Rule of Law in BiH is not the Constitution, although improvements will certainly be reached once the key priorities are implemented. But the legal culture that has developed in the long history of BiH is a culture of *rule by law* and not the *rule of law*.[75] Throughout history, BiH has always been part of political regimes – the Ottoman Empire, Austria-Hungary, the Kingdom of Yugoslavia, and the Socialist Federal Republic of Yugoslavia – that functioned as *rule by law* (except for Austria-Hungary). By consequence, this *rule by law* tradition is still deeply rooted in BiH, meaning that very often the objective of institutions in BiH is mere compliance with the laws.[76]

But judges and officeholders must comprehend that their role is first and foremost to protect the interests of the people: without it, the *rule of law* will remain dead letter. Besides constitutional reform, BiH needs to move on from the *rule by law* tradition to a *rule of law* culture based upon the respect of human rights. Clearly, BiH and its institutions need time to internalise the *rule of law* culture, but more than two decades of intense reform efforts have already passed, without impressive results,[77] at least regarding the cultural change. In fact, the non-implementation of many judgments against human rights-violations is detrimental already for this very reason. "Until (such a cultural change), BiH will be a state of the flawed *rule of law* in the Constitution, and with *rule by law* legal tradition".[78]

It is impossible to impose such an important cultural change from the outside. But it is also difficult to imagine that such a systemic change can come from within the judiciary alone (as not everyone is unhappy with the status

---

74 Priebe Report (2019), para 20. See also: Karčić, Fikret, "A Study on Legal Formalism in the Former Yugoslavia and its Successor States", *CIDS report* No.1, 2020.

75 For the difference between the *rule of law* and *rule by law* see: Tushnet, Mark, "Rule by Law or Rule of Law?", *Asia Pacific Law Review*, 2014, 22(2), 79–92.

76 Uzelac, Alan, Survival of the third legal tradition?, S.C.L.R., 2010, 49, 377–394, and Nurkić, Benjamin, "The Rule of Law in Bosnia and Herzegovina", *International Journal of Constitutional Law Blog*, Jun 16, 2022 (https://www.academia.edu/82224767/The_Rule_of_Law_in_Bosnia_and_Herzegovina_iconnectblog_com_2022_06_the_rule_of_law_in_bosnia_and_herzegovina).

77 European Court of Auditors (ECA), EU support for the rule of law in the Western Balkans: despite efforts, fundamental problems persist. Special Report EN 2022.

78 Nurkić, Benjamin, "The Rule of Law in Bosnia and Herzegovina," *International Journal of Constitutional Law Blog*, Jun 16, 2022.

quo). Rather, it needs to be demanded and accompanied by those who benefit most from the Rule of Law: citizens! This echoes the increasing demands by donors to include civil society and stakeholders in the reform process.[79] Judiciary reforms are an important part of democratic transformation. They need to be anchored in the foundational, constitutional values and linked to the fundamental and democratic rights of citizens.

Bibliography

Balić, Lejla, "Ustavni običaj u Bosni i Hercegovini – osvrt na izbor sudija Ustavnog suda Bosne i Hercegovine" *Godišnjak Pravnog fakulteta u Sarajevu*, 2009, 13–23.

Bartlett, Will, *International assistance, donor interests, and state capture in the Western Balkans, in Journal of Contemporary European Studies* (Special Issue: EU enlargement to the Western Balkans: The geopolitical turn or another postponement?), 2022, 184–200.

Bobek, Michal and Kosař, David "Global Solutions, Local Damages: A Critical Study in Judicial Councils in Central and Eastern Europe", *German Law Journal 171* (November 7, 2013), available at:https://ssrn.com/abstract=2351299.

Bogdandy, Armin Von "1. Founding Principles," in *Principles of European Constitutional Law*, eds. Bogdandy, Armin Von and Bast, Jürgen, (Hart/C.H. Beck/Nomos, 2009), 11–53.

Collins, Paul M. Jr. and Ringhand, Lori A. *Supreme Court Confirmation Hearings and Constitutional Change* (Cambridge: Cambridge University Press, 2013).

Dziedzic, Anna and Young, Simon N.M. eds. *The Cambridge Handbook of Foreign Judges on Domestic Courts.* (Cambridge: Cambridge University Press 2023).

European Commission for Democracy through Law (Venice Commission), "Compilation of Venice Commission Opinions and Reports concerning Judges," *CDL-PI* (2023)019, Strasbourg, 18 July 2023 (https://www.venice.coe.int/webforms/documents/?pdf=CDL-PI, (2023)019-e), and "Opinion on Legal Certainty and the Independence of the Judiciary in Bosnia and Herzegovina," *CDL-AD*, 2012, 014.

European Commission, "A new EU Framework to strengthen the Rule of Law," *COM*, 2014, 158 final/2.

European Court of Auditors, "EU support for the rule of law in the Western Balkans." (Special Report EN 2022, ECA Report 2022).

Expert Report on Rule of Law issues in Bosnia and Herzegovina, (Brussels, Priebe Report, December 5, 2019).

79 European Court of Auditors (ECA), Special Report EN 2022.

Grewe, Constance and Riegner, Michael, "Internationalized Constitutionalism in Ethnically Divided Societies: Bosnia-Herzegovina and Kosovo Compared," in *Max Planck Yearbook of United Nations Law, Volume 15*, eds. Bogdandy, Armin Von and Wolfrum, Rüdiger, 2011, 1–64 (https://www.mpil.de/files/pdf3/mpunyb_01_Riegner_152.pdf).

Išerić, Harun and Sahadžić, Maja, "Perils from Within and Without: The Constitutional Court of BiH Under Pressure," *VerfBlog*, 2023/7/27 (https://verfassungsblog.de/perils-from-within-and-without/).

Jovičić, Miodrag, *Savremeni federalizam* (Beograd: Savremena administracija, 1973).

Karčić, Fikret, "A Study on Legal Formalism in the Former Yugoslavia and its Successor States," *CIDS report No.1*, 2020.

Krneta, Slavica, "Prilog raspravi o potrebi uvođenja vrhovnog suda države BiH," *Ljudska prava* (2000), br. 2. god. 1., 96–97.

Kulenović, Nedim, *Court as a Policy-Maker? The Role and Effects of the Constitutional Court of Bosnia and Herzegovina in Democratic Transition and Consolidation*, (Analitika, Working Paper 5/2016, Sarajevo, 2016).

Kulenović, Nedim, *Faktična ustavna promjena u teoriji i praksi ustavnog prava, sa posebnom osvrtom na Ustav Bosne i Hercegovine* (Sarajevo: Doktorska disertacija, Univerzitet u Sarajevu-Pravni Fakultet, 2019).

Marko, Joseph, "Foreign Judges: a European Perspective," in *Hong Kong's Final Court of Appeal. The Development of the Law in China's Hong Kong*, eds. S.N.M. Young/Y. Ghai, (Cambridge: Cambridge University Press, 2014, 637–665).

Marković, Ratko, *Ustavno pravo* (Beograd: Službeni glasnik, 2009).

Mendelski, Martin, The Limits of the European Union's Transformative Power: Pathologies of Europeanisation and Rule of Law Reform in Central and Eastern Europe, SSRN Electronic Journal, September 18, 2014, https://ssrn.com/abstract=2728226.

Meškić, Zlatan, "Osnivanje Vrhovnog suda Bosne i Hercegovine kao uslov za članstvo u Evropskoj uniji," in *Jedan Vrhovni sud za BiH?* ed. Edin Šarčević, (Fondacija Centar za javno pravo, Sarajevo 2011), 109–140.

Milićević, Neđo, "Bosna i Hercegovina poslije Dejtona-nepodnošljivo skupa država," *Revija slobodne misli* br. 4, 4., 1996).

Moliterno, James E. et al., "Independence without accountability: The harmful consequences of EU Policy toward Central and Eastern European Entrants," *Fordham International Law Journal*, vol. 42, issue 2, (2018), 481.

Nurkić, Benjamin "The Rule of Law in Bosnia and Herzegovina," *International Journal of Constitutional Law Blog*, June 16, 2022 (http://www.iconnectblog.com/2022/06/therule-of-law-in-bosnia-and-herzegovina/).

Palermo, Francesco and Kössler, Karl, *Comparative Federalism. Constitutional Arrangements and Case Law*, (London, New York: Bloomsbury Publishing, 2017).

Pech, Laurent, The Rule of Law as a Well-Established and Well-Defined Principle of EU Law, *Hague J Rule Law* 14, 2022, 107–138, https://link.springer.com/article/10.1007/s40803-022-00176-8.

Phinnemore, David, "The Stabilisation and Association Process. A Framework for European Union Enlargement?" In *European Integration and Transformation in the Western Balkans*, ed. Arolda Elbasani, (Routledge, 2014).

Smailagić, Nedžad, "Entry "Constitutional Court of Bosnia and Herzegovina (Ustavni sud Bosne i Hercegovine)," *Max Planck Encyclopedia of Comparative Constitutional Law* [MPECCoL], June, 2023 (D. Foreign Judges…, 26–28) (https://oxcon.ouplaw.com/display/10.1093/law-mpeccol/law-mpeccol-e804#law-mpeccol-e804-div1–5).

Steiner, Christian and Ademović, Nedim, *Commentary on the BiH Constitution*, (Foundation Konrad Adenauer, 2010).

Tushnet, Mark, "Rule by Law or Rule of Law?" *Asia Pacific Law Review*, (2014) 22(2), 79–92.

Uzelac, Alan, "Survival of the third legal tradition?" *S.C.L.R.*, (2010), 49, 377–394.

Venice Commission, "Opinion on certain questions relating to the functioning of the Constitutional Court of Bosnia and Herzegovina," *CDL-AD* (2024)002-e, Strasbourg, 18 March 2024.

Venice Commission, "Opinion on legal certainty and the independence of the judiciary in Bosnia and Herzegovina," *CDL-AD*(2012)014, Strasbourg, 18 June, Opinion No. 648/2011.

Venice Commission, "Opinion on the Draft Law on the High Judicial and Prosecutorial Council of Bosnia and Herzegovina," *CDL-AD* (2014)008, Strasbourg, 24 March 2014, Opinion no. 712/2013.

Venice Commission, "Opinion on the method of electing judges to the Constitutional Court," *CDL-AD* (2024)015-e, Strasbourg, 24 June 2024.

Woelk, Jens and Išerić, Harun, "Don't throw out the baby with the water: How not to misread an EU request about foreign judges at the Constitutional Court of Bosnia and Herzegovina," in *50 Shades of Federalism* (https://shorturl.at/ElZdj).

Woelk, Jens, "Conditional or Sustainable? The Rule of Law and Judiciary Reforms in the Western Balkans," in *The Rule of Law in the EU*, eds. Carlo Ruzza and Luisa Antoniolli, (Challenges, Actors and Strategies, Springer, Cham), 245–262.

Legislation

Agreement on the establishment of the HJPC of BiH (Official Gazette of the FBiH, no. 16/04)

Amendment No. I to the Constitution of BiH (Official Gazette of BiH, no. 25/09)
Decisions of the High Representative, in 2000 and 2003, establishing the Court of BiH and the Prosecutor's Office of BiH

Law on Courts of BD (Official Gazette of the BD, no. 18/20)

Law on Courts of the FBiH (Official Gazette of the FBiH, no. 8/05, 22/06, 63/10, 72/10, 7/13, 52/14, and 85/21)

Law on Courts of the RS (Official Gazette of the RS, no. 37/12, 14/14, 44/15, 39/16, and 100/17)

Law on Procedure before the FBiH Constitutional Court (Official Gazette of the FBiH, no. 6/95 and 37/03)

Law on Public Prosecutor's Offices of RS (Official Gazette of the RS, no. 69/16)

Law on the Constitutional Court of the RS (Official Gazette of the RS, no. 104/11 and 92/12)

Law on the High Judicial and Prosecutorial Council of BiH – HJPC (*Visoko sudsko i tužilačko vijeće* – VSTV, Official Gazette of BiH, no. 25/04)

Law on the Prosecutor's Office of the BD (Official Gazette of the BD, no. 19/07)

Rules of Procedure (Official Gazette of the RS, no. 104/11 and 92/12)

Rules of Procedure of the Constitutional Court of the FBiH Court (Official Gazette of the FBiH, no. 40/10 and 18/16)

Rules of the Constitutional Court (text available in the Official Gazette of BiH, no. 94/14).

Statute of the BD (Official Gazette of the BDV, no. 2/10)

Statute of the BD (Official Gazette of the BDV, no. 2/10)

CHAPTER 11

The Complex State and Substate Constitutionalism

Maja Sahadžić

1 Context

After the Bosnian War, Bosnia and Herzegovina (BiH) became a multilevel system consisting of two entities – the Federation of BiH (FBiH) (composed of 10 cantons, hence federally organised) and the Republic of Srpska (RS (unitary organised) and one district – Brčko District (BD). Each entity and canton has its constitution, while the district has a statute. The constitutional system rests on three constituent peoples (Bosniaks, Croats, and Serbs) who often act as decentralising and centralising forces. Importantly, the system is established to maintain a weak state level and strong substate levels[1] based on the complex interplay between territory, identity, and substate constitutionalism. This gives insights into cohesive and divisive qualities of substate constitutionalism in BiH.[2]

This chapter examines the interaction between a broad substate constitutionalism and fragmenting and integrating forces based on differences in territory and identity. This often results in federalising and centralising pressures. First, this chapter examines the relationship between territory and identity. Second, it investigates how fragmenting dynamics are caused by broad substate constitutionalism. The equilibrium between federalising and centralising forces driven by political forces is the last topic discussed before the concluding remarks.

1 In BiH the term "state level" refers to the highest level of government such as the central level or the federal level, unlike in some other systems where it refers to the level of states (for example, the United States of America).

2 See: Balić, Lejla in this volume and Woelk and Vranješ in this volume on BiH as a complex state.

 | DOI:10.1163/9789004707887_012

2 Complex State and Federal Principles

BiH is often referred to as a "complex state", using the local term "*složena država*".[3] This rather neutral terminology is associated with the frequently extensive discussions concerning whether the post-conflict BiH has merely evolved or if the Federation of BiH (FBiH) and the Republic of Srpska (RS) were combined to form a new kind of BiH.[4] A noteworthy aspect of the Constitution of BiH (also referred to as the Dayton Constitution) is that BiH maintained its legal status as a state under international law.[5] Indeed, the Constitution suggests that the formerly unitary-organised BiH has decentralised as a result of the 1992–1995 Bosnian War and integrated identity diversity into its constitutional framework. The state's bottom-up restructuring, through the 1994 Washington Peace Agreement creating the FBiH and acknowledging the RS in its 1992 framework, however, also suggests that the FBiH and the RS were combined to create a new state. This provides much room for debating whether BiH is simply devolved, or if it is an aggregate created by merging the FBiH and the RS. The term "complex state" appears to have entered BiH academic discourse as a defining middle ground given that the aforementioned discussions are, in fact, disagreements founded on diverse legal reasoning and ideological viewpoints.[6] In one of its rulings, even the Constitutional Court of BiH acknowledged the unique (*sui generis*) characteristics of the

3 Balić, Lejla and Izmirlija, Midhat, "Consociation in Bosnia and Herzegovina: Practical Implementation of the Theoretical Principles," *South-East European Journal of Political Science* 1, no. 3 (2013), 121.

4 See: Vranješ, Nevenko, "Dejtonska i postdejtonska koncepcija političkog sistema Bosne i Hercegovine," in *Zbornik radova "Pravo između stvaranja i tumačenja"*, ed. Ćeranić, Dimitrije et al. (Istočno Sarajevo: Pravni fakultet Univerziteta u Istočnom Sarajevu, 2023). Barbarić, Dražen, "Struktura nedopuštene kohabitacije: analiza decizionističkoga modela politike u Bosni i Hercegovini," *Anali* 18, no. 1 (2021). Stanković, Marko, "Uspostavljanje BiH-federalizma: agregacija ili devolucija," in *Bosanskohercegovački federalizam*, ed. Šarčević, Edin, (Sarajevo: Fondacija Centar za javno pravo, 2020). Marković, Goran, "Federalizam i konsocijacija u ustavnom sistemu BiH," in *Bosanskohercegovački federalizam*, ed. Šarčević, Edin (Sarajevo: Fondacija Centar za javno pravo, 2020).

5 The Constitution of BiH, Article 1.

6 Balić, Lejla, "Pravna priroda i političke refleksije bosansko-hercegovačkog federalizma," in *Bosanskohercegovački federalizam*, ed. Šarčević, Edin, (Sarajevo: Fondacija Centar za javno pravo, 2020), 11. Simović, Darko, "Aporije etničkog federalizma u Bosni i Hercegovini – (ne)uspeli postkonfliktni federalni eksperiment," in *Bosanskohercegovački federalizam*, ed. Šarčević, Edin, (Sarajevo: Fondacija Centar za javno pravo, 2020), 196.

country's constitutional framework.[7] The phrase "complex state" is still widely employed in domestic academic debates since it intentionally lacks specificity, making it neither unitary nor federal.

However, over time, the idea that BiH is founded on federal principles has gained traction. This possibly has something to do with the recognition that federal principles have been used not only in federal states such as Belgium, but also in regionalised or even unitary states such as Italy and Spain. In other words, it has been recognised that territorial autonomy is a common means of accommodating identity variations, and federal principles are one such technique.[8] For example, adopting federal principles leads to the *devolution of power* – that is, the transfer of power from the state level to substate entities, the *allocation of power* – that is, the combination of power at the state and substate levels, and the *aggregation of power* – that is the accumulation of power at the state level.[9] Importantly, the devolution of power emphasises centrifugal forces, while the aggregation of power emphasises centripetal forces.[10] Significantly, federal principles also show that useful knowledge of constitutional design can be found at the substate level.[11] In systems featuring federal principles, substate *territorial autonomy* is a prevalent characteristic, if not an essential one.[12] However, substate entities also develop characteristics of *identity belonging* which is shown by the unification of groups based on a sense of honour, pride, and loyalty,[13] and interpretation of this belonging, which can be self-imposed or imposed from the outside (by political elites,

7 The Decision on merits of the Constitutional Court of BiH, U-1/11.

8 Kymlicka, Will, "Federalism and Secession: At Home and Abroad," *Canadian Journal of Law and Jurisprudence* 13, no. 2 (2000), 207, 10.

9 Bauböck, Rainer, "Multinational Federalism: Territorial or Cultural Autonomy?", *Willy Brandt Series of Working Papers in International Migration and Ethnic Relations*, no. 2 (2001), 15.

10 Keating, Michael, "Federalism and the Balance of Power in European States," (The Sigma Programme – Support for Improvement in Governance and Management, Paris: Organisation for Economic Co-operation and Development (OECD), 2007), 9–10.

11 Williams, Robert F. and Tarr, Alan G., "Subnational Constitutional Space: A View from the States, Provinces, Regions, Lander, and Cantons," in *Federalism, Subnational Constitutions, and Minority Rights*, ed. Tarr, Alan G., Williams, Robert F. and Marko, Joseph (Westport and London: Praeger, 2004), 4.

12 Popelier, Patricia, Aroney, Nicholas, and Delledone, Giacomo, "Subnational Constitutionalism, Defining Subnational Constitutions and Self-constituent Capacity," in *The Routledge Handbook on Subnational Constitutions and Constitutionalism*, ed. Popelier, Patricia, Delledone, Giacomo and Aroney, Nicholas, (London and New York: Routledge, 2021), 14.

13 Harris, Erika, "Identity, Territory, and Self-determination in Transborder Regions of Eastern and, Central Europe," *Euborders Working Paper Series*, no. 04 (2017), 3.

the Constitutional Court).[14] The combination of territorial autonomy and identity belonging leads to substate entities with distinct identities frequently posing threats to the system's stability, given that secessionist forces have long sought political autonomy in order to protect the interests of particular groups, so this is nothing new.[15] This appears to be precisely what is taking on in BiH presently.

3 Substate Level: Territorial Aspects

3.1 *The Importance of Terminology*

BiH, as a "complex state" or a state based on federal principles, is composed of the FBiH and the RS (the Entities) and the Brčko District (BD) as a single administrative unit under the sovereignty of BiH or a territory in the joint ownership of the Entities.[16] The term "state" in the Constitution of BiH exclusively refers to the state level.[17] Other substate-level entities are referred to as "Entities", "cantons", and "district".[18] The main purpose of this terminology is seemingly to highlight the state level's broad function and prevent circumstances in which the Entities would be regarded as states. In other words, by giving the top-down consolidation of the system at least some footing, this varied language aims to mitigate the effects of the bottom-up reconstruction of the system.

3.2 *Institutional Autonomy*

The internal makeup of the Entities and BD is not defined by the Dayton Constitution; instead, the Entities and BD establish internal setup, institutional organisation, and power distribution through their own constitutions (the Entities) and the statute (BD). Also, each of the ten cantons in the FBiH

14 Popelier, Aroney, and Delledone, "Subnational Constitutionalism, Defining Subnational Constitutions and Self-constituent Capacity," 15.

15 Harris, "Identity, Territory, and Self-determination in Transborder Regions of Eastern and, Central Europe," 4. Kymlicka, "Federalism and Secession: At Home and Abroad," 208.

16 On the definition of Brčko, see: The Constitution of BiH, Amendment I. Schreuer, "Arbitral Tribunal for Dispute over inter-entity boundary in Brcko area: Award in the Republika Srpska V. the Federation of Bosnia and Herzegovina (final award)," *International Legal Materials* 38 (1999), 539.

17 Article I 2. Constitution of BiH.

18 The Constitution of BiH, Article I 3, Article I 2, and Article IV 4.

specify internal affairs in their constitutions. First of all, this means that the Entities and BD enjoy full constitutional powers to establish their parliaments, governments, judicial systems, and constitutional courts. Here, it is impossible to overlook the connections between the asymmetric territorial design of BiH and identity through the principal parity of the constituent peoples that affect the makeup and operation of substate entities' institutions. As an illustration, the National Assembly of the RS, all cantonal assemblies, and the BD Assembly are unicameral, although the Parliament of the FBiH is bicameral. Additionally, the FBiH and the RS president and two vice presidents must represent distinct constituent peoples. Moreover, the Entities and BD do not consume constitutional powers in the same way. This is true because the ways in which substate entities consume constitutional powers are influenced by variations in their own territorial and institutional settings. Examples of how local powers are consumed differently include the decentralised FBiH, where there is an additional intermediary (cantonal) level between the FBiH and the local self-government, and the unitary RS, where there is no such intermediary level.

Given this wide institutional autonomy of the substate entities, the state level is often colloquially called "joint institutions". It is interesting to note that whereas mostly Serbs choose to use the term "joint institutions", Bosniaks prefer to refer to the state level as "the institutions of BiH". The choice of terminology also highlights the disparities in perceptions regarding the characteristics of the Bosnian constitutional system. While the Serb leadership interprets "joint institutions" as a form of shared government found in confederations, the Bosniak leadership views the state level as a multi-ethnic civic administration within an overarching state. Crucially, this is associated with the fact that the state level is perceived as weak or incomplete compared to the substate entities. For example, the BiH Constitution establishes the existence of the state-level legislature and executive, but it leaves the judiciary undefined with no Supreme Court acting as the final arbiter.[19] The Court of BiH[20] acts as a special court with no hierarchical links to the courts in the

19 See: Marković, Goran, "Treba li Bosni i Hercegovini jedan vrhovni sud: prilog raspravi," *Sveske za javno pravo/Blätter für Öffentliches Recht*, no. 4 (2011). Sahadžić, Maja, "Uspostavljanje Vrhovnog suda BiH, Aktualna pravna misao o teoretskoj nedosljednosti u praksi," *Sveske za javno pravo/Blätter für Öffentliches Recht*, no. 4 (2011).

20 The Court of BiH was established in 2002. Its existence is not foreseen in the Constitution of BiH.

Entities and BD, which has occasionally forced the Constitutional Court of BiH to deliberate on the interpretation and application of laws by the ordinary courts.[21]

One of the counteracting factors to the fact that broad substate autonomy took shape as a result of the fragmented and bottom-up process of constitutional (re)construction in BiH could be the supremacy of the Constitution of BiH. The substate constitutions and the Statute are, indeed, single documents that include all constitutional and statutory provisions for each substate entity in BiH. However, the Constitution of BiH reads that all substate entities, as well as their constitutions and laws, must adhere to it in full.[22] For example, once the Dayton Peace Agreement came into effect, the Entities' constitutions had to be changed to conform to the Constitution of BiH. Some anomalies persisted in the Entities' constitutions despite a thorough review, so the Constitutional Court of BiH resolved any remaining contradictions between the constitutions because the Constitution of BiH does not identify a further link to the constitutions of the Entities.[23]

3.3 *Division of Powers*

Further wide substate autonomy is visible in the division of powers where all substate entities, again, enjoy high autonomy while the state-level limitations are low if not minimal or non-existent. This is seemingly in line with discussions on the constitutional system's bottom-up reconstruction. For example, although the Constitution of BiH grants the state-level exclusive powers, these refer to a select few.[24] As a consequence, the Entities and BD retain vast residual powers, meaning that powers and functions that are not specifically

---

21 The Decision on the admissibility and merits of the Constitutional Court of BiH, AP-775/08.

22 The Constitution of BiH, Article III 3. b).

23 For example, in 2000 the Constitutional Court of BiH confirmed the principle of constituency when it adopted four partial decisions about the compliance of the Constitutions of the FBiH and the RS. In the third partial decision, the Court confirmed the principle of constituency on the whole territory of BiH. See: The Partial decision number 3 of the Constitutional Court of BiH, U-5/98.

24 The Constitution of BiH, Article III 1 enumerates: foreign policy, foreign trade policy, customs policy, monetary policy, finances of the institutions and for the international obligations of BiH, international law, immigration, refugee, and asylum policy and regulation, international and inter-Entity criminal law enforcement, including relations with Interpol, establishment and operation of common and international communications facilities, regulation of inter-Entity transportation, and air traffic control. Also, other powers can be traced elsewhere in the Constitution, such as in: Article IV 4, Article V 3, Article VI 3, Article VII and Article VIII.

allocated to the state level belong to the Entities and BD.[25] Furthermore, the Constitution of BiH expressly permits the Entities to establish special parallel relations with surrounding states that uphold BiH's territorial integrity and sovereignty, as well as to sign agreements with states and international organisations following the approval of the legislature at the state level.[26] Additionally, the Constitution of FBiH permits the cantons to sign foreign agreements, provided that both the FBiH and the state-level legislature agree.[27] Finally, the state level is entitled to assume additional powers over the matters necessary to preserve the sovereignty, territorial integrity, political independence, and international personality of BiH, respecting the distribution of powers and mutual agreement of the Entities.[28] However, because the Serb political leadership believe this will weaken the RS, they are strongly against the transfer of powers from the substate entities.[29] The RS leadership occasionally issues threats regarding independence referendums in reaction to conversations about the transfer of powers to the state level. It also rejects the whole idea of the state-level judiciary that has been established on the basis of one of those transfers. For example, in 2021, the Serb political leadership released a strategic document with a lengthy list of requests, including the declaration of independence of the RS, if the powers that have been transferred to the state level are not returned to the RS within six months, particularly those pertaining to the Armed Forces of BiH, the High Judicial and Prosecutorial Council of BiH (HJPC), the Court of BiH, and the Indirect Taxation Authority of BiH, including the dissolution of the Intelligence-Security Agency of BiH (OSA), revoking the approval for the establishment of the State Investigation and Protection Agency of BiH (SIPA), and establishing comparable agencies in the RS within a month. Among other previous threats was the abolition of numerous decisions made by the OHR in the National Assembly of the RS.[30] There has been a lot of controversy over this political adventurism in BiH and beyond. At one point, the sequence of events has included serious threats of secession and war, but also an invitation for a folk musician to perform for guests at the Presidency of BiH, an impromptu statement suggesting that war

25 The Constitution of BiH, Article III 3 a).

26 The Constitution of BiH, Article III 2 a) and d).

27 The Constitution of FBiH, Article V.1.2.3).

28 The Constitution of BiH, Article III 5 a).

29 Sahadžić Maja, "Bosnia and Herzegovina's constitutional crisis: is this time different?", *Centre on Constitutional Change, Centre on Constitutional Change*, 12/04, 2021, https://www.centreonconstitutionalchange.ac.uk/news-and-opinion/bosnia-and-herzegovinas-constitutional-crisis-time-different.

30 See: Sahadžić Bosnia and Herzegovina's constitutional crisis: is this time different?

is unlikely because the three sides in Bosnia are so broke that they could only fight each other by throwing chestnuts.[31]

This renders the Entities' mutual agreements all but impossible.[32] When there was a stalemate in the decision-making processes, the Office of the High Representative of BiH (OHR)[33] took a number of actions to get around this barrier, influence the transfer of powers,[34] and enable the efficient functioning of the system. At the same time, the practice of the so-called "parallel competences", or introducing policies in particular domains, such as the framework legislation on primary, secondary, and higher education, was initiated at the state level.[35] Since the current constitutional framework of BiH does not anticipate mechanisms of recovering transferred powers, it is unclear whether and how the Entities would be able to initiate such a procedure. Also, a one-way (bottom-up) transfer of power does appear to be rather counter-intuitive, and yet again, the top-down transfer can also appear counter-intuitive, especially where institutions have been created as permanent ones.

3.4 *Constitutional Amendments*

Remarkably, limited participation in state-level constitution-making appears to be attributable to the considerable substate constitutional powers. A cursory look at the substate constitutions and the Statute reveals that they have complete authority to amend their statutory and constitutional provisions. Also, compared to the process of altering the constitutions of the Entities, the Constitution of BiH's amending approach is more flexible. A two-thirds majority of those present and voting in the House of Representatives is required for the Constitution of BiH to be amended,[36] while double majorities

31 Sahadžić, Bosnia and Herzegovina's constitutional crisis: is this time different?

32 Interestingly enough, an agreement was reached about establishing unified armed forces at the central level.

33 The OHR (together with the High Representative for BiH) was created in 1995 to supervise the implementation of the Dayton Peace Agreement. Among other things, the High Representative for BiH can adopt and enforce decisions when there is a deadlock in decision-making. On the powers of the OHR see: Keil, Soeren and Kudlenko, Anastasiia, "Bosnia and Herzegovina 20 Years after Dayton: Complexity Born of Paradoxes," *International Peacekeeping* 22, no. 5 (2015), 481–82.

34 For example, regarding the laws that establish the High Judicial and Prosecutorial Council and VAT.

35 In 2000, the Constitutional Court of BiH recognised framework legislation as an important harmonising factor in the field of legislation. See: The Partial decision number 2 of the Constitutional Court of BiH, U-5/98.

36 The Constitution of BiH, Article X 1.

are needed for amendments to the Entities' constitutions. For example, a two-thirds majority in the House of Representatives and a simple majority in the House of Peoples comprising a majority of delegates from each constituent people, are needed to change the Constitution of FBiH.[37] Similar to this, a two-thirds majority in the National Assembly of the RS, as well as a majority of members from each of the constituent peoples and the Others from the Council of Peoples of the RS,[38] are needed for modification.[39] Admittedly, adjustments in BD and cantons are less stringent than those at the Entities level, since a two-thirds majority is required in the cantons[40] and a three-fourths majority is required to alter the BD Statute.[41]

At the state level, the conditions under which the Constitution of BiH arose may provide justification for using the flexible amendment mechanism. Ethnic cleansing and wanton destruction worsened following multiple failed plans for BiH,[42] which raised calls for the war to end. The Dayton Peace Agreement was intended to be a transitory instrument due to the pressing nature of the negotiations, their brief duration, and the presence of two pre-existing Entities. Meanwhile, the Constitution of BiH was intended to be a constitution for peace. The agreement itself has nothing to do with the bottom-up democratic exercise, but with an elite compromise. Perhaps this explains why the Constitution does not specifically demand the participation of the substate entities or the constituent peoples in the amendment procedure, even though its construction is virtually entirely based on ethnoterritorial features. Regretfully, the process of creating a state has hardly begun yet. At the substate level, two key observations are crucial: (1) procedural distinctions are dictated by distinct institutional frameworks of the substate entities; and (2) mandatory participation of the constituent peoples establishes the necessary majority for revisions.

37 The Constitution of FBiH, Article VII 1.2. a) and b).

38 This body was established by the intervention of the OHR during 2002 and 2003 to enable the so-called vital national interest procedure in the RS for the protection of the interests of the constituent peoples in cases when consensus cannot be reached. This body is not involved into any other legislative procedure.

39 The Constitution of the RS, Article 135 paragraph 2.

40 See, for example: *The Constitution of the Sarajevo Canton* (Official gazette of the Sarajevo Canton 1/96, 2/96, 3/96, 16/97, 14/00, 4/01, 28/4, 6/13, 31/17). The Constitution of the Sarajevo Canton, Article 42 paragraph 3.

41 The Statute of the BD, Article 33 paragraph 3.

42 Such as the Carrington-Cutileiro Plan, Vance-Owen Peace Plan, Owen-Stoltenberg Plan, Contact Group Plan, and plans introduced by the Bosniaks, Croats, and Serbs.

4 Substate Entities: Identity Aspects

4.1 *Constituent Peoples as Fundamental Identity*

The "complex state", however, would not have been conceivable or especially complex without the identity traits. The Dayton Constitution serves as evidence of the fundamental identity, as it suggests that the constituent power belongs to the three constituent peoples (Bosniaks, Croats, and Serbs),[43] who are acknowledged as the system's building blocks in the preamble of the constitution, admittedly along with Others and citizens of BiH.[44] The normative section of the Constitution of BiH specifically recognises how crucial the principles of parity and proportionate representation of the constituent peoples are to the institutional and procedural framework of BiH at all levels,[45] as the situation on the ground, at the moment of the ceasefire, was frozen and translated into their (constitutionally) guaranteed representation and participation in the legislative, executive, and judicial branches in post-conflict BiH. For example, even in the Constitutional Court of BiH, where there is no legal basis for the proportional appointment of judges, the principles of parity and proportional representation are so deeply ingrained that six national judges are elected from each constituent people (two Bosniaks, two Croats, and two Serbs) from both the FBiH and the RS.[46] Also, the constituent peoples' involvement is particularly emphasised in the decision-making processes, such as the "entity voting procedure" and the "vital national interest procedure", discussed elsewhere in this book.

4.2 *Embedded Territorial Identity*

Not only is there an obvious connection between each substate entity and constituent people – it is also institutionalised. With the adoption of four partial rulings regarding the conformity of the FBiH and the RS constitutions, in 2000 the Constitutional Court of BiH reaffirmed the principle of constituency. Aiming to overturn the territorial division of the constituent peoples according to the Entities in the system of government, the Court upheld the principle of constituency on the entire territory of BiH in its third partial decision suggesting that the constituent peoples must not be associated with par-

43 Barbarić, Dražen and Forić, Samir, "Constituent Peoples," in *Citizens, Constitution, Europe, Glossary of essential constitutional concepts in BiH*, ed. Sahadžić, Maja et al. (Sarajevo: Univerzitet u Sarajevu – Pravni fakultet, 2023), 273.

44 The Constitution of BiH, Preamble. See also: Sekulić, Tatjana in this volume.

45 See: Pearson Sven, "The "national key" in Bosnia and Herzegovina: a historical perspective," *Nationalities Papers* 43, no. 2 (2015).

46 Išerić, Harun, "Izbor domaćih sudija Ustavnog suda Bosne i Hercegovine kao ustavni običaj contra constitutionem," *Pravna misao*, no. 11–12 (2017), 11–12.

ticular parts of the territory in BiH.[47] However, it is still not entirely accurate to say that each constituent population is associated with the entirety of BiH's territory, despite the fact that this should be the presumption. The link between territory and identity is ubiquitous. This may best be identified by the comparison between the 1991 and the 2013 censuses. Almost all the population of cities and municipalities now consists of persons from a different constituent group than it did before the war. Cities and municipalities saw their population decline on multiple instances, and vice versa – increase. Once mostly dispersed and heterogeneous, the population became nearly totally territorially embedded due to the ethnic affiliation, with a small number of locations that still had pre-conflict identity markers. Both the Bosniak and Croat populations can be easily identified by following the borders of the FBiH, while the borders of the RS make it relatively easy to identify the Serb population. Territorial-ethnic separation[48] has happened and it also continued to perpetuate the consequences of the Bosnian War.[49]

4.3 *No Overarching Identity*

The fact that the term "citizens" is meaningless in this context seems to be an aggravating condition as there is no mention of a Bosnian-Herzegovinian nation in the Dayton Constitution.[50] It comes naturally to regard those who are not recognised as members of one of the constituent peoples as the "Others". Although groups typically retain their hybrid identities, or the so-called "multiscalar identities" when they disassociate,[51] some groups only

47 The Partial decision number 3 of the Constitutional Court of BiH, U-5/98. Banović, Damir and Marko, Joseph, "Collective and Individual Rights," in *Citizens, Constitution, Europe, Glossary of essential constitutional concepts in BiH*, ed. Sahadžić, Maja et al. (Sarajevo: Univerzitet u Sarajevu – Pravni fakultet, 2023), 261. Vranješ, Nevenko, "Dejtonska i post-dejtonska koncepcija političkog sistema Bosne i Hercegovine," 39–44. See also: Marko, Joseph in this volume.

48 Sahadžić, Maja, "Mild Asymmetry and Ethnoterritorial Overlap in Charge of the Consequences of Multinationalism. A Country Study of Constitutional Asymmetry in Bosnia and Herzegovina," in *Constitutional Asymmetry in Multinational Federalism, Managing Multinationalism in Multi-tiered Systems*, ed. Popelier Patricia and Maja Sahadžić (Cham: Palgrave Macmillan, 2019), 53.

49 Sahadžić, "Mild Asymmetry and Ethnoterritorial Overlap in Charge of the Consequences of Multinationalism. A Country Study of Constitutional Asymmetry in Bosnia and Herzegovina," 53.

50 Pobrić Nurko, *Ustavno pravo* (Mostar: Slovo, 2000), 63, 111.

51 Oliveira, José, Roca, Zoran, and Leitão, Nuno, "Territorial Identity and Development: From Topophilia to Terraphilia," *Regional Science Policy and Practice*, no. 3 (2019), 146, https://doi.org/10.1016/j.landusepol.2009.10.014.

retain their essential or core identities, or one-level identity, for various reasons.[52] In BiH, the disassociation of groups resulted in the preservation of mostly core identities within the constituent peoples, while the significance of a broader identity was either diminished or completely lost. Only Bosniaks do, to some extent, possess a hybrid identity. Therefore, the political leadership of Bosniaks continues to support the Bosnian-Herzegovinian identity. However, Serbs and Croats, who appear to value core identity more, have a very low connection to it.[53]

4.4 *Three Fragmenting Tendencies*

As a result, three tendencies become apparent. The first is consistent with Bosniaks' efforts to periodically push for a restoration of the unitary system and the civic identity of BiH.[54] The second tendency is associated with demands for the establishment of a third entity with a majority of Croats and the third tendency is linked to persistent threats to hold independence (or secession) referendums in the RS.[55] The Croats and Serbs fear losing their autonomy to centralising tendencies favoured by the Bosniaks, while the Bosniaks fear that the Serbs will eventually lead the RS to split away and that the Croats will eventually obtain more autonomy in cantons with a majority of Croats. To put it differently, threats of centralisation are constantly met with equally serious threats of greater power devolution, independence referendums, and secession, and *vice versa*.

This is also associated with the fact that the system is thought to be overly complex. This is particularly true in the FBiH, where there are ten cantonal constitutions in addition to the Constitution of the FBiH. The cantons are also split between predominantly Bosniak, predominantly Croat, and mixed cantons. Whilst Bosniaks are more numerous and oriented towards centralisation, Croats are less in number and supportive of decentralisation which makes their substate identity rendered ineffective or at least less significant. Compared to the FBiH, the RS has a unitary internal organisation and a predominantly Serb population. The RS is also a part of BiH as a bigger framework

52 Knight, David B., "Identity and Territory: Geographical Perspectives on Nationalism and Regionalism," *Annals of the Association of American Geographers* 72, no. 4 (1982), 515.

53 Perry, Valery, "Constitutional Reform in Bosnia and Herzegovina: Does the Road to Confederation go through the EU?", *International Peacekeeping* 22, no. 5 (2015), 492.

54 On unitary aspirations, see: Thorsten Gromes, "Federalism as a Means of Peace-Building: The Case of Postwar Bosnia and Herzegovina," *Nationalism and Ethnic Politics* 16, no. 3–4 (2010), 359, https://doi.org/10.1080/13537113.2010.526918.

55 For similar arguments, consult: Perry, "Constitutional Reform in Bosnia and Herzegovina: Does the Road to Confederation go through the EU?", 492.

that is founded on federal principles. This facilitates the daily political narratives about claims to autonomy that political leaders develop.

5 The Use of Substate Constitutionalism for Political Purposes

5.1 *The Perception of Substate Constitutionalism*

The ways in which substate entities employ substate constitutionalism for political ends vary. In the FBiH, there has never been a strong emphasis on substate constitutionalism. This circumstance possibly arises from the fact that Bosniaks and Croats share the FBiH as territory.[56] Indeed, the political leaders among the Bosniaks, as the most numerous, have frequently advocated centralisation and emphasised the significance of the Constitution of BiH, while political leaders among the Croats have been vociferous about the lack of the "third" or "Croat" entity, but not necessarily about having its constitution. As a small group in comparison to Bosniaks and Serbs, Croats are underrepresented and frequently unable to have an impact on state decision-making processes even though they make up a constituent people. Aside from that, the Croats have frequently bemoaned their lack of capacity to affect the results of elections. For example, their political elite has brought up the issue of Željko Komšić, elected to the Presidency of BiH on several occasions, as a purportedly non-legitimate representative of the Croats. Considering this claim, the third Croat entity's concept aims to strike a balance between their territorial and political autonomy within BiH.[57]

There appears to be a greater understanding of the significance of substate constitutionalism in the RS. Political leaders in the RS, irrespective of their political stance, promote a pressing need for the RS to maintain a unitary and autonomous posture. The Constitution of the RS has greatly supported widespread acceptance of this viewpoint among Serbs. Serbs also often emphasise three interrelated legal issues affecting Serbs: the regaining of

56 "Cantonisation" had been discussed in various proposals during the war; the current situation is the result of the Washington Agreement, which in 1994 anticipated the DPA. Under the influence of the United States of America, Bosniaks and Croats signed the Washington Agreement to put an end to their internal strife. In the parts of BiH where Bosniaks and Croats predominated, the Agreement formed the FBiH. Ten cantons with a preponderance of Bosniaks, Croats, or both, have been established under the FBiH Constitution, which was derived from the Agreement.

57 Zdeb, Aleksandra, "The Need to Have Something 'Of Their Own': Croat Parallel Institutions in Bosnia and Herzegovina," *Swiss Political Science Review* 22, no. 4 (2016), 547, 51–52.

powers previously transferred to the state level; the repeal by the National Assembly of the RS of laws and decisions adopted at the state level or by the OHR; and the appropriation of state powers. This occasionally incites secessionist sentiment and calls for independence referendums. The concept of secession and independence is almost unimaginable to Bosniaks. Because of this, efforts to repress it sometimes involve very explosive political and nationalist rhetoric.

Because of its tiny size and diverse population, BD is not well-versed in the topic of substate constitutionalism.

5.2 *The Interpretation of Substate Constitutionalism*

In both Entities, the understanding of substate constitutionalism's meaning and purpose is primarily derived from political actors.[58] The fact that political parties in BiH are mostly founded along ethnoterritorial lines, which is consistent with the country's divided political system, is one explanation.[59] Each constituent people has its political parties that dominate their ethnic strongholds. From this it follows that "the unwillingness of political elites to think and to mobilize populations outside an ethnopolitical framework is a reflection of how the population at large 'thinks' in ethnopolitical terms".[60] To put it differently, each constituent people's political leadership offers their perspective on how to implement substate constitutionalism, and the constituent peoples take note of and act upon it.

6 Conclusions

To make the "complex state" less dysfunctional, there have been multiple failed attempts to simplify the constitutional framework, including initiatives directed at limiting substate autonomy. Some attempts propose eliminating all Entities, cantons, and their own constitutions, some propose downsizing the number of cantons, but others propose establishing administrative

58 Touquet, Heleen and Vermeersch, Peter, "Bosnia and Herzegovina: Thinking Beyond Institution-Building," *Nationalism and Ethnic Politics* 14, no. 2 (2008), 270.

59 See also: Seizović, Zarije, "Političko pravni uzroci nacionalne mobilizacije i dekonstitucionalizacije u Bosni i Hercegovini," in *Paradigma Bosna, juče, danas, sutra* (Sarajevo: Dobra knjiga, 2014), 133–34.

60 Touquet and Vermeersch, "Bosnia and Herzegovina: Thinking Beyond Institution-Building," 271.publisher.

61 "Ustavne inicijative," accessed 18/12/2019, http://fcjp.ba/index.php/-79214.

regions, either with or without a constitution.[61] However, all three constituent peoples and their leaders seem to be against substate constitutional reform.

The question is how to advance. For example, a concept of "local ownership" that does not always include local authorities could provide some possibilities. This particularly is an important question given the local political actors' incapacity to introduce necessary changes in a complex BiH and the OHR's role, which is facilitating the peace implementation but is sometimes rather dividing. The next question is whether it is possible for citizens to assume responsibility for making significant decisions. After all, that is a fundamental component of democracy. The lack of a constitutional and legal framework for citizens' direct involvement (other from the RS) certainly restricts citizen's engagement in direct decision-making in BiH, especially under current power dynamics. Also, there is a lack of understanding among the public about their ability to participate in decision-making, as well as among the authorities about the importance of doing so. The question is whether empowering citizens would also enable modifications to the state organisational structure, a shift in the legitimacy of decision-making, and changes to the social, political, and economic environment.

For example, though underreported, recent international efforts have examined citizen assemblies, as reported elsewhere in this book.[62] Meanwhile, the subject of referendums as a means of resolving impasses in decision-making is addressed occasionally, although hesitantly. In BiH, it is a controversial subject to include citizens in the process of determining their destiny. And yet, voters should not be disregarded, as they do bear some responsibility along with their politicians in the process of reconstruction of the state and rebuilding an inclusive society.

Bibliography

Balić, Lejla and Izmirlija, Midhat, "Consociation in Bosnia and Herzegovina: Practical Implementation of the Theoretical Principles." *South-East European Journal of Political Science* I, no. 3 (2013), 121–34.

Balić, Lejla, "Pravna priroda i političke refleksije bosansko-hercegovačkog federalizma." In *Bosanskohercegovački federalizam*, edited by Šarčević, Edin, (Sarajevo: Fondacija Centar za javno pravo, 2020), 11–38.

62 See: Išerić and Herenda in this book.

Banović, Damir and Marko, Joseph, "Collective and Individual Rights." In *Citizens, Constitution, Europe, Glossary of Essential Constitutional Concepts in BiH*, edited by Sahadžić Maja, Banović Damir, Barbarić Dražen and Marković Goran, (Sarajevo: Univerzitet u Sarajevu – Pravni fakultet, 2023), 261–63.

Barbarić, Dražen and Forić, Samir, "Constituent Peoples." In *Citizens, Constitution, Europe, Glossary of Essential Constitutional Concepts in BiH*, edited by Sahadžić Maja, Banović Damir, Barbarić Dražen and Marković Goran, (Sarajevo: Univerzitet u Sarajevu – Pravni fakultet, 2023), 273–78.

Barbarić, Dražen, "Struktura nedopuštene kohabitacije: analiza decizionističkoga modela politike u Bosni i Hercegovini." *Anali* 18, no. 1 (2021), 113–33.

Bauböck, Rainer, "Multinational Federalism: Territorial or Cultural Autonomy?", *Willy Brandt Series of Working Papers in International Migration and Ethnic Relations*, no. 2 (2001), 3–69.

Gromes, Thorsten, "Federalism as a Means of Peace-Building: The Case of Postwar Bosnia and Herzegovina." *Nationalism and Ethnic Politics* 16, no. 3–4 (2010), 354–74. https://doi.org/10.1080/13537113.2010.526918.

Harris, Erika, "Identity, Territory, and Self-Determination in Transborder Regions of Eastern and, Central Europe." *Euborders Working Paper Series*, no. 04 (2017), 1–19.

Išerić, Harun, "Izbor domaćih sudija Ustavnog suda Bosne i Hercegovine kao ustavni običaj contra constitutionem." *Pravna misao*, no. 11–12 (2017), 17–47.

Keating, Michael, "Federalism and the Balance of Power in European States." 1–40. The Sigma Programme – Support for Improvement in Governance and Management. Paris: Organisation for Economic Co-operation and Development (OECD), 2007.

Keil, Soeren and Kudlenko, Anastasiia, "Bosnia and Herzegovina 20 Years after Dayton: Complexity Born of Paradoxes." *International Peacekeeping* 22, no. 5 (2015), 471–89.

Knight, David B. "Identity and Territory: Geographical Perspectives on Nationalism and Regionalism." *Annals of the Association of American Geographers* 72, no. 4 (1982), 514–31.

Kymlicka, Will, "Federalism and Secession: At Home and Abroad." *Canadian Journal of Law and Jurisprudence* 13, no. 2 (2000), 207–24.

Marković, Goran, "Federalizam i konsocijacija u ustavnom sistemu BiH." In *Bosanskohercegovački federalizam*, edited by Edin Šarčević, (Sarajevo: Fondacija Centar za javno pravo, 2020), 261–82.

Marković, Goran, "Treba li Bosni i Hercegovini jedan vrhovni sud: prilog raspravi." *Sveske za javno pravo/Blätter für Öffentliches Recht*, no. 4 (2011), 66–72.

Oliveira, José, Roca, Zoran and Leitão, Nuno, "Territorial Identity and Development: From Topophilia to Terraphilia." *Regional Science Policy and Practice*, no. 3 (2019), 141–58.https://doi.org/10.1016/j.landusepol.2009.10.014.

Pearson, Sven, "The "National Key" in Bosnia and Herzegovina: A Historical Perspective." *Nationalities Papers* 43, no. 2 (2015), 213–32.

Perry, Valery, "Constitutional Reform in Bosnia and Herzegovina: Does the Road to Confederation Go through the EU?". *International Peacekeeping* 22, no. 5 (2015), 490–510.

Pobrić, Nurko, *Ustavno pravo*. (Mostar: Slovo, 2000).

Popelier, Patricia, Aroney Nicholas and Delledone, Giacomo, "Subnational Constitutionalism, Defining Subnational Constitutions and Self-Constituent Capacity." In *The Routledge Handbook on Subnational Constitutions and Constitutionalism*, edited by Popelier, Patricia, Delledone, Giacomo and Aroney, Nicholas, (London and New York: Routledge, 2021), 1–19.

Sahadžić, Maja, "Bosnia and Herzegovina's Constitutional Crisis: Is This Time Different?", *Centre on Constitutional Change. Centre on Constitutional Change*, 12/04, 2021, https://www.centreonconstitutionalchange.ac.uk/news-and-opinion/bosnia-and-herzegovinas-constitutional-crisis-time-different.

Sahadžić, Maja, "Mild Asymmetry and Ethnoterritorial Overlap in Charge of the Consequences of Multinationalism. A Country Study of Constitutional Asymmetry in Bosnia and Herzegovina.", in *Constitutional Asymmetry in Multinational Federalism, Managing Multinationalism in Multi-Tiered Systems*, edited by Popelier, Patricia and Sahadžić, Maja, (Cham: Palgrave Macmillan, 2019), chap. 47–76.

Sahadžić, Maja, "Uspostavljanje Vrhovnog suda BiH, aktualna pravna misao o teoretskoj nedosljednosti u praksi." *Sveske za javno pravo/Blätter für Öffentliches Recht*, no. 4 (2011), 15–27.

Schreuer, Christoph H. "Arbitral Tribunal for Dispute over Inter-Entity Boundary in Brcko Area: Award in the Republika Srpska v. The Federation of Bosnia and Herzegovina (Final Award)." *International Legal Materials* 38 (1999), 534–50.

Seizović, Zarije, "Političko pravni uzroci nacionalne mobilizacije i dekonstitucionalizacije u Bosni i Hercegovini." In *Paradigma Bosna, juče, danas, sutra*, (Sarajevo: Dobra knjiga, 2014).

Simović, Darko, "Aporije etničkog federalizma u Bosni i Hercegovini – (ne)uspeli postkonfliktni federalni eksperiment." In *Bosanskohercegovački federalizam*, edited by Šarčević, Edin, (Sarajevo: Fondacija Centar za javno pravo, 2020), 188–231.

Stanković, Marko, "Uspostavljanje BiH-federalizma: agregacija ili devolucija." In *Bosanskohercegovački federalizam*, edited by Šarčević, Edin, (Sarajevo: Fondacija Centar za javno pravo, 2020), 39–55.

Touquet, Heleen and Vermeersch, Peter, "Bosnia and Herzegovina: Thinking Beyond Institution-Building." *Nationalism and Ethnic Politics* 14, no. 2 (2008), 266–88.

"Ustavne inicijative." accessed 18/12/2019, http://fcjp.ba/index.php/-79214.

Vranješ, Nevenko, "Dejtonska i postdejtonska koncepcija političkog sistema Bosne i Hercegovine." In *Zbornik Radova "Pravo između stvaranja i tumačenja"*, edited by Ćeranić, Dimitrije, Ivanović, Svjetlana, Lale, Radislav and Aličić, Samir, (Istočno Sarajevo: Pravni fakultet Univerziteta u Istočnom Sarajevu, 2023), 279–310.

Williams, Robert F. and Tarr, Alan G. "Subnational Constitutional Space: A View from the States, Provinces, Regions, Lander, and Cantons." In *Federalism, Subnational Constitutions, and Minority Rights*, edited by Tarr, Alan G., Williams, Robert F. and Marko, Joseph, (Westport and London: Praeger, 2004).

Zdeb, Aleksandra, "The Need to Have Something 'of Their Own': Croat Parallel Institutions in Bosnia and Herzegovina." *Swiss Political Science Review* 22, no. 4 (2016), 545–64.

Williams, Robert F. and Tarr, Alan G. "Subnational Constitutional Space: A View from the States, Provinces, Regions, Lander, and Cantons." In *Federalism, Subnational Constitutions, and Minority Rights*, edited by Tarr, Alan G., Williams, Robert F. and Marko, Joseph, (Westport and London: Praeger, 2004).

Zdeb, Aleksandra, "The Need to Have Something 'of Their Own': Croat Parallel Institutions in Bosnia and Herzegovina." *Swiss Political Science Review* 22, no. 4 (2016), 545–64.

CHAPTER 12

Intergovernmental Relations: The Road to Effective Federalism

Bojan Vlaški

1 Introduction

Almost three decades since the signing of the General Framework Agreement for Peace in Bosnia and Herzegovina (hereinafter: the Dayton Agreement), it seems that the reconciliation and stabilisation process, as a logical sequence of the Dayton Agreement, has never fully taken root. On the other hand, comparative federalism indicates the existence of mechanisms for the efficient implementation of core state functions, respecting the roles of both levels of government – federation and federal units. Different types of intergovernmental relations exist as mechanisms of this kind, especially intergovernmental agreements and intergovernmental bodies. To a greater or lesser extent, these mechanisms also characterise federalism in Bosnia and Herzegovina (hereinafter: BiH), although their application has so far been sporadic and partial, and accompanied by several obstacles.

After the introductory part, the structure of this chapter consists of three sections and a short conclusion. The second section, predominantly applying sociological and historical methods, provides an overview of conflictions (legal, internal- and foreign policy-related, selected by the author) that hinder the development of federalism in BiH. The subject of the third section are the mechanisms of intergovernmental relations (intergovernmental agreements and intergovernmental bodies) that can contribute to effectiveness of federalism, with comparative-legal references to exemplary models from selected federal systems. In the fourth section, the author applies a normative method to analyse the application of mechanisms of intergovernmental relations (intergovernmental agreements and intergovernmental bodies) and their potential for future stable development of federal relations in BiH. Finally, the fifth section of the chapter – the conclusion – summarises the challenges and perspectives of applying the mechanisms of intergovernmental relations in BiH also in the context of, *inter alia*, the European integration process.

 | DOI:10.1163/9789004707887_013

2 An Overview of Conflictions Hindering the Development of Federalism in BiH

Federalism in Bosnia and Herzegovina is characterised by a series of conflictions, resulting in obstacles for the development of a federal structure. These conflictions can be observed not only in (constitutional) legal theory, but also in political practice and the operation of the so-called international community.

Firstly, the relationship of domestic legal theory to the state system of BiH is multifaceted. Some authors consider BiH to be a unitary, highly decentralised state or a regional state.[1] Other authors define BiH as a federally organised state.[2] The third group of authors see BiH as a complex state union,[3] a federal–confederate state,[4] or even a (real) union.[5]

Furthermore, different and mutually exclusive positions of relevant political actors in BiH have been taken in political life. Political parties from the Federation of BiH (hereinafter: FBiH), with a predominantly Bosniak electorate, call in their programme documents for the establishment of a "regionalised state (and) elimination of blockages in decision-making by the institutions of BiH (while) the administrative-territorial reorganisation of the FBiH

1 Ibrahimagić, Omer, *Državno uređenje Bosne i Hercegovine* (Sarajevo: Vijeće Kongresa bošnjačkih intelektualaca, 2005), 88; Kurtćehajić, Suad, "Oblik državnog uređenja Bosne i Hercegovine zasnovanog na dejtonskom ustavu," *Pregled*, 3 (2012): 132.

2 Pobrić, Nurko, *Ustavno pravo* (Mostar: Slovo, 2000), 320–324; Begić, Kasim, "Uloga Ustavnog suda Bosne i Hercegovine," in *Federalne strukture u Evropi i Bosni i Hercegovini*, ed. Markert, Thomas and Winkelmann, Ingo, (Sarajevo: Ambasada SR Njemačke i Vijeće Evrope, 2001), 29; Zvonko Miljko, *Ustavno uređenje Bosne i Hercegovine* (Zagreb: Hrvatska sveučilišna naklada, 2006), 205; Trnka Kasim, *Ustavno pravo*, (Sarajevo: Fakultet za javnu upravu, 2006), 254; Kunić, Petar, *Promjene Ustava Bosne i Hercegovine – pro et contra: kritičke opaske na pojedina institucionalna rješenja: dosadašnja iskustva i moguća rješenja* (Banja Luka: Udruženje nastavnika i saradnika Univerziteta u Banjoj Luci, 2015), 14; Marković, Goran, *Ustavni lavirint – Aporije ustavnog sistema Bosne i Hercegovine* (Beograd: Službeni glasnik, 2021), 70.

3 Savić, Snežana, *Dejtonska Bosna i Hercegovina* (Banja Luka: Pravni fakultet Univerziteta u Banjoj Luci, 2003), 22. Cf.; Šarčević, Edin, *Dejtonski ustav* (Sarajevo: Fondacija "Konrad Adenauer" Predstavništvo u Bosni i Hercegovini, 2009), 78–80; Pilipović Milan, *Ustav Bosne i Hercegovine – normativno i stvarno* (Banja Luka: Pravni fakultet Univerziteta u Banjoj Luci, 2008), 73–74.

4 Kuzmanović, Rajko, *Ustavno pravo*, (Banja Luka: Pravni fakultet Univerziteta u Banjoj Luci, 2002), 308.

5 Mijanović, Gašo, "Podjela nadležnosti između institucija Bosne i Hercegovine i entiteta," in *Zbornik radova "Podjela nadležnosti između institucija Bosne i Hercegovine i entiteta"* (Banja Luka: 1999), 11–12.

can only be considered within the framework of reorganisation on the territory of the entire BiH,"[6] concluding that "the Dayton Constitution of BiH needs to be radically changed (…) that BiH should be organised as a decentralised state of regions (…) which implies the abolition of entities, cantons and the Brčko District,"[7] also calling for "changes in the constitution "with the aim of preventing obstructions and blockages of state institutions and abuses of the mechanism for protection of the vital interests of peoples, (…)," while "rejecting the concept of ethnic division of the country into three entities, expressing a permanent determination to build a civic BiH,"[8] and claiming that "the Constitution of BiH is discriminatory."[9]

Political parties from the FBiH with Croat electorate advocate for "BiH organised into several constitutional-administrative territorial units with the possibility of territorial discontinuity, which should be established in accordance with the principles of federalism and consociational democracy, with the consistent operationalisation of the fundamental principle from the preamble of the Dayton Constitution referring to the constituency of peoples,"[10] i.e., claim that it is necessary "for the purpose of achieving full membership in the EU to ensure, through the requisite and inevitable process of constitutional changes, the genuine equality of the Croat people with the other two, which implies the possibility of legitimate representation and protection of the vital national interest, as well as the administrative territorial reorganisation of BiH."[11]

Finally, the political parties based in the Republika Srpska (hereinafter: the RS) emphasise the principles of "three peoples and two entities as the way of functioning of post-war BiH (…)" and that the "constitutional changes are possible only through the legal procedure of amending the international treaty – that Annex 4, the Constitution of BiH, is – which entails an agreement between the two entities on changing the Constitution of BiH, and is to be

6 Programme Declaration SDA, 25. 9. 2023, https://sda.ba/assets/img/programska_deklaracija_sda.pdf.

7 Programme of the Social Democratic Party of Bosnia and Herzegovina, 25. 9. 2023, http://www.sdp.ba/upload/documents/dokumenti/PROGRAM_SDP_BiH.pdf.

8 Programme Orientation of Narod i pravda 2022–2026, 25. 9. 2023, https://www.narodipravda.ba/wp-content/uploads/2022/04/Kongresni-Dokumenti-A4-FINAL.pdf.

9 Naša stranka, Amendments to the Constitution of BiH, 25. 9. 2023, https://www.nasastranka.ba/uploads/documents/2-izmjene-ustava-bih_1667466656.pdf.

10 Elections Programme HDZ BiH, 25. 9. 2023, https://hdzbih.org/kandidati/HDZ_BiH_Izborni_program_2022.pdf.

11 HDZ 1990, Party Programme, 25. 9. 2023, https://hdz1990.ba/program-stranke/.

followed by constitutional amendments,"[12] that "the RS is an indisputable and immutable category" (...), as well as that "political actions and debates advocating for reorganisation of BiH contrary to the Dayton Peace Agreement are unacceptable," whereby the response to these ideas consists of "strengthening the position of the RS, based on the Dayton Agreement and the existing entity borders within BiH, with two entity units: RS and FBiH,"[13] stating that the vision of "the RS implies absolute protection and promotion of its constitutional Dayton capacities, their strengthening and complete emancipation of the Republic within the Dayton BiH, with full respect for the constitutional and legal position of the RS."[14]

The influence of the so-called "international community" is another factor that has been decisively shaping internal political conditions in BiH for decades. The beginnings of this influence go back to the joint declaration of the USA and the European Community of 10 March 1992 on the international recognition of the Yugoslav republics,[15] stating that BiH should receive international recognition if it "adopts without delay constitutional arrangements that will provide for a peaceful and harmonious development of this republic within its existing borders." Acting in accordance with this declaration, the political representatives of Muslims (Alija Izetbegović), Serbs (Radovan Karadžić) and Croats (Mate Boban) gave their consent on 18 March 1992 to the so-called Statement on Principles for New Constitutional Arrangements for BiH (according to Carrington–Cutileiro plan),[16] to continue negotiations and adopt a constitutional law amending the constitution of BiH. However, the crisis in BiH escalated on 6 and 8 April 1992, with the recognition of BiH independence by Germany and the USA, despite the absence of the adoption of the new constitutional arrangement for BiH. With Alija Izetbegović abandoning further negotiations on constitutional amendments (with undoubted encouragement of the then US ambassador to Yugoslavia, Warren

12 Programme Principles of the Alliance of Independent Social Democrats, 25. 9. 2023, https://snsd.org/wp-content/uploads/2012/03/Programski_principi_SNSD_6_Sabor.pdf.

13 Programme of the Serbian Democratic Party, 25. 9. 2023, https://www.sds.rs/UcitaneSlike//admin/Program_SDS.pdf.

14 PDP – Programme for the Reconstruction of the Republika Srpska, 25. 9. 2023, https://global-uploads.webflow.com/6459fecb7702f1001540f154/646dec4c63dae48be1b1326e_Program%20obnove%20Republike%20Srpske.pdf.

15 US-EC Declaration on the recognition of the Yugoslav Republics, 20. 10. 2023, http://aei-dev.library.pitt.edu/64582/1/US-EC_Declaration_on_the_recognition_of_the_Yugoslav_Republics.pdf.

16 Archives of Glas Srpske from March 1992, 20. 10. 2023, https://arhivapdf.glassrpske.rs/novine/1992/03/GlasSrpske19920319.pdf.

Zimmermann),[17] the Carrington–Cutileiro plan failed, after which war and the *de facto* disintegration of Bosnia and Herzegovina ensued. During the war, the so-called international community, through peace negotiations of the warring parties, created several peace plans with the aim of defining acceptable "constitutional arrangements" that were required by the declaration of 10 March 1992.[18] The crown of these peace negotiations was the signing of the Dayton Agreement.

The influence of the so-called international community also extends to the period of Dayton Agreement implementation. The time from 1997 to 2006 was marked by intense interventionism, which, among other things, manifested itself in the Office of the High Representative (hereinafter: the OHR) – in the unlawfully imposed constitutional amendments and laws, removing elected political representatives,[19] judges, prosecutors and public officials[20] from their positions, which was often accompanied by the deprivation of all civil rights,[21] the confiscation of assets of legal entities,[22] up to the illegal actions of SFOR of utilising physical coercion.[23] In legal science, the imposition of constitutional amendments and laws[24] was particularly criticised, for which there were

17 U.S. Policymakers on Bosnia Admit Errors in Opposing Partition in 1992, 20. 10. 2023, https://www.nytimes.com/1993/08/29/world/us-policymakers-on-bosnia-admit-errors-in-opposing-partition-in-1992.html.

18 For more, see: Zvonko Miljko, "Mirovni planovi i federaliziranje Bosne i Hercegovine," *Zbornik radova Pravnog fakulteta Sveučilišta u Mostaru*, XVI, (2003).

19 President Poplasen Dismissed, 30. 10. 2023, https://www.ohr.int/president-poplasen-dismissed/; Decision removing Ante Jelavic from his position as the Croat member of the BiH Presidency, 30. 10. 2023, https://www.ohr.int/decision-removing-ante-jelavic-from-his-position-as-the-croat-member-of-the-bih-presidency-2/.

20 Removals and Suspensions from Office, 30. 10. 2023, https://www.ohr.int/cat/hrs-decisions/removals-and-suspensions-from-office/page/2/?mo&y. It is indicative that the European Court of Human Rights (in the case Berić and Others v. BiH, 2005) did not accept to decide on the legal validity of some of the dismissals of officials, leaving the affected persons without any legal protection.

21 For more, see: Zeh, Juli, *Die Diktatur der Demokraten, Warum ohne Recht keine Staat zu machen ist* (Hamburg: edition Körber-Stiftung, 2012), 132, 135, 143–144, 151–152.

22 Hercegovačka banka uništena je zbog pokušaja pretvaranja Hrvata u manjinu, 30. 10. 2023, https://www.vecernji.ba/vijesti/hercegovacka-banka-unistena-je-zbog-pokusaja-pretvaranja-hrvata-u-manjinu-1482206; Decision appointing a Provisional Administrator for the Hercegovacka Banka, 30. 10. 2023, https://www.ohr.int/decision-appointing-a-provisional-administrator-for-the-hercegovacka-banka/.

23 Report on SFOR's actions against Serbian Orthodox Church in Pale, 30. 10. 2023, https://www.mitropolijadabrobosanska.org/starovlah/en/.

24 Zeh, *Die Diktatur der Demokraten, Warum ohne Recht keine Staat zu machen ist*, 49, 121–131; Gerald Knaus and Felix Martin, "Lessons from Bosnia and Herzegovina: Travails of the European Raj," *Journal of Democrcy*, Vol. 14, No. 3, (July 2003), 67–70.

attempts to legally reinforce such actions by: (1) referring to the authority under Annex X, Article 5, according to which the high representative is the final interpreter of the Agreement on Civilian Implementation of the Peace Settlement contained in that annex,[25] and (2) invoking the so-called Bonn powers resulting from item XI subitem 2 of the Bonn Declaration from December 1997,[26] a political act of the Peace Implementation Council,[27] which welcomes the intention (therefore, provides no authorisation) of the High Representative to adopt temporary measures from the domain of the Presidency of BiH and the Council of Ministers of BiH (but not the legislative bodies in BiH) and other measures. It undoubtedly emerges from the text of the Bonn Declaration that the so-called Bonn powers have a political, not a legal basis,[28] and that they do not enable the unlawful imposition of constitutional amendments and laws.

The interventionist influence of the so-called international community[29] has persisted until today, both on the basis of the text of the Dayton Agreement[30] and the *via facti* interventionism of the international Western community.[31] Here, it is important to note the difference between, on the one hand,

25 The non-persuasiveness of this argument is evident, since the authority of the high representative is limited to interpretation of Annex X to the Dayton Agreement, especially considering that the interpretation and creation of law are two separate juridical-logical operations.

26 PIC Bonn Conclusions, 30. 10. 2023, https://www.ohr.int/pic-bonn-conclusions-3/.

27 The Peace Implementation Council is a self-selected group of representatives of 43 countries and 12 international organisations, formed without a legal basis at the Peace Implementation Conference in London, on 8 and 9 December 1995, with the aim of animating international support for the Dayton Agreement. For more, see: Peace Implementation Council, 30. 10. 2023, https://www.ohr.int/international-community-in-bih/peace-implementation-council/.

28 Vlaški, Bojan and Romić, Marko, "Prav(n)a priroda akata visokog predstavnika za Bosnu i Hercegovinu – (u)pravna i(li) politička," in *Uporedni izazovi u savremenom pravu – in memoriam dr Stefan Andonović*, ed. Rajić Ćalić, Jovana (Beograd: Institut za uporedno pravo i Pravni fakultet Univerziteta u Kragujevcu, 2023), 104–108.

29 Truth be told, after 24 February 2022, it is difficult to talk about a single international community, since the contemporary world is increasingly leaning towards multipolarity. Therefore, for the diplomats gathered in the Peace Implementation Council and for Christian Schmidt, it would be more appropriate at the current moment to use the term "international Western community," which is under the US suzerainty.

30 The presence of foreign judges in the composition of the Constitutional Court of BiH, whose termination of office is one of the requirements on BiH's path to the EU.

31 In the form of actions by the Peace Implementation Council and also, as of 1 August 2021, actions of the German citizen Christian Schmidt, who without the consent of the UN Security Council, and without a valid legal basis entered the Office of the High Representative and significantly influenced internal political frictions by unlawful imposition

interventionism of the so-called international community until 31 July 2021 – when a kind of a "legal cloak"[32] of interventionist activities existed – and, on the other hand, the *via facti* interventionism embodied in the actions of Christian Schmidt when he joined the OHR. The current situation is the result of the general climate of the so-called division within the international community, not only in UN bodies, such as the Security Council and the General Assembly, but also in the activities of global and regional organisations that contribute to multipolarity of the contemporary world. The actions of Christian Schmidt represent only one of the global metastases of such division, making Schmidt nothing more than a diplomatic representative of the international Western community in BiH, which elected him with overwhelming majority in the Peace Implementation Council.

In the current turbulent global geopolitical circumstances, comparable to those in the beginning of the 1990s, all domestic actors should understand the sovereignty of BiH in the true sense of the word, by giving up unrealistic maximalist political goals (in the spirit of the principle of federal loyalty) and by turning to mutual cooperation and compromises in accordance with the Constitution of BiH, along with the elimination of malignant foreign influences from whichever part of the world they come. In this sense, it is important to underscore the 2019 Opinion of the European Commission, according to which "extensive international supervision is in principle incompatible with the sovereignty of Bosnia and Herzegovina and therefore with EU membership."[33] Although, bearing in mind historical experiences, the author of this chapter is not optimistic that mutual cooperation and compromises will really come to life in its entirety and in continuity, this chapter will give the contours of "roadside signs" that can be useful for their full realisation.

---

of constitutional amendments and laws. See: UN Documents for Bosnia & Herzegovina: Security Council Resolutions, 29. 11. 2023, https://www.securitycouncilreport.org/un_documents_type/security-council-resolutions/page/1?ctype=Bosnia±%26amp%3B±Herzegovina&cbtype=bosnia-herzegovina#038;cbtype=bosnia-herzegovina.

32 Starting with UN Security Council Resolution 1031 and subsequent resolutions, support was expressed for the high representative, his "Dayton powers," and with Resolution 1144 and the conclusions of the Bonn Declaration from December 1997 – ending with Resolution 1869. Truth be told, neither did these resolutions nor the UN Charter authorise the High Representative to change constitutions and pass laws in substitution of the democratically elected competent authorities in BiH, which he did through an extremely extensive interpretation of the so-called of Bonn powers.

33 Commission Opinion on Bosnia and Herzegovina's application for membership of the European Union, 30. 6. 2024, https://neighbourhood-enlargement.ec.europa.eu/document/download/6cbf9fa7-a288-4497-9e4a-17527bcbafc5_en?filename=20190529-bosnia-and-herzegovina-opinion.pdf.

3 Which Mechanism Can Increase the Effectiveness of Federalism?

Despite above obstacles to the development of federalism in BiH, comparative experiences indicate that federalism *per se* is not the cause of instability. Namely, the leading states of the contemporary world adopt a certain form of federalism. Most of the G7, G20, and BRICS member states are federally organised to a greater or lesser degree. In comparative legal theory, the EU is included in the model with confederal elements of "a complex organisation organised on the basis of international law, which is based both on the principle of interstate cooperation and on the principle of "complementing" the community order and the state order, a principle that had special innovative effects."[34] The efficiency of federalism is also manifested in public administrations of the EU, because among the member states that use technical assistance to strengthen the capacity of public administration, the federally organised member states are not priority beneficiaries, whose public administrations can accordingly be evaluated as efficient.[35] Finally, research data of the Swiss UBS bank reveal that federally regulated countries (Switzerland, Belgium, the USA, Australia, etc.) are at the top of the ranking list of countries with the greatest (median) wealth of citizens.[36]

The key framework for cooperation in contemporary federations are intergovernmental relations which, according to William Anderson, can be defined as "an important body of activities or interactions occurring between governmental units of all types and levels within the federal system."[37] On European soil, intergovernmental relations are encompassed by the term "cooperative federalism," which means "cooperation, collaboration of two levels of government, two categories of political-territorial units, federation, on the one hand, and federal units, on the other hand," i.e., it indicates "mutual cooperation of federal units among themselves, either without any authority of the federation, or with certain forms of its participation."[38] Intergovernmental rela-

34 de Vergotini, Đuzepe, *Uporedno ustavno pravo*, prevela: Mr Ljiljana Grubač, stručna redaktura prevoda: Prof. dr Marković, Ratko (Beograd: Službeni glasnik, 2015), 440.

35 Efficient public administration, Thematic objective 11, 30. 10. 2023, https://ec.europa.eu/regional_policy/policy/themes/better-public-administration_en.

36 UBS Global Wealth Report, 30. 10. 2023, https://www.ubs.com/global/en/family-office-uhnw/reports/global-wealth-report-2023.html.

37 Anderson, William, *Intergovernmental Relations in Review* (Minneapolis: University of Minnesota Press, 1960), 3.

38 Miodrag Jovičić, *Savremeni federalizam* (Beograd: Javno preduzeće "Službeni glasnik," Pravni fakultet Univerziteta u Beograd, 2006), 247, 255.

tions, or cooperative federalism, have two dimensions – vertical (relations between the federation and federal units, which as a rule do not mean hierarchy) and horizontal (mutual relations between federal units), and their basic mechanisms are: intergovernmental agreements and intergovernmental bodies.

3.1 *Intergovernmental Agreements*

Contractual cooperation in federalism has had its continuity for several centuries because, according to Georges Burdeau, at the foundation of federalism "lies the idea of an agreement, a contract (foedus), i.e., a deal between the participants of a single order."[39] Intergovernmental agreements can be written bilateral or multilateral legal acts (formal intergovernmental agreements), but also political acts, even oral agreements of political officials (informal intergovernmental agreements).

The subject of intergovernmental agreements can be any matter within the jurisdiction of signatory parties, as long as they are not contrary to the constitution and laws of the federation and signatory federal units. The question arises whether these agreements produce legal effects or whether they are political acts. In this regard, federations can be classified into two groups: (1) federations in which intergovernmental agreements are political acts, and produce legal effects exceptionally, through law, and (2) federations in which intergovernmental agreements are considered legal acts and as such produce legal effects. Although the conclusion of intergovernmental agreements in comparative federalism, as a rule, is not subject to regulation by special rules of procedure, in Canada[40] and Switzerland[41] this matter is regulated. As for regulating the procedure for amending and/or supplementing intergovernmental agreements, as a rule, these are done

---

39 Burdeau, Georges, *Traite de Science politique*, t. II, L'etat, 2. ed. (Paris: 1967), 461. Cited from: Jovičić, *Savremeni federalizam*, 37.

40 See: Adam, Marc-Antoine, Bergeron, Josée and Bonnard Marianne, "Intergovernmental Relations in Canada: Competing Visions and Diverse Dynamics," in *Intergovernmental relations in federal systems: comparative structures and dynamics*, eds. Poirier Johanne, Saunders, Cheryl and Kincaid, John (Ontario: Oxford University Press, 2015), 157.

41 In Switzerland, the Framework Intercantonal Agreement (*Interkantonale Rahmenvereinbarung*) was adopted, prescribing the rules for concluding horizontal intergovernmental agreements in connection with financial equalisation, while at the intercantonal level numerous guides, guidelines, and other templates have been adopted that facilitate the conclusion of intergovernmental agreements. For more, see: Iff, Andrea, et al., *Interkantonale und interkommunale Zusammenarbeit: Defizite bezüglich parlamentarischer und direktdemokratischer Mitwirkung* (Bern: KPM-Verlag, 2010), 39–43.

by agreement of the will of the signatory parties, with prohibition of any unilateral action.[42]

3.2 *Intergovernmental Bodies*

Intergovernmental bodies can be defined as organisational forms of vertical or horizontal connection of bodies of the federation and federal units. According to Agranoff, intergovernmental bodies are manifested in: (1) multitude of conferences, committees, and liaison bodies between the federation and federal units; (2) intergovernmental summits, such as conferences of prime ministers, and (3) concentration of authority for intergovernmental relations at all levels in the hands of special bodies and coordination officers.[43]

Intergovernmental bodies are a credible expression of cooperative federalism and enable a fuller participation of federal units in the performance of functions of the federation than is achieved by the work of the majority of upper houses of federal parliaments. Therefore, since the second half of the 20th century, intergovernmental bodies have gradually become key forums for discussions about numerous issues, the resolution of which depends on the smooth functioning of federal states, ensuring the exchange of information, coordinated action, especially in areas under the jurisdiction of federal units, when this is necessary and there is no consensus that these areas should be transferred to the jurisdiction of the federation through constitutional amendments. In short, in the words of Ronald Watts, "the institutions and processes for intergovernmental collaboration serve two important functions: conflict resolution and a means of adapting to changing circumstances."[44]

---

42 This rule applies, for example, in the USA, Switzerland, Canada and India. Zimmerman, Cf. Joseph F., *Interstate Relations – The Neglected Dimension of Federalism* (Westport, Connecticut, London: Praeger, 1996), 40–41; Strebel, Michael, *Executivföderalismus in der Schweiz?* (Baden-Baden: Nomos, 2014), 217–218; Singh, Mahendra Prasad and Saxena, Rekha, "Intergovernmental Relations in India: From Centralization to Decentralization," in *Intergovernmental relations in federal systems: comparative structures and dynamics*, eds. Poirier, Johanne, Saunders, Cheryl and Kincaid, John, (Ontario: Oxford University Press, 2015), 259.

43 Agranoff, Robert, "R.L. Watts and the Managing of IGR in Federal Systems," in *The Federal Idea, Essays in Honour of Ronald L. Watts*, eds. Chourchene, Thomas J., Allan, John R., Leuprecht, Christian and Verrelli, Nadia, (Montreal&Kingston, London, Ithaca: Institute of Intergovernmental Relations, School of Policy Studies, Queen's University, McGill-Queen's University Press, 2011), 273.

44 Watts, Ronald L., *Comparing Federal Systems in the 1990s* (Ontario: Institute of Intergovernmental Relations, Queen's University Kingston, 1996), 51.

It is possible to distinguish between several types of intergovernmental bodies according to different criteria. In literature, the following are distinguished: (1) intra-jurisdictional intergovernmental bodies, i.e., bodies of the federation whose composition includes representatives of the executive bodies of federal units (such as the German Bundesrat), and (2) inter-jurisdictional intergovernmental bodies, which are not federal bodies.[45] According to the participant criteria of inter-jurisdictional intergovernmental bodies, they can be divided into: (1) vertical intergovernmental bodies, and (2) horizontal intergovernmental bodies. According to the territorial principle, horizontal intergovernmental bodies can be divided into: (1) general, gathering representatives of executive (administrative) bodies from all federal units, and (2) regional, gathering representatives of executive (administrative) bodies from certain federal units, connected by geographical, economic, ethno-national, or other criteria. According to the criterion of (non)existence of a legal basis, the following are distinguished: (1) formal, and (2) informal intergovernmental bodies. Based on the composition of intergovernmental bodies, they can be: (1) executive-political bodies, which are made up of chief executives or ministers, and (2) administrative intergovernmental bodies, which are made up of managerial or other administrative officers. Administrative intergovernmental bodies can be divided according to (non)existence of legal subjectivity into: (1) informalised administrative intergovernmental bodies (conferences of administrative officers, working groups, professional associations, etc.), and (2) formalised administrative intergovernmental bodies, i.e. intergovernmental bodies of public administration, which, on the basis of the constitution, laws or intergovernmental agreements, are jointly formed by the federation and federal units, i.e., two or more federal units. According to regularity of sessions, the following can be distinguished: (1) standing, and (2) temporary (ad hoc) intergovernmental bodies.[46]

45 Cameron, David, "The Structure of Intergovernmental Relations," I*nternational Social Science Journal* (*Federalism*), 167, UNESCO Blackwell Publishers (March 2001): 121. Cited from: Rekha Saxena, *Situating Federalism: Mechanisms of Intergovernmental Relations in Canada and India* (New Delhi: Manohar, 2006), 155.

46 Vlaški, Bojan, *Organizacija javne uprave u federalizmu – posebno u Bosni i Hercegovini - doktorska disertacija* (*neobjavljeno*) (Beograd: Pravni fakultet Univerziteta u Beogradu, 2019), 172–173.

4 Intergovernmental Relations in BiH: Application and Potential

Federalism in BiH needs to affirm the elements of cooperation,[47] "which are almost non-existent in the text of the constitution of a unified state."[48] However, in practice, there are examples of concluding intergovernmental agreements and the existence of intergovernmental bodies, which often result in asymmetric arrangements in BiH.[49]

4.1 *Intergovernmental Agreements*

Intergovernmental agreements in BiH have their basis in Article III of the Constitution of BiH, but also in the provisions of individual laws. Two types of intergovernmental agreements can be distinguished in BiH: (1) constitutional agreements, and (2) administrative agreements. The subject of the former was the transfer of competences from the entities to the institutions of BiH, while the second group aims at the cooperation of administrative bodies for the purpose of performing administrative tasks more efficiently and effectively.

Constitutional agreements have a constitutional basis in Article III/5a of the Constitution of BiH, which, *inter alia*, establishes that "Bosnia and Herzegovina shall assume responsibility for such other matters as are agreed by the Entities," and in Article IV/4e of the Constitution of BiH, which stipulates that the BiH Parliamentary Assembly is, *inter alia*, responsible for "such other matters as are necessary to carry out its duties or as are assigned to it by mutual agreement of the Entities." In the constitutional practice so far, two intergovernmental constitutional agreements resulted in the transfer of competences from the entities to the institutions of BiH and the formation of new public administration bodies at the level of BiH (indirect taxation and defence).[50]

---

47 This approach arises from the adopted consociational model of the political system of Bosnia and Herzegovina. See: Vranješ, Nevenko, "Dejtonska i postdejtonska koncepcija političkog sistema Bosne i Hercegovine," in *Zbornik radova "Pravo između stvaranja i tumačenja" Tom I* (Istočno Sarajevo: Pravni fakultet Univerziteta u Istočnom Sarajevu, 2023), 301–306.

48 Markert, Thomas, "Prilog Venecijanske komisije o federalizmu u Bosni i Hercegovini," in *Federalne strukture u Evropi i Bosni i Hercegovini*, ed. Markert, Thomas and Winkelmann, Ingo, (Sarajevo: Ambasada SR Njemačke i Vijeće Evrope, 2001), 96.

49 Sahadžić, Maja, "Federal theory on constitutional asymmetries: revisited," *Queen Mary Law Journal 7* (Autumn 2016), 141–146.

50 Conclusions of the National Assembly of the Republika Srpska on consideration of the customs and tax system reform, *Official Gazette of the Republika Srpska*, 95/03; Decision of the Parliament of the Federation of BiH on granting consent to the Agreement on competences in indirect taxation, *Official Gazette of the Federation of BiH*, 64/03; Agree-

These were horizontal bilateral intergovernmental constitutional agreements that produced (constitutional) legal effects, after being certified by the signatures of entity prime ministers[51] with previously obtained consent of entity parliaments. Bearing in mind the fact that the procedure for concluding these agreements is not prescribed by the Constitution of BiH, the competence to regulate them belongs to the entities, although the entities have not yet taken steps in this direction. In this sense, *de constitutione et de lege ferenda* it is necessary to prescribe the mandatory prior consent of entity parliaments to the conclusion of intergovernmental (constitutional) agreements,[52] and the entity parliaments could also request their confirmation through a referendum, which is in place in some federations (e.g. in Switzerland and the USA).

Administrative agreements have as their subject matter achieving coordination and cooperation between different administrative bodies in BiH. These agreements can be horizontal or vertical, bilateral or multilateral, and they are significant because they functionally connect the administrative bodies at different levels of government in BiH. Administrative agreements in BiH are most often concluded in relation to police cooperation, although they also appear in other areas (environmental protection, fiscal policy, implementation of security measures, traffic), with the possibility of their application in migration management, water management, protection against natural disasters, health, tourism, etc. Moreover, administrative bodies and intergovernmental bodies were in some cases established by administrative agreements, namely: the Office of the Coordinator of the Brčko District of BiH (hereinafter: BD BiH) in the Council of Ministers of BiH (established in accordance with the Agreement on the Establishment of the Office of the Coordinator of the BD BiH concluded on 18 December 2005) and the BiH Fiscal Council, established in 2005 by the Agreement on the Establishment of the BiH Fiscal Council.[53]

---

ment between the Federation of BiH and the Republika Srpska on the transfer of jurisdiction in defence, *Official Gazette of the Republika Srpska*, 4/06.

51 For more, see: Ademović, Nedim, Marko, Joseph and Marković, Goran, *Ustavno pravo Bosne i Hercegovine* (Sarajevo: Konrad Adenauer Stiftung, 2012), 113; Steiner, Christian et al., *Ustav Bosne i Hercegovine Komentar* (Sarajevo: Fondacija Konrad Adenauer, 2010), 548.

52 Cf. Marković, Goran, *Bosanskohercegovački federalizam* (Beograd, Sarajevo: Službeni glasnik, University Press, 2012), 154.

53 See: Strukture upravljanja državom u BiH, Jačanjem institucionalnih kapaciteta i preuzimanjem vlasništva nad promjenama u procesu integracije u EU do funkcionalne države, Vanjskopolitička inicijativa BH, 36; Law on the Fiscal Council in BiH, *Official Gazette of BiH*, 63/08.

4.2 *Intergovernmental Bodies in BiH*

Irrespective of the distribution of legislative and executive competences, "in practice, almost everywhere, cooperation inevitably takes place between similar bodies of the federal administration and the administration of federal units," whereby such cooperation "(...) can in some cases take on institutionalised forms and be realised within the framework of special bodies."[54] Normative assumptions of intergovernmental cooperation are established in the Constitution of BiH and the Constitution of the Federation of BiH.

Article III/4 of the Constitution of BiH entitled "Coordination" stipulates the relations between the institutions of BiH and the entities, stating that "the Presidency may decide to facilitate inter-Entity cooperation on matters not within the responsibilities of Bosnia and Herzegovina." Moreover, the Rules of Procedure of the BiH Presidency[55] stipulate in Article 50 (1) that the BiH Presidency "in order to ensure inter-entity coordination on matters that are not within the competence of the state of Bosnia and Herzegovina (...) may invite the entities to attend the Cooperation Conference." Although "Coordination" and cooperation conferences have not been implemented in practice so far, informal meetings of entity prime ministers with the chair of the BiH Council of Ministers have been held from time to time, without making any legally binding decisions.

The foundations of intergovernmental cooperation in the FBiH can be found in the provisions of Article III/3 (4) and Article V/3 of the Constitution of the Federation of BiH, which foresee the possibility of establishing several different intergovernmental bodies: (1) Inter-Cantonal Council, (2) Cantonal Council, and (3) coordination bodies (e.g. commissions and working groups), to perform coordinating activities of the cantons in matters of common interest for two or more cantons. However, "the council has never been formed, nor is there any coordinating body between the FBiH and the cantons, or between the cantons, that would resolve these and similar matters" on a permanent basis.[56] Nevertheless, over the previous two decades, certain forms of informal intergovernmental cooperation were applied.[57] Given the significant scope of

54 Jovičić, *Savremeni federalizam*, 252.

55 Rules of Procedure of the BiH Presidency, *Official Gazette of BiH*, 10/13, 32/13, 22/14.

56 Taletović, Alen, "Organizacijski i funkcionalni problem organa uprave u FBiH," u *Zbornik radova -Međunarodna naučna konferencija "Javni i privatni aspekti nužnih pravnih reformi u BiH: Koliko daleko možemo ići?"* (Tuzla: 2014), 214.

57 These are, *inter alia*, meetings of the FBiH and cantonal prime ministers, meetings of the FBiH and cantonal ministers in some areas, visits of delegations from the Government of the Federation of BiH to some cantons, and occasional joint sessions of the Government of the Federation of BiH and the governments of some cantons. The subject of these

cantonal legislative and executive powers in the Constitution of the Federation of BiH, we believe that the institutionalisation and intensification of intergovernmental relations in the Federation of BiH are prerequisites for intergovernmental cooperation in the entire BiH, especially inter-entity cooperation.

As for horizontal intergovernmental cooperation in BiH, several meetings of entity prime ministers have been held so far. Moreover, as a result of these meetings, the governments of the Republika Srpska and the Federation of BiH held two joint sessions in 2017. At these sessions, several matters of interest to both entities were comprehensively discussed for the first time. The first joint session of the governments of the Republika Srpska and the Federation of BiH was held in Banja Luka on 9 March 2017. At this "founding" session of entity governments, the methodology was defined for future joint sessions. Before the joint session of the governments, bilateral meetings of individual ministers of the two governments were held in Banja Luka on the same day. The next joint session of entity governments was held after only seven months in Sarajevo, on 4 October 2017. Although 2017 gave rise to expectations of more intensive cooperation in the future, after an almost six-year break, the next joint session of entity governments was held on 8 June 2023 in Banja Luka.[58] Occasional informal meetings of ministers in entity governments were taking place for the purpose of coordinating activities of common interest (e.g. accession to the "Bologna Declaration," pension and disability insurance, veterans' affairs, maintenance and construction of transport infrastructure), as were occasional informal meetings of entity governments with the Government of BD BiH.[59]

Finally, several formal intergovernmental bodies were formed in BiH, of which we single out, according to the classification from section three of this chapter, two intra-jurisdictional, vertical, executive-political bodies: the Governing Board of the Indirect Taxation Authority and the Fiscal Council of BiH, and one inter-jurisdictional, horizontal, administrative intergovernmental body – Inter-Entity Body for Environment.

---

meetings and sessions were mainly in the fields of finance, economic development, social protection, construction of traffic and other infrastructure, education, forestry, etc.

58 At these sessions, cooperation was discussed in the following areas: implementation of obligations from the 2015–2018 Reform Agenda for Bosnia and Herzegovina, cooperation with the International Monetary Fund, combating grey economy, export of wood assortments, status of obsolete military assets, environmental protection, construction of traffic infrastructure, continuation of police cooperation, enforcement of criminal and misdemeanour sanctions, technical regulations, and science and technology.

59 For more, see: Vlaški, *Organizacija javne uprave u federalizmu – posebno u Bosni i Hercegovini – doktorska disertacija (neobjavljeno)*, 303–305.

5 Conclusion

Bearing in mind the insufficiently developed legal framework of intergovernmental relations in BiH, we believe that with parallel emancipation of BiH from tutorship by the so-called international community, and a clearly expressed political will for cooperation, it is necessary to increase the quantity and quality of the use of mechanisms of intergovernmental relations, i.e., intergovernmental (administrative) agreements, intergovernmental bodies and the mechanism of coordination of the European integration process. The importance of intergovernmental cooperation was vividly expressed on one occasion by the president of the Conference of Governments of Central Switzerland with the following words: "Cooperation in Central Switzerland will become even more important in the future. I am particularly referring to the areas of transport, health care, education in general, tourism, and security. In the police field, we have already laid a good basis for further development of cooperation through the new police cordon. There is no need for a 'Canton of Central Switzerland' (unification of six central Swiss cantons into one canton – B.V.) for successful cooperation – healthy competition between cantons strengthens the entire region – and that is why uniform regulation of all six Central Swiss cantons is not always necessary."[60] Following the model of developed federations, it is necessary to encourage cooperation in areas of common interest and formalise it, if necessary, by agreement. From the organisational perspective, it is necessary to institutionalise the existing informal intergovernmental bodies. Joint sessions of entity governments can be a particularly useful mechanism, bearing in mind the scope of entity competences according to the Constitution of BiH. One of the reasons that require "raising the bar" of horizontal and vertical administrative cooperation in BiH is undoubtedly the European integration process. However, increasing intergovernmental cooperation to achieve the standards set by the EU should not be an end in itself. Vertical and horizontal cooperation, as a neglected aspect of federalism in BiH, should restore citizens' trust in institutions, stop negative (e)migration trends, and further models of steady development of federalism and a more prosperous future. Ivo Andrić, a great connoisseur of the Bosnian and Herzegovinian mentality, wrote in *Bosnian Chronicle:* "Four faiths live in this narrow, mountainous and meagre strip of land ... expecting salvation from somewhere outside, each from the opposite direction." When "salvation" begins to be sought within BiH, it will be possible to build a spirit of comprom-

60 Strebel, *Executivföderalismus in der Schweiz?*, 220–221.

ise and a minimum of consensus on the future of BiH, which is a debt to future generations.

Bibliography

Adam, Marc-Antoine, Bergeron, Josée and Bonnard, Marianne, "Intergovernmental Relations in Canada: Competing Visions and Diverse Dynamics", in *Intergovernmental relations in federal systems: comparative structures and dynamics*, eds. Johanne Poirier, Cheryl Saunders and John Kincaid, (Ontario: Oxford University Press, 2015).

Ademović, Nedim, Marko, Joseph and Marković, Goran, *Ustavno pravo Bosne i Hercegovine* (Sarajevo: Konrad Adenauer Stiftung, 2012).

Agranoff, Robert, "R.L. Watts and the Managing of IGR in Federal Systems", in *The Federal Idea, Essays in Honour of Ronald L. Watts*, eds. Thomas J. Chourchene, John R. Allan, Christian Leuprecht and Nadia Verrelli, (Montreal&Kingston, London, Ithaca: Institute of Intergovernmental Relations, School of Policy Studies, Queen's University, McGill-Queen's University Press, 2011).

Anderson, William, *Intergovernmental Relations in Review*, (Minneapolis: University of Minnesota Press, 1960).

Annex IV to the General Framework Agreement for Peace in Bosnia and Herzegovina – Constitution of Bosnia and Herzegovina.

Arhiva Glasa Srpske iz marta 1992. godine, 20. 10. 2023, https://arhivapdf.glassrpske.rs/novine/1992/03/GlasSrpske19920319.pdf.

Begić, Kasim, "Uloga Ustavnog suda Bosne i Hercegovine", in *Federalne strukture u Evropi i Bosni i Hercegovini*, ed. Thomas Markert/Ingo Winkelmann (Sarajevo: Ambasada SR Njemačke i Vijeće Evrope, 2001).

Cameron, David, "The Structure of Intergovernmental Relations", *International Social Science Journal* (*Federalism*), 167, UNESCO Blackwell Publishers (March 2001).

de Vergotini, Đuzepe, *Uporedno ustavno pravo*, prevela: Mr Ljiljana Grubač, stručna redaktura prevoda: Prof. dr Ratko Marković (Beograd: Službeni glasnik, 2015).

Decision appointing a Provisional Administrator for the Hercegovacka Banka, 30. 10. 2023, https://www.ohr.int/decision-appointing-a-provisional-administrator-for-the-hercegovacka-banka/.

Decision removing Ante Jelavic from his position as the Croat member of the BiH Presidency, 30. 10. 2023, https://www.ohr.int/decision-removing-ante-jelavic-from-his-position-as-the-croat-member-of-the-bih-presidency-2/.

Efficient public administration, Thematic objective 11, 30. 10. 2023, https://ec.europa.eu/regional_policy/policy/themes/better-public-administration_en.

HDZ 1990, Program stranke, 25. 9. 2023, https://hdz1990.ba/program-stranke/.

Hercegovačka banka uništena je zbog pokušaja pretvaranja Hrvata u manjinu, 30. 10. 2023, https://www.vecernji.ba/vijesti/hercegovacka-banka-unistena-je-zbog-pokusaja-pretvaranja-hrvata-u-manjinu-1482206.

Ibrahimagić, Omer, *Državno uređenje Bosne i Hercegovine* (Sarajevo: Vijeće Kongresa bošnjačkih intelektualaca, 2005).

Iff, Andrea et al., *Interkantonale und interkommunale Zusammenarbeit: Defizite bezüglich parlamentarischer und direktdemokratischer Mitwirkung* (Bern: KPM-Verlag, 2010).

Izborni program HDZ-a BiH, 25. 9. 2023, https://hdzbih.org/kandidati/HDZ_BiH_Izborni_program_2022.pdf.

Jovičić, Miodrag, *Savremeni federalizam* (Beograd: Javno preduzeće "Službeni glasnik", Pravni fakultet Univerziteta u Beograd, 2006).

Knaus, Gerald and Martin, Felix, "Lessons from Bosnia and Herzegovina: Travails of the European Raj", *Journal of Democracy*, Vol. 14, No. 3, (July 2003).

Kunić, Petar, *Promjene Ustava Bosne i Hercegovine – pro et contra: kritičke opaske na pojedina institucionalna rješenja: dosadašnja iskustva i moguća rješenja* (Banja Luka: Udruženje nastavnika i saradnika Univerziteta u Banjoj Luci, 2015).

Kurtćehajić, Suad, "Oblik državnog uređenja Bosne i Hercegovine zasnovanog na dejtonskom ustavu", *Pregled*, 3 (2012).

Kuzmanović, Rajko, *Ustavno pravo*, (Banja Luka: Pravni fakultet Univerziteta u Banjoj Luci, 2002).

Markert, Thomas, "Prilog Venecijanske komisije o federalizmu u Bosni i Hercegovini", in *Federalne strukture u Evropi i Bosni i Hercegovini*, ed. Thomas Markert/Ingo Winkelmann, (Sarajevo: Ambasada SR Njemačke i Vijeće Evrope, 2001).

Marković, Goran, *Bosanskohercegovački federalizam* (Beograd, Sarajevo: Službeni glasnik, University Press, 2012).

Marković, Goran, *Ustavni lavirint – Aporije ustavnog sistema Bosne i Hercegovine* (Beograd: Službeni glasnik, 2021).

Miljko, Zvonko, "Mirovni planovi i federaliziranje Bosne i Hercegovine", *Zbornik radova Pravnog fakulteta Sveučilišta u Mostaru*, XVI, (2003).

Miljko, Zvonko, *Ustavno uređenje Bosne i Hercegovine* (Zagreb: Hrvatska sveučilišna naklada, 2006).

Naša stranka, Izmjene Ustava BiH, 25. 9. 2023, https://www.nasastranka.ba/uploads/documents/2-izmjene-ustava-bih_1667466656.pdf.

Odluka Parlamenta Federacije BiH o davanju saglasnosti na Sporazum o nadležnostima u oblasti indirektnog oporezivanja, "*Službene novine Federacije BiH*", br. 64/03.

PDP – Program obnove Republike Srpske, 25. 9. 2023, https://global-uploads.webflow.com/6459fecb7702f1001540f154/646dec4c63dae48be1b1326e_Program%20obnove%20Republike%20Srpske.pdf.

Peace Implementation Council, 30. 10. 2023, https://www.ohr.int/international-community-in-bih/peace-implementation-council/.

PIC Bonn Conclusions, 30. 10. 2023, https://www.ohr.int/pic-bonn-conclusions-3/.

Pilipović, Milan, *Ustav Bosne i Hercegovine – normativno i stvarno* (Banja Luka: Pravni fakultet Univerziteta u Banjoj Luci, 2008).

Pobrić, Nurko, *Ustavno pravo* (Mostar: Slovo, 2000).

Poslovnik o radu Predsjedništva BiH, "*Službeni glasnik BiH*", br. 10/13, 32/13 i 22/14.

President Poplasen Dismissed, 30. 10. 2023, https://www.ohr.int/president-poplasen-dismissed/.

Program Socijaldemokratske partije Bosne i Hercegovine, 25. 9. 2023, http://www.sdp.ba/upload/documents/dokumenti/PROGRAM_SDP_BiH.pdf.

Program Srpske demokratske stranke, 25. 9. 2023, https://www.sds.rs/UcitaneSlike//admin/Program_SDS.pdf.

Programska deklaracija SDA, 25. 9. 2023, https://sda.ba/assets/img/programska_deklaracija_sda.pdf.

Programska orijentacija Naroda i pravde 2022–2026, 25. 9. 2023, https://www.narodipravda.ba/wp-content/uploads/2022/04/Kongresni-Dokumenti-A4-FINAL.pdf.

Programski principi Saveza nezavisnih socijaldemokrata, 25. 9. 2023, https://snsd.org/wp-content/uploads/2012/03/Programski_principi_SNSD_6_Sabor.pdf.

Removals and Suspensions from Office, 30. 10. 2023, https://www.ohr.int/cat/hrs-decisions/removals-and-suspensions-from-office/page/2/?mo&y.

Report on SFOR's actions against Serbian Orthodox Church in Pale, 30. 10. 2023, https://www.mitropolijadabrobosanska.org/starovlah/en/.

Sahadžić, Maja, "Federal theory on constitutional asymmetries: revisited", *Queen Mary Law Journal* 7 (Autumn 2016).

Savić, Snežana, *Dejtonska Bosna i Hercegovina* (Banja Luka: Pravni fakultet Univerziteta u Banjoj Luci, 2003).

Saxena, Rekha, *Situating Federalism: Mechanisms of Intergovernmental Relations in Canada and India* (New Delhi: Manohar, 2006).

Singh, Mahendra Prasad and Saxena, Rekha "Intergovernmental Relations in India: From Centralization to Decentralization", in *Intergovernmental relations in federal systems: comparative structures and dynamics*, eds. Johanne Poirier, Cheryl Saunders and John Kincaid, (Ontario: Oxford University Press, 2015).

Sporazum između Federacije BiH i Republike Srpske o prenosu nadležnosti u oblasti odbrane, "*Službeni glasnik Republike Srpske*", br. 4/06.

Steiner, Christian et al., *Ustav Bosne i Hercegovine Komentar* (Sarajevo: Fondacija Konrad Adenauer, 2010).

Strebel, Michael, *Executivföderalismus in der Schweiz?* (Baden-Baden: Nomos, 2014).

Strukture upravljanja državom u BiH, Jačanjem institucionalnih kapaciteta i preuzimanjem vlasništva nad promjenama u procesu integracije u EU do funkcionalne države, Vanjskopolitička inicijativa BH.

Šarčević, Edin, *Dejtonski ustav* (Sarajevo: Fondacija "Konrad Adenauer" Predstavništvo u Bosni i Hercegovini, 2009).

Taletović, Alen, "Organizacijski i funkcionalni problem organa uprave u FBiH", u *Zbornik radova -Međunarodna naučna konferencija "Javni i privatni aspekti nužnih pravnih reformi u BiH: Koliko daleko možemo ići?"* (Tuzla: 2014).

Trnka, Kasim, *Ustavno pravo*, (Sarajevo: Fakultet za javnu upravu, 2006).

U.S. Policymakers on Bosnia Admit Errors in Opposing Partition in 1992, 20. 10. 2023, https://www.nytimes.com/1993/08/29/world/us-policymakers-on-bosnia-admit-errors-in-opposing-partition-in-1992.html.

UBS Global Wealth Report, 30. 10. 2023, https://www.ubs.com/global/en/family-office-uhnw/reports/global-wealth-report-2023.html.

US-EC Declaration on the recognition of the Yugoslav Republics, 20. 10. 2023, http://aei-dev.library.pitt.edu/64582/1/US-EC_Declaration_on_the_recognition_of_the_Yugoslav_Republics.pdf.

Vlaški, Bojan and Romić, Marko, "Prav(n)a priroda akata visokog predstavnika za Bosnu i Hercegovinu – (u)pravna i(li) politička", in *Uporedni izazovi u savremenom pravu – in memoriam dr Stefan Andonović*, ed. Jovana Rajić Ćalić (Beograd: Institut za uporedno pravo i Pravni fakultet Univerziteta u Kragujevcu, 2023).

Vlaški, Bojan, *Organizacija javne uprave u federalizmu – posebno u Bosni i Hercegovini – doktorska disertacija (neobjavljeno)* (Beograd: Pravni fakultet Univerziteta u Beogradu, 2019).

Vranješ, Nevenko, "Dejtonska i postdejtonska koncepcija političkog sistema Bosne i Hercegovine", u *Zbornik radova "Pravo između stvaranja i tumačenja" Tom I* (Istočno Sarajevo: Pravni fakultet Univerziteta u Istočnom Sarajevu, 2023).

Watts, Ronald L. *Comparing Federal Systems in the 1990s* (Ontario: Institute of Intergovernmental Relations, Queen's University Kingston, 1996).

Zaključci Narodne skupštine Republike Srpske o razmatranju pitanja reforme carina i poreskog sistema, "*Službeni glasnik Republike Srpske*", br. 95/03.

Zakon o Fiskalnom savjetu u BiH, "*Službeni glasnik BiH*", br. 63/08.

Zeh, Juli, *Die Diktatur der Demokraten, Warum ohne Recht keine Staat zu machen ist* (Hamburg: edition Körber-Stiftung, 2012).

Zimmerman, Joseph F. *Interstate Relations – The Neglected Dimension of Federalism* (Westport, Connecticut, London: Praeger, 1996).

Zimmerman, Joseph F. *Interstate Relations – The Neglected Dimension of Federalism* (Westport, Connecticut, London: Praeger, 1996).

CHAPTER 13

The Organisation of Local Self-Government in Bosnia and Herzegovina: Legal and Political Views

Nevenko Vranješ and Nikolina Babić

1 Notion and Concept of Local Self-Government

No universal definition exists of local self-government. Theory-wise, there are as many definitions as there are authors. Aleksandar Đurđev defines local self-government as "local government that has a degree of freedom, independence and material resources to realise its inherent and constitutionally guaranteed functions, whereby the primary, everyday life interests of citizens are coordinated and satisfied in it and through it."[1] Radivoje Marinković lays down additional elements, claiming that local self-government "is an organised system of exercising the rights of local self-government, through which citizens in local units directly and through their elected representatives govern public affairs of immediate interest to the local population, managing their own sources of income and acting according to the principle of constitutionality and legality."[2] Ratko Marković argues that local self-government is "a form of decision-making and governance in local communities, constituted in smaller parts of the state territory, directly by its inhabitants or through their representatives, who are directly elected, and other local authorities."[3] Snežana Đorđević defines local self-government as "the inalienable right of citizens to directly and through their elected representatives (authorities and bodies) make sovereign decisions on the most important matters for the local community and manage public affairs, in accordance with the Constitution and the law."[4] Đorđije Blažić argues that modern local self-government is the result of "the natural tendency of the local population to more or less independ-

1 Đurđev, Aleksandar, *Lokalna samouprava* (Novi Sad: Pravni fakultet, Centar za izdavačku delatnost, 1997), 1.

2 Marinković, Radivoje, *Lokalna samouprava: stare i nove nedoumice* (Beograd: Institut za političke studije, 1998), 77.

3 Marković, Ratko, *Ustavno pravo i političke institucije, dvadeset drugo ponovljeno izdanje* (Beograd: Pravni fakultet, 2017), 405.

4 Đorđević, Snežana, *Lokalna samouprava* (Beograd: CESID, 2002), 7.

 | DOI:10.1163/9789004707887_014

ently manage the affairs of the local community, to decide on all matters of special local interest through their representatives in local self-government bodies."[5] Similar elements of local self-government definition can be found with international authors. Thus, according to the *Encyclopedia of the Social Sciences*, local government implies a territorial, non-sovereign community possessing the legal right and the necessary organ to regulate its own affairs.6 Anderson notes that local governments have the following characteristics: territory, population, organisation, autonomy, separate legal regime, fiscal independence, and governance function.[7] Considering local governance, Beri argues that it constitutes self-management of public affairs in local units by authorities that represent local communities.[8] Addressing local self-government in Western Europe, Peter John cites local autonomy, freedom of decision, participation, local policies, stable finances, electoral system, etc. as elements of local government.[9]

By analysing the above definitions, it can be concluded that the key elements in defining local self-government are: the right of citizens to local self-government guaranteed by the constitution or law, autonomy, local population, local territory, interests and needs of the local population, direct participation of citizens in local affairs, local representative body, own sources of income, local affairs, etc. The autonomy of local self-government is imperative for its existence. Local self-government must be based on the decentralisation of power, i.e., local government must be completely separate from the central government, both in terms of rights and of independence. In this context, it is necessary for the local self-government unit to be financially independent and have the possibility to decide how it will carry out the tasks that inherently belong to it, which, *inter alia,* implies the existence of the local self-government unit's own and sustainable revenues. The essential elements of local self-government are local population and local territory, which is smaller than the state territory. Finally, direct participation of citizens in local affairs is also significant, as is the existence of local government by directly elected representative bodies. Bearing in mind that it is

5 Blažić, Đorđije, *Sistem lokalne samouprave (teorijsko, međunarodno-pravno, komparativno i pozitivno-pravno)* (Podgorica: Fakultet za državne i evropske studije, 2011), 82.

6 Robson, William A., *Encyclopedia of the Social Sciences, Vol-ix-x*, (New York: The Macmillan Company, 1937).

7 Anderson, William, *The Units of Government in United States*, (Chicago, 1945), 10.

8 Byrne, Tony, *Local Government in Britain*, Penguin Books, 1990, 1, cited from Marinković, Radivoje, *Lokalna samouprava*, (Beograd: Institut za političke studije, 1998), 76.

9 John, Peter, *Local Government in Western Europe* (London: Sage Publications, 2001), 6–8.

often not possible for citizens to directly participate in local affairs, due to organisational and technical aspects, it is important that local representative bodies are elected directly, while respecting the principles of universal and equal suffrage, freedom of choice and secrecy of voting. From the perspective of the European Charter on Local Self-Government, the most important principle of local self-government is the principle of subsidiarity. The principle of subsidiarity implies that public powers are assigned to those levels of government that are closest to the citizens, because this is the only way to achieve the efficiency and effectiveness of their performance. Specifically, subsidiarity means that local authorities have normative, executive, financial, managerial, and other legally prescribed forms of independence in relation to central authorities. This principle is also promoted by The Treaty on European Union in Art. 5, which reads that the institutions of the European Union perform only those tasks that cannot be performed at the level of central, regional and local authorities.[10] This principle achieves true decentralisation of local affairs.

In defining local self-government, this chapter considers the European Charter on Local Self-Government. On 15 May 1985, the Council of Europe adopted the European Charter on Local Self-Government, which entered into force on 1 September 1988, and was ratified by all 47 member states of the Council of Europe.[11] The European Charter on Local Self-Government is the key document that provides an international framework for local self-government, which Bosnia and Herzegovina signed and ratified on 12 July 2002. The Charter came into force in Bosnia and Herzegovina on 1 November of the same year.[12] The European Charter on Local Self-Government reads:

Local self-government denotes the right and the ability of local authorities, within the limits of the law, to regulate and manage a substantial share of public affairs under their own responsibility and in the interests of the local population. This right shall be exercised by councils or assemblies composed of members freely elected by secret ballot on the basis of direct, equal, universal suffrage, and which may possess executive organs responsible to them. This provision shall in no way affect recourse to assemblies of citizens, refer-

10 See: *Consolidated version of the Treaty on European Union*, https://eur-lex.europa.eu/legal-content/EN/TXT/?uri=CELEX:12016M/TXT, 18.07. 2024.

11 Vranješ, Nevenko, *Lokalna samouprava* (Banjaluka: Univerzitet u Banjoj Luci, Fakultet političkih nauka, 2020), 58.

12 Council of Europe, "Chart of signatures and ratifications of Treaty 122," Council of Europe, https://www.coe.int/en/web/conventions/full-list?module=signatures-by-treaty&treatynum=122 (accessed 13.09.2023).

endums, or any other form of direct citizen participation where it is permitted by statute.[13]

As established in the above analysis of local self-government definitions, the European Charter on Local Self-Government includes several essential elements in its definition of the concept: local self-government is determined by a legal norm and local government has certain rights that include the performance of its own affairs at the local level. Furthermore, the Charter mandates that local government should be elected in free elections, however, the election of the local government may in no way affect direct participation of citizens in local affairs using the tools of local democracy, assuming that the affairs are carried out in the interest of the local population. However, we must underscore that the Charter does not offer a universal model of local self-government organisation. It lays down the general principles of local self-government organisation, which the signatory countries respected when establishing their own, unique concepts of local self-government. In this light, the following principles of local self-government are recognised: (1) principle of decentralisation; (2) principle of legality; (3) principle of subsidiarity; (4) principle of depoliticisation; (5) principle of autonomy; (6) principle of professionalisation; (7) principle of mutual cooperation between state and local governments; (8) principle of efficiency and effectiveness of the work of local self-government bodies; (9) principle of equality; (10) principle of transparency; and (11) principle of incompatibility of public functions.[14] The principle of decentralisation and the principle of autonomy are closely related because they imply that local authorities are independent in performing their own, local, tasks, and thus are not subject to control of the utility of performing their respective tasks, but only control of legality. The principle of legality implies that local self-government is defined by the Constitution, and where this is not possible, it is determined by law. The principle of subsidiarity refers to the fact that tasks are performed at the level closest to the citizens, while respecting the principles of efficiency and effectiveness, i.e., performing tasks in the shortest possible time, using available resources, but making sure that the work is done well with minimal spending of resources and money. The principle of depoliticisation implies that the hierarchical level must be desig-

13 Savez opština i gradova Republike Srpske, "Evropska povelja o lokalnoj samoupravi," Savez opština i gradova Republike Srpske, https://www.alvrs.com/UcitaneSlike/admin/Dokumenti/evropska-povelja-o-lokalnoj-samoupravi-final-2.pdf (accessed 14.09.2023).

14 Vranješ, Nevenko, *Lokalna samouprava* (Banjaluka: Univerzitet u Banjoj Luci, Fakultet političkih nauka, 2020), 61.

nated up to which the influence of politics in the exercise of power is possible, i.e., that this influence is reduced to a minimum when fulfilling obligations. The principle of professionalisation complements the principle of depoliticisation, because it refers to the fact that employees in the administration should be competent, capable, impartial, objective, while creating conditions for their constant improvement and advancement. The principle of mutual cooperation between state and local governments means that local authorities will be consulted on issues affecting their work. The principle of equality is important for equal development of all local self-government units in a country, but also for equal treatment of all citizens by local authorities when meeting their needs. The principle of transparency means that local authorities should inform the local population of all information that is important for the work of local authorities, as well as inform the citizens about their rights and obligations. The principle of incompatibility of public functions refers to the fact that local officials cannot perform other functions or activities incompatible with their basic function in exercising local government.

2 Positive Law Status of Local Self-Government in Bosnia and Herzegovina

Bosnia and Herzegovina, in its present form, was created by the signing of the Dayton Peace Agreement in December 1995. The Dayton Agreement contains eleven annexes; it is the fundamental and most important document on the basis of which Bosnia and Herzegovina functions.[15] Bosnia and Herzegovina consists of two entities, the Republika Srpska and the Federation of Bosnia and Herzegovina, as well as a condominium without co-imperium – the Brčko District of Bosnia and Herzegovina. The division of competences between the institutions of Bosnia and Herzegovina and the entities is precisely defined by the Constitution. Article III of the Constitution of Bosnia and Herzegovina defines the responsibilities of the institutions of Bosnia and Herzegovina. More specifically, ten responsibilities of the state are listed.[16] This article also lays down that all governmental functions and powers not expressly assigned to the institutions of Bosnia and Herzegovina shall be those of the

15 For more, see: Nešković, Radomir, *NEDOVRŠENA DRŽAVA – Politički sistem Bosne i Hercegovine* (Sarajevo: Friedrich-Ebert-Stiftung, 2017), 223.

16 Office of the High Representative, *The General Framework Agreement for Peace in Bosnia and Herzegovina* (Sarajevo: Office of the High Representative, 1995) https://www.ohr.int/dayton-peace-agreement/?lang=en (accessed 17.09.2023).

entities. Given that the competence of local self-government is not expressly assigned to the institutions of Bosnia and Herzegovina, it follows that local self-government is in the competence of the entities. Local self-government in the Republika Srpska is envisaged by the Constitution of the Republika Srpska, the Law on Local Self-Government and the Law on Territorial Organisation of the Republika Srpska. In the Federation of Bosnia and Herzegovina, local self-government is defined by the Constitution of the Federation of Bosnia and Herzegovina, the Law on Federal Units (cantons) and the Law on the Principles of Local Self-Government in the Federation of Bosnia and Herzegovina. The Brčko District of Bosnia and Herzegovina is a specific unit, defined by Amendment I to the Constitution of Bosnia and Herzegovina as a unit of local self-government with its own institutions, laws and regulations.[17] Certainly, the European Charter on Local Self-Government must not be ignored, as its principles form the foundation for the development of local self-government in Bosnia and Herzegovina. Given the above, any consideration of the organisation of local self-government in Bosnia and Herzegovina and its position in the legal and political system of Bosnia and Herzegovina means consideration of the organisation of local self-government in the Republika Srpska, the Federation of Bosnia and Herzegovina and the Brčko District of Bosnia and Herzegovina. Local self-government in the Republika Srpska and in the Federation of Bosnia and Herzegovina are envisaged in an almost identical way, as prescribed by the European Charter on Local Self-Government. We find a similar situation in all members of former SFRY.

3 Organisation of Local Self-Government in the Republika Srpska

Organisation of local self-government in the Republika Srpska, in addition to the aforementioned constitutional and legal provisions, is regulated by the Law on Territorial Organization of the Republika Srpska, the Law on the Budget System of the Republika Srpska, the Law on the Status of Local Self-Government Unit Officials and other laws. Article 5 of the Constitution of the Republika Srpska reads that the constitutional arrangement of the Republika Srpska is based on, *inter alia*, local self-government. Article 66 also specifies that the freedoms and rights of man, equality before the law, the autonomous and equal position of enterprises and other organisations, and

17 Parlamentarna skupština Bosne i Hercegovine, *Amandman I na Ustav Bosne i Hercegovine* (Sarajevo: Službeni glasnik br. 25/09)

the constitutional position and rights of the units of local self-government, are the basis and a yardstick for the powers and the responsibilities of the republic agencies. The Constitution further stipulates that the territorial organisation of the Republika Srpska as well as the system of local government shall be regulated by law. However, Article 102 of the Constitution defines the responsibilities of municipalities that they exercise through their bodies, as follows:

> enact a development programme, town and country planning, budget, and annual balance sheet; regulate and provide for performing and development of municipal activities; regulate and provide for the use of urban construction sites and business premises; take care of construction, maintenance and use of local infrastructure, and other public facilities of importance to the municipality; take care of meeting specific needs of citizens in the areas of culture, education, health and social welfare, physical culture, public information, handicrafts, tourist trade and catering services, protection of the environment and other areas; execute laws, other regulations and general enactments of the Republic whose execution is entrusted to the municipality, provide for the execution of regulations and general enactments of the municipality; establish agencies, organisations and services to meet the needs of the municipality, and regulate their organisation and work; attend to other business as established by the Constitution and law, as well as by the statute of the municipality.[18]

Furthermore, the Constitution foresees that the performance of affairs of local government may be entrusted to the city. Therefore, even though the Constitution defines the responsibilities of the municipality and the possibility for the city to perform local administration affairs, this indicates that such a constitutional solution reflects a commitment to a single-level local self-government. Article 2 of the Law on Territorial Organisation of the Republika Srpska reads that the territory of the Republika Srpska consists of municipalities and cities. Article 4 defines a municipality as a basic territorial unit of local self-government formed for a part of a populated place, for one populated place or for several populated places, whereas Article 23 defines a city as

18 Narodna skupština Republike Srpske, *Ustav Republike Srpske* (Banjaluka: Službeni glasnik Republike Srpske br. 21/92 – prečišćeni tekst, 28/94, 8/96, 13/96, 15/96, 16/96, 21/96, 21/02, 26/02, 30/02, 31/02, 69/02, 31/03, 98/03, 115/05, 117/05).

a territorial unit that represents a coherent geographical, historical, administrative, social, and economic entity with an appropriate level of development.[19] Territorially, local self-government in the Republika Srpska is organised into 64 local self-government units, i.e., 53 municipalities and 11 cities, the cities being: Banja Luka, Bijeljina, Prijedor, Prnjavor, Gradiška, Derventa, Istočno Sarajevo, Doboj, Trebinje, Zvornik, and Laktaši. There are significant differences in the size of the territory of local self-government units in the Republika Srpska – with Kupres being the smallest municipality with a territory of 45 km^2, and the City of Istočno Sarajevo the largest with six municipalities in its composition and a territory of 1,448 km^2.[20] Also, it is noteworthy that some of the municipalities were created in the war and post-war period, as well as the fact that in certain municipalities, as well as one city, the name was changed due to intervention of the Constitutional Court of Bosnia and Herzegovina and deletion of the prefix "Serbian" from the names of several local self-government units in the Republika Srpska.[21] Post-war municipalities that were created by the division of territory between the Republika Srpska and the Federation of Bosnia and Herzegovina cover a small area. In addition, the disparity in the number of inhabitants is evident, with the estimated number of inhabitants in Istočni Drvar being 88, and in Banja Luka 186,094.[22] The Law on Local Self-Government of the Republika Srpska defines local self-government as:

> … the right of citizens to directly and through their freely and democratically elected representatives participate in the attainment of the common interests of the residents of the local self-government unit, as well as the right and the ability of local authorities, within the limits of the law, to regulate and manage a substantial share of public affairs under their own responsibility and in the interests of the local population. Local self-government is exercised in cities, i.e., municipalities, and is carried out by local self-government unit authorities and citizens, in accordance with the Constitution of the Republika Srpska (hereinafter:

---

19 Narodna skupština Republike Srpske, *Zakon o teritorijalnoj organizaciji Republike Srpske* (Banjaluka: Službeni glasnik Republike Srpske br. 69/09).

20 Republički zavod za statistiku, *Gradovi i opštine Republike Srpske, 2021* (Banjaluka: Republički zavod za statistiku, 2021), 12.

21 Vranješ, Nevenko, *Lokalna samouprava* (Banjaluka: Univerzitet u Banjoj Luci, Fakultet političkih nauka, 2020), 117.

22 Republički zavod za statistiku, *Gradovi i opštine Republike Srpske, 2021* (Banjaluka: Republički zavod za statistiku, 2021), 12.

> the Constitution), the law and the statute of the local self-government unit.[23]

Furthermore, Article 5 of the Law establishes that local self-government units have the status of a legal entity, while Article 7 reads that they own property, which is managed by local self-government unit authorities. Article 8 defines municipality as a basic territorial unit of local self-government, formed for a part of a populated place, for one populated place or for several populated places; Article 10 stipulates that a city can be established by law in an urban area that forms a unique geographical, social, economic, historical and territorial whole with an appropriate level of development, and if it has more than 50,000 inhabitants and had the status of a developed local self-government unit over the past three years, based on the decision on the level of development of the local self-government unit.

Exceptionally, a municipality can acquire the status of a city regardless of the number of inhabitants, if the employment rate in the municipality is above the republic average. As for competences, the tasks of the city and municipality are, according to the Law on Local Self-Government, established in the same way as the tasks of the local self-government unit, and these can be tasks that the local self-government unit performs independently, as well as delegated tasks. The local self-government unit performs tasks independently in the areas of organising the work of the local self-government unit; provision of services; construction and spatial planning; housing and utility activities; culture; child and youth care; primary, secondary and higher education; health and social protection of the population; sports and physical culture; crafts, trade, tourism and catering; protection of natural assets and the environment; protection of citizens and material goods from natural and other major disasters, as well as providing legal aid to citizens. These tasks are the same irrespective of whether performed by the municipality or the city. Exceptionally, Article 11 stipulates that a city that does not have a municipality in its composition may, in addition to the competences assigned to the municipality, organise legal representation before courts and other bodies in property disputes, fees and services collection disputes, and labour disputes, in accordance with the law, as well as collection, collection control and enforced collection of own source revenues to the city budget. The city may also exceptionally organise the issuance of a joint invoice for the services rendered by public enterprises, i.e., enterprises of which it is the founder, as well as for fees

23 Narodna skupština Republike Srpske, *Zakon o lokalnoj samoupravi Republike Srpske* (Banjaluka: Službeni glasnik Republike Srpske br. 97/16).

and other income determined by the city authorities in accordance with the law. Furthermore, the law may assign additional responsibilities to the city. However, to date, there has been no law granting cities in the Republika Srpska additional powers compared to municipalities. Article 12 of the same Law establishes that a city that has several municipalities in its composition has overall regulatory competences in terms of spatial planning, land use, environmental protection and urban plans; executes all competences assigned by law to municipalities in the areas of water supply, sewage, public transport, waste management, secondary education, health care, tourism and trade, fire and civil protection; collects own revenues and manages city assets; organises the inspection assigned by law to the municipality; implements city laws and regulations; establishes appropriate forms of coordination to ensure that the municipalities in its composition perform their functions in a uniform and efficient manner and also performs other competences established by the law and city statute.[24] Power in local self-government units is organised through the city or municipality assembly and the city or municipal mayor, as well as the city or municipal administration. The city or municipal mayor and the assembly of the city or municipality are directly elected for a period of four years. The number of councillors in the assembly is determined by the statute in accordance with the electoral legislation, and the Election Law of the Republika Srpska establishes in Article 42b that the number of councillors ranges from 11 to 31, depending on the number of voters registered in the voter list of the local self-government unit.[25] The law prescribes the forms of participation of citizens through referendum, citizens' assembly, citizens' initiative, local community, citizens' hours in assemblies, and other forms of participation. We note here a weak affirmation of the referendum as the strongest instrument of direct democracy.[26]

Local self-government in the Republika Srpska is single-level and monotypic, considering that the city and municipality are the only units of local self-government and that they have the same competences determined by law, without their differences in demography, territory, development level, and available resources being taken into account. In addition, there is no differentiation into rural or urban municipalities in terms of the degree of their urban-

24 The only city in the Republika Srpska that has more than one municipality is Istočno Sarajevo, consisting of six municipalities: Istočno Novo Sarajevo, Istočni Stari Grad, Istočna Ilidža, Pale, Sokolac and Trnovo.

25 Narodna skupština Republike Srpske, *Izborni Zakon Republike Srpske* (Banjaluka: Službeni glasnik Republike Srpske br. 34/02).

26 Used exclusively when examining the trust of mayors of municipalities or city mayors.

isation. The only differentiation criterion for local self-government units in the Republika Srpska is the level of development, by which they are classified into extremely underdeveloped, underdeveloped, medium-developed, and developed local self-government units.[27] However, this differentiation exists for the sake of revenue distribution between the Republika Srpska and the local self-government units – so that the local self-government units can effectively carry out their competences, where specific assistance is provided for special support for extremely underdeveloped and underdeveloped units. Article 76 of the Law on Local Self-Government of the Republika Srpska stipulates that criteria for establishing the level of development of local self-government units are defined by the National Assembly of the Republika Srpska every three years, and the level of development is determined by the Government of the Republika Srpska every 30 September for the following year.[28] By the decision of the Government of the Republika Srpska of 29 September 2022, as many as 36 local self-government units, out of 64, were placed under the categories of underdeveloped and extremely underdeveloped local self-government units.[29] According to the criterion of the degree of participation of citizens in the performance of local government affairs, local self-government in the Republika Srpska can be classified as semi-indirect local self-government, considering that local government is exercised by the city or municipal assembly and the city or municipal mayor, but in its Article 106, the Law on Local Self-Government lays down forms of direct participation of citizens – referendum, citizens' assembly, citizens' initiative, local community, citizens' hours in assemblies, and other forms provided for by law.[30]

4 Organisation of Local Self-Government in the Federation of Bosnia and Herzegovina

The Federation of Bosnia and Herzegovina consists of federal units – cantons, of which there are 10 and which have broader competences than local self-government units, such as the legislature, the judiciary, and the police. In the

27 Narodna skupština Republike Srpske, *Zakon o lokalnoj samoupravi Republike Srpske* (Banjaluka: Službeni glasnik Republike Srpske br. 97/16).

28 Ibid.

29 Vlada Republike Srpske, *Odluka o stepenu razvijenosti jedinica lokalne samouprave u Republici Srpskoj za 2023. godinu* (Banjaluka: Službeni glasnik Republike Srpske br. 99/22, 2022).

30 Narodna skupština Republike Srpske, *Zakon o lokalnoj samoupravi Republike Srpske* (Banjaluka: Službeni glasnik Republike Srpske br. 97/16).

Federation of Bosnia and Herzegovina, local self-government is defined by the Constitution of the Federation of Bosnia and Herzegovina, the Law on Federal Units (Cantons) and the Law on Principles of Local Self-Government in the Federation of Bosnia and Herzegovina. The Constitution of the Federation of Bosnia and Herzegovina stipulates that local self-government is exercised by municipalities and cities.[31] Article 2 of the Law on the Principles of Local Self-Government in the Federation of Bosnia and Herzegovina defines that local self-government stands for the right and the ability of local authorities, within the limits of the law, to regulate and manage a substantial share of public affairs under their own responsibility and in the interests of the local population.[32] The definition of local self-government is identical to the definition of the Republika Srpska. Precisely, this is the solution found in the European Charter on Local Self-Government. Furthermore, the Law confirms that local self-government is organised and exercised in municipalities and cities as units of local self-government, where a municipality is a unit of local self-government established by the law on condition of meeting the prescribed criteria, and a city is a local unit of self-government defined as an urban and infrastructure-based system of elements, which are interconnected by everyday needs of the population. The Law also lays down that cities will be established, besides the Constitution, pursuant to federal laws on the basis of an agreement on association of two or more municipalities, or on the basis of a decision rendered by the municipal council of a municipality, provided that the municipality has at least 30,000 residents, or at least 10,000 people living in its urban centre as an integral urban area.

Exceptionally, a municipality of special historical and cultural importance may be declared a city. As in the Republika Srpska, local self-government units have the status of a legal entity and the right to their own property and financial resources, which they manage independently. Territorially, the Federation of Bosnia and Herzegovina has 58 municipalities and 22 cities. There is disparity in the size of the territory of municipalities and cities, where, for example, the municipality of Doboj Jug has an area of 10.2 km^2, and the city of Mostar 1,175 km^2, or the municipality of Dobretići, has 652 inhabitants, and

31 Ustavotvorna skupština Federacije Bosne i Hercegovine, *Ustav Federacije Bosne i Hercegovine* (Sarajevo: Službene novine Federacije BiH, br. 1/94, 13/97, 16/02, 22/02, 52/02, 63/03, 9/04, 20/04, 33/04, 71/05, 72/05, 88/08).

32 Parlament Federacije Bosne i Hercegovine, *Zakon o principima lokalne samouprave u Federaciji Bosne i Hercegovine* (Sarajevo: Službene novine Federacije BiH br. 49/06, 51/09).

the city of Sarajevo has 304,065 inhabitants.[33] The Constitution of the Federation of Bosnia and Herzegovina stipulates the division of competences between the federal and cantonal authorities, clearly establishing the exclusive competences of the Federation, the common competences of the cantons and the Federation, with a special emphasis on the competences of the cantons. Given that local self-government is not defined as the exclusive competence of the Federation, it is concluded that this falls under the competence of the cantons. The confirmation of this claim can be found in Article 4 of the Constitution, where, defining the responsibilities of the canton, it reads that the following are included: regulating local land use, including by zoning; regulating and promoting local business and charitable activities; regulating and ensuring the availability of local energy production facilities.[34] Also, Article 3 of the Law on Federal Units (Cantons) reads that the territory of a canton consists of municipalities and parts of municipalities determined by that law.[35] The Law on the Principles of Local Self-Government of the Federation of Bosnia and Herzegovina defines the independent competences of local self-government units, stating that local self-government units have the right to deal with all matters of local importance that are not exempted from its competences or added to the competences of another authority pursuant to the Constitution and law.[36] In addition, the requirements for and the manner of performing entrusted tasks are envisaged. Also in the Federation of Bosnia and Herzegovina, with respect to competences of local self-government units, no differentiation is made between local self-government units, regardless of their economic, demographic, or developmental differences. Although the Constitution of the Federation of Bosnia and Herzegovina reads that the responsibilities of a city include: finance and tax policy, in accordance with federal and cantonal legislation; joint infrastructure; urban planning; public transport; other responsibilities assigned to the city by the canton or municipalities, the mere listing of the responsibilities of a city does not constitute an essential difference, considering that everything listed is also in the independ-

33 Savez općina i gradova Federacije Bosne i Hercegovine, "Članice" https://www.sogfbih.ba/clanice-tabela (accessed 25.09.2023).

34 Ustavotvorna skupština Federacije Bosne i Hercegovine, *Ustav Federacije Bosne i Hercegovine* (Sarajevo: Službene novine Federacije BiH, br. 1/94, 13/97, 16/02, 22/02, 52/02, 63/03, 9/04, 20/04, 33/04, 71/05, 72/05, 88/08).

35 Ustavotvorna skupština Federacije Bosne i Hercegovine, *Zakon o federalnim jedinicama (kantonima – županijama)* (Sarajevo: Službene novine Federacije BiH, br. 9/96).

36 Parlament Federacije Bosne i Hercegovine, *Zakon o principima lokalne samouprave u Federaciji Bosne i Hercegovine* (Sarajevo: Službene novine Federacije BiH br. 49/06, 51/09).

ent competence of the municipalities. Power in local self-government units (municipalities and cities) in the Federation of BiH is exercised by municipal or city councils that have representative and normative authority and through city or municipal mayors that have executive authority. Municipal and city administrations have been established for the purpose of implementing the decisions of the council and the mayor in local self-government units. City or municipal councils, as well as city or municipal mayors, are directly elected for a term of four years. The Law on the Principles of Local Self-Government also foresees direct forms of citizen participation in the exercise of local government, such as referendum, local citizens' assembly, citizens' initiative and other forms of direct declaration of will, elaborated further by the statute of the local self-government unit.

It may be stated that local self-government in the Federation of Bosnia and Herzegovina is single-level, given that cantons are federal units, not local self-government units, and that it is monotypic because positive law does differentiate the competences of municipalities and cities. Furthermore, local self-government in the Federation of Bosnia and Herzegovina can be classified under the category of semi-indirect local self-governments, because positive law also recognises forms of direct participation of citizens in the exercise of power.

The law stipulates that citizens directly decide on matters within the competence of local self-government units through referendums, local citizens' assemblies, and other forms of direct declaration of will. Here, too, we note a weak affirmation of the referendum, except for the motion of no confidence against mayors.

The key problem of local self-government in the Federation of Bosnia and Herzegovina is reflected in the fact that a certain number of cantons (including the largest, Sarajevo Canton) do not have laws on local self-government, significantly affecting the position and development of local self-government.

5 Brčko District of Bosnia and Herzegovina

The Brčko District of Bosnia and Herzegovina is a specific unit, given that it is a condominium without co-imperium of the Republika Srpska and the Federation of Bosnia and Herzegovina, whose status was resolved by the Final Arbitral Decision for Brčko, passed on 5 March 1999.[37] By Amendment I to the

37 Nešković, Radomir, *NEDOVRŠENA DRŽAVA – Politički sistem Bosne i Hercegovine* (Sarajevo: Friedrich-Ebert-Stiftung, 2017), 303.

Constitution of Bosnia and Herzegovina, Brčko District is defined as a unit of local self-government with its own institutions, laws, and regulations. The Statute of the Brčko District in Chapter I, Article 1 confirms that Brčko is a single administrative unit of local self-government existing under the sovereignty of Bosnia and Herzegovina and that the District derives its powers of local self-government by virtue of each entity having delegated all of its powers of governance as previously exercised by the two entities and the three municipal governments within the pre-war municipality of Brčko.[38] The legislative power is exercised by the District Assembly. The executive power is exercised by the District Government. The judicial power is exercised by the District Courts. The District also has its own Police, Public Attorney's Office, Prosecutor's Office, Finance Directorate, Audit Office, Office of the Co-ordinator in the Council of Ministers of Bosnia and Herzegovina, Office for Public Property, Securities Commission, and Employment Office. Here, a specific situation arises where, on the one hand, there are two entities, of which the Republika Srpska has a unitary structure, and the Federation of Bosnia and Herzegovina has a federal structure, but both entities have the same arrangement of local self-government. Brčko District, although designated as a local self-government unit, has significantly greater powers than local self-government units in the Republika Srpska or the Federation of Bosnia and Herzegovina. First, it has legislative powers, which the local self-government units in the entities do not have; it has its own police, courts, prosecutor's offices, and public attorney's office. In other words, it is an atypical unit of local self-government under direct sovereignty of Bosnia and Herzegovina, whose territory is jointly owned (condominium) by entities and has its own legal order in organisational and functional terms.[39] From a positive law point of view, neither the District statute nor other regulations specify the forms of citizen participation in local democracy in the District, except that there is a Law on Local Communities, which we find is a significant deficiency.

38 Stručna služba Brčko Distrikta, *Statut Brčko Distrikta Bosne i Hercegovine (prečišćen tekst)* (Brčko Distrikt: Stručna služba Brčko Distrikta Bosne i Hercegovine, 2010).

39 Vranješ, Nevenko and Vlaški, Bojan, *The Brčko District, Citizen, Constitution, Europe, Glossary of essential constitutional concepts in BiH,* (Sarajevo: University of Sarajevo, Faculty of Law, 2023), 358–359.

6 Council of Europe's Assessment of the State of Local Self-Government in Bosnia and Herzegovina

The Congress of Local and Regional Authorities (CLARE), through its Monitoring Committee, supervises the compliance of the positive legal and functional framework of the local self-government units of the signatory states with the principles and provisions of the European Charter on Local Self-Government. Bosnia and Herzegovina has ratified all thirty provisions of the Charter. According to the latest Report of the Monitoring Committee of the Congress of Local and Regional Authorities, of the above 30 provisions, 19 are in compliance with the Charter, five are partially in compliance and five are not in compliance. One provision, concerning the financial resources of local authorities, remains to be determined.[40]

Based on the above, the implementation of the principles of the European Charter on Local Self-Government in Bosnia and Herzegovina, and especially in the Republika Srpska, was rated quite highly by the Congress of Local and Regional Authorities of the Council of Europe.[41] For the sake of comparison, Croatia, as a member of the European Union, has only 16 provisions in compliance, Austria 21, Hungary 12, Serbia 16, Greece 10, etc. The situation in the Republika Srpska is significantly better compared to the Federation of BiH, and the report cites non-harmonisation of cantonal laws with the federal legislation on local self-government as the key reason. This compliance is a kind of guarantee that the local self-government in Bosnia and Herzegovina is on the path of compatibility with the countries of the European Union. This is very important, since the *acquis communautaire* is implemented at the local and regional level and by local and regional authorities.

7 Conclusion

Local self-government in Bosnia and Herzegovina is organised at the level of the entities and the Brčko District of Bosnia and Herzegovina. All these levels have adopted the most complete definition of local self-government as pro-

---

40 Congress of Local and Regional Authorities, *Bosnia and Herzegovina - Monitoring Report*, (Congress of Local and Regional Authorities, 2019) https://www.congress-monitoring.eu/en/44-pays.html (accessed 20.05. 2024).

41 Cf. *Bosnia and Herzegovina – Monitoring Report*, https://www.congress-monitoring.eu/en/44-pays.html and https://rm.coe.int/local-and-regional-democracy-in-bosnia-and-herzegovina-monitoring-comm/168098072a (accessed 04.05.2024).

vided by the European Charter on Local Self-Government, emphasising that local self-government is the right and the ability of local authorities, within the limits of the law, to regulate and manage a substantial share of public affairs under their own responsibility and in the interests of the local population. The analysis of the Constitution of Bosnia and Herzegovina shows that local self-government is under the competence of the entities. Although the entities have different arrangements, i.e., the Republika Srpska is organised unitarily, while the Federation of Bosnia and Herzegovina is organised federally, we conclude by analysing the aforementioned positive regulations that the organisation of local self-government is almost identical. In both entities, local self-government is single-level and monotypic. Entities do not differentiate between or take into account the specificities of local self-government units when determining their competence. The problem of disproportionate size of local self-government units in terms of territory and number of inhabitants is also present in both entities. Furthermore, it was identified that according to the criterion of citizens' participation in the exercise of local government, local self-government in both entities is semi-indirect. In addition to directly elected bodies of the executive and representative authorities in the entities (which is not the case in the Brčko District of BiH), forms of direct participation of citizens in the exercise of power do exist, such as referendums, citizens' initiatives, local communities, etc. However, the affirmation of these forms is questionable and not utilised much especially with respect to citizens' views on development projects. Brčko District is an example of an atypical unit of local self-government in BiH, given that the Constitution of Bosnia and Herzegovina and the Statute of Brčko District designate it as a unit of local self-government, but compared to local self-government units in the Republika Srpska and the Federation of Bosnia and Herzegovina, it has much greater powers, and can therefore be classified as a form of a third entity. The current organisation of local self-government in the entities (especially its monotypic structure and omnibus competences) does not follow their actual needs or the needs of the local population and may be subject to future reform. Optimism comes from the fact that, in a formal sense, local self-government in Bosnia and Herzegovina is quite aligned with the European Charter on Local Self-Government, which increases its capacity for European integration, since the majority of the *acquis communautaire* system is based on local and regional policies.

In the future, both entities must face the reform of local self-government in the domain of more functional territorial organisation. They also must address the issue of small and unsustainable municipalities. It is necessary to establish quantitative criteria for the organisation of municipalities in the Republic of

Srpska and give a different legal and factual meaning to cities in both entities. Furthermore, both entities should better regulate and implement forms of direct democracy. Finally, it is necessary to constitutionally guarantee the right to local self-government in both entities.

Bibliography

Anderson, William, *The Units of Government in United States*, (Chicago: Public Administration Service, 1945).

Blažić, Đorđije, *Sistem lokalne samouprave (teorijsko, međunarodno-pravno, komparativno i pozitivno-pravno)*. (Podgorica: Fakultet za državne i evropske studije, 2011).

Byrne, Tony, *Local Government in Britain*, (Penguin Books, 1990), prema Marinković, Radivoje, *Lokalna samouprava*, (Beograd: Institut za političke studije, 1998).

Congress of Local and Regional Authorities, *Bosnia and Herzegovina – Monitoring Report*, (Congress of Local and Regional Authorities, 2019. https://www.congress-monitoring.eu/en/44-pays.html (accessed 20.05.2024).

Council of Europe, "Chart of signatures and ratifications of Treaty 122." Council of Europe. https://www.coe.int/en/web/conventions/full-list?module=signatures-by-treaty&treatynum=122 (accessed 13.09.2023).

Đorđević, Snežana, *Lokalna samouprava*, (Beograd: CESID, 2002).

Đurđev, Aleksandar, *Lokalna samouprava*, (Novi Sad: Pravni fakultet, Centar za izdavačku delatnost, 1997).

John, Peter, *Local Government in Western Europe*, (London: Sage Publications, 2001).

Marinković, Radivoje, *Lokalna samouprava: stare i nove nedoumice*, (Beograd: Institut za političke studije, 1998).

Marković, Ratko, *Ustavno pravo i političke institucije, dvadeset drugo ponovljeno izdanje*, (Beograd: Pravni fakultet, 2017).

Narodna skupština Republike Srpske, *Izborni Zakon Republike Srpske*. Banjaluka: Službeni glasnik Republike Srpske br. 34/02. br. 97/16.

Narodna skupština Republike Srpske, *Ustav Republike Srpske*. Banjaluka: Službeni glasnik Republike Srpske br. 21/92 – prečišćeni tekst, 28/94, 8/96, 13/96, 15/96, 16/96, 21/96, 21/02, 26/02, 30/02, 31/02, 69/02, 31/03, 98/03, 115/05, 117/05.

Narodna skupština Republike Srpske, *Zakon o lokalnoj samoupravi Republike Srpske*. Banjaluka: Službeni glasnik Republike Srpske br. 97/16.

Narodna skupština Republike Srpske, *Zakon o teritorijalnoj organizaciji Republike Srpske*. Banjaluka: Službeni glasnik Republike Srpske br. 69/09.

Nešković, Radomir, *NEDOVRŠENA DRŽAVA – Politički sistem Bosne i Hercegovine*, (Sarajevo: Friedrich-Ebert-Stiftung, 2017).

Office of the High Representative, "The General Framework Agreement for Peace in Bosnia and Herzegovina." Sarajevo: Office of the High Representative, 1995. https://www.ohr.int/dayton-peace-agreement/?lang=en (accessed 17.09.2023).

Parlament Federacije Bosne i Hercegovine, *Zakon o principima lokalne samouprave u Federaciji Bosne i Hercegovine*. Sarajevo: Službene novine Federacije BiH br. 49/06, 51/09.

Parlamentarna skupština Bosne i Hercegovine, *Amandman I na Ustav Bosne i Hercegovine*. Sarajevo: Službeni glasnik br. 25/09. https://www.ohr.int/ohr-dept/legal/laws-of-bih/pdf/001%20-%20Constitutions/BH/BH%20Amendment%20I%20to%20BH%20Constitution%2025-09.pdf (accessed 17.09.2023).

Republički zavod za statistiku, *Gradovi i opštine Republike Srpske, 2021.*, (Banjaluka: Republički zavod za statistiku, 2021).

Robson, William A. *Encyclopedia of the Social Sciences, Vol-ix-x*, (New York: The Macmillan Company, 1937).

Savez općina i gradova Federacije Bosne i Hercegovine, "Članice." https://www.sogfbih.ba/clanice-tabela (accessed 25.09.2023).

Savez opština i gradova Republike Srpske, "Evropska povelja o lokalnoj samoupravi." Bijeljina: Savez opština i gradova Republike Srpske. https://www.alvrs.com/UcitaneSlike/admin/Dokumenti/evropska-povelja-o-lokalnoj-samoupravi-final-2.pdf (accessed 14.09.2023).

Stručna služba Brčko Distrikta, Statut Brčko Distrikta Bosne i Hercegovine (prečišćen tekst) (Brčko Distrikt: Stručna služba Brčko Distrikta Bosne i Hercegovine, 2010.

Ustavotvorna skupština Federacije Bosne i Hercegovine, *Ustav Federacije Bosne i Hercegovine*. Sarajevo: Službene novine Federacije BiH, br. 1/94, 13/97, 16/02, 22/02, 52/02, 63/03, 9/04, 20/04, 33/04, 71/05, 72/05, 88/08.

Ustavotvorna skupština Federacije Bosne i Hercegovine, *Zakon o federalnim jedinicama (kantonima – županijama)*. Sarajevo: Službene novine Federacije BiH, br. 9/96.

Vlada Republike Srpske, *Odluka o stepenu razvijenosti jedinica lokalne samouprave u Republici Srpskoj za 2023. godinu*. Banjaluka: Službeni glasnik Republike Srpske br.99/22, 202.

Vranješ, Nevenko and Vlaški, Bojan, *The Brčko District, Citizen, Constitution, Europe, Glossary of essential constitutional concepts in BiH*, (Sarajevo: University of Sarajevo, Faculty of Law, 2023).

Vranješ, Nevenko, *Lokalna samouprava*, (Banjaluka: Univerzitet u Banjoj Luci, Fakultet političkih nauka, 2020).

CHAPTER 14

Securitised by NATO: Bosnia and Herzegovina in Times of International Rivalry

Neven Andjelic

1 Introduction

Realist theories of International Relations position the state's self-preservation as the country's primary national interest. Traced back to Hobbesian description of a human state of nature as "war of all against all," "*bellum omnium contra omnes*," in which individuals' nature received projected views on human collectives like a state,[1] realist theories dominated the post-WWII period. "The instinct of self-preservation, in a world made up of independent nations," establishing realism in International Relations, wrote Morgenthau, "operates to make each desire power in order to secure itself against the danger of external aggression."[2] Realists see state self-preservation "not only inevitable, but an essential stabilizing factor in a society of sovereign nations."[3]

Bosnia and Herzegovina, however, is a unique country where parts of political elites diverge from this fundamental principle of International Relations. Leader of the strongest political party among Bosnian Serbs and the second largest in the country, Milorad Dodik, frequently argued that "Bosnia is an impossible, tragicomic state."[4] On another occasion he described it as "impos-

1 Hobbes, Thomas, "*De Cive*," (London: Printed by J.C. for R. Royston, at the Angel in Ivie –Lane. 1651), http://www.public-library.uk/ebooks/27/57.pdf. 10. See also: George Shelton, "*Morality and Sovereignty in the Philosophy of Hobbes*," (London: Palgrave Macmillan, 2016), 22.

2 Morgenthau, Hans J., "*Politics among Nations: The Struggle for Power and Peace*," (New York: Alfred A. Knopf, 1949), 127.

3 Morgenthau, Hans J., "*Politics among Nations: The Struggle for Power and Peace*," (New York: Alfred A. Knopf, 1949), 125.

4 Dodik, Milorad, "Dodik: BiH je nemoguća, tragikomična država, naš cilj je samostalna RS," Hercegovina,info, June 16, 2014, https://www.hercegovina.info/vijesti/bih/dodik-bih-je-nemoguca-tragikomicna-drzava-nas-cilj-je-samostalna-rs/75682/.

 | DOI:10.1163/9789004707887_015

sible, unnecessary and undesirable for Serbs."[5] A critical question, therefore, is who is interested in preserving BiH if its domestic leaders are antagonistic towards their own state? Bosnia and Herzegovina was preserved and established as a functioning independent state primarily by the will of the US and supported by the Western allies during the period when the western dominance went unchallenged in the 1990s. However, Russia and China are actively seeking a new global security arrangement that would reflect changed geopolitics. The western isolation of Russia following its aggression against Ukraine is frequently breached by Dodik and other Bosnian Serbs' politicians in attempts to reflect global divisions in Bosnia and Herzegovina. Thus, the existence and security of the state is intricately linked to international security dynamics and global alliances.

A broader international security arrangement keeps the country together in the absence of internal consensus. However, a lack of agreement on the future global security model, and the search for the solution by increasingly violent means, created a state of conflict between the major powers. Whether it will be a unipolar, bipolar, or multipolar world, keeps several crisis points contested. Different authors put conflicting views, even in the same journal, *Foreign Policy*, in the space of less than a year. While two academics claim, "the world is multipolar and that isn't bad news for the United States,"[6] another author argues, "the world is not multipolar," and warns this understanding "could lead to serious policy mistakes."[7] The High Representative of the EU for Foreign Affairs and Security Policy, Josep Borell, described the international system as "complex multipolarity," that succeeded a unipolar world lasting "from 1989 to 2008," and a bipolar one prior to this.[8] However, there are views that "bipolar world is more likely than a unipolar or multipolar one."[9]

5 Dodik, Milorad, "Dodik: BiH je nemoguća, nepotrebna i nepoželjna za Srbe," Hrvatski medijski servis, July 18, 2018, https://hms.ba/dodik-bih-je-nemoguca-nepotrebna-i-nepozeljna-za-srbe/.

6 Ashford, Emma and Cooper, Evan, "Yes, the World Is Multipolar And that isn't bad news for the United States," Foreign Policy, October 5, 2022, https://foreignpolicy.com/2023/10/05/usa-china-multipolar-bipolar-unipolar/.

7 Bekkevold, Jo Inge, "*No, the World Is Not Multipolar*," Foreign Policy, September 22, 2023, https://foreignpolicy.com/2023/09/22/multipolar-world-bipolar-power-geopolitics-business-strategy-china-united-states-india/.

8 Borell, Josep, "How to revive multilateralism in a multipolar world?" European External Action Service, March 16, 2021, https://www.eeas.europa.eu/eeas/how-revive-multilateralism-multipolar-world_en.

9 Xuetong, Yan, "A Bipolar World is More Likely Than a Unipolar or Multipolar One," Carnegie Endowment for International Peace, April 20, 2015, https://carnegieendowment.org/posts/2015/09/a-bipolar-world-is-more-likely-than-a-unipolar-or-multipolar-one?lang=en.

The new international order, regardless of the number of poles, will have at least one other dominant power that views or might be viewing Bosnia and Herzegovina differently than the United States. Even the change of administration in the White House created a confusion among the allies and shift in some of the West's strategic interests.

The contested points, regardless, already exist, while some of them, like Ukraine, escalated into a violent all-out war, after eight years of low-intensity conflict. Several frozen conflicts re-emerged, like in the Middle East and the Caucasus, thus underlining the volatility of the contested zones. Although inviting some comparisons to the contested territory, Bosnia and Herzegovina seems to have a stable security arrangement that prevents the risk of violent escalation of political disagreements. The presence, even numerically almost symbolic, of Western international troops effectively deters other powers from exerting influence over BiH's internal affairs. While joining the NATO alliance would solidify the country's geopolitical position, the current formal and informal arrangements provide a significant degree of security and stability.

In the next sections, this chapter will integrate relevant theoretical references of International Relations on state self-preservation in the contested international system. By doing so, it will highlight the lack of internal consensus regarding the future of the state. The implications of global geopolitical realignment for Bosnia and Herzegovina will be addressed by providing a comprehensive analysis of international and domestic factors that shape its security structure.

2 History of NATO Engagement in Bosnia and Herzegovina

The country's independence arrived following the end of the Cold War and the investigative phase of establishing a new security architecture in post-communist and post-Soviet Europe. The new and still uncertain phase in the geopolitics of the 1990s had a catastrophic consequence in Bosnia and Herzegovina, where, following the adoption of the Maastricht Treaty, the deeply integrated European Union lacked political will and security capacity to stop the war. At the same time, the USA were wary of the rising potential of the pan-European economic rival[10] when the Soviet Union collapsed, Russia was

10 Featherstone, Kevin and Ginsberg, Roy H., "The United States and the European Union," 2nd ed, (New York: St Martins's Press, 1996).

in chaos,[11] and China was preoccupied with the post-Tiananmen society while initiating a giant economic leap.[12]

The result of the fundamental rethink of a long-standing foreign policy and security doctrines in the 1990s meant, firstly, a US-sponsored Washington Agreement in 1994, followed by an American-led intervention to stop the war in 1995 and the consequent Dayton Peace Agreement. After 45 years of existence, NATO had the historical first combat action in 1994, when they shot down four Bosnian Serb fighter-bombers.[13] By intervening and stopping the war, American-led security and diplomatic efforts imposed peace deals that kept the country in place through close international supervision, including a large NATO-led International Force (IFOR).[14] Troops from the NATO member-states and "a large number of countries who had never been together formed Operation Joint Endeavor," including Russia. The operation was described as "a unique case in the history of peace operations. It is the first operation NATO has conducted out-of-area, or out of its normal area of protection."[15]

NATO expanded in the late 1990s as former Warsaw Pact member states, firstly from Central and Eastern Europe and later from the South-eastern part of the continent, joined the alliance. The process drew some ambiguous reactions from Moscow and conflicting statements from the Western officials and witnesses about the agreed security understanding between NATO and Russia. Some official statements from Moscow showed an apparent understanding that former Warsaw Pact members would not join NATO, and when they did, it was seen as a betrayal. In numerous fait accompli analyses, various interpretations appeared, leading to a possible conclusion that although "the charge of betrayal is technically untrue, (it) has a psychological truth."[16] The

11 Sakwa, Richard, "Putin: Russia's Choice," (London: Routledge, 2007).

12 Kobayashi, Shigeo, Baobo, Jia and Sano, Junya, "The 'Three Reforms' in China: Progress and Outlook," Sakura Institute of Research, Inc., *RIM*, No.45 (September 1999) https://www.jri.co.jp/english/periodical/rim/1999/RIMe199904threereforms/.

13 NATO, "Did you know that the first combat action by NATO forces took place in 1994, 45 years after the creation of the Alliance?", accessed October 10, 2023, https://shape.nato.int/page2148121621.

14 Sobel, Richard, "Trends: United States Intervention in Bosnia," *The Public Opinion Quarterly* Vol. 62, No. 2 (Summer, 1998), 250–278.

15 Layton, Richard L., "Command and Control Structure," in: "*Lessons From Bosnia: The IFOR Experience,*" ed. Wentz, Larry K., (Office of the Assistant Secretary of Defense (OASD), Command & Control Research Program (CCRP), Washington, DC, 20301. January 1998), 35.

16 Wintour, Patrick, "Russia's belief in Nato 'betrayal' – and why it matters today," The Guardian, January 12, 2023, https://www.theguardian.com/world/2022/jan/12/russias-belief-in-nato-betrayal-and-why-it-matters-today.

issue would be recalled by Russian President Vladimir Putin in his speech at the Munich Security Conference in 2007,[17] prior to and during Russia's invasion of Ukraine,[18] and in many scholarly works and journalistic articles in the West.[19]

All former communist countries that would eventually join the European Union previously joined NATO. While the lack of NATO membership is not incompatible with accession to the European Union, the fact is that all former communist countries, unlike militarily neutral countries like Austria, Sweden, and Finland that joined the EU in 1995, first joined the ranks of NATO. Cyprus and Malta, which joined the EU alongside eight post-communist countries, remained outside NATO, like Ireland that joined the EU in 1973. This raises a question about the seriousness of BiH political elites in their efforts to join the EU, as a former communist country, if they are divided on the issues of NATO membership. Nevertheless, despite its lack of membership in the alliance, NATO is ever so present in the post-conflict Bosnia and Herzegovina. Even Sweden and Finland eventually joined the alliance following the escalation of the conflict in the east of Europe, thus suggesting that neutrality might not be an option in contemporary Europe. The very existence of post-WWII Austria is based on the agreement it would be neutral, while Ireland is situated on the opposite end of Europe. All the evidence suggests that the future of Bosnia and Herzegovina outside of NATO is not viable.

The names of the deployed forces, their structure, and numbers have been changing from the original Implementation Force (IFOR), set up to secure peace in Bosnia and Herzegovina based on the Dayton Agreement, replaced soon by the Stabilisation Force (SFOR), both led by NATO, until the significantly scaled-down presence of the international military in the form of EUFOR since 2004. Despite the geopolitical challenges, UN Security Council Resolution 2757, adopted unanimously, shows universal support for the mandate of the multinational stabilisation force EUFOR-Althea. The mission, al-

---

17 Putin, Vladimir, "Speech and the Following Discussion at the Munich Conference on Security Policy," President of Russia, February 10, 2007, http://www.en.kremlin.ru/events/president/transcripts/24034.

18 Clark, J. P. and Pfaff, C. Anthony, Principal Investigators, "Striking the Balance: US Army Force Posture in Europe, 2028 – A Study Sponsored by the Office of the Secretary of the Army, *Strategic Studies Institute and the US Army War College Press*, June 2020, https://press.armywarcollege.edu/cgi/viewcontent.cgi?article=1906&context=monographs.

19 Marcetic, Branko, "When officials say the quiet part about Russia and NATO out loud," Responsible Statecraft, September 19, 2023, https://responsiblestatecraft.org/russia-ukraine-nato-expansion/.

beit relatively small, is effectively averting any internal and external actors with the ambition to destabilise the country and the region.

Political parties with support based on specific numerically dominant BiH ethnic groups have contrasting attitudes and reasoning about state security and membership in international organisations. Like in neighbouring Serbia, Bosnian Serbs show rhetorical animosity towards NATO and the Western world, and block further moves by Bosnia and Herzegovina to join the military alliance. Meanwhile, Bosnian Croats show a willingness to join NATO members that include Croatia, and Bosniaks see the membership as a warranty for the country's preservation and as protection against interference from both Serbia and Croatia.

The state structure provided by the Dayton Peace Agreement formally left the continuing coexistence of two armies that fought each other until NATO intervention in 1995. In practice, each of the three dominant ethnic groups controlled a military force with little confidence in the other two's peaceful intentions. Observers noted that "Bosnia therefore had *de jure* two armies (one for the FBiH and one for the RS). *De facto*, however, Bosniak and Croat troops were not fully united until a comprehensive military reform in 2005/6."[20]

While peace and stability have been secured in the country, developments in these fields have not been static. An American-led initiative unified the armies and created the Ministry of Defence at the state level in 2004, thus finally defining Bosnia and Herzegovina as a state according to the famous definition by Weber of the state as the only agency with the monopoly to legitimately use violence.[21] The outcome of the process provided more security to all communities than the previously existing model provided by the Dayton Peace Agreement. NATO officers noted, "the Bosnian Joint Staff has emerged as the most multi-ethnic and well-balanced group of diverse individuals in the country, and is something of a role model."[22]

Bosnia and Herzegovina joined the Partnership for Peace programme in 2006. Two years later, the Individual Partnership Action Plan (IPAP) was agreed upon with the alliance. BiH Presidency submitted the application for the Membership Action Plan in 2009 and was later invited to join the plan.

20 Keil, Soeren and Kudlenko, Anastasia, "Bosnia and Herzegovina twenty years after Dayton: complexity born of paradoxes. International Peacekeeping," 22 (5) (2015), 1–19. http://dx.doi.org/DOI:10.1080/13533312.2015.1103651.

21 Weber, Max, "Politics as Vocation (Extract)," (1919) accessed October 10, 2023, https://www.balliol.ox.ac.uk/sites/default/files/politics_as_a_vocation_extract.pdf.

22 Drewienkiewicz, K J, "Foreword," in *Destination NATO: Defence Reform in Bosnia and Herzegovina, 2003–13*, ed. Rohan Maxwell and John Andreas Olsen (London: Whitehall Paper 80, Royal United Services Institute, 2013), 1–5.

This is when the internal disagreements within Bosnia and Herzegovina undermine the overall concept of collective stability and security. Different politicians interpret differently whether the country is within the MAP and whether its submission to NATO could come under the title of Annual National Programme.[23] In an academic analysis from 2015, the authors stated that "20 years after the war ended the country is not yet ready to assume responsibility for its own defence. Reform efforts in military policy have mainly been driven by international actors, most notably NATO,"[24] thus leaving a question of the state's security and defence capacity.

It is not a coincidence that internal disagreements on NATO membership escalated around 2009. It is widely assumed that the unipolar international system ended with the 9/11 attacks and the global financial crisis of 2007–2008. Thus, the external changes were almost immediately acted upon by the internal forces and will remain unsettled until the new global understanding.

Despite the frequent internal disagreements and occasional incidents, violent acts are largely missing, as it is reported on an annual basis by the European Commission.[25] The international efforts have been decisive in scaling down the conflict and bringing up three types of peace interventions: peace-making by militarily intervening in 1995, with the follow-up operations of peace-keeping during the first post-conflict decade and peace-building efforts since. The main question, therefore, is about the success of the peace-building process and whether the country, without external intervention, could finish the process.

Miloš Šolaja, an academic from Banja Luka argued that "the EUFOR mission in BiH has long served only the Europeans, enabling them to present themselves as a security pillar." He claims that "EUFOR has no clear strategy or satisfactory personnel and organisational framework," and that the country should better "develop its own defence and security policy."[26] Đuro Kozar, a

23 Živković, Vukašin, "NATO Perspective of Kosovo and Bosnia and Herzegovina," European Western Balkans, February 8, 2019, https://europeanwesternbalkans.com/2019/02/08/nato-perspective-kosovo-bosnia-herzegovina/.

24 Keil, Soeren and Kudlenko, Anastasia, "Bosnia and Herzegovina twenty years after Dayton: complexity born of paradoxes. International Peacekeeping," 22 (5) (2015), 1–19.

25 European Commission, "Bosnia and Herzegovina: Key Documents," European Neighbourhood Policy and Enlargement Negotiations (DG NEAR), https://neighbourhood-enlargement.ec.europa.eu/enlargement-policy/bosnia-and-herzegovina_en#key-documents.

26 Šolaja, Miloš, cited in "Može li EUFOR izvršiti svoju misiju u BiH?," Deutche Welle, February 24, 2023, https://www.dw.com/hr/mo%C5%BEe-li-eufor-izvr%C5%A1iti-svoju-misiju-u-bih/a-64801392.

leading defence analyst from Sarajevo differs by stating that EUFOR "has an executive mandate to use force" and can call on the intervention by contributing member states.[27]

3 Neutrality and EU and NATO Accession

During the peace-building phase in the country's development, it is clear that Bosnia and Herzegovina successfully transformed its military and security forces compared to its original structures during the peace-keeping period of the first post-conflict decade. However, it still lacks the capacity to provide for its own security without external intervention and supervision, where EUFOR and NATO make up the main security pillars. Internal actors lack the vision, capacity and will to consider the changed international environment since 1995.

Following Russia's invasion of Ukraine, traditionally neutral Sweden and, since the end of WWII, neutral Finland joined NATO. In a clear political statement contrary to the lack of actual economic, political, and social reforms, the European Union granted candidate status to Ukraine and Moldova in June 2022. Consequently, the candidate status was granted eventually even to Bosnia and Herzegovina in December 2022, despite the lack of progress in achieving 14 key priorities stated by the European Commission's Opinion in 2019. The EU's decision to grant these countries candidate status, despite the claims of conditionality principle, is a clear sign of the repositioning in the current security architecture of Europe.

At the security level, the "principle of collective defence is at the very heart of NATO's founding treaty. It remains a unique and enduring principle that binds its members together, committing them to protect each other and setting a spirit of solidarity within the Alliance."[28] Applying Article 5 of the NATO treaty would drag all members of the Atlantic Alliance into the conflict if Ukraine, Moldova, or Georgia were accepted as members based on the principle of solidarity of all member states. By not having full territorial control over their countries, these three states might invoke Article 5 to reestablish their full territorial sovereignty. Bosnia and Herzegovina has complete control

27 Kozar, Đuro, cited in Huseinović, Samir "Može li EUFOR izvršiti svoju misiju u BiH?," Deutche Welle, February 24, 2023, https://www.dw.com/hr/mo%C5%BEe-li-eufor-izvr%C5%A1iti-svoju-misiju-u-bih/a-64801392.

28 NATO, "Collective defence and Article 5." Last updated July 4, 2023, https://www.nato.int/cps/en/natohq/topics_110496.htm.

over its territory and is not involved in any violent conflict, thus making no potential danger of bringing all members of the Atlantic Alliance into the conflict.

A fundamental rethink of European security and the BiH positioning within that frame is required from the country's political elites. The war in Ukraine has renewed debates about the EU's common foreign and security policy, underlining the issue of the overall reliance on NATO, i.e., the US. Ironically, the last time this debate was similarly intensive was during the war in Bosnia and Herzegovina, which exposed the lack of the EU's security capacity. It is these shortages in European integrations that removed the possible forcefulness of the EU's interventionist policies towards Bosnia and Herzegovina where political leadership of Bosnian and Herzegovinian Serbs refuse to integrate into European security structures officially and express the antagonistic rhetoric towards NATO. After all, while NATO membership is not required, integrating into European security structures is a requirement for the EU membership that all political parties support, in words, if not actions. NATO membership has become a necessity, under current geopolitical order and has proven that all post-communist countries acceded to it before joining the EU. Neutrality, as propagated by political parties based in the Republika Srpska, is a stance that is no longer feasible.

The perceived neutrality of Bosnia and Herzegovina is not linked to its potential prosperity in such a position. There is no economic miracle, and emigration waves of citizens depopulate the country in search of living standards and stability of the West. Nations that attempt to play a neutral position tend to have an interest and a strategy for exploring such a position to their advantage. Except for the visionless declaratory remarks by the leadership of the Republika Srpska, there was no sign of any strategy for how a neutral stand would benefit Bosnia and Herzegovina.

A view that Bosnia and Herzegovina can survive as a neutral country, balancing in the new world order the interests of Russia and the West, openly ignores reality: who provides for the state security already, who are the main trading partners and investors, and what is the union that all political elites claim they want to join? The current world simply does not provide for neutrality, to have similar equidistance towards Brussels and Moscow. This conclusion is drawn even without considering how morally or politically it is untenable to urge neutrality in the contemporary world.

Countries in such a position offer to stage international dialogues, broker peace or host international peace conferences and organisations. Bosnia and Herzegovina is not active in any of these areas. The lack of a strategic vision is one of many signs of political and security immaturity in the country. The boundaries of Bosnia and Herzegovina could be understood as pretty much open to both the "neutral" Serbia and towards NATO members, Montenegro and Croatia due to the weak security military structures within the country. The Armed Forces of Bosnia and Herzegovina is basically a natural disaster response unit when required, or a resource for symbolically contributing to the UN peace missions. The country's security is effectively outsourced to EUFOR-Althea force while relying on the hope of honest and friendly behaviour by the neighbours.

Joining the EU means accommodating the member states' common foreign and security policy. Parliamentarians in Bosnia and Herzegovina voted down twice the proposal to adapt its foreign policy towards Ukraine to the EU's policy.[29] While the country's political elites declare their determination to integrate fully into European political and economic structures, politicians in Bosnia and Herzegovina work against such integrations in practice. The opposition delegate's proposal "To adopt a conclusion requesting the BiH Council of Ministers to fully harmonise policies, measures and positions with the official positions of the European Union regarding Russian aggression against Ukraine"[30] was rejected by Bosnian Serb representatives in the House of Peoples of the state parliament, and representatives of the largest Bosnian Croats' party who also did not support it by either voting against the proposal or by abstaining.[31]

Even geography directs political and security conclusions. Between the Russian Naval Facility in the northern Syrian port of Tartus, the lawless territory to the Turkish border, and the Atlantic Ocean, there are only 21.2 kilometres of coastline not controlled by NATO: the coast of Bosnia and Herzegov-

29 Andjelic, Neven, "BiH je primarni cilj državnih aktivnosti Hrvatske" Oslobođenje, July 16, 2022, https://www.oslobodjenje.ba/dosjei/teme/bih-je-primarni-cilj-drzavnih-aktivnosti-hrvatske-774905.

30 Bećirović, Denis, "Skandal u Domu Naroda: Delegati HDZ-a nisu podržali usklađivanje BiH sa stavovima EU o ruskoj agresiji na Ukrajinu," Slobodna Bosna, March 24, 2022, https://www.slobodna-bosna.ba/vijest/242590/skandal_u_domu_naroda_delegati_hdz_a_nisu_podrzali_uskladjivanje_bih_sa_stavovima_eu_o_ruskoj_agresiji_na_ukrajinu_video.html.

31 Oslobođenje, "Čović i delegati HDZ-a glasali protiv inicijative za uvođenje sankcija Rusiji," Oslobodjenje Portal, March 24, 2022, https://f01-novi.oslobodjenje.ba/vijesti/bih/covic-i-delegati-hdz-a-glasali-protiv-inicijative-za-uvodenje-sankcija-rusiji-745085. See also: Slobodna Bosna, "Skandal u Domu Naroda: Delegati HDZ-a nisu podržali usklađivanje BiH sa stavovima EU o ruskoj agresiji na Ukrajinu," Slobodna Bosna, March 24, 2022, https://www.slobodna-bosna.ba/vijest/242590/skandal_u_domu_naroda_delegati_hdz_a_nisu_podrzali_uskladjivanje_bih_sa_stavovima_eu_o_ruskoj_agresiji_na_ukrajinu_video.html.

ina. If the imaginary journey is taken along the coastline from the Syrian-Turkish border to the Russian exclave of Kaliningrad and includes the Black Sea coast, only the shores of Russia, Georgia, Ukraine, and Bosnia and Herzegovina are not NATO-land. Due to Russia's geopolitical interests and military engagements, Georgia and Ukraine do not control their whole sovereign territory. At the same time, Bosnia and Herzegovina has complete sovereign control of its border and coastline.

Geographical location and the presence of some form of troops from the Western military alliance, the political interests of the dominant powers, and geopolitical positioning create a relatively safe international environment for the country. Adding the Baltic Sea coast and continuing to Russia's Arctic, while considering recent Finish and Swedish membership in NATO, it is possible to see complete control of European and Asia Minor coastline by NATO almost from Tartus in Syria to Murmansk in Russia, with just a few notable exceptions. A look at the map of the Western Balkans offers another geography-influenced view of security. All countries belong to NATO except Serbia, Kosovo, and Bosnia and Herzegovina, which make up a hole in the NATO-secured lands.

This chapter shows the connection between NATO membership and control over sovereign state territory. However, it is possible to raise doubts over the full sovereignty of the state if some other force, even an international one, has a legitimate right to use violence over that territory. Multilateralism provides elements of security for the state that proved to be weaker in the system based on bilateralism, as the empirical examples from the neighbourhood of Russia demonstrate. However, one could question the level of sovereignty of the small-power states engaged in the alliance controlled by the super-power. The trade-off of membership in NATO is the introduction of a benign foreign power, or a group, in political and security matters that used to be in the exclusive domain of a sovereign state.

4 Summary

The international community, in particular NATO institutions, showed the duality of policies towards Bosnia and Herzegovina and the broader region. Following the initial concerns for peace and security in Bosnia and Herzegovina and the strong involvement in setting up the structures, NATO was more ambivalent to the slowness of BiH political elites. It was only following the challenges by Russia that more urgent and determined actions developed. By this time, domestic politicians had learnt to ignore threats from the international community and realised that their personal interest was in exploiting the current situation. Dario Čepo perceived the situation as a "normative conflict mainly between the preservation of the political status quo within the Dayton constitutional setting and the integration into higher order structures that could jeopardise positions of elites who thrive within the existing post-conflict configurations."[32]

Since the Dayton Peace Agreement, the political elites in power lack the capacity, competence, and political will to provide security by internal forces. Even when changes in personalities occur, i.e., new leaders or parties come into position, the pattern of dysfunctional governance remains. While they lack the competence to provide security, the elites do not show a vision of getting external actors to do it for them. Internal disagreements among those who agreed to share power and form large governing coalitions paralyse attempts to develop common policies that, if implemented, might lead to progress. The ruling coalition also disagrees on what set of external actors to engage with and how to get them to provide security for Bosnia and Herzegovina.

While the requirement of a 2% defence budget was achieved by the majority of the NATO members, the EU states are determined to increase their spending further. Bosnia and Herzegovina spent 0.8% on defence in 2022 which is a continuation of the trend that coincided with the establishment of the state-level Ministry of Defence. The spending never reached the NATO guideline of 2%, and since 2015 it never reached even 1 percent.[33]

The solution centres on the transformation of political elites. This could be realised in two ways: the BiH electorate voting them out of power or external actors compelling the local elites to accept the realities of the contemporary world and the new international system. The former approach underscores the democratic process, while the latter highlights the potential for external influence. This transformation would necessitate a robust utilisation of the Bonn's powers by the High Representative of the International Community,

32 Čepo, Dario, "Euro-Atlantic Integrations of BiH: Shifting Gears and Reinterpreting Motives in Foreign Affairs," in *Bosnia and Herzegovina's Foreign Policy since Independence,* eds. Hasić, Jasmin and Karabegović, Dženeta, (London: Palgrave Macmillan, 2019), 73.

33 Ministarstvo odbrane Bosne i Hercegovine, Predstavnički dom parlamentarne skupštine BiH, odgovor na poslaničko pitanje, broj 04-50-993-46/23, 29.11.2023. https://static.parlament.ba/doc/162622_2298%20-%c5%a0emsudin%20Dedi%c4%87-%20odgovor%20MOBiH.pdf; World Bank, Military Expenditure (% of GDP) – Bosnia and Herzegovina, https://data.worldbank.org/indicator/MS.MIL.XPND.GD.ZS?locations=BA; Macrotrends, Bosnia Military Spending/Defense Budget 1992–2025, https://www.macrotrends.net/global-metrics/countries/BIH/bosnia/military-spending-defense-budget.

a collective endorsement of such measures by states represented in the Peace Implementation Council, and a decisive role of the US in the process. "The fact that no country alone is sufficiently strong to feel secure against any possible combination of opposing states," wrote Hans Morgenthau at the beginning of the Cold War and the then new world order, "makes necessary the formation of alliances and counter-alliances through which each state seeks to ensure the needed support in case its safety is menaced from without."[34]

The twenty-first century presents a challenge of establishing a new international system where, like in the 1950s, less powerful nations have to seek alliances. If the nation of Bosnia and Herzegovina remains divided, one should recall Thomas Hobbes, if not biblical references earlier, stressing "*a Kingdome divided in it selfe cannot stand*," (Sic!) and question the state's self-preservation. The analogy has been used in politics as leaders often seek national unity to support their decisions. Most famously, it was Abraham Lincoln seeking a nomination to the Senate stating, "A house divided against itself cannot stand."[35] As Bosnian Serbs' political leadership frequently expresses a lack of interest in preserving the state, the divided kingdom syndrome plays into their hands. Given the RS' leadership's frequent visits to Moscow since 2022, it is clear that any further deterioration of the security structure in Bosnia and Herzegovina would strengthen Russia's position. Therefore, the international community, i.e., the Western alliance, must provide security arrangements for Bosnia and Herzegovina if they want to maintain the current order. The global challenges other actors present to the West-dominated rules-based international system require the decision.

This chapter's main argument is that state security is provided by external actors dominated by NATO members regardless of the lack of membership in the organisation. However, membership does mean actual participation as a fully sovereign state. The examples from the Baltic Sea region confirm such necessity. The three former Soviet republics – Estonia, Latvia, and Lithuania – first reformed and joined NATO shortly before being granted membership in the EU. Their history and geopolitical position underlined the priority and urgency to organise their national security with NATO support. In the process, they firmly and successfully lobbied to have fully developed armies, albeit

---

34 Morgenthau, Hans J., "*Politics among Nations: The Struggle for Power and Peace*," (New York: Alfred A. Knopf, 1949), 127.

35 Lincoln, Abraham, "House Divided Speech," Lincoln Home, citing Illinois Republican State Convention, Springfield, Illinois June 16, 1858 as quoted in: Neely Jr., Mark E., "*The Abraham Lincoln Encyclopedia*," (New York: Da Capo Press, Inc., 1982), https://www.nps.gov/liho/learn/historyculture/housedivided.htm.

small according to the sizes of their nations, because some strategists in Brussels had the original idea of each of them having specialist types of units where NATO would provide the real potentially fighting forces. Closer to Bosnia and Herzegovina, in times of potential national political crisis and divisions, Montenegro and North Macedonia joined NATO in relatively rapid processes, thus securing national unity and security.

In both cases an issue of democratic decision making was liberally implemented. In Montenegro, the signs were the referendum would fail and the ruling coalition passed the decision with their parliamentary majority never offering an opportunity to citizens to decide. The referendum on NATO membership failed in North Macedonia, but then the parliamentary majority adopted the decision to join the alliance regardless. Thus, despite the presence of significant opposition to the membership among the population of potential members, the organisation allowed Montenegro and North Macedonia to implement decisions on joining NATO by interpreting democratic decision making in a liberal way and clearly providing security arrangements that would suit broader interests in a new geopolitical positioning.

The presence and support by NATO is a case of some supervision over the non-member state, protecting the country from possible dangers, therefore bordering a protectorate status in the current state of play on the global stage. British Parliament's House of Lords and an American think tank Freedom House argued that "without reengagement [in BiH] from the transatlantic alliance, corrupt elites will continue using state institutions to empower themselves at the expense of Bosnian citizens' fundamental freedoms."[36]

European Council on Foreign Relations offered a similar argument, stating that "NATO allies have put Bosnia on the agenda for the Vilnius summit as one of three 'vulnerable states' alongside Moldova and Georgia. But to stop a 'Transnistria scenario' emerging in Bosnia, they need to urgently increase the costs of escalation for Dodik."[37] The NATO Summit communique clearly summed up the position of the alliance and the situation in Bosnia and Herzegovina: "We encourage Bosnia and Herzegovina to take advantage of NATO's

36 "Western Balkans and the Dayton Peace Agreement," House of Lords Library, October 6, 2023, https://lordslibrary.parliament.uk/western-balkans-and-the-dayton-peace-agreement/ quoting *"Nations in Transit 2023 Report: War Deepens Regional Divide,"* Freedom House, accessed October 8, 2023, https://freedomhouse.org/report/nations-transit/2023/war-deepens-regional-divide.

37 Ruge, Majda, "Deterrence starts in the Balkans: How NATO allies can prevent military escalation in Bosnia and Herzegovina," European Council on Foreign Relations, July 11, 2023, https://ecfr.eu/article/deterrence-starts-in-the-balkans-how-nato-allies-can-prevent-military-escalation-in-bosnia-and-herzegovina/.

support and intensify efforts to make progress on reforms in key areas, including the much-needed political, electoral, rule of law, economic, and defence reforms, without prejudice to a final decision on NATO membership."[38]

The alliance's official statements use diplomatic language and miss the point that, when confronted with the potential of a country allying itself with Russia or seeking declaratory neutrality, NATO approved the will of parliamentary majorities regardless of the signs that a significant number, even the majority of citizens might disagree. In Bosnia and Herzegovina, political elites show no signs of ever agreeing on such a step. The consociational political model prevents the possibility of forcing the decision through the parliament by the objections of one ethnic group's representatives. However, the international community does have an opportunity, albeit not democratic, to impose the decisions through the High Representative. The alternative options include a long-term approach, which will influence a shift in popular support, and the option in place since the first NATO engagement in the country. It consists of the alliance *de facto* in charge of security arrangements in Bosnia and Herzegovina.

Military spending in Bosnia and Herzegovina is very low considering the NATO standards and the latest tendencies within the EU member states. Considering everything presented, the contemporary international system shows signs of creating a multipolar order where most of the countries seek alliances that suit them. The elites in Bosnia and Herzegovina lack a consensus and therefore the stalemate needs to be solved. Several options include legal and political steps that require external actors' involvement. The democratic solution to the problem is the replacement of the nationalist parties by electoral means. However, the current electoral law strongly favours votes in their support and the change is therefore a highly unlikely outcome of any elections.

The change of the electoral law is connected with the constitutional changes that would allow them which again is an impossible task for the internal actors. A national referendum on NATO membership was not held by the latest new members, Sweden, Finland, and Montenegro, while the result of it was ignored in North Macedonia. However, the modus operandi of Bosnia and Herzegovina prevents the imposition of the decision by the parliamentary majority regardless of the democratic legitimacy. Therefore, the only possibility to amend the status of the country is to make constitutional changes that would provide for a new electoral law and a new decision-making system and legislative procedures.

---

38 NATO, "Vilnius Summit Communiqué," July 11, 2023, https://www.nato.int/cps/en/natohq/official_texts_217320.htm.

Bibliography

Andjelic, Neven, "BiH je primarni cilj državnih aktivnosti Hrvatske" Oslobođenje, July 16, 2022, https://www.oslobodjenje.ba/dosjei/teme/bih-je-primarni-cilj-drzavnih-aktivnosti-hrvatske-774905.

Andjelic, Neven, "Bosnia-Herzegovina: the (in)security between the NATO-land and NATO-less country," *The World Orders Forum*, May 8, 2023, https://www.wgresearch.org/_files/ugd/bdf8dc_49cdd78deae24446b35d090bb3034f3c.pd.

Andjelic, Neven, "Nations in Transit 2023: Bosnia-Herzegovina," *Freedom House*, accessed October 8, 2023, https://freedomhouse.org/country/bosnia-and-herzegovina/nations-transit/2023.

Ashford, Emma and Cooper, Evan, "Yes, the World Is Multipolar And that isn't bad news for the United States," Foreign Policy, October 5, 2022, https://foreignpolicy.com/2023/10/05/usa-china-multipolar-bipolar-unipolar/.

Aybet, Gülnur and Bieber, Florian, "From Dayton to Brussels: The Impact of EU and NATO Conditionally on State Building in Bosnia & Hercegovina," *Europe-Asia Studies* 63, no. 10 (2011), 1911–37. http://www.jstor.org/stable/41302200.

Bećirović, Denis, "Skandal u Domu Naroda: Delegati HDZ-a nisu podržali usklađivanje BiH sa stavovima EU o ruskoj agresiji na Ukrajinu," Slobodna Bosna, March 24, 2022, https://www.slobodna-bosna.ba/vijest/242590/skandal_u_domu_naroda_delegati_hdz_a_nisu_podrzali_uskladjivanje_bih_sa_stavovima_eu_o_ruskoj_agresiji_na_ukrajinu_video.html.

Bekkevold, Jo Inge, "*No, the World Is Not Multipolar*," Foreign Policy, September 22, 2023, https://foreignpolicy.com/2023/09/22/multipolar-world-bipolar-power-geopolitics-business-strategy-china-united-states-india/.

Borell, Josep, "How to revive multilateralism in a multipolar world?" European External Action Service, March 16, 2021, https://www.eeas.europa.eu/eeas/how-revive-multilateralism-multipolar-world_en.

Čepo, Dario, "Euro-Atlantic Integrations of BiH: Shifting Gears and Reinterpreting Motives in Foreign Affairs," in *Bosnia and Herzegovina's Foreign Policy since Independence*, eds. Hasić, Jasmin and Karabegović, Dženeta, (London: Palgrave Macmillan, 2019), 71–95.

Clark, J. P. and Pfaff, C. Anthony, Principal Investigators, "Striking the Balance: US Army Force Posture in Europe, 2028 – A Study Sponsored by the Office of the Secretary of the Army, *Strategic Studies Institute and the US Army War College Press*, June 2020, https://press.armywarcollege.edu/cgi/viewcontent.cgi?article=1906&context=monographs.

Dodik, Milorad, "Dodik: BiH je nemoguća, nepotrebna i nepoželjna za Srbe," Hrvatski medijski servis, July 18, 2018, https://hms.ba/dodik-bih-je-nemoguca-nepotrebna-i-nepozeljna-za-srbe/.

Dodik, Milorad, "Dodik: BiH je nemoguća, tragikomična država, naš cilj je samostalna RS," Dodik: BiH je nemoguća, tragikomična država, naš cilj je samostalna RS," Hercegovina.info, June 16, 2014, https://www.hercegovina.info/vijesti/bih/dodik-bih-je-nemoguca-tragikomicna-drzava-nas-cilj-je-samostalna-rs/75682/.

Drewienkiewicz, K J, "Foreword," in *Destination NATO: Defence Reform in Bosnia and Herzegovina, 2003–13*, eds. Maxwell, Rohan and Olsen John Andreas, London: Whitehall Paper 80, Royal United Services Institute (2013), 1–5.

Featherstone, Kevin and Ginsberg, Roy H. "The United States and the European Union," 2nd ed, (New York: St Martins's Press, 1996).

Freedom House, *"Nations in Transit 2023 Report: War Deepens Regional Divide,"* Freedom House, accessed October 8, 2023, https://freedomhouse.org/report/nations-transit/2023/war-deepens-regional-divide.

Hobbes, Thomas, *"De Cive,"* (London: Printed by J.C. for R. Royston, at the Angel in Ivie–Lane. 1651), http://www.public-library.uk/ebooks/27/57.pdf.

House of Lords, "Western Balkans and the Dayton Peace Agreement," House of Lords Library, October 6 2023, https://lordslibrary.parliament.uk/western-balkans-and-the-dayton-peace-agreement/.

Huseinović, Samir, "Može li EUFOR izvršiti svoju misiju u BiH?," Deutche Welle, February 24, 2023, https://www.dw.com/hr/mo%C5%BEe-li-eufor-izvr%C5%A1iti-svoju-misiju-u-bih/a-64801392.

Keil, Soeren and Kudlenko, Anastasia, "Bosnia and Herzegovina twenty years after Dayton: complexity born of paradoxes," *International Peacekeeping*," 22 (5) (2015), 1–19. http://dx.doi.org/DOI:10.1080/13533312.2015.1103651

Kobayashi, Shigeo, Baobo, Jia and Sano, Junya, "The 'Three Reforms' in China: Progress and Outlook," Sakura Institute of Research, Inc., *RIM*, No.45 (September 1999).

Kozar, Đuro, "Može li EUFOR izvršiti svoju misiju u BiH?," Deutche Welle, February 24, 2023, https://www.dw.com/hr/mo%C5%BEe-li-eufor-izvr%C5%A1iti-svoju-misiju-u-bih/a-64801392.

Layton, Richard L. "Command and Control Structure," in: "*Lessons from Bosnia: The IFOR Experience*," ed. Wentz, Larry K., (Office of the Assistant Secretary of Defense (OASD), Command & Control Research Program (CCRP), Washington, DC, 20301. January 1998), 35.

Lincoln, Abraham, "House Divided Speech," Lincoln Home, citing Illinois Republican State Convention, Springfield, Illinois June 16, 1858 as quoted in: Neely Jr., Mark E., "*The Abraham Lincoln Encyclopedia*," (New York: Da Capo Press, Inc., 1982), https://www.nps.gov/liho/learn/historyculture/housedivided.htm.

Macrotrends, Bosnia Military Spending/Defense Budget 1992–2025, https://www.macrotrends.net/global-metrics/countries/BIH/bosnia/military-spending-defense-budget.

Marcetic, Branko, "When officials say the quiet part about Russia and NATO out loud," Responsible Statecraft, September 19, 2023, https://responsiblestatecraft.org/russia-ukraine-nato-expansion/.

Maxwell, Rohan and Olsen, John Andreas, eds. "Destination NATO: Defence Reform in Bosnia and Herzegovina, 2003–13," *Whitehall Paper 80*, London: Royal United Services Institute (2013).

Ministarstvo odbrane Bosne i Hercegovine, Predstavnički dom parlamentarne skupštine BiH, odgovor na poslaničko pitanje, broj 04-50-993-46/2329., 11.2023. https://static.parlament.ba/doc/162622_2298%20-%c5%a0emsudin%20Dedi%c4%87-%20odgovor%20MOBiH.pdf.

Morgenthau, Hans J. "*Politics among Nations: The Struggle for Power and Peace*," (New York: Alfred A. Knopf, 1949).

NATO, "Collective defence and Article 5." Last updated July 4, 2023, https://www.nato.int/cps/en/natohq/topics_110496.htm.

NATO, "Did you know that the first combat action by NATO forces took place in 1994, 45 years after the creation of the Alliance?," accessed October 10, 2023, https://shape.nato.int/page2148121621.

NATO, "Vilnius Summit Communiqué," July 11, 2023, https://www.nato.int/cps/en/natohq/official_texts_217320.htm.

Oslobođenje, "Čović i delegati HDZ-a glasali protiv inicijative za uvođenje sankcija Rusiji," Oslobodjenje Portal, March 24, 2022, https://f01-novi.oslobodjenje.ba/vijesti/bih/covic-i-delegati-hdz-a-glasali-protiv-inicijative-za-uvodenje-sankcija-rusiji-745085.

Preljević, Hamza, "UNsatisfied? The Rocky Path to NATO Membership – Bosnia and Herzegovina: A New Approach in Understanding the Challenges," *Croatian International Relations Review* XXIII (80) 2017, 33–59.

Putin, Vladimir, "Speech and the Following Discussion at the Munich Conference on Security Policy," President of Russia, February 10, 2007, http://www.en.kremlin.ru/events/president/transcripts/24034.

Ruge, Majda, "Deterrence starts in the Balkans: How NATO allies can prevent military escalation in Bosnia and Herzegovina," European Council on Foreign Relations, July 11, 2023, https://ecfr.eu/article/deterrence-starts-in-the-balkans-how-nato-allies-can-prevent-military-escalation-in-bosnia-and-herzegovina/.

Sakwa, Richard, "Putin: Russia's Choice," (London: Routledge, 2007).

Shelton, George, "Morality and Sovereignty in the Philosophy of Hobbes," (London: Palgrave Macmillan, 2016).

Slobodna Bosna, "Skandal u Domu Naroda: Delegati HDZ-a nisu podržali usklađivanje BiH sa stavovima EU o ruskoj agresiji na Ukrajinu," Slobodna Bosna, March 24, 2022, https://www.slobodna-bosna.ba/vijest/242590/skandal_u_domu_naroda_de

legati_hdz_a_nisu_podrzali_uskladjivanje_bih_sa_stavovima_eu_o_ruskoj_agresiji_na_ukrajinu_video.html.

Sobel, Richard, "Trends: United States Intervention in Bosnia," *The Public Opinion Quarterly* Vol. 62, No. 2 (Summer, 1998), 250–278.

Šolaja, Miloš, cited in "Može li EUFOR izvršiti svoju misiju u BiH?," Deutche Welle, 24 February 2023, https://www.dw.com/hr/mo%C5%BEe-li-eufor-izvr%C5%A1iti-svoju-misiju-u-bih/a-64801392.

Weber, Max, "Politics as Vocation (Extract)," (1919) accessed October 10 2023, https://www.balliol.ox.ac.uk/sites/default/files/politics_as_a_vocation_extract.pdf.

Wintour, Patrick, "Russia's belief in Nato 'betrayal' – and why it matters today," The Guardian, January 12, 2023, https://www.theguardian.com/world/2022/jan/12/russias-belief-in-nato-betrayal-and-why-it-matters-today.

Woehrel, Steven, "Bosnia: Current Issues and U.S. Policy," *Congressional Research Service*, The Library of Congress,101 Independence Ave, SE, Washington, DC, (February 29, 2012).

World Bank, Military Expenditure (% of GDP) – Bosnia and Herzegovina, https://data.worldbank.org/indicator/MS.MIL.XPND.GD.ZS?locations=BA

Xuetong, Yan, "A Bipolar World is More Likely Than a Unipolar or Multipolar One," Carnegie Endowment for International Peace, April 20, 2015, https://carnegieendowment.org/posts/2015/09/a-bipolar-world-is-more-likely-than-a-unipolar-or-multipolar-one?lang=en.

Živković, Vukašin, "NATO Perspective of Kosovo and Bosnia and Herzegovina," European Western Balkans, February 8, 2019, https://europeanwesternbalkans.com/2019/02/08/nato-perspective-kosovo-bosnia-herzegovina/.

CHAPTER 15

Brussels versus Dayton? The Constitutional Impact of Future EU Accession

Jens Woelk

1 Stuck in Transition: Why Discuss Constitutional Issues in BiH?

Although the relations between Bosnia and Herzegovina (BiH) and the European Union (EU) have revolved around the perspective of future accession to the EU for two decades, there is still limited discussion on the constitutional impact of the integration path towards the EU. This is true even today, after the European Commission has identified in 2019 which issues of constitutional relevance need to be addressed and changed. Neither did receiving the official status as a candidate for EU accession in December 2022 trigger a debate about constitutional reform. This important issue for the future of the country seems to remain wishful thinking. EU accession (or even the opening of negotiations for it) is perceived, at best, as a far-distant hypothesis.[1]

And despite all criticism, the Constitution of BiH has proven its resistance against change,[2] not least because of the absence of a common vision among the political actors and elites. Both a common vision and constitutional amendments will be necessary at some point if BiH shall become an EU Member State. This is shown by the experience in the EU Member States, most of which have introduced integration clauses in their constitutions. BiH is stuck in transition for the last two decades. The indications provided by the EU, which question the status quo, may serve as guidance for moving towards a sustainable system.

After introducing the constitutional impact of EU membership and the ways found in Member States to address this important issue, this chapter

1 Understandably, according to a recent study by the European Bank for Reconstruction and Development (EBRD), Can the Western Balkans Converge towards EU Living standards? February 2024 (https://rb.gy/onyhiw), regarding the living conditions in the Western Balkans, "a full catch-up could, on current trends, take 70 years or more".

2 See the introductory chapter by Nedim Hogić in this volume. The only amendment to the Constitution of BiH has been constitutionalising the Brčko Arbitration Award in 2009, establishing the autonomous Brčko District (Article VI, 4).

 | DOI:10.1163/9789004707887_016

will briefly clarify the starting point for Bosnia and Herzegovina and its limited sovereignty in the first phase of reconstruction after the war. The promise of EU accession and the EU taking over from the International Community in relations with the region and with BiH will be discussed before looking into the substance of necessary constitutional change. The chapter ends with considerations on the actual possibilities for change.

2 The Constitutional Dimension of EU Integration for Member States

Membership in the EU raises numerous constitutional issues. This is a consequence of the specific supranational character of the EU legal system, most notably the direct effect and the supremacy of EU legal sources, which limit the sovereignty of Member States. The legal basis for compliance is the principle of loyal cooperation, obliging Member States to give efficient implementation to EU law in their legal systems (Article 4.3 TEU). Already, the preparation for EU accession requires constitutional adaptation: There needs to be "technical" alignment of the domestic legal system to implement the *acquis communautaire*, i.e., the existing body of EU law,[3] in certain areas. This technical adaptation may as well have a constitutional dimension, e.g., through relevance for human rights or for the independence and organisation of the judiciary. Even more so, the EU's (political) Copenhagen criteria for accession require all candidate states to guarantee the respect and implementation of common constitutional values.[4] Importantly, there is no blueprint: a certain degree of diversity is even expressly guaranteed since the Lisbon Treaty, at least concerning fundamental constitutional principles or structures (Article 4.2 TEU).[5]

3 It is estimated that the EU acquis is composed of 110,000 pages (2009); Turkish Government, FAQ negotiation process. (https://www.ab.gov.tr/faq-for-negotiation-process_44460_en.html).

4 Democracy, Human Rights, including the rights of persons belonging to minorities, and the Rule of Law. These common values are conditions for accession since the Copenhagen Summit in 1993. In 2009, with the entry into force of the Lisbon Treaty, they have become part of Article 2 TEU, enshrining the basic values of the European Union.

5 Art. 4.2 TEU: "The Union shall respect the equality of Member States before the Treaties as well as their national identities, inherent in their fundamental structures, political and constitutional, inclusive of regional and local self-government." However, in case of controversy, it is the European Court of Justice to decide; see, among the few cases, e.g., Judgment in Case C-208/09, Ilonka Sayn-Wittgenstein v Landeshauptmann von Wien, 22 December 2010.

On the one hand, the experience of different enlargement rounds, and in particular those involving former dictatorships (Greece, Portugal, and Spain), as well as former socialist countries (Baltic and Central and Eastern European countries), required the EU to develop criteria related to the constitutional sphere.[6] On the other hand, the EU's deeper integration since the Maastricht Treaty (1992), with several Treaty reforms or accession to the EU, triggered constitutional amendments in many Member States for addressing the need of a secure constitutional basis for EU membership and its consequences in the domestic legal system.[7] Typically, EU integration clauses in EU Member States' constitutions regulate the following key issues to ensure compliance with EU law and facilitate the process of integration: the transfer of certain sovereign powers to EU institutions; the recognition of the supremacy of EU Law; the ratification of EU Treaties to ensure democratic legitimacy;[8] and judicial cooperation and implementation, ensuring uniform interpretation and application of EU law.

These are general issues raised by EU membership, which are usually addressed by Member States in broad or specific integration clauses within the Constitution, or at least implicitly, e.g., through judgements of the Constitutional or Supreme Courts.[9] The Italian Constitution, with its Article 11, provides an example of a generic and broad clause allowing for the limitation of the country's sovereignty, on conditions of equality with other States, for the objectives of peace and justice (in fact, it was originally thought for UN membership); this has later been complemented by the recognition of EU Law as a limit for the State and regional legislators (Article 117.1). Among the examples of specific integration clauses regulating different aspects, there are very detailed regulations in Austria (Articles 23a to 23f Federal Constitution) and Croatia (Articles 143 to 146 Croatian Constitution). Article 23 of the German Basic Law (GG), introduced in 1992, can be regarded as an intermediate solu-

6 Hoffmeister, Frank, "Constitutional Implications of EU Membership: A View from the Commission", *Croatian Yearbook of European Law and Policy* (CYELP) 3, 2007, 59–97.

7 See: Albi, Anneli, "'Europe' Articles in the Constitutions of the Central and Eastern European Countries", *Common Market Law Review*, 42 (2), 2005, 399–423, and Claes, Monica, "Constitutionalizing Europe at its Source: The 'European Clauses' in the National Constitutions: Evolution and Typology", in *Yearbook of European Law*; Oxford Vol. 24, Fasc. 1, 2005, 81–125.

8 In some countries, besides an explicit constitutional amendment, a referendum is necessary for ratifying a reform of the EU Treaties, for instance, in France (Art. 88-IV, French Constitution).

9 In Ireland, a 1987 decision of the Supreme Court established that ratification of any significant amendment to the Treaties of the European Union requires an amendment to the Constitution (in Ireland, all constitutional amendments require approval by referendum); Raymond Crotty v. An Taoiseach and Others [1987] IESC 4 (9 April 1987).

tion: It specifically addresses EU integration, summarising the main issues in one article – including values and the ratification process, with much detail regarding the participation of Parliament and the *Länder*.

While those general issues concern all Member States, they need to be separately addressed by each single Member State. Thus, the solutions for adapting their constitutions vary, but a general trend towards adopting specific EU-integration clauses can be observed. These may also address country-specific issues, such as the impact of EU integration on the federal structure in Austria and Germany. In the case of Bosnia and Herzegovina, there are unique structural issues which require constitutional amendments before the country can accede to the EU.

3 International Reconstruction after the War and Limited Sovereignty

The Dayton Constitution is silent about European integration. Of course, this silence is easily explained by its primary functions of ending the war and consolidating the post-conflict situation in the first phase of BiH's transition.[10] The focus of the negotiations leading to the Dayton Peace Agreement (DPA), of which the Constitution is part (Annexe 4), clearly was finding a compromise to keep the country together, which was achieved through combining a federal structure with power-sharing features.[11] The essence of the resulting "complex State" is a system of guarantees for the three major groups, i.e., the "constituent peoples".[12] Thus, the constitutional system is characterised by a structural bias in favour of the status quo,[13] which is reinforced and perpetu-

10 It is quasi-mandatory to quote Richard Holbrooke, To End a War (1999), describing the negotiations at the air base and the making of the Dayton Constitution.

11 On this combination, see various chapters in this volume, starting from Nedim Hogić's introductory chapter.

12 In December 1995, at the DPA was signed by three Heads of State representing the constituent peoples: Alija Izetbegović, President of Bosnia and Herzegovina; Slobodan Milošević, President of Federal Republic of Yugoslavia; and Franjo Tuđman, President of Croatia. This avoided the formal recognition of the leaders of secessionist forces from Herceg-Bosna and Republika Srpska and guaranteed the (formal) support of the agreement by the two neighbouring countries which had been involved in the war.

13 According to Arend Lijphard, a Power sharing system is characterised by the following four main elements: grand-coalition in government; guaranteed representation in the institutions and in the public administration, as well as in the judiciary; autonomy of the groups; veto rights, Lijphard, Arend, "Constitutional Design for Divided Societies", 15

ated in the political reality by a power-cartel of ethno-nationalist parties at the centre, as well as by a tendential antagonism of the territorial entities. By consequence, the political landscape of Bosnia and Herzegovina (BiH) has been dominated by static elements.

To improve the functioning of the system and to guarantee the right of return and the restitution of property to refugees and internally displaced persons, the dynamic elements of the DPA and the Constitution have been reinforced by two institutional actors: the Office of the High Representative (OHR) and the Constitutional Court of BiH. Therefore, the first decade of BiH's constitutional transition can be characterised as international reconstruction with strongly limited sovereignty. The International Community acted as the driver of change. Soon, it was criticised for establishing an international "semi-protectorate",[14] as direct international involvement guaranteed the most important functions of a sovereign State, such as external and internal security (SFOR and IPTF),[15] democracy,[16] Human Rights,[17] and the Rule of Law.[18]

Journal of Democracy 96, 2004. They are all present in BiH. See the chapters in Part 1 of this volume.

14 Most famously by Gerald Knaus and Felix Martin, "Lessons from Bosnia and Herzegovina: Travails of the European Raj", 14 *Journal of Democracy* 60, 2003, 61–63; but also by the Venice Commission: European Commission for Democracy through Law (2005), "Opinion on the constitutional situation in Bosnia and Herzegovina and the powers of the High Representative", Venice, 11 March 2005.

15 SFOR (Stabilisation Force) was a NATO-led multinational peacekeeping force deployed in Bosnia and Herzegovina from December 1996 to December 2004 to ensure the implementation of the Dayton Peace Agreement, while IPTF (International Police Task Force) was a UN civilian police mission established to oversee law enforcement activities and help reform the local police forces in the country (operational from December 1995 to December 2002).

16 The involvement of the Organization for Security and Co-operation in Europe (OSCE) in overseeing and supporting elections in Bosnia and Herzegovina effectively ended in 2006, following a gradual handover of electoral responsibilities to local authorities (see OSCE report on the 2006 elections: https://www.osce.org/files/f/documents/c/7/23945.pdf).

17 In the aftermath of the war, the Human Rights Chamber (DPA, Annexe VI) and the Commission for Real Property Claims of Displaced Persons and Refugees (DPA, Annexe VII) played essential roles in addressing human rights violations and facilitating the return of property to displaced persons. Both were composed of a majority of foreign and a minority of local members; the HRC ceased its activity in 2003, its functions were incorporated into the Constitutional Court of BiH.

18 Foreign judges played an important role in the phase of international reconstruction, in particular for war crimes.

The increasing disengagement of the International Community since 2005/6 should have been compensated by a major shift in the transition process: the attractive perspective of future accession to the EU was thought to create the dynamics for a self-sustaining and beneficial reform process for stabilising the country. The concept of "local ownership" was to substitute international imposition.[19] In a way, the philosophy of European integration, i.e., creating added value through cooperation and by limiting the sovereignty of the member states, was to be repeated on a smaller scale.[20] This was the optimistic design for the second phase of BiH's constitutional transition: autonomous reforms, externally guided and assisted by the EU. While it is right in its premise that sustainable change can only be created and consolidated from within, it profoundly miscalculated the preconditions, as well as the incentives, and underestimated the resistance by elites in Bosnia and Herzegovina.

This soon became dramatically clear with the failure of the adoption of the 'April Package' in 2006.[21] Conceived as a "repatriation" project, comprehensive constitutional reform was intended to resolve the original sin of the Dayton Constitution, i.e., its legitimacy deficit. After a decade of international rule, the adoption by the Parliamentary Assembly of BiH was to formally ratify the common basis for future development and to prepare full sovereignty under Bosnian responsibility, after the progressive withdrawal of the International Community. The plan failed by a narrow margin, and BiH entered the second phase of transition without amendments of the Dayton Constitution.

---

19 On the rise of the local ownership agenda in the Balkans, see, e.g., Stefanie Kappler and Nicolas Lemay-Hébert, "Hybrid local ownership in Bosnia-Herzegovina and Kosovo: From discursive to material aspects of ownership", in *Local Ownership in International Peacebuilding*, Lee, Sung Yong and Özerdem, Alpaslan (eds.) (London: Routledge, 2015).

20 With hindsight, this appears naïve. But those were the years immediately after the successful enlargement of 2004, which had "re-united" the two halves of Europe. In 2012, the Nobel Peace Prize was awarded to the EU "for over six decades [having] contributed to the advancement of peace and reconciliation, democracy, and human rights in Europe", with the EU's contribution "to reconciliation in the Balkans in the aftermath of the wars there and the dissolution of Yugoslavia" explicitly mentioned in the motivation (https://www.nobelprize.org/prizes/peace/2012/eu/facts/).

21 The April Package failed to win approval by two votes in the House of Representatives of BiH; see: Hogić, Nedim in this volume. On the process leading to the April Package-proposal and its substance, see: Don Hays, Jason Crosby, "From Dayton to Brussels: Constitutional Preparations for Bosnia's EU accession", *United States Institute of Peace*, Special Report 175, October 2006 (https://www.usip.org/sites/default/files/resources/SRocto6_2.pdf).

4 The EU and the Western Balkans: Waiting for a Brighter Future?

As early as 2000, in a regional approach, the Stabilisation and Association Process for the Balkans was launched by the EU, and since the Thessaloniki European Council summit in June 2003, the EU has opened the accession perspective to all Western Balkan States: "The future of the Balkans is within the European Union".[22] Immediately, it was clarified, though, that the "countries (...) will become an integral part of the EU, once they meet the established criteria",[23] thus, the important principle of conditionality was introduced.[24] While four states were progressively recognised as candidates (North Macedonia, 2005, Montenegro, 2010, Serbia, 2012, and Albania, 2014) and even started negotiations (Montenegro, 2012; Serbia, 2014; only in July 2020 the draft negotiating framework for Albania and North Macedonia was presented to EU Member States), for a long time, Kosovo and BiH remained in the category of "potential candidates".[25]

The enlargement process had lost its priority for the EU for at least 15 years. Public opinion in many EU Member States had become more critical; there was no major political success, and after the failure of adopting the Constitutional Treaty in 2005, the EU itself experienced various crises which absorbed its attention and political energy.[26] The uncertainty in the region increased since 2008, after the unilateral declaration of independence

22 EU-Western Balkans Summit, Thessaloniki, 21 June 2003, Declaration (para. 2): In the first paragraph, there is a common commitment to joint (constitutional) values, and the Stabilisation and Association Process is reaffirmed as the common framework for developing the "privileged relationship" between the EU and the Western Balkans (paras. 3, 4).

23 Thessaloniki European Council, 19–20 June 2003, Presidency Conclusions (paras. 40–43).

24 On EU conditionality and its effects in BiH and in the Western Balkans, see, e.g.: Džihić, Vedran, and Wieser, Angela, "Incentives for Democratization? Effects of EU Conditionality on Democracy in Bosnia & Hercegovina." *Europe-Asia Studies* 63(10), 2011, 1803–1825; and Džankić, Jelena, Soeren, Keil, and Kmezić, Marko, *The Europeanization of the Western Balkans: A Failure of EU Conditionality?* (Switzerland: Palgrave Macmillan, 2019).

25 See: European Neighbourhood Policy and Enlargement Negotiations (DG NEAR), Enhanced EU engagement with the Western Balkans. (https://neighbourhood-enlargement.ec.europa.eu/enlargement-policy/enhanced-eu-engagement-western-balkans_en), last checked: 8 August 2024.

26 The economic and financial crisis was followed by the migration crisis, Brexit, and the COVID-19 pandemics.

by Kosovo, which is still not recognised by five EU Member States, despite the EU's engagement in a huge Rule of Law-mission (EULEX).[27] In 2014, EC President Juncker even declared that there would be no enlargement under his mandate.[28]

Nevertheless, the process continued, conducted as a rather technical exercise by the European Commission. But it was evident that the enlargement process had lost its momentum, raising serious credibility issues for the EU in the Western Balkans, aptly nicknamed the "waiting room".[29] The "Rule of Law-crisis" and the EU's difficulties with addressing and enforcing a fundamental common principle vis-à-vis the Member States Hungary and Poland further eroded trust and motivation for reform.[30] In 2022, the reanimation of the stalling enlargement process became part of the EU's reaction to Russia's invasion of Ukraine, above all due to geopolitical considerations.[31] In this context, candidate status was granted to BiH in December 2022; one year later, the European Council decided it will "open accession negotiations, once the necessary degree of compliance with the membership criteria is achieved".[32] Again, this raises the question of conditionality.

27 EULEX is the largest civilian mission under the EU's Common Security and Defence Policy (CSDP). It supports the Kosovo authorities in establishing sustainable and independent rule-of-law institutions (https://www.eulex-kosovo.eu/). Under its current mandate, extended until 14 June 2025, EULEX undertakes monitoring, mentoring, and advising activities and has limited executive functions.

28 In reflection of this, even the title of Commissioner for Enlargement and Neighbourly Relations was altered to Neighbourhood Policy and Enlargement as an expression of the downgrade in relation to neighbourhood policy.

29 Those countries "in the waiting room" for many years increasingly suffer from "pre-enlargement fatigue", as underlined by Belloni, Roberto and Brunazzo, Marco, "After 'Brexit': The Western Balkans in the European Waiting Room", *European Review of International Studies*, Vol. 4, No. 1, 2017, 21–38, and Woelk, Jens, "From Enlargement Perspective to 'Waiting for Godot'? Has the EU Lost its Transformative Power in the Balkans?" in *Highs and Lows of European Integration: Sixty Years after the Treaty of Rome*, Antoniolli, Luisa, Bonatti, Luigi, and Ruzza, Carlo, eds., (Springer, Wien, 2018), 27–47.

30 On the "Rule of Law-crisis", for instance, Ruzza, Carlo, and Antoniolli, Luisa, eds., *The Rule of Law in the EU: Challenges, Actors and Strategies* (Springer, Cham, 2024), 245–262.

31 As part of the EU support to Ukraine, the country was awarded candidate status in June 2022, together with Moldova and (with some conditions) Georgia. However, the risk of a 'fast-track'-enlargement was to be avoided, considering the situation of the Western Balkans, which are also exposed to Russian influence.

32 European Council Conclusions.

5 The Relations between BiH and the EU: "From Dayton to Bruxelles"?

The second phase of Bosnia and Herzegovina's transition has often been summarised by the slogan "From Dayton to Brussels".[33] This meant that local ownership of the transformation process was supposed to replace massive international intervention and direct interference, guided by the objective of becoming a member of the EU. This objective was widely considered as a desirable, generally accepted "carrot", able to create the momentum for triggering necessary reforms. The "stick" of internationally imposed coercive measures was not (to be) used anymore. This logic is in line with the voluntary character of European integration, built on cooperation and limited sovereignty. On the one hand, the experience of "Europeanisation" of the Baltic Republics and the Central and Eastern European Countries in the 1990s was fresh, the EU prepared for comprehensive reform and enlargement at the same time, and the optimistic expectation was that these positive developments would help in ending the Western Balkan's post-conflict depression. On the other hand, it soon became clear to many that the specific context of the region would require adaptation of the EU's approach, i.e., not merely "State-(re)building" after conflict, but a targeted "EU Member State-building".[34]

Parallel to the International Community's progressive withdrawal, the EU has deeply engaged with BiH within the framework of the Common Foreign and Security Policy (CFSP) and the Common Security and Defence Policy (CSDP). The EU Special Representative (EUSR) is, at the same time, also Head of the Delegation of the European Union (EUD).[35] Between 2003 and 2012, the EU ran a police mission (EUPM) as a successor of IPTF, and it still operates a EUFOR mission (operation ALTHEA) with troops and an executive mandate, which should guarantee a stable and secure environment in the

33 Hitchner, R. Bruce, "From Dayton to Brussels: The Story Behind the Constitutional and Governmental Reform Process in Bosnia and Herzegovina", in *The Fletcher Forum of World Affairs*, 30(1), 125–135.

34 Bieber, Florian, "Building Impossible States? State-Building Strategies and EU Membership in the Western Balkans", *Europe-Asia Studies* 63(10), 2011, 1783–1802; Woelk, Jens, "EU Member State-Building in the Western Balkans: (Prolonged) EU-protectorates or new model of sustainable enlargement? Conclusion." *Nationalities Papers* 41(3), 2013, 469–482; see the whole Special Issue on this topic.

35 The EU Delegation to Bosnia and Herzegovina in Sarajevo is one of the largest EU representations in the world (https://www.eeas.europa.eu/delegations/bosnia-and-herzegovina_en?s=219).

country (upon mandate by the UN Security Council). Again, direct engagement was substituted by softer instruments more respectful of formal sovereignty, without, however, giving up influence.

Currently, several agreements build the legal basis of the bilateral relationship between the EU and BiH. They include the Visa Facilitation and Readmission Agreements (2008), the Interim Agreement on Trade and Trade-Related Issues (2008), and, most importantly, the Stabilisation and Association Agreement (SAA), in force since 2015. Conditionality, i.e., compliance with predefined objectives, agreed upon in negotiations, shall guarantee the reforms necessary for immediate participation in certain programmes and preparing for future EU accession. Conditionality is monitored by the European Commission.[36] It is supported through significant technical and financial assistance, which is provided through IPA programmes (Instrument for Pre-Accession Assistance); estimated EU financial assistance to BiH between 1996 and 2021 amounts to 3.5 billion euros.[37] The EU is also BiH's main trading partner (exports almost 75% of goods and services to the EU, and imports from the EU about 60% of total imports).

Despite the assistance and support from the EU and other donors, progress on the way toward EU accession has been extremely slow and characterised by continuous misperceptions and mistakes. A recent report by the European Court of Auditors criticises the EU support in the Rule of Law-area, as (too) much remains to be done despite huge efforts and considerable financial support.[38] Although various commitments made by local political leaders regarding important reforms have not been respected, the country has always been allowed to move forward anyway, thus softening or even questioning the strict "conditionality" of the EU's enlargement process.[39] The Court of Auditors also criticises the insufficient involvement of civil society.

---

36 The results are published in annual reports; see, e.g., European Commission, 2023 Enlargement Package (8 November 2023). (https://neighbourhood-enlargement.ec.europa.eu/enlargement-policy/strategy-and-reports_en).

37 Bilateral IPA II indicative funding allocations in the period 2014–2020 amount to €552.1 million. (https://neighbourhood-enlargement.ec.europa.eu/enlargement-policy/overview-instrument-pre-accession-assistance/bosnia-and-herzegovina-financial-assistance-under-ipa_en).

38 European Court of Auditors, EU support for the rule of law in the Western Balkans: despite efforts, fundamental problems persist, Special Report 01/2022. (https://op.europa.eu/webpub/eca/special-reports/eu-support-to-the-rule-of-law-in-Western-Balkans-01-2022/en/)

39 Zhelyazkova, Asya et al., "European Union Conditionality in the Western Balkans: External Incentives and Europeanization", in *The Europeanization of the Western Balkans: A*

A prime example of the lack of serious consequences is police reform (which had been made a condition for the SAA).[40] The question of having control over a police force is a constitutional one (i.e., related to competences) and is affecting power structures. The constitutional dimension of the issue, dealt with in terms of "technical" conditionality, had been underestimated by international actors which asked for greater centralisation of police forces. Also, as there is not one EU blueprint on how to organise police forces, there was no compelling ratio to follow. In the end, the SAA entered into force with enormous delay, almost 7 years after its initial signing and 4 years after ratification by all Member States, but above all, without the commitments, undertaken by the signatories, having been respected. No true reform in substance, but no consequences. Other reforms stalled, too. Rather than leading to local ownership, international reform programmes have instead been conquered and manipulated by local elites.[41]

In such conditions, addressing constitutional reform was not imaginable at all. Indeed, despite being necessary for implementing the 2009 *Sejdić-Finci* decision and others by the European Court of Human Rights,[42] constitutional reform became a taboo between 2010 and 2019. For more than a decade, only carrots were available (plus some bland criticism), but no stick has been used anymore.[43] The whole process was *de facto* "downgraded" to a technical exercise; but even at that level without major progress, as the annual monitoring reports of the European Commission show.[44] Bosnia has become stuck in

Failure of EU Conditionality?, edited by Džankić, Jelena, Soeren, Keil, and Kmezić, Marko (Switzerland: Palgrave Macmillan, 2019), 15–39.

40 See, e.g., International Crisis Group (ICG), Bosnia's Stalled Police Reform: No Progress, No EU, Europe Report No. 164, Sarajevo/Bruxelles, 6 September 2005 [www.crisisweb.org], and Giulio Venneri, "'Conquered' vs. 'Octroyée' Ownership: Police Reform and Conditionality in the EU's Peace/Statebuilding of Bosnia and Herzegovina", Review of European Studies 5(3), 57–72, 2013.

41 This is Venneri, Giulio, 2013.

42 See below (5) and Chapter 6 by Marko, Joseph in this volume.

43 In fact, the High Representative practically did not use the Bonn Powers between 2007 and 2020. The EU's coercive powers are limited to (financial) sanctions, most notably the suspension of assistance funds, which, in turn, prevent the objectives from being reached. Together with the need for success for justifying its own engagement and assistance, this leads to a soft application of conditionality.

44 Previously called "progress reports", since 2018, the monitoring reports are called, more soberly, "annual reports".

transition, which plays into the hands of those whose goal is to preserve the status quo as long as possible.[45]

6 Preparing the Constitution for Future Accession: What Needs to Be Changed and Why?

After BiH had submitted its candidacy for EU membership in 2016, the European Commission prepared its feasibility study on the country's readiness for future accession. The "Opinion on the Application for membership", published in May 2019, lists 14 key priorities.[46] These conditions, in the areas of democracy, state functionality, governance, the Rule of Law, fundamental rights, and public administration reform, need to be fulfilled before the European Commission can recommend the opening of accession negotiations. As of today, there is almost no follow-up on the key conditionality requirements, despite formal commitments at the highest political level.[47] According to the European Commission's report from 2023, only a few of the 14 defined criteria have been met.[48]

Without expressly calling for a major overhaul of the Dayton Constitution, at least **six key issues** require constitutional amendments. Most had already been identified 14 years earlier by the Venice Commission.[49] They refer to

45 There has constantly been a tension on the part of internationals between the perceived need to control and the rhetoric of creating ownership locally to be able to gradually withdraw from what has become a costly undertaking. The conflicts in the International Community resulting from these contrasting approaches have been masterly played by local politicians mostly interested in controlling incoming resources, often by staging crisis.

46 European Commission (2019), Opinion on the application for membership, 29 May 2019, COM(2019) 261 final, 14–16. (https://neighbourhood-enlargement.ec.europa.eu/system/files/2019-05/20190529-bosnia-and-herzegovina-opinion.pdf).

47 There is an impressively long list of political declarations of commitment by Bosnian politicians and numerous Action Plans, which are, however, rarely followed up or implemented, as highlighted, e.g., by the BTI Transformation Index – Atlas: Bosnia and Herzegovina Country Dashboard (https://bti-project.org/en/reports/country-report/BIH).

48 European Commission (2023), Bosnia and Herzegovina 2023 Report, SWD (2023) 691 final (8 November 2023); see, for the assessment of the 14 key priorities, 9–14 (p. 10, for Key priority 4: "Fundamentally improve the institutional framework, including at constitutional level").

49 European Commission for Democracy through Law (2005), CDL-AD (2005) 004, Opinion on the Constitutional Situation in Bosnia and Herzegovina and the Powers of the High Representative. The Venice Commission criticised the confusing overlap of territorial

values, the effective implementation of the rule of law, democracy, human rights, and the implementation of the judgements of the ECtHR. They also regard functionality: Due to BiH's territorial fragmentation, much more coordination is needed for guaranteeing the (future) implementation of EU law. The certainty of competencies, as well as the status of State institutions created by agreement with the Entities (i.e., those not directly foreseen in the Constitution), need to be guaranteed. Ethnic veto powers must not be construed as final and unchecked powers, as this would mean uncertainty in the implementation of EU Law and regarding the fulfilment of Bosnia and Herzegovina's membership obligations. The Office of the High Representative should close before the country becomes a member of the EU.[50]

Thus, the Opinion officially certifies that EU accession will not take place without changes to the Dayton Constitution. After more than a decade of silence, constitutional reform is back on the agenda. Like the Venice Commission's Opinion (2005), the European Commission's Opinion (2019) also calls for a significant change to the status quo. To meet the structural requirements of adapting to EU Law and integration, the two key elements of the Dayton compromise are put in question: the current balances between the ethnic and the civic principles need to be changed, favouring the latter, and the widely decentralised, asymmetrical system of territorial government needs to become more functional through coordination and cooperation. In addition, international influence shall phase out.

It comes as no surprise that the Opinion insists on the implementation of the **ECtHR case law** regarding the guarantee of equality and non-discrimination of citizens (para. 4f). In fact, since 2009, several judgements of the ECtHR have declared the exclusion of citizens from some political offices by the very Constitution a violation of the European Convention of Human Rights (ECHR). The ECtHR had to decide in different cases on complaints by citizens of BiH who claimed to be discriminated against and deprived of their right to stand for election for specific institutions, as they either were not members of one of the three constituent peoples, did not declare as such, or were excluded because of their residence. Article II.2 of the Constitution BiH provides for direct application of the ECHR and its Protocols, which

structures and ethnicity as well as the composition of State Presidency and House of Peoples, the weakness of the structures at State level, and the lack of both a clear definition and a limitation of the so-called "vital interest" – veto. The latter should be limited to core matters of "identity interest" of the three constituent peoples, such as language, culture, and religion.

50 EC (2019), Opinion, 14 (in particular, the recommendations under para 4).

"have priority over all other law". The landmark decision in 2009, the case of *Sejdić and Finci v. BiH,* was followed by the decisions in the cases of *Zornić v. BiH* (2014), *Pilav v. BiH* (2016), *Šlaku v. BiH* (2016), and *Pudarić v. BiH* (2020),[51] all reinforcing the necessity to amend the Constitution to end the discrimination of citizens. None of these decisions has been implemented so far. All decisions concerned the exclusion from the right to stand for election. The recent *Kovačević v. BiH* judgement (2023) extended that jurisprudence to active voting rights.[52] The continuous violation of fundamental rights due to the lack of implementation of the above decisions is an important reason for insisting on constitutional reform.[53] However, ending discrimination based on ethnic affiliation and the exclusion of minorities or citizens will not be possible without strengthening the civic principle and limiting special rights for constituent peoples to specific and circumscribed guarantees. This, of course, contrasts with the interests of ethno-national parties and elites.

The second area in which constitutional change appears necessary is related to functionality issues. EU Member States have an obligation to guarantee the **effective implementation** of EU Law (Art. 10 TEU). This obligation is the reason for requesting "legal certainty in the distribution of competences across all levels of government" (para. 4a) as well as, in the judicial sphere, "legal certainty, including the establishment of a judicial body entrusted with ensuring the consistent interpretation of the law throughout BiH" (para. 4e). In federal, regional, or decentralised systems, coordination and cooperation between institutions and levels of government must compensate for institutional fragmentation.

The EC observes that "(w)ith 14 **executives** across the country exercising competences relevant for implementing the EU acquis, either considerable efforts and significant strengthening of the country's capacities at all levels or some pooling of resources and capacities are needed for Bosnia and Herze-

---

51 ECtHR judgments: Sejdić and Finci v. BiH ([GC], App nos. 27996/06 and 34836/06, ECHR 2009), Zornić v. BiH, App no. 3681/06 (ECtHR, 15 July 2014), Pilav v. BiH, App no. 41939/07 (ECtHR, 9 June 2016), Šlaku v. BiH, App no. 56666/12 (ECtHR, 26 May 2016), and Pudarić v. BiH, App no. 55799/18 (ECtHR, 8 December 2020).

52 Kovačević v. BiH, App no. 43651/22 (ECtHR, 29 August 2023). See: Woelk, Jens, "Opening Pandora's Box?: On the Kovačević Case and the European Court of Human Rights' fundamental criticism of the electoral system in Bosnia and Herzegovina", *VerfBlog*, 2023/9/01 (https://verfassungsblog.de/opening-pandoras-box/); and Marko, Joseph, "The Kovačević Case Revisited: The ECtHR Grand Chamber May De-Block the Constitutional Impasse in Bosnia and Herzegovina", *VerfBlog*, 2024/3/28 (https://verfassungsblog.de/the-kovacevic-case-revisited/). The decision has been appealed and will be decided by the ECtHR's Grand Chamber, probably in autumn 2024.

53 EC (2019), Opinion, 7.

govina to cope with the obligations of EU membership. This is notably the case at the cantonal level, where capacities to deliver on EU membership obligations are insufficient".[54] In other words: simplify the territorial structures or coordinate and create sufficient capacities at all levels. It is recognised that "the governments have taken some steps to ensure coordination on EU integration matters, including by establishing a coordination mechanism on EU matters". However, the latter is yet to become fully operational. The Opinion also criticises that "Bosnia and Herzegovina does not have a national programme for the adoption of the EU acquis. The programme is a legal obligation under the SAA and is essential for planning and streamlining the EU legal approximation process throughout the country."[55] This is an important indicator for lacking continuous coordination in practice. Thus, for overcoming the problems of institutional complexity and fragmentation, specific mechanisms and procedures need to be developed, starting by strengthening the role of the Directorate for European Integration. Examples are provided by federal Member States, such as Belgium (continuous consultation in a joint conference-format and rotation in representation) and Austria (joint cooperation body of the nine *Länder* for coordination, with offices in Vienna and Bruxelles, plus the conference of the Presidents of the *Länder* for coordination at the political level).

As *ultima ratio*, according to the Opinion, a constitutional **substitution clause** should be introduced, which allows the State to temporarily exercise the competences of other levels of government to prevent and remedy breaches of EU law.[56] Such a clause is common in the Constitution of Member States with federal or regional systems, e.g., Italy.[57] As subnational entities are responsible for the implementation of EU Law (and thus also for inertia or infringements in those fields), but (only) the State is responsible for breaches vis-à-vis the EU, powers of substitution are needed to enable the State to avoid infringements in the first place. These powers are a temporary derogation of the internal competence order and are themselves to be substituted by the adoption of the necessary legal measures by the competent sub-national entities. The very existence of such a procedure is usually beneficial for greater

54 EC (2019), Opinion, 8.

55 EC (2019), Opinion, 11.

56 EC (2019), Opinion, 14 (para 4 b).

57 Art. 120.2 Italian Constitution provides the central government with powers of substitution, to be exercised after consultation with the concerned region and the Standing Conference of State and Regions, respecting the principle of loyal cooperation.

attention and discipline in the subnational entities' autonomous implementation activities.[58]

The Opinion also insists on further constitutional guarantees for the **independence of the judiciary**, including its self-governance institution, the High Judicial and Prosecutorial Council (HJPC).[59] As judicial decisions are mutually recognised throughout the EU, the independence of judicial institutions is fundamental. In BiH, two issues have been problematic: undue interference with the judiciary (politics, corruption ...)[60] and political challenges to the status of institutions at the State level established by Transfer Agreements, in which the entities ceded their respective powers.[61] This option is expressly foreseen by Article III.5 of the BiH Constitution, but has given rise to political controversy after political leaders from the RS have called for their unilateral cancellation. While a unilateral withdrawal from the Agreements does not appear legally possible, the status and certainty of these important judicial institutions would certainly be strengthened by their inclusion in the Constitution.

European integration is foremost legal integration based upon the work and cooperation of independent judiciaries in the Member States and with the European Court of Justice (ECJ). In this integrated framework, direct interaction between national courts and the ECJ through the preliminary reference procedure is a central element guaranteeing the uniform application and interpretation of EU law (Art. 267 TFEU). In BiH, four distinct legal systems operate (State, FBiH, RS, and Brčko District) without hierarchical organisation; there is no **Supreme Court at the State level** ensuring the consistent interpretation of the law throughout the whole country.[62] Although this is quite unique in comparative terms, even a remedy short of the establishment of a Supreme Court could guarantee uniform interpretation, for instance, a

58 Complementary may be a provision regarding the domestic distribution of potential financial sanctions in cases of inertia or infringement, based upon causality. An example of a predetermined key is Article 104.6 of the German Basic Law.

59 See: Woelk, Jens, in this volume.

60 Expert Report on the Rule of Law (2019).

61 With the Transfer Agreements, the two Entities transferred parts of their powers in the judicial sector to the State for establishing a State Court and a State Prosecutor Office (for war crimes and serious economic crimes), as well as the High Judicial and Prosecutorial Council for the autonomous administration of the judiciary (including recruitment and disciplinary procedures). See Venice Commission: "Opinion on Legal Certainty and the Independence of the Judiciary in Bosnia and Herzegovina", *Council of Europe* (June 18, 2012), 8.

62 See: Woelk, Jens, in this volume.

pre-established coordination panel in which all highest courts are represented. However, such an institution needs to be practical as well as authoritative. This is a further example of the limits of complexity when adapting the structures of BiH with the aim to integrate them into the European Union.

A combination of the considerations on strengthening the civic principle and the need for more certainty in the implementation of EU Law is at the basis of the Opinion's objection to **ethnic criteria** in the composition and decision-making of several administrative bodies (e.g., Competition Council and State Aid Council), as they pose risks for the implementation of the EU acquis.[63] The same goes for the ethnic-based veto rights in the Parliament and the entity legislative assemblies. The logic is clear: direct effect and supremacy of EU Law, as guarantors for its effective and uniform application in the Member States, must not be limited in any way. This affects the very nerve of the power-sharing system in BiH, as veto rights are the ultimate guarantee for the constituent peoples (and the ethno-national parties). However, the open formulations of those veto rights and their frequent political abuse in practice makes them a factor of uncertainty which, from the EU's perspective, cannot be tolerated.

Finally, the Opinion also addresses the two **remnants of the period of international reconstruction**: the foreign judges at the Constitutional Court of BiH and the International Community's High Representative.

The European Commission recommends a reform of the Constitutional Court, "including addressing the issue of international judges, and ensur(ing) enforcement of its decisions".[64] Apart from the fact that there are other jurisdictions in the world where foreign judges sit on the benches of Constitutional or Supreme Courts, this does not necessarily mean sending foreign judges away. The Constitution itself provides that the Parliamentary Assembly may decide by law a different method of selection of the three judges selected by the ECtHR President. According to the EC, "(e)nacting this provision might ensure a stronger domestic participation in their selection process".[65] This focus on their selection is very different from the political debate about having foreign judges at the Constitutional Court at all.[66]

---

63 EC (2019), Opinion, 12.

64 EC (2019), Opinion, 15 (para 4 d). See: Woelk, Jens in this volume.

65 EC (2019), Analytical Report accompanying the Opinion, 29 May 2019, SWD (2019) 222 final, 11–12.

66 See, for this debate: Išerić, Harun, and Sahadžić, Maja, "Perils from Within and Without: The Constitutional Court of BiH Under Pressure", *VerfBlog*, 2023/7/27 (https://verfassungsblog.de/perils-from-within-and-without/), and Harun Išerić, Jens Woelk, "Don't throw out the baby with the water: How not to misread an EU request about foreign

Although not established in the BiH Constitution itself, but in Annex 10 to the Dayton Peace Agreement, the Opinion considers the OHR and its extensive 'Bonn powers' as "in principle incompatible with the sovereignty of BiH and therefore with EU membership". However, the European Commission acknowledges that the closure of the OHR, a process "underway since 2008", is subject to conditions. While the Opinion had been published after more than a decade in which the Bonn Powers had not been used anymore, in the meantime, the High Representative has become active again by imposing legislation through international decrees.[67] Apart from the question of coordination within the International Community (for years, the OHR is contested by Russia), the continuous reliance on the powers of the High Representative certainly reveals the fragile character of a system for which external guarantees still appear essential (at least as reserve powers). Also, the changes required by EU conditionality, which go beyond the Dayton Peace Accords, are beyond the OHR's mandate and thus cannot be imposed.

While most of the above issues would require amendments of different parts of the Constitution, introducing a specific **integration clause** as a general basis for integration would make much sense to provide the necessary constitutional basis for limitations of BiH sovereignty as far as necessary for its international and supranational integration. Such a clause, with the limited scope of serving as a competence-base for State coordination vis-à-vis obligations resulting from the EU integration process, was already part of the 2006 "April Package"-proposal (Art. III 6 c).[68] Although the proposal was

judges at the Constitutional Court of Bosnia and Herzegovina", *50 Shades of Federalism*, 2024 (https://shorturl.at/6wEaE).

67 The renewed use of Bonn Powers started with the controversial decision by the outgoing High Representative, Valentin Inzko, to impose genocide denial and the glorification of war criminals as criminal offences. Herenda, Tahir, "Political Horse-Trading at High Costs: Genocide Denial, Power-Sharing and the Freedom of Expression in Bosnia and Herzegovina", *VerfBlog*, 2022/2/14 (https://verfassungsblog.de/political-horse-trading-at-high-costs/). The successor, Christian Schmidt, imposed decisions to guarantee elections, which have been much criticised. See: Woelk, Jens, and Sahadžić, Maja, "Cutting the Gordian Knot in Bosnia and Herzegovina: The High Representative Imposes Constitutional and Legislative Amendments on Election Eve", *VerfBlog*, 2022/10/07 (https://verfassungsblog.de/cutting-the-gordian-knot-in-bosnia-and-herzegovina/?).

68 See: Venice Commission, "Preliminary Opinion on the Draft Amendments to the Constitution of Bosnia and Herzegovina", Strasbourg, April 7, 2006, CDL(2006)027. The integration clause is positively evaluated, as it "give(s) to the State level the responsibility to negotiate with the European Union and to adopt and implement all measures necessary for the implementation of commitments to the European Union", 6.

not adopted, this precedent, as well as the experience of most EU Member States, suggests the inclusion of a specific integration clause in the BiH Constitution. In terms of substance, this clause should: (a) indicate European integration as an overarching constitutional objective for all authorities and refer to the EU values as shared values; (b) provide a constitutional basis for the transfer of sovereignty rights to the EU and other international organisations; (c) contain provisions on internal State responsibility in coordination, as well as participation of the Entities and of the Parliamentary Assembly BiH in the decision-making process related to EU matters; and (d) regulate the principles of procedures for implementing EU Law (including implied powers!). Together with the other necessary constitutional amendments, such a specific integration clause would provide orientation in the transformation process by clearly indicating the primary objective of becoming a Member State of the EU and binding all institutions at all levels to that objective.

7 How to Get There: Is Formal Constitutional Change Even Possible in BiH?

The EU has officially certified that Bosnia and Herzegovina needs to change the Dayton Constitution in several neuralgic points. It is true (and obvious) that accession to a supranational organisation with common rules for all members requires adaptation and change. Many Member States have prepared for accession with the adoption of integration clauses or sections in their Constitution, for instance Austria, Slovenia and Croatia. The issues addressed by those constitutional provisions primarily regard the adaptation of internal structures and competencies to the impact of EU Law, with its direct effect and supremacy, as well as the obligation to guarantee efficient and effective implementation. These are technical issues of constitutional relevance. In the context of Bosnia and Herzegovina's complexities, this functionality-agenda already creates the need for a major change to guarantee sufficient coordination and representation by one voice. But more is required.

The main problems are related to the specific constitutional identity of the Dayton Constitution, and in particular to the compromise in favour of the rights of the three "constituent peoples", also vis-à-vis the individual rights of all citizens. The Council of Europe (Venice Commission and European Court of Human Rights) have repeatedly made it clear that the Dayton constitutional arrangement is of transitional character, justified by the need to end the war, and that the status quo cannot be considered a permanent settlement.[69] Now, the European Commission also asks for change of the status quo, including adjusting the balance between the civic and the ethnic principles.

Of course, this goes to the very heart of the current constitutional system of BiH. It is true that Article 4.2 TEU, since the Lisbon Treaty, protects certain features of Member States' Constitution from the pressures of EU supremacy. Thus, Bosnia and Herzegovina might emphasise some fundamental elements of its peculiar identity in a specific "identity clause".[70] However, from the perspective of the EU, derogations from the EU acquis cannot be but punctual: a systemic derogation of fundamental rights and principles of EU Law would question the uniform application of EU Law, on the EU's side, and the will to be a like-minded Member, on BiH's side. The guarantee of fundamental rights for all, as well as non-discrimination, is essential for European integration.

Thus, the dilemma: constitutional reforms are necessary. And they regard core issues of the Dayton compromise.

Reforming the Constitution would mark the beginning of the end of the country's transition, as it would mean taking over the "ownership" of the transformation process and not only creating the preconditions for future EU accession. However, while the elements have been identified and there is a general direction (lesser emphasis on ethnic division, more functionality), there is no specific blueprint for reform, as this would mean imposition. "The European Commission does not prescribe a specific method on how a candidate should address these issues. (...) There is an obligation of result to provide for the supremacy of Community law by accession. The choice on how and when to opt for a constitutional model which is best reconcilable with the candidate's own national tradition certainly remains in the hands of the democratically elected representatives of the candidate country itself."[71]

Even though European integration is a shared goal, according to declarations, it cannot be considered neutral to the positions of the Entities: strengthening the State threatens the autonomy of the RS and favours the political preferences of Bosniaks; Croats insist on creating a third entity or at least major control of some territory. There is still no common vision for the

69 See the clear message in the Venice Commission's Opinion (2005), repeated by the ECtHR in its Sejdić-Finci case law.

70 In 1992, with its ratification of the Maastricht Treaty, Germany has adopted such an "identity clause": Article 23.1 of the Basic Law allows Germany membership in the EU as long as it respects Germany's fundamental constitutional principles.

71 Hoffmeister, Frank, "Constitutional Implications of EU Membership: A View from the Commission", *Croatian Yearbook of European Law and Policy* (CYELP) 3, 97, 2007.

country, and the polarisation produced by war has been preserved and prevails in the political positions of the parties representing the groups. The institutional and territorial entrenchment of ethnicity, combined with the limited number of institutional players, regularly creates antagonism rather than fostering creative solutions.[72] Bosnian Serb politicians insist on the integrity of the RS and regularly seek to undermine State institutions, even questioning the State itself.

Thus, although EU accession is a shared goal, it still seems secondary to the aim of preserving the relative power of one's own group. The attraction of the accession objective is too weak, what it means for Bosnia and Herzegovina too abstract, and its possible realisation too distant in the future to trigger motivation for elaborating a concrete common vision of the State. Thus, if constitutional reform shall happen, the International Community and the EU will have to become involved in the process leading to proposals by creating safe spaces for public debate, guaranteeing the procedures and facilitating the process – without imposing the outcome.

As the substance of the constitutional changes inevitably touches the fundamental compromise, the absence of a common vision needs to be overcome. By contrast with the imposition by external actors, which is a constant feature in Bosnian history, the change from an externally imposed to a generally accepted constitutional system could be considered as a true defining moment for Bosnia and Herzegovina. Ending the process of transition, it should be formally marked by a constituent act, such as the adoption of a new Constitution or amendments of the Dayton Constitution, legitimated by the people. Thus, the process leading to constitutional reform needs to be public and transparent, include civil society, as well as to start and end in Parliament. It will need to be (technically) assisted by international and EU experts.[73] And it needs to become part of the EU's strategy and narrative. Chapter 35 in the accession negotiations, dedicated to constitutional reform, could provide a useful format, making the issue visible and important, as well

---

72 Back in 2004, a provocative proposal by the European Stability Initiative (ESI), Making Federalism Work: A Radical Proposal for Practical reform (January 2004) [www.esiweb.org], suggested to overcome the deadlock resulting from this antagonism by increasing the number of institutional actors representing territorial interests. To this end, the Federation should be abolished, and territorial government in BiH be based on 12 constituent units (10 Cantons, RS, and Brčko-District).

73 For Joseph, Edward P., and Hitchner, R. Bruce, "Making Bosnia Work: Why EU Accession is Not Enough", *USIPeace Briefing*, June 2008, 7, these are the lessons to be learned from the failure of the April Package.

as concentrating the different but connected elements in one forum. It would also require the EU to develop its own strategy.

The year 2021, a year without elections, had widely been seen as an opportunity for comprehensive reform in Bosnia and Herzegovina. Twenty-five years after the Dayton Peace Agreement, the time appeared ripe for change. But despite high expectations, not much was achieved. Negotiations with party leaders failed, again. Their insistence on the status quo and short-term gains is understandable, from their point of view: legislations are far too short compared to the challenge of a comprehensive constitutional change. An EU Delegation-led innovative experiment with a citizens' assembly produced innovative proposals, but these were never discussed publicly or in Parliament.[74] This confirms the criticism of the lack of involvement of civil society in the reform dialogue.[75] More courage is needed, in particular by the EU leadership, which needs to be clear about the importance of major changes and constitutional amendments, both for the country's sustainability and for its preparation for EU accession. Public debate beyond the institutions needs to be encouraged, but not against them. Framing constitutional reform as part of Chapter 35 could help: While forms of deliberative democracy might open new perspectives and guarantee pluralism by involving civil society and stake holders, it is essential to feed the resulting recommendations from that debate into the institutional decision-making process.

Both power sharing and federalism require a constructive attitude to make things work. The case of Bosnia and Herzegovina illustrates that a substitution

74 The recommendations of the 57 randomly selected citizens on elections and constitutional reform differ significantly from the proposals of the international community and political parties. Among them, the abolition of the House of Peoples is truly innovative; other recommendations are in line with the conclusions of the Venice Commission's 2005 analysis or the 2006 April Package. See chapter 17 by Harun Išerić and Tahir Herenda in this volume.

75 The European Commission's assessment of the current situation is desolating: "The Opinion's key priority 11 on ensuring an enabling environment for civil society still needs to be addressed, notably by upholding European standards on freedom of association and freedom of assembly. Meaningful and systematic consultations with civil society have yet to be ensured as part of an inclusive policy dialogue. A framework for the transparent funding of civil society organisations still needs to be adopted. The reintroduction of criminal penalties for defamation in the Republika Srpska entity, which entered into force in August 2023, severely impacts the environment for civil society. Legislative initiatives in parliamentary procedure in the Republika Srpska entity to target civil society organisations as foreign agents, if adopted, would mark a regrettable and undeniable major step backwards." European Commission, Bosnia and Herzegovina 2023 Report, SWD(2023) 691 final (8 November 2023), 18–19.

of reluctant political actors by external intervention and guarantees is possible, at least for a short time after a conflict. However, the price to pay for over-ruling in the first phase, and *laissez-faire* after that, is the consolidation of ethno-nationalist structures, which perpetuate the lack of consensus regarding common goals between those elites which are supposed to cooperate. The resulting situation, which today characterises Bosnia and Herzegovina, profoundly contrasts with the essence of European integration, which is all about voluntary, not imposed, cooperation.

There is no easy way out of the constitutional dilemma.[76] But the alternative is the status quo. With no guarantee for how long. One generation after Dayton, the 'fundamentals' need to be tackled. They are the elephant in the room.

ECtHR Judgments

Sejdić and Finci v. BiH ([GC], App nos. 27996/06 and 34836/06, ECHR 2009).
Zornić v, BiH App no 3681/06 (ECtHR, 15 July 2014).
Pilav v, BiH App no 41939/07 (ECtHR, 9 June 2016), Šlaku v. BiH, App no 56666/12 (ECtHR, 26 May 2016).
Pudarić v, BiH App no 55799/18 (ECtHR, 8 December 2020).
Kovačević v, BiH App no. 43651/22 (ECtHR, 29 August 2023).

Bibliography

Albi, Anneli, "'Europe' Articles in the Constitutions of the Central and Eastern European Countries," *Common Market Law Review*, 42 (2), (2005), 399–423.
Belloni, Roberto and Brunazzo, Marco, "After 'Brexit': The Western Balkans in the European Waiting Room," *European Review of International Studies*, Vol. 4, No. 1, (2017), 21–38.
Bieber, Florian, "Building Impossible States? State-Building Strategies and EU Membership in the Western Balkans", *Europe-Asia Studies* 63(10), (2011), 1783–1802.
Claes, Monica, "Constitutionalizing Europe at its Source: The 'European Clauses' in the National Constitutions: Evolution and Typology," in *Yearbook of European Law*, (Oxford, 2005) Vol. 24, Fasc. 1, 81–125.

76 The word "dilemma" is quite frequently used in B-H-S, quasi as if it were only a rather difficult question. Maybe this gives hope ...

Džankić, Jelena, Keil, Soeren and Kmezić, Mario, *The Europeanization of the Western Balkans: A failure of EU conditionality?*, (Switzerland: Palgrave Macmillan, 2019).

Džihić, Vedran and Wieser, Angela, "Incentives for Democratization? Effects of EU Conditionality on Democracy in Bosnia & Hercegovina." *Europe-Asia Studies* 63(10), (2011), 1803–1825.

European Bank for Reconstruction and Development (EBRD), "Can the Western Balkans converge towards EU living standards?", February 26, 2024 (https://rb.gy/onyhiw).

European Commission, "Analytical Report accompanying the Opinion," SWD(2019) 222 final, May 29, 2019.

European Commission, "Bosnia and Herzegovina 2023 Report," SWD 691 final, November 8, 2023.

European Commission, "Enlargement Package", November 8, 2023, (https://neighbourhood-enlargement.ec.europa.eu/enlargement-policy/strategy-and-reports_en).

European Commission, "Opinion on the application for membership," COM(2019) 261 final, May 29, 2019, 14–16 (https://neighbourhood-enlargement.ec.europa.eu/system/files/2019-05/20190529-bosnia-and-herzegovina-opinion.pdf).

European Court of Auditors, "EU support for the rule of law in the Western Balkans: despite efforts, fundamental problems persist," *Special Report* 01/2022 (https://op.europa.eu/webpub/eca/special-reports/eu-support-to-the-rule-of-law-in-Western-Balkans-01-2022/en/).

European Neighbourhood Policy and Enlargement Negotiations (DG NEAR), "Enhanced EU engagement with the Western Balkans", November 8, 2023, (https://neighbourhood-enlargement.ec.europa.eu/enlargement-policy/enhanced-eu-engagement-western-balkans_en).

European Stability Initiative (ESI), "Making federalism work: A radical proposal for practical reform", January 8, 2004 [www.esiweb.org].

Hays, Don and Crosby, Jason, "From Dayton to Brussels. Constitutional Preparations for Bosnia's EU accession," *United States Institute of Peace*, Special Report 175, October 2006 (https://www.usip.org/sites/default/files/resources/SRoct06_2.pdf).

Herenda, Tahir, "Political Horse-Trading at High Costs: Genocide Denial, Power-Sharing and the Freedom of Expression in Bosnia and Herzegovina," *VerfBlog*, 2022/2/14 (https://verfassungsblog.de/political-horse-trading-at-high-costs/).

Hitchner, R. Bruce, "From Dayton to Brussels: The Story Behind the Constitutional and Governmental Reform Process in Bosnia and Herzegovina," *The Fletcher Forum of World Affairs* 30(1), (2006), 125–135.

Hoffmeister, Frank, "Constitutional implications of EU membership: a view from the Commission," *Croatian Yearbook of European Law and Policy* (CYELP) 3, (2007), 59–97.

Holbrooke, Richard, *To End a War*, Modern Library, 1999.

International Crisis Group (ICG), "Bosnia's Stalled Police Reform: No Progress, No EU," *Europe Report* No. 164, Sarajevo/Bruxelles, September 6, 2005 [www.crisis-web.org].

Išerić, Harun and Sahadžić, Maja, "Perils from Within and Without: The Constitutional Court of BiH Under Pressure," *VerfBlog*, 2023/7/27 (https://verfassungsblog.de/perils-from-within-and-without/).

Išerić, Harun, Woelk, Jens, "Don't throw out the baby with the water: How not to misread an EU request about foreign judges at the Constitutional Court of Bosnia and Herzegovina," *50 Shades of Federalism*, 2024, (https://shorturl.at/6wEaE).

Joseph, Edward P. and Hitchner, R. Bruce, "Making Bosnia Work. Why EU Accession Is Not Enough," *USIPeace Briefing*, June 2008.

Kappler, Stefanie and Lemay-Hébert, Nicolas, "Hybrid local ownership in Bosnia-Herzegovina and Kosovo. From discursive to material aspects of ownership," in *Local Ownership in International Peacebuilding*, Lee, Sung Yong, Özerdem, Alpaslan (eds.), (Routledge, 2015).

Knaus, Gerald and Martin, Felix, "Lessons from Bosnia and Herzegovina: Travails of the European Raj," 14 *Journal of Democracy*, (2003), 60, 61–63.

Lijphard, Arend, "Constitutional Design for Divided Societies," 15 *Journal of Democracy*, (2004), 96.

Marko, Joseph, "The Kovačević Case Revisited: The ECtHR Grand Chamber May De-Block the Constitutional Impasse in Bosnia and Herzegovina," *VerfBlog*, 2024/3/28 (https://verfassungsblog.de/the-kovacevic-case-revisited/).

Ruzza, Carlo, Antoniolli, Lusia, (eds.), *The Rule of Law in the EU. Challenges, Actors and Strategies*, (Springer, Cham, 2024).

Venice Commission, "Opinion on Legal Certainty and the Independence of the Judiciary in Bosnia and Herzegovina," Council of Europe (June 18, 2012), 8.

Venice Commission, "Preliminary Opinion on the Draft Amendments to the Constitution of Bosnia and Herzegovina," (Strasbourg, April 7, 2006), CDL (2006)027.

Venice Commission, Opinion on the Constitutional Situation in Bosnia and Herzegovina and the Powers of the High Representative, Venice, (European Commission for Democracy through Law, March 11, 2005), CDL-AD (2005) 004.

Venneri, Giulio, "'Conquered' vs. 'Octroyée' Ownership: Police Reform and Conditionality in the EU's Peace/Statebuilding of Bosnia and Herzegovina", *Review of European Studies* 5(3): 57–72, (2013).

Woelk, Jens, "EU Member State-Building in the Western Balkans: (Prolonged) EU-protectorates or new model of sustainable enlargement? Conclusion." *Nationalities Papers* 41(3), (2013), 469–482.

Woelk, Jens, "From Enlargement Perspective to "Waiting for Godot"? Has the EU Lost its Transformative Power in the Balkans?" in *Highs and Lows of European Integra-*

tion. Sixty Years After the Treaty of Rome, Antoniolli, Luisa, Bonatti, Luigi, Ruzza, Carlo, (eds.), (Springer, Wien, (2018)), 27–47.

Woelk, Jens, "Opening Pandora's Box?: On the Kovačević Case and the European Court of Human Rights' fundamental criticism of the electoral system in Bosnia and Herzegovina," *VerfBlog*, 2023/9/01 (https://verfassungsblog.de/opening-pandoras-box/).

Woelk, Jens, Sahadžić, Maja, " Cutting the Gordian Knot in Bosnia and Herzegovina: The High Representative Imposes Constitutional and Legislative Amendments on Election Eve," *VerfBlog*, 2022/10/07 (https://verfassungsblog.de/cutting-the-gordian-knot-in-bosnia-and-herzegovina/?).

Zhelyazkova, Asya, Damjanovski, Ivan, Nechev, Zoran and Schimmelfennig, Frank, "European Union Conditionality in the Western Balkans: External Incentives and Europeanization," in *The Europeanization of the Western Balkans: A failure of EU conditionality?*, edited by Džankić, Jelena, Keil, Soeren and Kmezić, Marko, (Switzerland: Palgrave Macmillan, 2019), 15–39.

CHAPTER 16

The Constitution of Citizenship in Bosnia and Herzegovina: Perspective of the Others and of the Citizens

Tatjana Sekulić

1 Introduction

The aim of this chapter is to highlight the state of the art in citizenship evolution in Bosnia and Herzegovina from a politico-historical perspective. We will briefly look at its modern statehood as it was acquired in the socialist and federal Yugoslavia (1943/1945/1990–91), as it was violently challenged during the Yugoslav wars in the 1990s, and as it was profoundly restructured by the General Framework Agreement for Peace in BiH (Dayton Agreement) in 1995. The opening of the horizon of EU integration and accession in the early 2000s revealed several ambivalences and contradictions of the new socio-political order of the state and society, where the citizenship regime became one of the crucial points of the EU conditionality.

Citizenship is considered here as a multifaceted condition: as the legal status of being a citizen of an internationally recognised national state, but also in relation to the concept of identity and belonging to a specific (ethno)national community.[1] Moreover, the status of being a citizen presupposes individual freedom to participate in political life of the society, with full recognition of rights, liberties, and duties in the civic and social arenas, in relation to the concept of membership in a liberal democratic polity. In the case of complex pluri-national states such as BiH, where the violence of the four-year war (1992–1995) had produced highly homogenised political bodies of constituent peoples on an ethnonational basis, the liberal democratic principle of citizen-

1 See: Balibar, Étienne, *Cittadinanza* (Torino: Bollati Boringhieri, capitolo V, "Cittadinanza ed esclusione", 2012), 86–110; Benhabib, Seyla, "Transformations of Citizenship: The Case of Contemporary Europe". *Government and Opposition,* Vol. 37, No. 4 (Autumn 2002), 439–465; and Benhabib, Seyla, *The Right of the Others. Aliens, Residents and Citizens*. (Cambridge: Cambridge University Press, 2012); Claus Offe and Ulrich K. Preuß, *Citizens in Europe. Essays on Democracy, Constitutionalism and European Integration* (Colchester: ECPR Press, 2016).

 | DOI:10.1163/9789004707887_017

ship clashes with the fragmented polity, where trust and mutual recognition between three dominant groupings has been constantly questioned. Exploring the liminal, residual space between these two conceptions of citizenship will make it possible to reveal the ways in which rights, practices, and access to participation in the substantial citizenship are used in Bosnia and Herzegovina to perpetuate a specific constitutional order dominated by an illiberal, anti-democratic logic of the leading elites.

What are the consequences of the BiH constitutional order imposed by the Dayton Peace Agreement from the perspective of the citizenship regime, i.e., the real possibility for *all* citizens to participate in the political, economic, social, and cultural life of the political community as a whole, beyond the mere legal status? How has the European Union managed the country's accession process since 2000? What are the effects and limits of its politics and policies of conditionality on the creation of the new constitutional order of the state and society in Bosnia and Herzegovina? These three questions define the frame within which the complexity of the case has been explored and analysed in the broader context of the EU integration and enlargement process.

The constitutional definition of citizenship in Bosnia and Herzegovina is addressed through the most significant politico-historical phases in the first section of the chapter. Secondly, the EU discourse on BiH citizenship is explored using the Critical Discourse Studies methodology in analysing official reports of the European Commission. Thirdly, the sobbing process of the country's accession is reflected upon in relation to the specific EU conditionality policies, and, in general, in relation to the new global re-ordering.

2 Politico-historical Conceptualisation of BiH Citizenship

The analysis of the issue of citizenship in the case of Bosnia and Herzegovina starts with the analytical distinction between citizenship as nationhood and the claim for citizenship as membership in a democratic polity of the country. A basic definition of the national citizenship category as "a legal and social status which combines some form of collectively shared identity with the entitlement to social and economic benefits and the privileges of political membership through the exercise of (democratic) rights" was proposed by Seyla Benhabib.[2] This definition could be analytically applied both to the Socialist Federal Republic of Yugoslavia, with strong limitations of the liberal demo-

2 Benhabib, Seyla, "Twilight of Sovereignty or the Emergence of Cosmopolitan Norms? Rethinking Citizenship in Volatile Times," *Citizenship Studies*, 2007, 11(1), 19–36.

cratic rights, and post-Dayton BiH citizenship constitutionality. Two dimensions emerge from this definition as fundamental for the citizenship constellation in BiH: the collectively shared identity and the political membership, in the perspective of democratisation as Europeanisation of the accession country's society. John Erik Fossum[3] reminds us that democracy as such, and as a socio-political regime, cannot itself determine the demos (2009). Drawing on the theory of deliberative democracy, in which Jürgen Habermas defined democracy as a normative concept, we ask with Fossum several essential questions: how should people relate to each other? What is considered more relevant in a specific context – membership in a community defined by a specific ethnonational/cultural/religious identity, or in a community defined by the political principle of demos, where membership as status and as participation is evenly shared among equals in a common citizenship?

The constitution of a complex state has been burdened since 1990 by ethnonational subjects of political power, who received democratic legitimacy for their exclusionary politics through the first elections in 1990 and 1991. They decided not only who was part of the community, but also how and in what sense he/she was part of the community; what kind of (ideological) identity was allowed to enter the new distribution of power; and what kind of legitimacy of the new citizenship order was proposed and accepted, defining new basic norms of the community as just and valid. In our analytical case, the definition of communities on an ethnonational basis determined the definition of the *demoi*,[4] as three constitutional peoples that occupied the entire political space of action. By consequence, individuals self-identified and normatively recognised as 'Others' and 'minorities' were relegated to the residual spaces of political life, almost without voice. This made a specific citizenship regime a tool of exclusion from political rights,[5] and of ethnonational engineering, as proposed by Shaw and Štiks in their analysis of citizenship regimes after Yugoslavia (2013).[6]

The consequence of the constitutional definition of citizenship, according to the Dayton Peace Agreement, is that citizenship rights as status – being a holder of a BiH passport – did not mean having full rights of liberal democratic citizenship, to be exercised and fulfilled in the entire country. Indeed, in our

---

3 Fossum, John Erik, "Citizenship, Democracy and the Public Sphere," in Rumford, Chris (ed.), *The Sage Handbook of European Studies* (London: Sage publications, 2009).

4 Bellamy, Richard, and Castiglione, Dario, "Three Models of Democracy, Political Community, and Representation in the EU". *Journal of European Public Policy*, 2013, 20:2, 206–223.

5 Kochenov, Dimitry, *Citizenship* (Cambridge, MA: The MIT Press, 2019).

6 Shaw, Jo, and Štiks, Igor, *Citizenship after Yugoslavia* (London: Routledge, 2013).

case, 'being framed as national' as the basis of citizenship[7] does not refer to the borders of the state but to those of one community, one entity, and even one canton. Institutional barriers to participation, both in terms of the community and in terms of territorial governance and administration, have consistently produced violations of citizenship rights in recent decades, as reported by the European Commission, ECtHR judgements, NGO human rights monitors, and other agencies and institutions. Moreover, this is a pattern similar to that of the Yugoslav citizenship regime, where the opaque definition of the sovereign political subject of the Federation as a multi-layered political entity[8] – constituent peoples/nations *or* socialist republics, without full recognition of individual rights of the citizens – provided fertile ground for legitimising the hegemonic violent politics of the new ethnonational elites since 1990.

In the following sections, we will briefly outline the historical legacy between the two constitutional regimes of citizenship of the country.

2.1 *BiH Constitution within SFR Yugoslavia*

In the historical perspective of the constitutional genesis of Bosnia and Herzegovina, from the establishment of the Socialist Republic within SFR Yugoslavia in November 1943, the Constitution used the definition of titular peoples, i.e., constituent nations, and Others – nationalities and minorities, later including Muslims and "Yugoslavs" – only *after* mentioning the other two status dimensions, "working people and citizens". The amended Constitution of the Socialist Republic of Bosnia and Herzegovina affirms in the second paragraph of the Introduction that:

> The working people and citizens, the peoples of Bosnia and Herzegovina – Croats, Serbs and Muslims and members of other nations and nationalities – exercise their sovereign rights and their class and national interests in the Socialist Republic of Bosnia and Herzegovina, as a state, and as a self-governing community.
>
> Constitution of SR BiH 1985: 8

Why could this definition work to a certain extent in the former Yugoslavia? And why does it show all its limits in post-Dayton BiH? The Yugoslav Feder-

7 Recchi, Ettore, and Kuhn, Theresa, "Europeans' Space-Sets and the Political Legitimacy of the EU" in *A Political Sociology of Transnational Europe*, Kauppi, Niilo (ed.) (Colchester: ECPR Press, 2013, 191–222).

8 Bauböck, Rainer, "The Three Levels of Citizenship within the European Union" (*German Law Journal*, 2014, Vol. 15, n. 5, pp. 752–763).

ation was composed of six Socialist Republics where the 'constituent peoples' had a privileged position within a general condition of limited political rights of all citizens. The system of political representation in the institutions, from the local to the republican and federal levels, was strongly controlled by the Communist Party, which was organically interwoven with all segments of society. The universal class interest of the 'working people' was ideologically emphasised as being more important compared to the interests of the national groupings. Nationalism was indicated as one of the greatest perils for the political system and for social cohesion of the Federation. Thus, it was confronted not only by the 'brotherhood and unity' socialising narrative but also by a sophisticated system of representation where the constituent peoples could exercise their privileged status in relation to recognised nationalities and other minorities.[9] At the same time, the socialist modern state of Yugoslavia did not find an innovative way of separating (ethno)national identity and the territorial principle of belonging. Constituent peoples *had* their Republics, in the cases of Slovenia, Croatia, Serbia (with two autonomous regions), Montenegro, and Macedonia. The largest Albanian minority enjoyed a degree of autonomy in the Autonomous Province of Kosovo and, after the constitutional reform of 1974, increased participation at the highest levels of the socialist state institutions, including the Communist League, on the condition that representatives were party members and demonstrated loyalty to the Socialist Federation and its principles. In this sense, Bosnia and Herzegovina was an exception within the Federation, because of its plural ethnonational composition, but also because of the delayed recognition of the Muslim national community's constitutional status in the late 1960s, which was ratified only with the 1971 census and the 1974 Constitution. Moreover, its exceptionality was related to territorial distribution and the high proximity of citizens belonging to three constituent peoples, not only co-existing in the same cities and villages as neighbors but also living together as family members, relatives, friends, school and work fellows. BiH was characterised by a significant presence of people belonging to the formal category of Others, as well as declared members of the other three constituent peoples of Yugoslavia (i.e., nationals of Slovenia, Montenegro, and Macedonia), "Yugoslavs", or members of recognised nationalities and other minorities.

Where was the place, and what was the role of the 'citizens' of the Socialist Republic of BiH and of the SFR Yugoslavia? What was the substance of this

9 Sekulić, Gajo, "Godina 1989: Šta je zbiljski srušeno rušenjem Berlinskog zida?" in *1989–2009. Godine prevrata: Početak inkluzije ili ekskluzije?*, ed. Mujagić, Nermina (Sarajevo: the Heinrich Böll Foundation, 2009).

citizenship beyond the mere status of State and Republic nationals, and beyond the ubiquitous '(ethno)national key' in all forms and at all levels of political, bureaucratic, and technocratic participation and representation? There is no room in this chapter to enter profoundly in this important discussion, but it remains necessary to better understand what was lost with the destruction of the Yugoslav model of socialism, as a heritage of participation experiences in community life in the workplaces, schools, town squares, neighborhoods, civic and political institutions, and organisations.

In that sense, we will only mention the model of self-management introduced gradually in the system since the late 1950s, as an experiment of socialist liberal democratic participation in the political and social life of citizens, yet within the illiberal framework of a one-party regime. Does it even make sense to talk about democratising effects of self-management on the post-totalitarian Yugoslav society after the full victory of ethnonational politics and discourses since 1991? The democratic transition of post-Yugoslav new states and societies wiped out this heritage not only due to the widespread and violent forms of nationalism, but even more due to the less transparent but still violent transition to capitalism.[10] Neither nationalism nor capitalism as such, in its dominant neoliberal form, appreciate citizens as politically and economically independent and empowered individuals, aware of their rights, liberties, and duties, actively participating in the life of the community on local, national, European, and global levels.

The Dayton Peace Agreement (1995), and the Washington Agreement (1994) before it, established a state structure in which it was clear from the outset that it privileged the ethnic principle over the principle of fundamental human rights, and the social, civic, cultural, and political rights derived from the status of a liberal democratic citizenship regime. The constitutional structuring of the relationship between individuals as citizens and groups as constituent nations, established in Dayton (Ohio), revealed itself to be highly resistant to any change towards a more inclusive citizenship constellation based on the liberal democratic principles. While the new constitutional order pri-

10 See: Altvater, Elmar et al. (Eds.), *Demokratie oder Kapitalismus? Europe in der Krise.* (Blätter Verlagsgesellschaft GmbH, 2013), Auflage: 1; Azmanova, Albena, *Capitalism on Edge: How Fighting Precarity Can Achieve Radical Change Without Crisis or Utopia.* (New York: Columbia University Press, 2020); Habermas, Jürgen, Demokratie oder Kapitalismus? Vom Elend der nationalstaatlichen Fragmentierung in einer kapitalistisch integrierten Weltgesellschaft. *Blätter* 5/2013, 59–70; Mujkić, Asim, "Bosnian Days of Reckoning: Review of the Sequence of Protests in Bosnia and Herzegovina 2013–14, and Future Prospects of Resistance." *Southeastern Europe* 40 (2), 217–242, 2016.

oritised recognition and respect of collective rights related to ethno-national groupings, it consequently weakened individual citizenship rights for all. Why has political power become so inseparable from the status of the constituent peoples, despite the awareness that fundamental human rights and freedoms, as well as the very principle of political equality of *all* citizens of the common state, are normatively, institutionally, and practically violated? And that a part of its political body is discriminated against based on affiliation with a particular ethno-national community, despite the subjective character of that affiliation, i.e., self-identification?

2.2 *Perspective of the Others, and of the Citizens*

The Dayton Constitution reaffirmed the Yugoslav constitutional categories of constituent peoples, Others, *and* citizens, reproducing the paradox of the duality of ethnonational affiliation as a politically dominant fact, combined with the liberal conception of citizenship as a polity membership. All complaints to the European Court of Human Rights have been based on the dimension of fundamental human rights and freedoms as a more general framework within which the rights associated with citizenship are defined. In addition, the status of a citizen – in our case, the multi-layered citizenship of BiH, of the two entities, of the ten cantons of the Federation BiH, and the Brčko District – is re-defined in relation to two principles: ethno-national self-identification as a subjective principle, and residence as an objective principle and as a fact. In the first case, the identity of a person is recognised by belonging to one and only one of the groupings within the state borders (in its territorial and symbolic meaning), while the second case refers to the objective principle of residence, because of which each person is invited to formally declare only one place of residence for a certain period of time. In this second case, the sub-principle of *domicile*, which is different from *residence*, becomes a corrective that allows individuals who have the status of citizens with a place of residence outside the state, or even dual citizenship, to have access to the political life of the state under certain conditions.

The impasse on this duality was detected by the ECtHR judgements, from the very first case of Sejdić & Finci v. BiH (2009). This case law entered the EU conditionality discourse on political rights for participation in the highest representative bodies, i.e., the tripartite Presidency and the House of Peoples on the State level, and for the right to elect his/her representatives in the State political bodies. The claim to fully respect these rights, based on the Council of Europe and UN treaties on fundamental human rights (no discrimination based on ethnicity, race, gender, class, religion, etc. for participation in the political life of a liberal democratic polity) and constitutionally guaranteed by the words '*and* citizens',[11] constrained the European Commission to demand the political and constitutional solution of this impasse. The resilience of the ethnonational elites to these demands is amazing. They resist to any pressure, blocking and backsliding in the EU accession process of the country.

The status of being a citizen of this complex state remains hindered with the forced structural solutions of GFAP, brought out with the aim to stop the war, legitimising the primacy of the ethnonational principle over the democratic liberal principle of citizenship.

3 EU Discourses on BiH Citizenship

The European Court of Human Rights made its first decision in 2009, in the case of Sejdić & Finci v. BiH, followed by other cases[12] that confirmed the same constitutional discrepancy. The most recent decision is the case of Kovačević v. Bosnia and Herzegovina (2023) on active voting rights and residence. In all these cases, it was the perspective of the normative category of Others – as members of non-constituent peoples – that unveiled the normative unsustainability of the combination of two opposing principles, with the subjective and exclusive ethnonational affiliation principle prevailing over the inclusive principle of citizenship. If citizenship means full participation in rights, freedoms, and duties of a liberal democratic parliamentary state (as BiH is defined by its Constitution), then these rights, freedoms, and duties are guaranteed for everyone, and for each one; otherwise, they belong to no one.[13]

Still, even the judgements of the ECtHR contain justification for the international actors involved in the Dayton Peace Agreement and its constitutional regime:

> The constitutional provisions pertaining to the ethnic privileges for the "constituent peoples" were not included in the Agreed Basic Principles which constituted the basic outline for what the future Dayton Agree-

11 Constitution of Bosnia and Herzegovina, Article 2, Paragraphs 17, 27, 39.

12 European Court of Human Rights decisions in the cases of *Dervo Sejdić and Jakob Finci* v. *Bosnia and Herzegovina* (27996/06 and 34836/06 of 22 December 2009); *Azra Zornić* v. *Bosnia and Herzegovina* (3681/06 of 15 July 2014); *Ilijaz Pilav* v. *Bosnia and Herzegovina* (41939/07 of 9 June 2016); and *Samir Šlaku* v. *Bosnia and Herzegovina* (56666/12 of 26 May 2016). See also: Hogić, Nedim, (Chapter 3) in this volume, and Woelk, Jens, in this volume (Chapter 10).

13 Ferrajoli, Luigi, *Per una Costituzione della Terra. L'umanità al bivio* (Milano: Feltrinelli editore, 2022), 61.

> ment would contain (see: paragraphs 6.1 and 6.2 of the Further Agreed Basic Principles of 26 September 1995). Reportedly, the international mediators reluctantly accepted these arrangements at a later stage because of strong demands to this effect from some of the parties to the conflict (…) Fully aware that these arrangements were most probably conflicting with human rights, the international mediators considered it to be especially important to make the Constitution a dynamic instrument and provide for their possible phasing out.[14]
>
> KOVAČEVIĆ V. BOSNIA AND HERZEGOVINA. Judgement, 29 August 2023: 2–3

During the 1990s, the citizens of BiH passed through the devastation of their individual, social, political, economic, and cultural lifeworlds. Many of them were not just passive victims and bystanders but also actors of the devastation on the one hand, and actors of resistance to the logic of ethnonationalism, violence, and hatred on the other. The constitutional order of the country, with all its contradictions and paradoxes, was defined in Dayton (Ohio) by the actors of devastation, with the complicity of the so-called International Community. Thus, the only way to build up the new constitutional order is to amend the Dayton Constitution by the logic of resistance to ethnonationalism, violence, and hatred.

Since the end of the war, and especially since the Stability Pact Summit held in Sarajevo in July 1999, the European Union became the main international political actor in re-establishing the economic and social structure reinforcing the political architecture of the vulnerable state. The complexity of the accession process of the country, tackled in the Chapter 15 of this book, passed through several phases, not always in a progressive pattern, but also confirming the stagnation or even backsliding in the reforms, especially in the fields of the Rule of Law, Judiciary, and Fight of corruption.[15]

In this section, we will focus only on the discursive construction of the concept of citizen/citizenship, as it emerges from the European Commission's annual reports on the progress of BiH in preparing for the EU accession. The

---

14 The quotation invokes the following publications: Nystuen, Gro, *Achieving Peace or Protecting Human Rights? Conflicts between Norms Regarding Ethnic Discrimination in the Dayton Peace Agreement*, Martinus Nijhoff Publishers, 2005, 192 and 240–241; and O'Brien, James C., *The Dayton Agreement in Bosnia: Durable Cease-Fire, Permanent Negotiation*, in Zartman, William I., and Kremenyuk, Victor (eds.), *Peace versus Justice: Negotiating Forward- and Backward-Looking Outcomes* (Rowman & Littlefield Publishers, 2005, 105).

15 Sekulić, Tatjana, *The European Union and the Paradox of Enlargement: The Complex Accession of the Western Balkans* (Basingstoke: Palgrave Macmillan, 2020).

analysis includes the following reporting years: November 2010 Report (almost a year after the ECtHR's legally binding decision in the Sejdić-Finci v. BiH case); November 2015 Report (year of the 'migrant crisis'); Opinion on the application for membership and Analytical Report of May 2019 (as a reply to the application for membership submitted by the BiH Government in February 2016 and the answers to the questionnaire in February 2018); October 2020 Report (first year of the pandemic); October 2021 Report (end of the pandemic crisis); October 2022 Report (anticipating the conferral of candidate status); and November 2023 Report (the first on BiH as a candidate country). While the period 2010–2019 corresponds to the second Barroso and the Juncker Commissions, characterised by the so-called "enlargement fatigue" and a five-year moratorium on further accessions, from 2020 onwards, the first von der Leyen Commission, under the burden of the pandemic and the Ukrainian crisis (but not only), introduced significant changes for all Western Balkan countries. European Commission reports and opinions are seen here as 'regulatory texts', capable of enforcing the 'intertextual hierarchy' of who decides what.[16] In this sense, the candidate and potential candidate states are seen as the recipients of these policies. However, the European Commission, as the final producer of the text, has the power to control and guide the decisions. Despite the obvious power asymmetry of the specific relationship, we considered these texts to be highly significant for our analysis, as they contain a polyphony of voices and "show traces of different discourses and ideologies" that reveal the active role of local actors, both institutional and civil.[17]

3.1 *Report Analysis*

The empirical analysis aims to shed light on one of the aspects of the EU agency in strengthening the constitution of the fragile state of Bosnia and Herzegovina as a polity, while at the same time empowering its citizens, beyond their ethno-national affiliations, to act as political subjects capable of deciding on their future. To this end, we looked not only at the number of occurrences but also at the way in which the words 'citizen(s)' and 'citizenship' were positioned within the text of the reports and acquired different

---

16 See: Smith, Dorothy E. (ed.), *Institutional Ethnography as Practice* (Lanham-Oxford, Rowman and Littlefield Publishers, 2006).

17 See: Wodak, Ruth and Meyer, Michael, *Methods of Discourse Studies* (London, Sage Publications, 6th Edition, 2016); Sekulić, Tatjana, *The European Union and the Paradox of Enlargement: The Complex Accession of the Western Balkans* (Basingstoke: Palgrave Macmillan, 2020), 74–76.

meanings. Three dominant significances were found: (a) citizen and citizenship in the sense of political membership in a polity as a dominant feature of a liberal democratic national state; (b) citizen and citizenship as intertwined with the fundamental human rights dimension of personhood; (c) citizenship as nationality, i.e., as membership of a single national state.

The EC Report, published in November 2010, followed important events such as the failure of the 'Butmir process'[18] one year earlier and the ECtHR judgement in the Sejdić and Finci v. BiH case. Despite the small number of occurrences of the words citizen(s) and citizenship – just 9 in 64 pages – the Report clearly identified the problem related to the subject of full political citizenship as a constitutional issue, with consequences on the Electoral Law:

> Discriminatory provisions that prevent citizens who do not identify themselves as belonging to the three constituent peoples from standing as candidates for the Presidency and the House of Peoples of the Parliamentary Assembly remained in the Constitution and the Electoral Law when the general elections held in October 2010 were called.[19]

Moreover, the authors of the Report underlined the subjective character of ethnonational affiliation, based on self-identification of citizens, upgraded to a political principle of participation, as incompatible with the European Convention on Human Rights and Fundamental Freedoms. The clash among three meanings of citizenship – individual citizen as a subject of the polity, as a holder of human rights and fundamental freedoms, and as a member of the national state – pointed out in this report, cannot be resolved but through constitutional reform. Despite BiH citizens having the liberty to travel to and within the European Union without visas as of 2010, which was an important step forward, the requirements advanced by the EC were not resolved in the subsequent period.

November 2015 EC Report was published in the middle of the 'migrant crisis' that brought back the issue of WB6 accession on the European agenda. Croatia's accession to the EU in July 2013 also meant for BiH that it now shared a border with the European Union. Meanwhile, the accession process was moved laterally to the intergovernmental level of the Berlin Process.[20] The

18 See: Hogić, Nedim, (Chapter 3) in this volume.

19 European Commission (2010). *Bosnia and Herzegovina 2010 Report*: 5.

20 The Berlin Process has enabled important political and economic steps forward to be promoted and implemented. Its impact should be seen as positive and complementary

words citizen(s) and citizenship occurred more frequently than in the previous report – 20 times in 71 pages – highlighting the impasse created due to the lack of will of the country's political elites to tackle the constitutional reforms and resolve the contradictions. The Introduction section reported that:

> The legal and institutional framework remains weak and inadequate. The lack of enforcement of the law negatively affects citizens and institutions.[21]

The political pressure and the policy agency of the EU revealed insufficient and inefficient to support the requested reforms in the country in the five-year period; the text reports several sectors, beyond the Constitution itself and the Electoral Law, in which the situation was problematic and in stagnation: public administration reform; access to public information and services; human rights and minorities domain; justice, freedom and security. Still, most of the occurrences of the two key words were related to the conception of citizenship in terms of 'nationality', when speaking about visa liberalisation (underlined again as a huge achievement), bilateral agreements related to Kosovo, the issue of dual citizenship, and finally the issue of readmission agreements and security, related to those BiH citizens whose asylum request to the EU member countries was denied, and, the Balkan Route of migrants.

In February 2016, BiH formally applied for membership, without the enthusiastic consensus of the European Commission,[22] and two years later, in February 2018, the answers to the questionnaire – a total of 3,897 – were delivered to Commission President Jean-Claude Juncker. The authorities failed to reach an agreement on answers to 22 questions. In May 2019, the European Commission's Opinion on the application for membership and the Analytical Report were published as a feasibility study based on the responses to the questionnaire. This time, the report was very transparent, with 67 occurrences of the words 'citizen(s)' and 'citizenship' in 184 pages of text, containing clear criticism of the political and social situation in the country. We quote here some of the most noteworthy instances:

---

to mainstream accession procedures. For further information, see: Coletti & D'Urso, 2021.

21 European Commission (2015). *Bosnia and Herzegovina: 2015 Report.*

22 Sekulić, Tatjana, *The European Union and the Paradox of Enlargement. The Complex Accession of the Western Balkans* (Basingstoke: Palgrave Macmillan, 2020).

> Significant reforms are needed to ensure that all citizens can effectively exercise their political rights, irrespective of their ethnicity and residence.[23]
>
> There is no citizens' budget at any level of government. For the public to be in a position to understand the budget meaningfully, citizen participation in the budget process should be enhanced.[24]
>
> All levels of government show signs of political capture, directly affecting the daily life of citizens, notably in health, education, employment and public procurement matters.[25]
>
> Bosnia and Herzegovina will have to amend its legal framework, including its Constitution and election laws, to ensure EU citizens' rights upon accession, including the right to vote and stand as candidates in municipal and European Parliament elections.[26]

The first three sentences refer to the national and local levels, defining critical points related not only to the political dimension of citizenship but also to the social and civic dimensions of everyday life and the financial support to citizens' empowerment. The last quote refers to the supranational level of the citizenship constellation, conditioned by the legal framework, the non-negotiable definition of EU citizenship, and its derived status from citizenship in the Member States.[27]

---

23 European Commission. 2019b. *Communication from the Commission to the European Parliament and the Council. Commission Opinion on Bosnia and Herzegovina's application for membership of the European Union.* https://ec.europa.eu/neighbourhood-enlargement/sites/near/files/20190529-bosnia-and-herzegovina-opinion.pdf, 11.

24 https://ec.europa.eu/neighbourhood-enlargement/sites/near/files/20190529-bosnia-and-herzegovina-opinion.pdf, 24.

25 https://ec.europa.eu/neighbourhood-enlargement/sites/near/files/20190529-bosnia-and-herzegovina-opinion.pdf, 28.

26 https://ec.europa.eu/neighbourhood-enlargement/sites/near/files/20190529-bosnia-and-herzegovina-opinion.pdf, 56.

27 See: Bauböck, Rainer and Guiraudon, Virginie, "Introduction: realignments of Citizenship: Reassessing Rights in the Age of Plural Memberships and Multi-level Governance", *Citizenship Studies*, 2009, 13:5, 439–450; Delanty, Gherard, "European Citizenship: A Critical Assessment". *Citizenship Studies*, 11:1, 2007, 63–72; Marchetti, Maria Cristina, *L'Europa dei cittadini. Cittadinanza e democrazia nell'Unione Europea* (Milano: FrancoAngeli, 2015).

Among a large number of critical observations on the – unsatisfying – state of implementation of the Copenhagen criteria and the standards defined by the *acquis communautaire*, the report recalled the negative demographic trends in the country, which are almost the same for the whole population, without distinction along the ethnic lines, with 1 million BiH citizens currently living on the territory of the European Union, 85,000 people having renounced their BiH citizenship since 1996 (more than 4,000 per year in 2017 and 2018), and high emigration flows confirmed in subsequent years.[28]

The opinion of the European Commission, based on the findings of the Analytical Report, contains fourteen key priorities as a condition for the conferment of candidate status, two of which explicitly mention the word 'citizenship':

> Key priority 4f – "Ensure equality and non-discrimination of citizens, notably by addressing the *Sejdić-Finci* ECtHR case law."[29]
>
> Key priority 9 – "Strengthen the protection of the rights of all citizens, notably by ensuring the implementation of the legislation on non-discrimination and on gender equality."[30]

Furthermore, all five key priorities contained in the section on fundamental rights (9–13) are an expression of the concept of democratic liberal citizenship. This means that any recognition, respect, and praxis of the collective rights normative are conditioned by prioritising recognition, respect, and protection of individual rights, which, rooted in the principle of personhood, guarantee the universality of human rights for *each* and *every* human being as a person.

In the course of 2020, however, EU institutions have invested new vigour into the prospect of enlargement – not just in declarations. In March 2020, a new enlargement methodology was officially adopted, which seeks to make the process "more predictable, more credible ... more dynamic and subject to stronger political steering"[31] by foreseeing, among other things, gradual inte-

---

28 European Commission. 2019a. *Analytical Report on Bosnia and Herzegovina*, 89.

29 European Commission. 2019a. *Analytical Report on Bosnia and Herzegovina*: Democracy/ Functionality section, 15.

30 European Commission. 2019a. *Analytical Report on Bosnia and Herzegovina*: Fundamental Rights section, 15.

31 Communication from the Commission to the European Parliament, the Council, the European Economic and Social Committee and the Committee of the Regions. 2020 Communication on EU Enlargement Policy, Brussels, 10 October 2020.

gration of the candidates in various EU policies if the reforms are duly implemented, but also a reversal of the process in case progress is lacking. The Zagreb Summit in May 2020 provided an opportunity for the EU to reiterate its renewed commitment to the European perspective of all Western Balkan countries. In the same period, the European Council approved the opening of negotiations with Albania and North Macedonia, a decision that Commission President von der Leyen described as "truly historic," proclaiming that "the future of the whole region lies in the EU. We share the same history, we share the same destiny."[32]

The EC's October 2020 report highlighted the dramatic context of the pandemic:

> Thousands of citizens are at risk of losing their jobs, and temporary government support measures (unemployment benefits, deferrals/waivers to tax and social security contributions, etc.) have an important fiscal impact.[33]

The assessment of progress towards harmonisation with EU principles and laws was expressed in extremely negative terms, with the word citizen (and citizenship) appearing frequently – 48 times in 125 pages – in the most negative assessments. It was clear that, with the new (global) crises, the situation had deteriorated with regard to the political criteria, the Rule of Law, the judicial system, human rights, and fundamental freedoms of citizens, minorities, and vulnerable groups, including women, children, and the elderly, regardless of their ethnonational origin. Following the first case dealt with by the ECtHR, many other complaints have been filed and decided, requiring the same crucial condition: "constitutional amendments to ensure equality of political rights among all citizens".[34]

The EC Report, published in October 2021, mentioned the word 'citizen(s)' (and citizenship) 45 times in 125 pages. Citizens were recalled regarding health (due to the pandemic, public health systems were a priority), low vaccination rates, foreign fighters, and radicalisation tendencies, but the major attention remained on the political criteria, Rule of Law and judiciary, rights, and freedoms:

---

32 State of the Union Address by President von der Leyen at the European Parliament Plenary, Brussels, 16 September 2020. https://ec.europa.eu/commission/presscorner/detail/ov/SPEECH_20_1655.

33 European Commission (2020). *Bosnia and Herzegovina 2020 Report*, 3.

34 European Commission (2020). *Bosnia and Herzegovina 2020 Report*, 25.

> Lack of commitment to judicial reform from political actors, and the poor functioning of the judicial system continued to undermine the citizens' enjoyment of rights and the fight against corruption and organised crime.[35]

> As regards fundamental rights, significant reforms are needed to ensure that all citizens are able to effectively exercise their political rights and thus bring the country's constitutional and legislative framework into line with the Sejdić-Finci case-law of the ECtHR.[36]

One characteristic of the report can be mentioned: increased attention to the concrete individual as a political subject and as a social being, holder of specific citizens' rights and freedoms, negatively affected by the system:

> Corruption indicators further deteriorated and all levels of government show signs of political capture directly affecting the daily life of citizens.[37]

> However, it still does not reflect the real situation on the ground as a significant number of citizens do not initiate proceedings, nor they seek judicial protection for fear of being fired.[38]

The report maintained its analytical and normative dimensions, addressing the call for concrete action to various institutions in the country.

One year later, the EC report published in October 2022 reflects a profoundly changed geopolitical context following the Russian aggression against Ukraine in February of that year. The new approach of the EU institutions and policies towards further enlargement, with strong geopolitical connotations already drafted by the von der Leyen Commission during the pandemic crisis, now became an undiscussed necessity for the security and defence of the EU and its members. Because of the new foreign, security, and defence policy, the 'business as usual' conditionality pressure on BiH elites and institutions had somewhat eased, as the country was heading towards the confirmation of its candidate status in December 2022 without resolving the majority of the 14 key priorities. At the same time, the diplomatic and effective presence of the European Commission was strengthened due to the increased threat of com-

35 European Commission (2021). *Bosnia and Herzegovina 2021 Report*, 16.
36 European Commission (2021). *Bosnia and Herzegovina 2021 Report*, 15, 25.
37 European Commission (2021). *Bosnia and Herzegovina 2021 Report*, 15.
38 European Commission (2021). *Bosnia and Herzegovina 2021 Report*, 87.

petitive geopolitical actors in the region. The 2022 Report aimed to justify the EU's decision to grant candidate status by focusing more on the (limited) achievements and less on the shortcomings in the implementation of reforms, as in the following statement:

> The legislative and institutional framework on fundamental rights is largely in place.[39]

Nevertheless, many of the crucial critical points relating to the political criteria, the Rule of Law, the judiciary, human rights, and freedoms were assessed as not having been met, as the required constitutional reform and the Electoral Law to comply with the binding rulings of the ECtHR and the EU criteria had not been adopted. The way in which the Report used the words 'citizen(s)' and 'citizenship' – 47 times in 122 pages – followed the usual pattern, and the sentences in which the words were positioned were almost repetitions of the previous ones:

> The lack of political commitment to judicial reform and the poor functioning of the judicial system continued to undermine the citizens' enjoyment of rights and the fight against corruption and organised crime.[40]
>
> The Sejdić-Finci, Zornić, Šlaku, Pilav and Pudarić ECtHR rulings on electoral rights require constitutional amendments to ensure equality among all citizens; they have still not been implemented and remain under enhanced supervision.[41]

The report, however, insisted more than before on one of the crucial principles of the EU integration, free movement of capital, goods, services, and people; in that sense, the authors underlined that:

> Bosnia and Herzegovina is late in implementing its obligations under the SAA, which requires the country to amend its legislation on the acquisition of real estate so that from 2021 EU citizens should be treated in the same manner as citizens of Bosnia and Herzegovina.[42]

---

39 European Commission (2022). *Bosnia and Herzegovina 2022 Report*, 28.

40 European Commission (2022). *Bosnia and Herzegovina 2022 Report*, 5.

41 European Commission (2022). *Bosnia and Herzegovina 2022 Report*, 28.

42 European Commission (2022). *Bosnia and Herzegovina 2022 Report*: Chapter on Free Movement of Capital, 74.

The first EC Report on Bosnia and Herzegovina as a candidate country was published in November 2023. The structure of the report did not change. Almost all the 'shortcomings' identified in the 2019 Analytical Report remained problematic. The use of the word 'citizen(s)' (and only in a few cases citizenship) decreased to 34 occurrences, in the same chapters and sections: political criteria, Rule of Law and justice, human rights and freedoms, more often in relation to regional cooperation, and the perspective of EU citizenship. The evaluative nature and normative character of the text once again revealed the main critical point of the Dayton constitutional impasse, where the institutional "structuring structures", as Pierre Bourdieu called them, reproduced the discrimination of citizens based on the subjective and totalising principle of ethnonational affiliation, objectivised and crystallised as the main political principle. The final assessment, repeated over time, was again underlined in 2023: Ensure equality and non-discrimination of citizens, notably by addressing the Sejdić-Finci ECtHR case law.[43] As it was said in the Report,

> The country needs to urgently finalise the pending constitutional and electoral reforms. These reforms should be advanced as an utmost priority. Significant reforms are needed to ensure that all citizens are able to effectively exercise their active and passive voting rights and thus bring the country's constitutional and legislative framework into line with the *Sejdić-Finci* case-law of the ECtHR.[44]

> Minorities and unaffiliated citizens remain barred from running for the Presidency and House of Peoples.[45]

Moreover, a quick check of intersectional criteria of belonging, such as gender, class, sexual orientation, and political affiliation, seems to amplify the effect of being defined as a member of an ethnonational minority, even in the case of being a member of one of the constituent peoples with a 'wrong' place of residence. Just to illustrate, the institutions of the State were called upon to act to:

> Strengthen the protection of the rights of all citizens, notably by ensuring the implementation of the legislation on non-discrimination and on gender equality.[46]

43 European Commission (2023). *Bosnia and Herzegovina 2023 Report*: key priority 4, 10.
44 European Commission (2023). *Bosnia and Herzegovina 2023 Report*, 36.
45 European Commission (2023). *Bosnia and Herzegovina 2023 Report*, 46.
46 European Commission (2023). *Bosnia and Herzegovina 2023 Report*: key priority 9, 12.

Gender equality remains extremely important for the analysis of the citizenship regime in the country, as all EC documents examined reported that although "equality between women and men is largely provided for in the legislation [...] Women are under-represented in politics and public life [...][47]. Moreover, the intersectional amplification of the disadvantaged position of a large part of the citizenry was clearly underlined in the texts throughout the years of EC reporting, as mentioned in 2020:

> The rules of procedure requiring gender balance in the appointment of members of the collegiums and of delegations to international organisations are largely ignored. There are no measures to promote the political representation of disadvantaged groups of women.

We leave a deeper analysis of the gender issue for future work, as it is time to draft a tentative conclusion to this chapter.

4 Summary: EU Accession Conditionality and the New Constitutional Regime in BiH

Constitutional reform in Bosnia and Herzegovina is as much a European problem as it is a problem of the country itself. The 'troubles and issues' of the process of democratisation and Europeanisation of the BiH polity and society, analysed in this section, are not endemic; they resonate with the complex transition of many post-communist countries of Central and Eastern Europe, where illiberal and authoritarian tendencies have continued to undermine the development of a liberal democratic political culture. The same tendencies can be observed today in the old democracies of Western and Southern Europe, and in the USA, where political regimes are in decline and increasing right-wing radicalisation is observed. The 2024 European Parliament elections, among many others, can be perceived as an example of these processes in several member countries, and the new USA administration established in January 2025 confirms such fears. In the current European and global (geopolitical) context, the search for a solution to the constitutional impasse in Bosnia and Herzegovina is even more urgent, but due to the described political trends, it has also become more difficult.

47 European Commission (2020). *Bosnia and Herzegovina 2020 Report*, 31–32.

The problem of citizenship is currently treated in the Western interdisciplinary literature mostly as the problem of conceptualising and constitutionalising the common EU citizenship as inclusive for all citizens of the member states. The other dimension of the same concept concerns the 'migrant question', both in terms of intra-EU migration considered as mobility, and especially in terms of regular long-term extra-EU migrants and their citizenship status as *denizens*. Rainer Bauböck speaks of constellations of citizenship in terms of "a structure in which individuals are simultaneously linked to several such (territorial) political entities"[48] – on the local, regional, federal, national, and EU levels, each of them additionally under the tension of migrant's integration.

The Western European countries with a tradition of immigration are faced with the much more complex issue of multicultural citizenship, and thus of integrating into the polity a growing number of people with a migrant background: men, women, and children, holders of universal fundamental human rights and freedoms, often coming with different cultural backgrounds.[49] From this point of view, the solution to the constitutional crisis in Bosnia and Herzegovina seems to be much easier and within reach, since the culture of diversity is, or at least was, the main traditional feature of this country. But it did not work, as the reader could see in Chapters 3 and 10 of this book.

The lack of political will on the part of the dominant ethno-national elites emerges here as the main cause of the impasse, the lack of will that is going back to the specific individual interests of maintaining the privileged political-

---

48 In his seminal article of 2010, Bauböck supported that "This rough definition applies, firstly, to all democratic federations, in which the rights of citizens are determined not only by federal authorities but also by autonomous sub-state governments. It applies, secondly, to the EU, in which union citizenship is determined by the nationality laws of the member-states and complements national citizenship with transnational rights of free movement between member-states and supranational rights of political participation in European Parliament elections. Thirdly, citizenship constellations are not only generated by the political integration of states into a larger polity but also by migration between them. The legal status and rights of migrants are determined by the laws of their country of residence and of external citizenship." In Bauböck, Rainer, "Studying citizenship constellations", *Journal of Ethnic and Migration Studies*, 2010, 36(5), 847–859.

49 See: Bauböck, Rainer, "The Three Levels of Citizenship within the European Union", *German Law Journal*, 2014, Vol. 15, n. 5, 752–763; Modood, Tariq, *Essays on Secularism and Multiculturalism* (ECPR Press Rowman & Littlefield International, 2019); Soysal, Nuhoğlu Yasemin, *Limits of Citizenship: Migrants and Post-national Membership in Europe* (University of Chicago Press, 1995).

economic position in the brutally capitalised society, through the war. Here, we are not only talking about a 'captured state',[50] but also about a captured citizenship,[51] which has been seized by mechanisms of capillary control of access to resources: education, work, welfare, business, EU and other external funds, civil and political participation in the life of the country. Moreover, there is no longer any room for justifying the impasse with the arguments of war trauma, both of victims and perpetrators, since these arguments have already been largely instrumentalised to reinforce the violently created barriers between groupings and between citizens.

Finally, there is a need for civic and political actors who are much more capable of putting the pieces of a broken society back together into a new and different whole, metaphorically using the philosophy behind the Japanese practice of *kintsugi*. Reassembling the pieces into which the object has been fragmented so that the lines of fracture remain visible, preserving the memory of both the object itself and the causes that led to its destruction, and at the same time reinforcing the skills of those who act to hold everything together with golden glue.

Is there still this Bosnian-Herzegovinian capability to use the traditional practical knowledge of living together to create and reproduce its new forms over time, based on its cultural roots and above 'mere' and abstract reconciliation? We are convinced that this quality is something worth building on in order to create a new sense of belonging and togetherness as a basis for a new constitutional patriotism. It can be grounded in European cosmopolitanism and supported by a different and more effective EU agency, beyond the rhetoric of "Europe in Diversity", to build the new citizenship constellation in Bosnia and Herzegovina. But much remains to be done.

---

50 See: Marko, Joseph, "Bosnia-Herzegovina: The Role of the Judiciary in a Divided Society," *Constitutional Review* 5(2), 194–221, 2019; Mujkić, Asim, "Bosnian Days of Reckoning: Review of the Sequence of Protests in Bosnia and Herzegovina 2013–14, and Future Prospects of Resistance," *Southeastern Europe* 40(2), 217–242, 2016.

51 See: Milan, Chiara, *Social Mobilization Beyond Ethnicity: Civic Activism and Grassroots Movements in Bosnia and Herzegovina* (London and New York: Routledge, 2020); Piacentini, Arianna, *Ethnonationality's Evolution in Bosnia-Herzegovina and Macedonia: Politics, Institutions and Intergenerational Dis-continuities* (Basingstoke: Palgrave Macmillan, 2020); Chrzová, Barbora, "Bosnian-Herzegovinian Citizens in the Making – The Citizenship Debate in the Time of Social Mobilizations". *Nationalities Papers*, 52:1, 2024, 60–78.

Bibliography

Altvater, Elmar et al. (Eds.), *Demokratie oder Kapitalismus? Europe in der Krise.* (Blätter Verlagsgesellschaft GmbH; 2013), Auflage: 1.

Azmanova, Albena, *Capitalism on Edge: How Fighting Precarity Can Achieve Radical Change Without Crisis or Utopia.* (New York: Columbia University Press, 2020).

Balibar, Étienne, *Cittadinanza,* (Torino: Bollati Boringhieri, capitolo V, "Cittadinanza ed esclusione", 2012), 86–110.

Bauböck, Rainer and Guiraudon, Virginie, "Introduction: realignments of citizenship: reassessing rights in the age of plural memberships and multi-level governance", *Citizenship Studies,* 2009, 13: 5, 439–450.

Bauböck, Rainer, "Studying citizenship constellations", *Journal of ethnic and migration studies,* 2010, 36 (5), 847–859.

Bauböck, Rainer, "The Three Levels of Citizenship within the European Union", *German Law Journal,* 2014, Vol. 15, n.5, 752–763.

Bellamy, Richard and Castiglione, Dario, "Three models of democracy, political community and representation in the EU". *Journal of European Public Policy,* 2013, 20:2, 206–223.

Benhabib, Seyla, "Transformations of Citizenship: The Case of Contemporary Europe". *Government and Opposition.* Vol. 37, No. 4 (AUTUMN 2002), 439–465.

Benhabib, Seyla, "Twilight of sovereignty or the emergence of the cosmopolitan norms? Rethinking citizenship in the volatile times", *Citizenship studies,* 2007, 11 (1), 19–36.

Benhabib, Seyla, *The Right of the Others. Aliens, Residents and Citizens.* (Cambridge: Cambridge University Press, 2012).

Bourdieu, Pierre, *La Distinction: Critique sociale du jugement,* (Paris: Les Éditions de Minuit, 1979).

Chrzová, Barbora, "Bosnian-Herzegovinian Citizens in the Making – The Citizenship Debate in the Time of Social Mobilizations". *Nationalities Papers,* 52: 1, 2024, 60–78.

Coletti, Raffaela and D'Urso, Dario (Eds.), *L'Unione europea e i Balcani: la scommessa dell'allargamento,* (Roma; Donzelli, Quaderni Cespi n.4, 2021).

Delanty, Gherard, "European Citizenship: A Critical Assessment". *Citizenship Studies,* 11:1, 2007, 63–72.

Ferrajoli, Luigi, *Per una Costituzione della Terra. L'umanità al bivio,* (Milano: Feltrinelli editore, 2022).

Fossum, John Erik, "Citizenship, Democracy and the Public Sphere, in Rumford C. (ed.), *The Sage Handbook of European Studies,* (London: Sage publications, 2009).

Habermas, Jürgen, Demokratie oder Kapitalismus? Vom Elend der nationalstaatlichen Fragmentierung in einer kapitalistisch integrierten Weltgesellschaft. *Blätter* 5/2013, 59–70.

Kochenov, Dimitry, *Citizenship* (Cambridge MA: The MIT Press, 2019).

Marchetti, Maria Cristina, *L'Europa dei cittadini. Cittadinanza e democrazia nell'Unione Europea*, (Milano: FrancoAngeli, 2015).

Marko, Joseph, "Bosnia-Herzegovina: The Role of the Judiciary in a Divided Society." *Constitutional Review* 5(2), 194–221, 2019.

Milan, Chiara, *Social Mobilization Beyond Ethnicity Civic Activism and Grassroots Movements in Bosnia and Herzegovina.* (London and New York: Routledge, 2020).

Modood, Tariq, *Essays on Secularism and Multiculturalism.* (ECPR Press Rowman & Littlefield International, 2019).

Mujkić, Asim, "Bosnian Days of Reckoning: Review of the Sequence of Protests in Bosnia and Herzegovina 2013–14, and Future Prospects of Resistance." *Southeastern Europe* 40 (2), 217–242, 2016.

Nystuen, Gro, *Achieving Peace or Protecting Human Rights? Conflicts between Norms Regarding Ethnic Discrimination in the Dayton Peace Agreement*, Martinus Nijhoff Publishers, 2005, 192 and 240–41.

Offe, Claus and Preuß, Ulrich K. *Citizens in Europe. Essays on Democracy, Constitutionalism and European Integration.* (Colchester: ECPR Press, 2016).

Piacentini, Arianna, *Ethnonationality's Evolution in Bosnia Herzegovina and Macedonia: Politics, Institutions and Intergenerational Dis-continuities.* (Basingstoke: Palgrave Macmillan, 2020).

Recchi, Ettore and Kuhn, Theresa, "Europeans' Space-Sets and the Political Legitimacy of the EU" in *A Political Sociology of Transnational Europe*, Kauppi, Niilo (ed.) (Colchester: ECPR Press, 191–222, 2013).

Sekulić, Gajo, "Godina 1989: Šta je zbiljski srušeno rušenjem Berlinskog zida?" in *1989–2009. Godine prevrata: Početak inkluzije ili ekskluzije?*, ed. Mujagić, Nermina, (Sarajevo: the Heinrich Böll Foundation, 2009).

Sekulić, Tatjana, *The European Union and the Paradox of Enlargement. The Complex Accession of the Western Balkans* (Basingstoke: Palgrave Macmillan, 2020).

Sekulić, Tatjana, *Violenza etnica. I Balcani tra etnonazionalismo e democrazia* (Roma: Carocci, 2002).

Smith, Dorothy E. (ed.), *Institutional Ethnography as Practice* (Lanham-Oxford, Rowman and Littlefield Publishers, 2006).

Soysal, Nuhoğlu Yasemin, *Limits of Citizenship. Migrants and Post-national membership in Europe* (University of Chicago Press, 1995).

Štiks, Igor and Shaw, Jo, *Citizenship after Yugoslavia*, (London: Routledge 2013).

Wodak, Ruth and Meyer, Michael, *Methods of Discourse Studies* (London, Sage Publications, 6th Edition, 2016).

Zartman, William I. and Kremenyuk, Victor (eds), *Peace versus Justice: Negotiating Forward – and Backward-Looking Outcomes*, Rowman & Littlefield Publishers, 2005, 105.

Documents

European Commission (2010). *Bosnia and Herzegovina 2010 Report.*

European Commission (2015). *Bosnia and Herzegovina 2015 Report.*

European Commission. 2019a. *Analytical Report on Bosnia and Herzegovina.* https://ec.europa.eu/neighbourhood-enlargement/sites/near/files/20190529-bosnia-and-herzegovina-analytical-report.pdf

European Commission. 2019b. *Communication from the Commission to the European Parliament and the Council. Commission Opinion on Bosnia and Herzegovina's application for membership of the European Union.* https://ec.europa.eu/neighbourhood-enlargement/sites/near/files/20190529-bosnia-and-herzegovina-opinion.pdf

European Commission (2020). *Bosnia and Herzegovina 2020 Report.*

European Commission (2021). *Bosnia and Herzegovina 2021 Report.*

European Commission (2022). *Bosnia and Herzegovina 2022 Report.*

European Commission (2023). *Bosnia and Herzegovina 2023 Report.*

Ustav Socijalističke Republike Bosne i Hercegovine (1985). Sarajevo: NIO Službeni list SRBiH.

UN Resolution on Bosnia and Herzegovina n. 757, 22 May 1992. https://digitallibrary.un.org/record/142881.

Ustav Bosne i Hercegovine – Устав Босне и Херцеговине – Constitution of Bosnia and Herzegovina, Office of High Representative, 1996. https://digitallibrary.un.org/record/142881.

Ustav Bosne i Hercegovine – Устав Босне и Херцеговине – Constitution of Bosnia and Herzegovina, Office of High Representative, 1996.

CHAPTER 17

Citizens' Assembly in Bosnia and Herzegovina: Opening the Window to Deliberative Democracy

Harun Išerić and Tahir Herenda

1 Introduction to Citizens' Assembly

As of July 2024, the OECD Database of Representative Deliberative Processes and Institutions records 733 various deliberative processes and institutions worldwide, with more than half being established after 2019,[1] all across the globe and on different government levels, building up on the deliberative wave over time.[2] Deliberative processes and institutions have emerged as a response to increasing disenchantment with politics, election fatigue, and declining confidence in the political system, with the aim of making democracy more resilient.[3] Examples of deliberative processes include citizens' juries, deliberative polls, and citizens' assemblies (CA s).[4] This chapter reflects on the specific cases of CAs: one in the city of Mostar (CA Mostar) and another encompassing citizen from the whole Bosnia and Herzegovina (BiH) (CA BiH). Our methodology involved a comprehensive review of existing literature on deliberative democracy, particularly in deeply divided societies. We examined the structure, composition, and mandate of these two CAs, as well as the topics they deliberated upon. We also looked at the involvement of local authorities and political elites in these processes. Our analysis was enriched by the examination of similar deliberative processes in other divided societies, such as Northern Ireland and Belgium. In addition to the literature review, we also

1 "OECD Database of Representative Deliberative Processes and Institutions", OECD, accessed October 30, 2022. https://airtable.com/apppPtOagL1JQ6KqK/shrHEM120gzPs0nQG/tbl1eKbt37N7hVFHF/viwxQgJNyONVHkmS6?blocks=hide.

2 OECD, *Innovative Citizen Participation and New Democratic Institutions: Catching the Deliberative Wave: Highlights 2020* (Paris: OECD Publishing, 2020), 20.

3 Congress of Local and Regional Authorities of the Council of Europe, *Beyond Elections: The Use of Deliberative Methods in European Municipalities and Regions* (Strasbourg: Council of Europe, 2022), 17.

4 Dimitri Courant, "Citizens' Assemblies for Referendums and Constitutional Reforms: Is There an 'Irish Model' for Deliberative Democracy?" *Frontiers in Political Science*, January 8, 2021, https://www.frontiersin.org/articles/10.3389/fpos.2020.591983/full.

 | DOI:10.1163/9789004707887_018

utilised primary sources such as reports, rulebooks, and recommendations produced by these assemblies. We analysed the implementation of these recommendations and the response of the respective authorities. We aimed to understand how dialogue and consensus-building among citizens can contribute to democratic processes, even in deeply divided societies.

CA is defined as a body constituted from a randomly, civic lottery-selected citizens to deliberate on issues of public concern or interest[5] over an extended period. Other authors emphasise that CA is a place where groups of citizens "learn together, listen, and respect one another".[6] Motives to convene CAs vary. Among the most usual ones are to re-establish trust in a political system,[7] to fight political populism and extreme-right political parties, as well as to foster the success of traditional political parties,[8] to restore the motivation of citizens to participate in the political decision-making process,[9] to inform the public of the complexity of public action and the good-quality work done by public officials,[10] and to combat democratic erosion in Western democracies.[11] Furthermore, CA provides an additional injection of legitimacy for difficult and challenging political decisions, including those with far-reaching consequences for citizens, as well as in cases that may provoke voter retaliation.

CAs exist on local, macro, and micro levels, such as the global, EU, national, regional, and local levels. CAs can be convened by governments, CSO s, or intergovernmental organisations.[12] In some cases, CAs have been convened

5 Janković, Ivana, "Deliberative Democracy – Theory and Practice: The Case of the Belgrade Citizens' Assembly", *Philosophy and Society* 33, 1 (Institute for Philosophy and Social Theory, 2022), 34.

6 Janković, *Deliberative Democracy – Theory and Practice*, 45.

7 Berbner, Bastian, "The Unlikely Friendship That Helped Legalize Same-Sex Marriage in Ireland", We Are Not Divided, September 2, 2022. https://wearenotdivided.reasonstobecheerful.world/the-unlikely-friendship-that-helped-legalize-same-sex-marriage-in-ireland/.

8 Macq, Hadrien, and Jacquet, Vincent, "Institutionalising participatory and deliberative procedures: The origins of the first permanent citizens' assembly", *European Journal of Political Research* 62, 1 (John Wiley & Sons Ltd, 2021), 166.

9 Janković, *Deliberative Democracy – Theory and Practice*, 32.

10 Macq and Jacquet, *Institutionalising participatory and deliberative procedures*, 168.

11 O'Cinneide, Colm, "The Citizens' Assembly Viewed in External Perspective: Useful, but Not a Deliberative *Deus Ex Machina*", IACL-AIDC, December 12, 2018, https://blog-iacl-aidc.org/debate-the-citizens-assembly-in-ireland/2018/12/12/the-citizens-assembly-viewed-in-external-perspective-useful-but-not-a-deliberative-deus-ex-machina.

12 Courant, *Citizens' Assemblies for Referendums and Constitutional Reforms.*

in cooperation with governmental actors and a third party, such as an intergovernmental organisation that acts as a mediator between a government and the CA. A CA can be an ad-hoc or an institutionalised, permanent body.[13] The agenda of a CA could be strictly set by the convening authority or partially by CA participants. The issues presented on the agenda could be controversial and deeply contested or of high public interest, including (complex issues such as) legal and constitutional reform, same-sex marriages, abortion, euthanasia, but also those that affect every-day life of ordinary citizens, such as waste management, natural disasters, and, most recently, climate change and sustainability.[14] The composition of CAs also varies, since some of them have included politicians, dominantly MP s,[15] or representatives of special and interest groups, alongside ordinary citizens. In any case, a CA brings a group of citizens together, bearing in mind various demographic criteria like gender, ethnicity, geography, social background, education, etc. Such a group has to be balanced in order to represent a cross-section of citizens in every sense.[16] In other words, it should be a micro cosmos of the respective society. In addition to supporting the legitimacy of the CA, studies have shown that diversity enhances the quality of the decision-making process.[17]

According to Mulvad and Popp-Madsen, we can distinguish between four different types of political mandates given to CAs: a purely *consultative* mandate; an *agenda-setting* mandate, where the CA "is endowed with the power to actually frame the subsequent legislative handling of a given matter", a *co-legislative* mandate, where decision-making power is shared between an elected parliament and a CA in a form of bi-cameral approach; and a *legislative* mandate.[18] The process of deliberation consists of three phases: learning about the issues on the agenda and competence-building, deliberation in small groups, and formulating and adopting recommendation(s) by the

---

13 See: OECD, *Innovative Citizen Participation and New Democratic Institutions*, 35–37. Courant, Dimitri, *"Citizens' Assemblies for Referendums and Constitutional Reforms.* Macq, Hadrien, and Jacquet, Vincent, *Institutionalising Participatory and Deliberative Procedures."*

14 For the critique, see: Machin, Amanda, "Democracy, Agony, and Rupture: A Critique of Climate Citizens' Assemblies," *Polit Vierteljahresschr*, March 07, 2023, https://link.springer.com/article/10.1007/s11615-023-00455-5.

15 Courant, *Citizens' Assemblies for Referendums and Constitutional Reforms*, 14–15.

16 OECD, *Innovative Citizen Participation and New Democratic Institutions*, 9.

17 Rock, David, and Grant, Heidi, "Why Diverse Teams Are Smarter", Harvard Business Review, November 4, 2016, https://hbr.org/2016/11/why-diverse-teams-are-smarter.

18 Mulvad, Andreas Møller, and Popp-Madsen, Benjamin Ask, "Sortition-infused democracy: Empowering citizens in the age of climate emergency," *Thesis Eleven* 167, 1 (SAGE Publications, 2021), 81–82.

whole CA. Deliberation entails a process in which individuals weigh the merits of competing arguments together in discussion.[19]

The work of CAs is usually supported by independent experts whose composition ought to be varied and inclusive, representing a fair balance of both supportive and opposing viewpoints on discussed matters. Independent experts provide reports, opinions, and answers to questions raised by CA members. When issues discussed are the ones dealing with everyday life, personal testimonies could also constitute a part of the CA. If there are certain specific stakeholders for the issues discussed, they could also be invited to testify. Such involvement of stakeholders contributes to the greater legitimacy of the CA. Another essential part of the CA is a moderator, who facilitates the debate in a neutral and professional manner. There could be more than one moderator facilitating the discussion and exchange of ideas within the working groups.

The final part of the CA is submitting a report and adopted recommendations to the respective authority – the one that has convened it. As a rule, CA recommendations are not binding. In the words of the French President Macron: "You can't say that just because 150 citizens wrote something, it's the Bible or the Koran."[20]

2 Deliberative Democracy in Divided Societies

The main idea of deliberative democracy is to facilitate a grassroots dialogue, and preferably consensus, on important and divisive issues in society. Proponents of deliberative democracy claim that this type of direct confrontation of different ideas and opinions results in a better and more complete understanding of an issue, which then paves the way to a common view of the issue and its solution. Crucially, the core value of such deliberation is mutual respect.[21]

The most testing environment for such a hypothesis is a deeply divided society. Such societies are marked by mutually reinforcing cleavages,[22]

19 James S. Fishkin, "Random Assemblies for Lawmaking? Prospects and Limits," *Politics & Society* 46, 3 (SAGE Publications, 2018), 361.

20 Sonia Phalnikar, "France's Citizen Climate Assembly: A Failed Experiment?," *Deutsche Welle*, February 16, 2021, https://www.dw.com/en/frances-citizen-climate-assembly-a-failed-experiment/a-56528234.

21 Gutmann, Amy, and Thompson, Dennis F. *Democracy and Disagreement.* (Belknap Press of Harvard University Press, 1996), 79.

22 Lijphart, Arend, "Majority Rule versus Democracy in Deeply Divided Societies." *Politikon* 4, no. 2 (December 1977), 113–126. https://doi.org/10.1080/02589347708704717, 117.

which result in a polarised public sphere in which political parties, the media, and other social and cultural institutions are grouped along identity markers such as ethnicity, religion, or language, for example. In these societies, communication within the group is rich, but inter-group communication is very limited.[23] The only real inter-group dialogue is performed by the political elites, but due to the nature of division in these societies, these interactions are often mired with ethnic outbidding, which in turn results in a *zero-sum game* atmosphere.

This lack of a culture of dialogue and a polarised public sphere has led many to be pessimistic regarding the potential for deliberative democracy within these policies. For example, comparing a divided society with a collapsing marriage, Shapiro notes that "Once honest exchange gets under way, however, they might unearth new irreconcilable differences, with the effect that the relationship worsens and perhaps even falls apart in acrimony."[24] Although this lack of enthusiasm has been echoed by many other voices, another group of authors has elaborated that there are reasons for optimism regarding deliberative democracy in divided societies.[25]

In order to gain a clearer view of deliberative democracy in divided societies, we will shortly consider examples from Northern Ireland and Belgium. The Belgian example is of particular interest, given that it is one of the few examples (alongside Bosnia)[26] of a state that combines federalism and consociationalism. In an attempt to contribute to a clearer understanding of deliberative democracy in divided places, Pow and Garry analysed two mini-publics held in Northern Ireland: one whose subject was social care for older people, as an ethnically non-contested issue, while the second was held on the issue of constitutional status, an issue on which the stances of the two groups differed drastically. The difference between the issues enriched the comparison, allowing the authors to pinpoint the effect of deeply divisive issues on the

23 Dryzek, John S. "Deliberative Democracy in Divided Societies: Alternatives to Agonism and Analgesia." *Political Theory* 33, no. 2 (2005), 218–242. http://www.jstor.org/stable/30038413, 230.

24 Shapiro, Ian, "Enough of Deliberation: Politics Is about Interests and Power." In *Deliberative Politics: Essays on Democracy and Disagreement*, edited by Macedo, Stephen, Oxford University Press, 1999, 32.

25 For an overview of the debate, see: Juan E. Ugarriza and Didier Caluwaerts (2014). Deliberation in Contexts of Conflict: An Introduction. In: *Democratic Deliberation in Deeply Divided Societies*, eds. Ugarriza, Juan E., and Caluwaerts, Didier, Palgrave Macmillan, London. https://doi.org/10.1057/9781137357816_1, 2–3.

26 See Chapter 5 of this volume: Marković, Goran, "Relationship between Consociation and Federalism in Bosnia and Herzegovina".

quality of deliberation. While in both deliberations a vast majority of participants agreed that they shared their opinions freely and that the discussion was respectful, the perceived quality of the discussion was actually higher in the discussion that touched upon the more contested issue.[27] Additionally, individuals that see themselves as neither nationalist nor unionist perceived the contested issue debate as more respectful and free.[28] In terms of opinion change concerning the ethnically contentious deliberation, only a small fraction of individuals in each category – nationalists, unionists, and those who did not align with either group – altered their opinions. Conversely, within the ethnically non-contentious deliberation, a significant number of nationalists and individuals who did not associate with either group reported a shift in their perspectives, whereas a minority of unionists experienced the same change.[29] However, other authors dealing with deliberative democracy in Northern Ireland pointed out that the potentials of deliberation are wasted if there are no real results stemming from the discussions, and that a lack of real policy change bears a risk of disaffection.[30]

Analysing deliberative democracy in Belgium, Caluwaerts and Reuchamps came up with mixed findings. They analysed two experiments conducted in Belgium during politically challenging times to investigate whether intergroup deliberation can promote appreciation between different linguistic groups. The first experiment gathered Belgian citizens from both Dutch- and French-speaking parts of the country in nine deliberative groups. Three groups were homogeneously Dutch-speaking, three others were French-speaking, and the final three were composed of both French and Dutch speakers. The second experiment was larger, known as the G1000 Citizens' Summit, and had participants seated at linguistically homogeneous or bilingual tables. In both experiments, participants were asked to discuss a controversial topic related to the current political deadlock in the country. They did not find that the high quality of deliberation leads to attitude changes, but

27 Pow, Jamie, and Garry, John. "What Happens When Mini-Publics Are Held in a Deeply Divided Place? Evidence from Northern Ireland." *PS: Political Science & Politics* 56, no. 4 (October 2023), 572–578. https://doi.org/10.1017/S1049096523000409, 574.

28 Pow and Garry, "What Happens When Mini-Publics Are Held in a Deeply Divided Place?", 574.

29 Pow and Garry, "What Happens When Mini-Publics Are Held in a Deeply Divided Place?", 574.

30 Hayward, Katy, "Deliberative Democracy in Northern Ireland: Opportunities and Challenges for Consensus in a Consociational System," in *Democratic Deliberation in Deeply Divided Societies*, eds. Ugarriza, Juan E., and Caluwaerts, Didier (Palgrave Macmillan, London, 2014), https://doi.org/10.1057/9781137357816_2, 28.

they did however find that the attitude change was caused by the composition of the group. If members of a group are confronted with the out-group members in the bilingual tables, there was a more positive out-group attitude, while the homogenous groups were more likely to be negative to the out-group. However, conclusions made by the two are limited due to the small number of participants in the deliberation.[31]

Although the examples given above are not suitable for generalisation, they certainly prove that deliberative democracy can be a useful exercise in divided societies and that a considerable level of consensus and attitude change is possible, even when talking about contentious inter-group issues.

3 The Potential for Inter-ethnic Consensus in Bosnia and Herzegovina

The two CAs held in BiH share certain similarities with the examples above. As in Northern Ireland, the two assemblies dealt with issues of vastly varying importance for the citizens. The citizens' assembly held in the city of Mostar in 2021 touched upon cleanliness and maintenance of public spaces, including waste management, public parks, and other issues of that nature. This CA can be considered as dealing with ethnically non-contentious issues. The other CA, which encompassed citizens from the whole country, dealt with more general issues, such as constitutional and electoral reform. These issues are, as one can expect in a power-sharing regime, highly contentious and a potent source of divisive rhetoric.

The Citizens' Assembly in Mostar was convened as part of the Council of Europe's broader efforts to enhance democratic participation in Bosnia and Herzegovina, particularly in response to a decade-long political deadlock that left Mostar without local elections. Organised by the Congress of Local and Regional Authorities within the framework of the project "Building Democratic Participation in the City of Mostar," the assembly aimed to restore citizen engagement in decision-making and rebuild trust in public institutions. The initiative built on the findings of the Reflection Group on Mostar, established in 2017 to develop sustainable democratic solutions, and was further reinforced by the European Court of Human Rights ruling in Baralija v. Bosnia and Herzegovina, which called for electoral reform in the city. By

31 Caluwaerts, Didier, and Reuchamps, Min, "Does Inter-Group Deliberation Foster Inter-Group Appreciation? Evidence from Two Experiments in Belgium." *Politics* 34, no. 2 (June 2014), 101–115. https://doi.org/10.1111/1467-9256.12043.

implementing a deliberative democracy approach through mini-publics, the project sought to create a structured yet inclusive space for citizens to engage in dialogue with local decision-makers.[32]

The composition of the Mostar assembly was multiethnic, although it was not in proportion with the general composition of the population (150 Croats, 70 Bosniaks, 19 Serbs, 11 Others).[33] The multiethnicity of the assembly was a deliberate decision; the Rulebook of the Assembly prescribes that the membership of the Assembly is to reflect, *inter alia,* the ethnic composition of the city.[34] Given the fact that the recommendations of this assembly related to a number of non-contentious issues, it is of no surprise that 30 out of 32 of them had 90% or more of the members in agreement. The other two had 87.5% and 85% levels of consensus, respectively.[35]

The assembly held in Mostar was the first of its kind in BiH, and, being situated in a city whose divisions are stark even for the standards of Bosnian society, the fact that a high level of consensus was reached was met with positive reactions. Decision-making issues in Mostar are notorious, and they originate from its post-war political and ethnic complexities. The 2004 Statute, imposed by the Office of the High Representative (OHR), aimed to balance power between Croats and Bosniaks, but political deadlock continued. The Constitutional Court in 2010 and the European Court of Human Rights in 2019 highlighted problems with Mostar's electoral system, leading to reforms and the first local elections in over a decade in 2020. Despite these efforts, effective governance remains hampered by ethnic divisions and the need for consensus.[36]

---

32 Council of Europe Office in Sarajevo, "Building Democratic Participation in the City of Mostar," Council of Europe, accessed March 18, 2025, https://www.coe.int/en/web/sarajevo/building-democratic-participation-in-the-city-of-mostar.

33 Report on registration for the Mostar Citizens' Assembly, *Mostar gradimo,* accessed October 03, 2023, https://mostargradimo.ba/wp-content/uploads/2021/06/Izvjestaj-o-registraciji-za-Skupstinu-gradana.xlsx.

34 Mostar Citizens' Assembly Rulebook, *Mostar gradimo*, accessed June 18, 2024, https://mostargradimo.ba/wp-content/uploads/2021/07/28072021Rulebook-ENG-web-2774-2955-3924.1.pdf.

35 Recommendations by the Mostar Citizens' Assembly, *Mostar gradimo,* accessed October 03, 2023. https://mostargradimo.ba/wp-content/uploads/2021/08/Final-recommendations_ENG-courtesy-translation.pdf.

36 Woelk, Jens, "'Everything is Bridgeable' in a Post-Conflict Situation? The Situation of Local Government in Bosnia and Herzegovina," in *Local Governance in Multi-layered Systems*, eds. Nicolini, Matteo and Valdesalici, Alice, Ius Gentium: Comparative Perspectives on Law and Justice, vol. 108 (Springer, Cham, 2023), 264–366. https://doi.org/10.1007/978-3-031-41792-4_16.

However, one needs to bear in mind the fact that the issues on which the citizens in Mostar deliberated are of such a nature that one cannot reasonably expect anything else but a high level of consensus.

In that regard, we need to look at the second CA, which occurred in BiH. The process was launched and supported by the European Union, with the support of the United States Embassy and the OSCE Mission to BiH.[37] The involvement of the EU in organising the second Citizens' Assembly in Bosnia and Herzegovina was a double-edged sword regarding its legitimacy. While it provided the necessary funding and demonstrated an alternative democratic process to local politicians, it also fuelled suspicions about potential hidden agendas, which could undermine public trust in the process.[38]

This CA dealt with more divisive issues. The decision-making procedure reflected this fact, since a two-third majority was required for a decision to be accepted, while if 15% of the members totally disagreed with the decision, it had to be amended through additional discussion.[39]

The organisers of the assembly had a "no wrong answers" policy in order to encourage open debate, while the process itself underwent three phases: the first being the learning phase, in which rules of deliberation acceptable for everyone were established, and the citizens were able to talk with experts in constitutional and electoral law. The second phase was dubbed the consultation phase, and here the members were free to either informally consult their friends and family members or consult with the wider public. The third phase was the decision-making process itself. The deliberations took two weekends in total.[40]

Out of the 19 recommendations that were subject to the decision-making process in the CA, only 2 did not have the necessary two-thirds majority (they

37 Delegation of the European Union to Bosnia and Herzegovina, "BiH Citizens' Assembly Gave Recommendations on Constitutional and Electoral Reform," accessed March 18, 2025, https://www.eeas.europa.eu/delegations/bosnia-and-herzegovina/bih-citizens%E2%80%99-assembly-gave-recommendations-constitutional-and-electoral-reform_en?s=219.

38 Balcani Caucaso Transeuropa, "Bosnia and Herzegovina: Experiments in Deliberative Democracy," accessed March 18, 2025, https://www.balcanicaucaso.org/eng/Areas/Bosnia-Herzegovina/Bosnia-and-Herzegovina-experiments-in-deliberative-democracy-220852.

39 Recommendations of the Citizens' Assembly of Bosnia and Herzegovina, *Skupština građana,* accessed October 03, 2023. https://www.skupstinagradjana.ba/images/Recommendations_for_citizens_report_v6_1.pdf.

40 Recommendations of the Citizens' Assembly of Bosnia and Herzegovina, *Skupština građana,* accessed October 03, 2023. https://www.skupstinagradjana.ba/images/Recommendations_for_citizens_report_v6_1.pdf.

did, however, have a simple majority of 61.8% each). Although the general topic for which the CA was called implies that issues that were to be debated and deliberated upon are divisive, a closer look tells us that the vast majority of the recommendations dealt with issues where a cross-ethnic consensus was to be expected. Recommendations such as the introduction of e-technologies into the electoral process, obligatory vote for citizens, transparent and independent electoral committees, etc., can hardly be considered as issues which divide the population of Bosnia and Herzegovina. In our opinion, only two out of nineteen recommendations can be considered as pertaining to unequivocally divisive issues. The first is the abolishment of the Houses of the Peoples in the Parliamentary Assembly of Bosnia and Herzegovina and the Parliament of the Federation of Bosnia and Herzegovina, and the Council of Peoples of the National Assembly of the Republika Srpska, as upper chambers of the legislative bodies in which ethnic vetoes can be invoked. However, the recommendation also entails that the vital national interest veto will be transferred to a new unicameral legislative body, i.e., the veto would be kept.[41] This rationalisation of the legislative procedure mustered an 80.3% support, showing a potential for a wide base of consensus on this pervasive issue. This recommendation is particularly interesting in the light of Sejdić-Finci group of cases, and the Kovačević case, since it shows a path to resolution of a number of violations of active and passive electoral rights of the citizens of Bosnia and Herzegovina.[42] The second recommendation focuses on two reforms of the Presidency of Bosnia and Herzegovina. First, a fourth member should be included, not belonging to the three constituent peoples, which would enable all members of the presidency a year on the post of the Chair of the Presidency. Second, all four members are to be elected indirectly. According to the proposition, members of the Presidency are to be nominated by *ad hoc* caucuses of constituent peoples and the Others from their own ranks. This solution, which would effectively implement the Sejdić-Finci group of ECtHR judgements while resolving the Bosniak-Croat "conflict" regarding electoral reform, had a 78.2% support.[43]

41 Recommendation no. 4, Recommendations of the Citizens' Assembly of Bosnia and Herzegovina, *Skupština građana,* accessed October 03, 2023. https://www.skupstinagradjana.ba/images/Recommendations_for_citizens_report_v6_1.pdf.

42 See: Marko, Joseph, in this volume, and Balić, Lejla, in this volume.

43 Recommendation no. 3, Recommendations of the Citizens' Assembly of Bosnia and Herzegovina, available on: *Skupština građana,* accessed October 03, 2023. https://www.skupstinagradjana.ba/images/Recommendations_for_citizens_report_v6_1.pdf.

Other issues that could be considered divisive related to general discrimination and affirmative action regarding women in politics, but these issues cannot be considered ethnically divisive, as the ideological rift that these issues relate to cuts across the cleavages of Bosnian society.

Although the two recommendations that were analysed in more detail present a limited sample, one can be cautiously optimistic about the prospects of CAs in BiH. After all, the two issues that were subject to the citizens' decision-making process have been the two most notorious and divisive issues in the public life of Bosnia and Herzegovina in the last decade or more. However, we must echo the concerns voiced regarding CAs in Northern Ireland – the discussions held by the citizens should result in real-life changes if the optimism regarding the potential of deliberation is to be kept; otherwise, the threat of disaffection looms large. In that regard, one can certainly appreciate the fact that the recommendations of the CA Mostar have the potential for both a wide base of consensus and a fair chance of being implemented by the authorities.

4 Implementation of the Citizens' Assemblies' Recommendations in Bosnia and Herzegovina

In the final phase of its work, a CA adopts a report about its work and recommendations that are submitted to the authority that has convened the CA.[44] The authority can choose to implement recommendations (all or some), to reject, to modify, or ignore them. The OECD report on deliberative processes (encompassing not only CAs), which included 55 cases, shows that in 76% of cases, public authorities have implemented more than half of the recommendations. In 36% of cases, all recommendations have been implemented. Only in 11% of cases none of the recommendations were implemented.[45]

Implementation of recommendations highly depends on the authority that has convened the CA and set its agenda. As Dunetz points out, for a CA to be successful, there has to be a commitment given ahead of time regarding how and when the government will respond to the recommendations.[46] In some

44 "How to Run a Citizens' Assembly: A Handbook for Local Authorities Based on the Innovation in Democracy Programme," accessed October 30, 2023. https://www.thersa.org/globalassets/reports/2020/IIDP-citizens-assembly.pdf.

45 OECD, *Innovative Citizen Participation and New Democratic Institutions*, 32.

46 Dunetz, David, "Towards Democratic Innovation in Israel: The Case for Citizens' Assemblies," *Heinrich-Böll-Stiftung*, September 01, 2020. https://il.boell.org/sites/default/files/2020-11/Towards-Democratic-Innovation-in-Israel_The-Case-for-Citizens-Assemblies.pdf.

cases, governments have had unconditionally accepted the binding nature of recommendations if a certain threshold of votes by the CA was reached.[47] In other cases, governments have agreed to submit the recommendations to a referendum[48] before even knowing what these recommendations were going to be.

Janković explains that without government backing, most deliberative events have little or no effect on public opinion and the decision-making process. "In order to show its full potential and genuinely influence public policy, deliberative bodies need to collaborate with regular governmental institutions."[49] Whether the recommendation is going to be implemented might also depend on its potential to bridge the division between the government and the public.[50] Recommendations, especially those on controversial and dividing social issues, are seen as inputs and confidence for the government in need to make certain decisions.[51] In these cases, CAs have the best effect.[52]

In order for the spirit of the CA to keep on living, authorities would meet with citizens participating in CAs in follow-up meetings to discuss the implementation of recommendations, in order not to lose the CA spirit.[53] One of the OECD's good principles for deliberative processes is monitoring the implementation of the recommendations with regular public progress reports.[54] Governments should be responsible, and respond, and explain the rationale for accepting or rejecting a recommendation[55] in an implementation report.

Implementation of CAs' recommendations has been in direct correlation with the level of inclusion of the local authorities in the preparation of CAs,

47 E.g., in case of city Gdansk (Poland), it was 80%. Marcin Gerwin, "Designing the Process of Delivering Recommendations by the Citizens' Assembly," *newDemocracy Foundation*, https://www.newdemocracy.com.au/docs/researchnotes/ContentHost/Marcin_Delivering_Recommendations_Dublin.pdf.

48 Courant, *Citizens' Assemblies for Referendums and Constitutional Reforms*, 4, 9.

49 Janković, *Deliberative Democracy – Theory and Practice*, 45.

50 Phalnikar, *France's Citizen Climate Assembly*.

51 Cahillane, Laura, "Delaying Tactics or Useful Deliberative Exercises? The Irish Citizens' Assembly and the Convention on the Constitution," IACL-AIDC, December 04, 2018, https://blog-iacl-aidc.org/debate-the-citizens-assembly-in-ireland/2018/12/3/delaying-tactics-or-useful-deliberative-exercises-the-irish-citizens-assembly-and-the-convention-on-the-constitution.

52 Cahillane, *Delaying Tactics or Useful Deliberative Exercises?"*

53 Boswell, John, "Seeing Like a Citizen: How Being a Participant in a Citizens' Assembly Changed Everything I Thought I Knew about Deliberative Mini-Publics," *Journal of Deliberative Democracy* 17(2) (University of Westminster Press, 2021).

54 OECD, *Innovative Citizen Participation and New Democratic Institutions*, 9.

55 OECD, *Innovative Citizen Participation and New Democratic Institutions*, 31.

as well as in deliberation. Although neither CA Mostar nor CA BiH were organised or established by a national authority, but by an external factor – in the case of CA Mostar, it was the Council of Europe (CoE), more precisely the Congress of Local and Regional Authorities (Congress), and in the case of CA BiH, it was the Delegation of the EU in BiH (EU Delegation) – the involvement of domestic authorities differentiated, with CA Mostar having local government involved thoroughly and from the beginning, while there was a lack of such inclusion in the case of CA BiH.

With regards to CA Mostar, the local government has been involved in the process from the beginning and through various means, which ultimately contributed to the effectiveness of the implementation of recommendations. As part of the preparation for CA Mostar, the city administration has signed a memorandum of understanding with the CoE, undertaking an obligation to address and discuss each recommendation adopted by the CA in the city council, to inform the CoE about discussions and decisions made by the city council, to ensure the sustainability of proposed solutions, and to consider the implementation of CA Mostar in 2022/2023.[56] The composition of the CA Mostar Oversight Board, tasked with overseeing assembly proceedings, including the selection of CA participants and deciding on the filed complaints, included representatives of the mayor's office and of each political party/collation represented in the city council.[57] It was optional for political parties/collations to appoint a representative, and each one of them did so, which speaks of the interest of local politicians to be part of the process. Furthermore, the local political elite were involved in the setting of the CA agenda. According to the Congress, such involvement was deemed essential "as they would have to support the process and ensure the implementation of recommendations."[58] Finally, political representatives were also involved in the deliberation by answering questions and concerns raised by CA participants.

On the other hand, the EU Delegation made no credible effort to include domestic politicians. There was an invitation to members of the Interdepartmental Working Group for Electoral Reform in BiH to participate as an observer to which there was no response. During the deliberation, the EU Delega-

56 Memorandum of co-operation between the Council of Europe and the City Mostar for the implementation of the project Building Democratic Participation in City Mostar, *Mostar gradimo*, https://mostargradimo.ba/wp-content/uploads/2021/07/MoU-Signed-ENG.pdf.

57 Mostar Citizens' Assembly Rulebook, *Mostar gradimo*, https://mostargradimo.ba/wp-content/uploads/2021/07/28072021Rulebook-ENG-web-2774-2955-3924.1.pdf.

58 Congress of Local and Regional Authorities of the Council of Europe, *Beyond Elections*, 31.

tion asked representatives of political parties represented in the House of Representatives of the Parliamentary Assembly of Bosnia and Herzegovina (PA BiH) to present their views to members of CA BiH; however, not a single party from the BiH entity Republika Srpska did so. Contrary to the CA Mostar experience, representatives of the whole political spectrum of the PA BiH were not included in the initiative phase of CA BiH or in determining the topic and questions to be answered by CA BiH. CA BiH was conceived as an organisation with limited political involvement, which eventually affected the implementation of its recommendations.

Once recommendations were adopted by CA Mostar,[59] the city council unanimously adopted an action plan for their implementation[60] and planned the necessary funding in the 2022 budget. Additionally, the mayor was asked to report quarterly on the implementation of the action plan.[61] The implementation of recommendations was also financially[62] supported by the Council of Europe, as well as by other means.[63] When the city council was adopting a conclusion on the implementation of recommendations in July 2022, it emphasised the need for the city to strengthen the implementation and asked the mayor to submit one more report at the end of 2022.[64]

The CoE, as well as CA Mostar, did not operate in a political vacuum or in isolation from the city administration and local politicians. On the contrary,

59 Some recommendations address issues that are not within the competencies of the city administration but cantonal level. See, for example, recommendation no. 3 in the part "Reorganisation of the public utility companies" of the Action plan for the implementation of the Citizens' Assembly recommendations, *Mostar Gradimo*. https://mostargradimo.ba/wp-content/uploads/2022/01/Akcioni-plan-za-implementaciju-Skupstine-gradana-Mostara-1-1.pdf.

60 Action plan for the implementation of the Citizens' Assembly recommendations, https://mostargradimo.ba/wp-content/uploads/2022/01/Akcioni-plan-za-implementaciju-Skupstine-gradana-Mostara-1-1.pdf.

61 Conclusion for the Action plan for the implementation of the Citizens' Assembly recommendation, *Mostar gradimo*. https://mostargradimo.ba/wp-content/uploads/2022/01/Sluzbeni-glasnik-Grada-Mostara-broj-23-2021.pdf.

62 Council of Europe Congress supports implementation of the Citizens' Assembly recommendations in the City of Mostar, *Council of Europe Office in Sarajevo*, May 6, 2022, https://www.coe.int/en/web/sarajevo/-/council-of-europe-congress-supports-implementation-of-the-citizens-assembly-recommendations-in-the-city-of-mostar.

63 Council of Europe Office in Sarajevo, "Action Plan for BiH 2022–2025," *Council of Europe Office in Sarajevo*. https://rm.coe.int/action-plan-bosnia-and-herzegovina-2022-2025-eng/1680a54231.

64 Conclusion of the City Council on the Report on the Implementation of the Action Plan, *Mostar gradimo*, https://mostargradimo.ba/wp-content/uploads/2022/10/Conclusion-on-the-Report-on-the-Action-Plan.docx.

the politicians were involved in the work of the CA through various means. Such an enabling environment, as well as the fact that the issues contested were not ethnically coloured, eventually resulted in the city council's commitment to fully implement all adopted recommendations. On the other hand, since the work of the CA was terminated when it adopted recommendations, it was only up to the CoE, as well as the city council, to be persistent in overseeing the implementation of recommendations by the city administration. So far, the city council adopted two reports on the implementation of the action plan.

One identified deficiency is the exclusion of CA Mostar in the implementation process, although there was a high interest of CA participants to be involved. According to the survey conducted among CA participants, a year after the CA adopted the recommendations,[65] almost every respondent who participated in the survey (40% (18) of CA participants) expressed their interest to contribute to the implementation of recommendations. Furthermore, each of them was interested in participating in the next CA edition, and 13 of them stated that visible progress is seen in fields for which recommendations have been made. In that sense, one of the adopted CA recommendations addresses the mayor, asking him to investigate with the Congress team how citizens' assemblies could be institutionalised in Mostar.[66] The percentage of those who completed the survey is less than half and it may indicate the lack of interest for the CA, either because they have not contributed to the implementation of recommendations or they were disappointed with the city's response or the dynamic of the implementation phase. However, considering that almost everyone who completed the survey stated that progress in implementing recommendations was visible, it indicates that the oversight exercised by the CoE and the city council seems to be adequate. On the other hand, CA involvement in implementing recommendation could foster the process as more domestic and in control of domestic players, contributing to further development of democratic culture of keeping elected representatives accountable for the promises made and getting citizens more engaged in the democratic process. It would also keep the CA spirit alive.

65 Citizens' Assembly members' views – 1 year after, *Mostar gradimo*, July 26, 2022, https://mostargradimo.ba/misljenje-ucesnika-skupstine-gradana-godinu-dana-poslije-2/.

66 Recommendations by the Mostar Citizens' Assembly, *Mostar gradimo*, https://mostargradimo.ba/wp-content/uploads/2021/08/Final-recommendations_ENG-courtesy-translation.pdf. Institutionalised CA is not a new phenomenon. OECD database has recorded over 40 such examples.

Implementation of recommendations adopted by CA BiH was totally opposite to the process led in the city of Mostar. According to CA BiH rules, all 17 adopted recommendations have been transmitted to the BiH PA (state-level body with competences to implement constitutional and electoral reforms) via the EU Special Representative. Recommendations were indeed presented to the representatives of the caucuses, but without any further political implications. On the other hand, there were no proper presentations to other stakeholders to whom the recommendations were directed, such as the Delegation of the EU, BiH Central Election Commission, entity parliaments, BiH Prosecutor's Office, public broadcasting system, etc. The position of the convening authority indicates a lesser interest to insist on the implementation of recommendations, either because it did not support the recommendations as these differed significantly from the reform proposed by the EU[67] or simply because it was not eager to promote them among the political elites, the media, or the public in general.

Although CA BiH is terminated, one of the activities listed is for the Central Election Commission to inform CA BiH on the election observation conclusions. Also, CA BiH Rules state that recommendations should be taken into consideration when appropriate decisions are made. To follow up on this rule, there should have been oversight exercised by CA BiH. Obviously, there was desire of CA BiH participants to keep CA BiH operating, but there were no concrete recommendations adopted on its institutionalisation, as was the case in the city of Mostar. The EU Delegation also failed to follow up on the recommendation requiring the involvement of CA BiH in the implementation process and to use the potential it had for the second edition of CA BiH or to assess the potential institutionalisation of CA.

CA BiH recommendations were presented to the public during the political negotiations about the constitutional and electoral reform under the supervision of the international community (the so-called Neum negotiations). The EU, which was deeply involved in these negotiations, invited political leaders to find inspiration in the deliberation process and the recommendations it has produced.[68] At the same time, there is no information available in the public

67 Woelk, Jens, and Sahadžić, Maja, "Cutting the Gordian Knot in Bosnia and Herzegovina: The High Representative Imposes Constitutional and Legislative Amendments on Election Eve," *VerfBlog,* October 7, 2022, https://verfassungsblog.de/cutting-the-gordian-knot-in-bosnia-and-herzegovina/.

68 Press and Information Team of the Delegation to Bosnia and Herzegovina, "BiH Citizens' Assembly presents its recommendations on constitutional and electoral reform to the BiH Parliament", Delegation of the European Union to Bosnia and Herzegovina & European Union Special Representative in Bosnia and Herzegovina, March 17, 2022, https://

whether the EU in any way insisted on a discussion about the recommendations during the political negotiations, or whether it had even brought it up as a topic. Furthermore, on the website of CA BiH, there is no news of any public or media campaign or promotion of recommendations targeting the general public or politicians. Considering the lack of engagement of the EU Delegation to ensure sincere and thorough involvement of MPs in the preparation and operation of CA BiH, as well as the deficiency in promoting CA BiH recommendations in the media and the public or lobbying for their implementation, it seems that the EU was never sincerely invested in the process. Bearing in mind the difficult environment in which CA BiH operated, caused by the fact that the BiH Constitution is hard to amend, the constitutional crises and long, exhausting negotiations on electoral reform, and the deeply polarised political scene, as well as the very sensitive and ethnically contested issues decided by CA BiH, the EU had to be aware that the absence of its political involvement from the beginning of the work of CA BiH doomed the implementation of recommendations to failure.

An overview of the implementation of recommendations adopted by CA Mostar, as well as CA BiH, indicates that earlier involvement of political elites in the proceedings of CAs could contribute to the implementation of the recommendations. This does not mean that domestic politicians should be given the floor to influence the decision-making process, but that they need to be involved either symbolically or be given the floor to answer questions raised by CA participants. It would make them feel part of the process, for they are the ones in charge of the follow-up. The EU Delegation should have discussed the operation of CA BiH at least with the PA BiH leadership to ensure a parliamentary debate. The failure to do so has resulted in the fact that CA BiH recommendations are, at this moment, a dead letter, as politicians have shown no political will or interest to bring them into the parliamentary arena. The failure of the EU to plan how to communicate, respond to, and use the recommendations in the policy process or their work in BiH, including negotiations on constitutional and electoral reform, has resulted in great disappointment and undermined the trust of citizens in the political system, but also in the EU. Furthermore, it seems the EU Delegation considered the recommendations to be for one-time use (for the Neum negotiations), although these tackle pressing social issues for the country, which will be in the spotlight in the future.

---

www.eeas.europa.eu/delegations/bosnia-and-herzegovina/skup%C5%A1tina-gra%C4%91ana-bih-prezentirala-svoje-preporuke-o-ustavnoj-i_bs.

Building up on positive experience with the first edition of CA Mostar, in 2024, the CoE supported two CAs at the local level: the second CA Mostar[69] and the first CA Banja Luka.[70] Both CAs took place in February 2024. CA Mostar was dedicated to the economy and tourism, while CA Banja Luka focused on entrepreneurship and youth.

5 Conclusion

The two examples of citizens' assemblies in BiH give us many reasons for optimism. On the grassroots level, the consensus that was established during the work of both assemblies shows that the depth of division at the level of political elites and in the public sphere in general does not necessarily translate to the level of ordinary citizens. In that regard, the examples from the EU-led CA BiH is especially encouraging. The examples of CAs in BiH dovetail neatly with the experiences of Northern Ireland and Belgium, in that they prove the sceptics wrong by showing that constructive dialogue on a variety of topics is achievable regardless of the divisiveness of the issues discussed.

However, the potential of deliberative democracy is much bigger than the mere establishment of understanding inside a small group of citizens. In order to sustain the momentum gained by the deliberations of citizens and to make a more significant impact, a concerted effort is required. In that regard, the experiences from Bosnia and Herzegovina are mixed. The Mostar assembly, while more modest in terms of the divisiveness of the issues discussed, has a significant potential to contribute to the city's development and well-being of people in a more meaningful way.

On the other hand, the most significant contribution of the EU-led assembly seems to be the inter-group dialogue focused on divisive issues, established on an individual basis, while the extra-assembly effects are yet to materialise. The Bosnian experience, therefore, shows that the citizens' assemblies need to be designed not only to discuss important issues but to ensure that the deliberations of citizens have an impact outside of the halls in which they were held. However, even when limited in their outside effects, these assemblies hint that the cleavages in the Bosnian society are not unbridgeable.

---

69 Second CA Mostar and further development of the deliberative process in local level in BiH is part of the CoE Office in Sarajevo, Action Plan for BiH 2022–2025.

70 Banja Luka was chosen, following the 2022 CoE call for allocation of 40,000.00 euros for the local self-government with the best application for the deliberative process.

To establish a legal basis for domestic authorities to convene citizens' assemblies in the future, amendments to the entity laws on local self-government have been drafted with the support of the CoE. These amendments would formally recognise the CA as a form of direct citizen participation in local self-government affairs. At the cantonal, entity, and state levels, the relevant parliamentary rules of procedure may allow legislative bodies to initiate and establish a CA to discuss specific issues.

Furthermore, once the Office of the High Representative (OHR) enacted amendments to the Constitution of the FBiH[71] to enhance the transparency and accountability of the FBiH legislature, it required each house to enable citizens' participation, including youth participation, in its work. The OHR also mandated that the rules of procedure of each house prescribe appropriate forms of direct citizen participation in matters falling under the responsibilities of the FBiH Parliament. Additionally, the OHR obligated all levels of government (self-government, canton, and the entity) to develop appropriate structures for the inclusive participation of youth in matters concerning their future within one year of the amendments' entry into force. This created an important opportunity for the government to strengthen the role of CAs as a means of implementing these obligations. However, evaluations of the adopted amendments – where conducted – indicated that these obligations were not fully upheld. As a result, the OHR had to further intervene to ensure compliance with its decision. To enhance the effectiveness of deliberative democracy in BiH, future CAs must be embedded within a legal framework that ensures political follow-through. This could involve parliamentary commitments to debate and consider CA recommendations. Moreover, increasing the direct involvement of domestic institutions in organising CAs, rather than relying on external actors, could mitigate concerns about legitimacy and foster greater political and public buy-in.

CAs could also play a significant role in EU integration. An important lesson learnt from CA BiH is that citizens have the courage to take bold and decisive decisions necessary for the country's future. In that context, the national CA's future potential is intertwined with the hard decisions the government will have to make during EU integration, including comprehensive constitutional

71 Decision Enacting Amendments to the Constitution of the Federation of Bosnia and Herzegovina, *Office of the High Representative,* October 2, 2022, https://www.ohr.int/decision-enacting-amendments-to-the-constitution-of-the-federation-of-bosnia-and-herzegovina-3/.

reforms.[72] Citizens' assistance in that process, as well as shared liability of politicians and ordinary citizens for choices made, could foster the decision-making process at the state level and become one of the wheels of integration.

Bibliography

Action plan for the implementation of the Citizens' Assembly recommendations, *Mostar gradimo*, https://mostargradimo.ba/wp-content/uploads/2022/01/Akcioni-plan-za-implementaciju-Skupstine-gradana-Mostara-1-1.pdf.

Balcani Caucaso Transeuropa, "Bosnia and Herzegovina: Experiments in Deliberative Democracy," October 10, 2022, https://www.balcanicaucaso.org/eng/Areas/Bosnia-Herzegovina/Bosnia-and-Herzegovina-experiments-in-deliberative-democracy-220852.

Boswell, John, "Seeing Like a Citizen: How Being a Participant in a Citizens Assembly Changed Everything I thought I Knew about Deliberative Mini-Publics," *Journal of Deliberative Democracy* 17, 2 (University of Westminster Press 2021).

Cahillane, Laura, "Delaying Tactics or Useful Deliberative Exercises? The Irish Citizens' Assembly and the Convention on the Constitution," *IACL-AIDC*, December 04, 2018, https://blog-iacl-aidc.org/debate-the-citizens-assembly-in-ireland/2018/12/3/delaying-tactics-or-useful-deliberative-exercises-the-irish-citizens-assembly-and-the-convention-on-the-constitution.

Caluwaerts, Didier and Reuchamps, Min, "Does Inter-Group Deliberation Foster Inter-Group Appreciation? Evidence from Two Experiments in Belgium." *Politics* 34, no.2 (June 2014), 101–15. https://doi.org/10.1111/1467-9256.12043.

Citizens' Assembly members' views – 1 year after, *Mostar gradimo*, July 26, 2022, https://mostargradimo.ba/misljenje-ucesnika-skupstine-gradana-godinu-dana-poslije-2/.

Conclusion for the Action plan for the implementation of the Citizens' Assembly recommendation, *Mostar gradimo*, https://mostargradimo.ba/wp-content/uploads/2022/01/Sluzbeni-glasnik-Grada-Mostara-broj-23-2021.pdf.

Conclusion of the City Council on the Report on the implementation of the Action Plan, *Mostar gradimo*, https://mostargradimo.ba/wp-content/uploads/2022/10/Conclusion-on-the-Report-on-the-Action-Plan.docx.

72 European Commission. "Opinion on Bosnia and Herzegovina's EU Membership application". COM (2019) 261 final, Brussels, May 29, 2019. https://archive.europa.ba/?page_id=63860. See: Woelk, Jens, in this volume (Chapter 15).

Congress of Local and Regional Authorities of the Council of Europe, *Beyond elections: The use of deliberative methods in European municipalities and* regions (Strasbourg: Council of Europe, 2022).

Council of Europe Office in Sarajevo, "Building Democratic Participation in the City of Mostar," Council of Europe, https://www.coe.int/en/web/sarajevo/building-demo cratic-participation-in-the-city-of-mostar.

Council of Europe Congress supports implementation of the Citizens' Assembly recommendations in the City of Mostar, *Council of Europe Office in Sarajevo*, May 6, 2022, https://www.coe.int/en/web/sarajevo/-/council-of-europe-congress-supports-implementation-of-the-citizens-assembly-recommendations-in-the-city-of-mostar.

Council of Europe Office in Sarajevo, "Action Plan for BiH 2022–2025," *Council of Europe Office in Sarajevo*, https://rm.coe.int/action-plan-bosnia-and-herzegovina-2022-2025-eng/1680a54231.

Courant, Dimitri, "Citizens' Assemblies for Referendums and Constitutional Reforms: Is There an "Irish Model" for Deliberative Democracy?," *Frontiers in Political Science*, January 8, 2021, https://www.frontiersin.org/articles/10.3389/fpos.2020.591983/full.

Delegation of the European Union to Bosnia and Herzegovina, "BiH Citizens' Assembly Gave Recommendations on Constitutional and Electoral Reform," March 2, 2022, https://www.eeas.europa.eu/delegations/bosnia-and-herzegovina/bih-citiz ens%E2%80%99-assembly-gave-recommendations-constitutional-and-electoral-r eform_en?s=219.

Dryzek, John S. "Deliberative Democracy in Divided Societies: Alternatives to Agonism and Analgesia." *Political Theory* 33, no.2 (2005): 218–42. http://www.jstor.org/stable/30038413.

Dunetz, David, "Towards Democratic Innovation in Israel: The Case for Citizens' Assemblies," *Heinrich-Böll-Stiftung*, September 01, 2020, https://il.boell.org/sites/de fault/files/2020-11/Towards-Democratic-Innovation-in-Israel_The-Case-for-Citizens-Assemblies.pdf.

European Commission. "Opinion on Bosnia and Herzegovina's EU membership application". COM(2019) 261 final, Brussels, May 29, 2019. https://archive.europa.ba/?page_id=63860.

Fishkin, James S. "Random Assemblies for Lawmaking? Prospects and Limits," *Politics & Society* 46, 3 (SAGE Publications 2018).

Gerwin, Marcin, "Designing the Process of Delivering Recommendations by the Citizens' Assembly," *New Democracy Foundation*, https://www.newdemocracy.com.au/docs/researchnotes/ContentHost/Marcin_Delivering_Recommendations_Dub lin.pdf.

Gutmann, Amy and Thompson, Dennis F. *Democracy and Disagreement* (Belknap Press of Harvard University Press, 1996).

Hayward, Katy, "Deliberative Democracy in Northern Ireland: Opportunities and Challenges for Consensus in a Consociational System," in *Democratic Deliberation in Deeply Divided Societies*, eds. Ugarriza, Juan E. and Caluwaerts, Didier, (Palgrave Macmillan, London, 2014), https://doi.org/10.1057/9781137357816_2.

"How to run a citizens' assembly A handbook for local authorities based on the Innovation in Democracy Programme," GOV UK, accessed October 30, 2023, https://www.thersa.org/globalassets/reports/2020/IIDP-citizens-assembly.pdf.

Janković, Ivana, "Deliberative Democracy – Theory and Practice: The Case of the Belgrade Citizens' Assembly", *Philosophy and Society* 33, 1 (Institute for Philosophy and Social Theory 2022).

Lijphart, Arend, "Majority Rule versus Democracy in Deeply Divided Societies." *Politikon* 4, no.2 (December 1977), 113–26. https://doi.org/10.1080/02589347708704717.

Machin, Amanda, "Democracy, Agony, and Rupture: A Critique of Climate Citizens' Assemblies," *Polit Vierteljahresschr*, March 07, 2023, https://link.springer.com/article/10.1007/s11615-023-00455-5.

Macq, Hadrien and Jacquet, Vincent, "Institutionalising participatory and deliberative procedures: The origins of the first permanent citizens' assembly", *European Journal of Political Research* 62, 1 (John Wiley & Sons Ltd 2021).

Memorandum of co-operation between the Council of Europe and the City Mostar for the implementation of the project Building democratic participation in City Mostar, *Mostar gradimo*, https://mostargradimo.ba/wp-content/uploads/2021/07/MoU-Signed-ENG.pdf.

Mostar Citizens Assembly Rulebook, *Mostar gradimo*, accessed June 18, 2024, https://mostargradimo.ba/wp-content/uploads/2021/07/28072021Rulebook-ENG-web-2774-2955-3924.1.pdf.

Mostar Citizens Assembly Rulebook, *Mostar gradimo*, https://mostargradimo.ba/wp-content/uploads/2021/07/28072021Rulebook-ENG-web-2774-2955-3924.1.pdf.

Mulvad, Andreas Møller and Popp-Madsen, Benjamin Ask, "Sortition-infused democracy: Empowering citizens in the age of climate emergency," *Thesis Eleven* 167, 1 (SAGE Publications 2021).

O'Cinneide, Colm, "The Citizens' Assembly Viewed in External Perspective: Useful, but not a Deliberative Deus Ex Machina", IACL-AIDC, December 12, 2018, https://blog-iacl-aidc.org/debate-the-citizens-assembly-in-ireland/2018/12/12/the-citizens-assembly-viewed-in-external-perspective-useful-but-not-a-deliberative-deus-ex-machina.

"OECD Database of Representative Deliberative Processes and Institutions", OECD, accessed October 30, 2022, https://airtable.com/apppPtOagL1JQ6KqK/shrHEM12ogzPsonQG/tbl1eKbt37N7hVFHF/viwxQgJNyONVHkmS6?blocks=hide.

OECD, *Innovative Citizen Participation and New Democratic Institutions: catching the deliberative wave: highlights 2020* (Paris: OECD Publishing, 2020).

Phalnikar, Sonia, "France's citizen climate assembly: A failed experiment?," Deutsche Welle, February 16, 2021, https://www.dw.com/en/frances-citizen-climate-assembly-a-failed-experiment/a-56528234.

Pow, Jamie and Garry, John, "What Happens When Mini-Publics Are Held in a Deeply Divided Place? Evidence from Northern Ireland." *PS: Political Science & Politics* 56, no.4 (October 2023), 572–78, https://doi.org/10.1017/S1049096523000409.

Press and information team of the Delegation to Bosnia and Herzegovina, "BiH Citizens' Assembly presents its recommendations on constitutional and electoral reform to the BiH Parliament", Delegation of the European Union to Bosnia and Herzegovina & European Union Special Representative in Bosnia and Herzegovina, March 17, 2022, https://www.eeas.europa.eu/delegations/bosnia-and-herzegovina/skup%C5%A1tina-gra%C4%91ana-bih-prezentirala-svoje-preporuke-o-ustavnoj-i_bs.

Recommendation no.3, Recommendations of the Citizens Assembly of Bosnia and Herzegovina, available on: *Skupština građana*, accessed October 03, 2023, https://www.skupstinagradjana.ba/images/Recommendations_for_citizens_report_v6_1.pdf.

Recommendation no.4, Recommendations of the Citizens Assembly of Bosnia and Herzegovina, *Skupština građana*, accessed October 03, 2023, https://www.skupstinagradjana.ba/images/Recommendations_for_citizens_report_v6_1.pdf.

Recommendations by the Mostar Citizens' Assembly, *Mostar gradimo*, accessed October 03, 2023, https://mostargradimo.ba/wp-content/uploads/2021/08/Final-recommendations_ENG-courtesy-translation.pdf.

Recommendations of the Citizens Assembly of Bosnia and Herzegovina, *Skupština građana*, accessed October 03, 2023, https://www.skupstinagradjana.ba/images/Recommendations_for_citizens_report_v6_1.pdf.

Report on registration to the Mostar Citizens' Assembly, *Mostar gradimo*, accessed October 03, 2023, https://mostargradimo.ba/wp-content/uploads/2021/06/Izvjestaj-o-registraciji-za-Skupstinu-gradana.xlsx.

Rock, David and Grant, Heidi, "Why Diverse Teams Are Smarter", *Harvard Business Review*, November 04, 2016, https://hbr.org/2016/11/why-diverse-teams-are-smarter.

Shapiro, Ian, "Enough of Deliberation: Politics Is about Interests and Power." In *Deliberative Politics: Essays on Democracy and Disagreement*, edited by StephenMacedo (Oxford University Press, 1999).

Ugarriza, Juan E. and Caluwaerts, Didier, "Deliberation in Contexts of Conflict: An Introduction" in *Democratic Deliberation in Deeply Divided Societies*, edsUgarriza,

Juan E. and Caluwaerts, Didier, (Palgrave Macmillan, London, 2014) https://doi.org/10.1057/9781137357816_1.

Woelk, Jens and Sahadžić, Maja, "Cutting the Gordian Knot in Bosnia and Herzegovina: The High Representative Imposes Constitutional and Legislative Amendments on Election Eve," *VerfBlog*, October 07, 2022, https://verfassungsblog.de/cutting-the-gordian-knot-in-bosnia-and-herzegovina/.

Woelk, Jens, "'Everything is Bridgeable' in a Post-Conflict Situation? The Situation of Local Government in Bosnia and Herzegovina," in *Local Governance in Multi-Layered Systems*, eds. Nicolini, Matteo and Valdesalici, Alice, Ius Gentium: Comparative Perspectives on Law and Justice, vol 108 (Springer, Cham, 2023), 264–366, https://doi.org/10.1007/978-3-031-41792-4_16.

Woelk, Jens, "'Everything is Bridgeable' in a Post-Conflict Situation? The Situation of Local Government in Bosnia and Herzegovina," in *Local Governance in Multi-Layered Systems*, eds. Nicolini, Matteo and Valdesalici, Alice, Ius Gentium: Comparative Perspectives on Law and Justice, vol 108 (Springer, Cham, 2023), 264–366, https://doi.org/10.1007/978-3-031-41792-4_16.

CHAPTER 18

Conclusions: The Constitution as Guarantee and Foundation for Sustainable Evolution

Maja Sahadžić and Tatjana Sekulić

As the Dayton Peace Agreement marks its 30th anniversary in December 2025, it symbolises the end of one generation since Bosnia and Herzegovina's (BiH) post-war reconstruction began. However, the country continues to face significant challenges and disputes, particularly in its political-institutional framework and ethnic divisions. Moving forward, addressing these obstacles will be crucial for securing a more stable and sustainable future for BiH.

Thus, the purpose of this volume was to examine three foundational issues of the post-Dayton BiH: territorial government, organisation of institutions, and the perception and preservation of identity. At the same time, these three foundational issues served as the main discussion points centred around fundamental constitutional principles, institutional and territorial organisation, and European integration. Given that the book is based on a two-year effort of research and exchange, the discussion of those points came up in every chapter in its own way, as part of a mutual learning process regarding the various viewpoints and positionings of the authors.

Starting with the fundamental constitutional principles, the authors in the book addressed **basic values and normative principles**, including rights, freedoms, and duties, by challenging fundamental ground rules for expressing the political, social, economic, and, most importantly, identity variations in BiH. Specifically, the authors analysed which rights are essential for effectively safeguarding individuals and/or groups, and how this is related to the foundations for a sustainable future in BiH. With these queries, the authors attempted to examine whether and how the individual rights of citizens can be reconciled with the collective rights of groups. To do so, it was necessary to discuss the dual understanding of individual and collective rights and whether this duality contributes to or detracts from the issue. Added to this, it was also necessary to question how equality of dual rights and citizenship should be framed in a so-called "complex state" like BiH.

Undoubtedly, the BiH constitutional system acknowledges values and principles that are crucial for any state that is multi-national. Following Nedim Hogić's brief introduction to the politics and history of constitutional devel-

 | DOI:10.1163/9789004707887_019

opment in BiH, several authors in this volume attempted to prove this, albeit with a twist. Damir Banović, for example, maintained that there was a need for reforms, including a minimal understanding of an overarching identity and a consensus on the structure of the constitutional and political system. The notion of constituency of peoples, which forms the foundation of the society of BiH, complicates the former. Like many other systems, BiH is a place of layered identities, and it has to keep this stratification in place to keep the system together. This is consistent with Dražen Barbarić's suggestion that it would be incorrect to forsake the concept of constituency of peoples in order to turn BiH into a civic state regime, since it would not inevitably unite the three ethnic communities into a single civic society. The latter is consistent with Goran Marković's assertion that the existence of federal and consociational features in BiH is determined by the objectively given nature of the society, as well as the political and historical context in which the Dayton Constitution was drafted, and not by one's desires and preferences. As demonstrated by Barbarić, the coexistence of federalist and consociational components need not inevitably result in the system's paralysis or failure, provided that fundamental ideals and principles, such as the constituency of peoples, are not violated. Joseph Marko, however, opened the door to a potential "third way" based on the conception of political equality, which suggests particular normative standards to be applied in upcoming reform initiatives to reconcile the current divisions.

Furthermore, under **institutional and territorial organisation**, the authors addressed the institutional organisation in BiH by questioning what kind of institutional structure is capable of converting the values, normative principles, rights, and duties into a working representational and participatory system. Specifically, the authors discussed if elected political representatives should defend the cultural identities of groups or serve the electorate simply by putting relevant socio-economic interests to the forefront. Importantly, the authors examined if these options have to be chosen one way or if there is a way to create a model that can balance two goals. Also, the authors analysed the type of system that can best ensure the values, normative principles, rights, and duties combined with the legislative, executive, and judicial branches. Specifically, the authors evaluated the kind of federal structure that BiH presently has and how it can be used or developed to move forward.

This book demonstrated that while discussing values and principles in theory is one thing, it appears that putting them into practice through significant constitutional and legal reforms is quite another. As Lejla Balić pointed out, the European Court of Human Rights (ECtHR) established in the *Kovačević v. BiH* judgement that the concept of exclusive ethnic representation is contrary to democracy, as it reduces individual choices; so, in the first instance, the Court rejected the argument that exclusive ethnic representation ensures dialogue between the constituent peoples. Furthermore, as Marko Romić contended, the question of whether the Dayton Constitution and the division of powers will be taken literally or widely construed in the future would create a new concept of executive power that the original Dayton solutions did not anticipate. To address the complexity of the institutional and territorial organisation in BiH, Bojan Vlaški proposed using instruments of intergovernmental relations, such as intergovernmental (administrative) agreements, intergovernmental bodies, and the mechanism of coordination more frequently, while Jens Woelk highlighted the significance of creating a culture of the rule of law, which would replace the lengthy tradition of the rule by law and bring in a culture of accountability and transparency. Based on this, Maja Sahadžić proposed the idea of "local ownership" and calls for citizens to be more actively involved in the development of rule of law procedures, while Neven Andjelic highlighted the need for BiH voters to play a more active role in opposing the Office High Representative's (OHR) heavy reliance on Bonn's powers. According to the observations of Nevenko Vranješ and Nikolina Babić, one reason for optimism is that BiH's local self-government is officially in line with the European Charter on Local Self-Government, which makes it a relatively unproblematic aspect of the country's institutional and territorial dilemma.

Finally, under **European integration**, the authors analysed what is required to fit the complex BiH system into the European Union (EU). The authors questioned the unique difficulties as a result of EU conditionality during the EU integration process and what kind of initiatives are needed for a crucial step in building a lasting peace. This proved to be related to the difficulties of accommodating internal structures and procedures in order for BiH to become a member of the EU.

As Woelk pointed out, the Council of Europe's European Court of Human Rights, as well as the Venice Commission, have stated time and time again that the Dayton constitutional arrangement is only temporary and was necessary in order to put a stop to the war. The European Commission, which also requests a change in the status quo, now supports this. Nevertheless, maintaining one's own group's relative dominance still seems to take precedence above the shared objective of EU membership. Returning to values and principles, Tatjana Sekulić emphasised the need for civil and political actors who possess greater capacity to reconstruct a broken society, in which both the state and the citizenry are still captured by the ethnonational political logic and practices, into a new and distinct whole. Harun Išerić and Tahir Herenda claimed that these should be citizen's assemblies, which represent the level of common citizens.

The Dayton Peace Agreement imposed such constitutional arrangements on the country, creating a minimum indispensable condition for ending the war while preserving the state within its internationally recognised borders. These arrangements are no longer sufficient to build a truly just and peaceful society in BiH, capable of meeting EU membership requirements. **An open public dialogue on the constitution** that leads to substantive reforms is crucial to this goal, to which this work will hopefully make a valuable and substantial contribution. One generation after the imposition of the agreement to end the war, other actors (politicians and the international community, but also 'common' citizens) need to organise such open and inclusive public dialogue and guarantee its procedures.

The three foundational issues discussed in the volume for Bosnia and Herzegovina are crucial for any multilevel governance system that is constructed from the bottom up, starting from the local level and working its way up to European integration. This is because the volume has looked closely at the dynamic aspects of internal change, especially when it comes to eventual EU accession. While the status quo still seems to be the preferred option for many, it cannot be overlooked that the situation in Bosnia and Herzegovina – and elsewhere – has considerably changed and evolved over the last 30 years.

Importantly, the authors – constitutional and legal experts, political scientists, and sociologists from a variety of ethnic and cultural backgrounds – share their results of an interdisciplinary and intercultural dialogue that advances our understanding of BiH's complex constitutional framework. Their collaboration on this book, and earlier on the research project that underpinned it, has produced innovative conceptual frameworks and, at times, suggested policy instruments that could prove invaluable in any future post-conflict situation in multinational states.

The future of Bosnia and Herzegovina's constitutional framework rests on the delicate balance between preserving the peace established by Dayton and fostering the political will needed to enact reforms that will build a more cohesive, democratic, and inclusive society for generations to come. A constitution shall not only ensure stability and the rule of law but also serves as a living document, capable of guiding a society through future challenges by providing mechanisms for amendment and reform. In this way, a constitution is both a stabilising force and a vehicle for progress, playing a pivotal role in the future evolution of the country by balancing tradition with the capacity for integration.

However, the recent constitutional and political turbulence, which has unfolded in March 2025 – sparked by the sentencing of the President of the Republic of Srpska to a year in prison and a six-year ban from public office for flouting the decisions of the OHR in Bosnia and Herzegovina – has once again thrown a spotlight on the deeper tensions at play. The defiance of the Republic of Srpska's leadership, depicted in adopting legislation aimed at restoring the so-called original Dayton framework, highlights a larger truth that constitutions are meant to be stabilising forces and vehicles for progress, not relics of past compromises.[1] The crisis illustrates how the very foundational principles upon which Bosnia and Herzegovina's political and legal order rests, together with institutional and territorial arrangements inherited from the Dayton Peace Agreement, once necessary for ending violence, now serve as an impediment to democratic consolidation and EU integration.

In light of this, the analyses in this volume feel more urgent than ever, although the crisis has not been treated in single chapters as the volume was submitted before it started. The last constitutional and political crisis is a symptom of deeper structural dysfunction that reveals the limits of the Dayton constitution in its current form. There is a growing consensus, both internally and externally, that the constitution was never intended as a permanent solution, but rather a necessary transitional arrangement. It was a political life raft, not a blueprint for long-term governance. What is needed now is a forward-looking constitutional reform process, one that reaffirms the values and principles articulated in this book and translates them into a viable institutional design for a more solid democratic and participatory basis of the state and of the society. Only through such transformation can BiH move toward European integration.

References

Davidović, Miloš, and Maja Sahadžić, "The Tipping Point in Bih's Constitutional Struggle," *Verfassungsblog*, 15/04/2025, 2025, https://verfassungsblog.de/bih-constitutional-struggle-dodik/.

Hänel, Rena, "Dodik's Defiant Secessionist Constitution," *Verfassungsblog*, 15/04/2025, 2025, https://verfassungsblog.de/dodik-secessionist-constitution/.

1 See: Miloš Davidović and Maja Sahadžić, "The Tipping Point in BiH's Constitutional Struggle," *Verfassungsblog*, 15/04/2025, 2025, https://verfassungsblog.de/bih-constitutional-struggle-dodik/; Rena Hänel, "Dodik's Defiant Secessionist Constitution," *Verfassungsblog*, 15/04/2025, https://verfassungsblog.de/dodik-secessionist-constitution/, 2025.

Index

www.ingramcontent.com/pod-product-compliance
Lightning Source LLC
Chambersburg PA
CBHW051356240926
51852CB00001B/48
9789004707870